SIGNAL BOY

Summer 1939 – Signal Boy Adams – aged 16. HMS *Eagle* in Hong Kong.

Signal Boy

My Life as I Remember it

ROBERT ADAMS

SERENDIPITY

First published in 2002 by
Serendipity
Suite 530
37 Store Street
Bloomsbury
London

British Library Cataloguing-in-Publication data
A catalogue record for this book is available from the British Library

ISBN 1-84394-013-2

Printed and bound in the UK by Alden Digital, Oxford

Dedication

To all my wonderful family who are a constant joy in my life, especially Eileen, who through fifty-two years as my wife has helped to make a lot of this happen.

And a special thanks to Julia and Jim who had the courage and foresight to provide me with (and get me hooked on) a computer at seventy-five years old

There is a witching in the sea,
Its songs and stories
And in the mere sight of a ship
and the sailor's dress,
especially to a young mind,
which has done more to man navies
and fill merchantmen
than all the Press Gangs of Europe.

'Two years before the Mast'
Richard Henry Dana 1840

Contents

SIGNAL BOY
ROBERT ADAMS
MY LIFE, AS I
REMEMBER IT

Foreword

Major John P. Synnott RM (Retd.)

IT IS A LITTLE OVER FIFTY-FIVE YEARS since I first met Bob Adams. His main interest at that time was to collect my sister with whom I had just spent the afternoon. He proceeded to whisk her away on the pillion of his motor bicycle to her home in Worthing. The warmth of her welcome to him was an early indicator that he was likely to become my future brother-in-law.

In this personal, lucid and frank account of events over a period of seventy-eight years he has blended historical and other events with his thoughts, emotions and personal conflicts. By so doing he has revealed with much candour those standards of fidelity and conduct which have characterised him over the many years of our acquaintanceship.

In January 1938 Bob fulfilled an early ambition to enter the Royal Navy and was admitted as a Boy Seaman. Thus he submitted to the rigours of a disciplinary and professional training demanded by the Service which had changed little since the turn of the century. Note the reference to 'caning', a punishment common to both boy offenders and Midshipmen. From this initial training he managed to qualify at an early age for promotion to Chief Yeoman of Signals and could have advanced further had he so desired. Bob spent much of World War II at sea in a variety of ships, first experiencing action at the tender age of seventeen in the Far East. Thereafter, he was to serve in virtually every theatre of the war. His account of these years, fraught with danger and discomfort, is recorded with the same light touch as in other more relaxed periods of his distinguished career.

He retired in 1963 after twenty-five years service and had to make the change to civilian life. This involved abandoning many of the long established practices and precepts of his previous career. Moreover, the early 60s had introduced a newly liberated society who openly challenged previously held moral and social virtues. Philip Larkin, in a poem, wrote, 'Sexual intercourse began in 1963,' but for the family Adams, 1963 marked the beginning of a search for permanent employment and re-settlement in a non-service environment. This was never going to be easy. There were a succession of false dawns before they embarked for a 'new life' in Canada. Even for a family accustomed to travel this was a bold and courageous move. It proved successful and provided the settlement and stability they sought and this is where the chronicle ends.

J.P.S.

Alverstoke, March 2002

by Joy Street

I FIRST MET BOB ADAMS when I was thirteen years old and my name was then Joyce Bonsall. I appear in the early pages of *Signal Boy*.

My teenage years were filled with wonderfully happy times. Whilst at school our free time was spent playing up the 'rec' (Tarring recreation ground) with our friends called 'the gang', cycling, walking on the hills (the South Downs), swimming off the beach at Grand Avenue, Worthing or going to the pictures at the new Plaza Cinema and the new Odeon Cinema which are now a bingo hall and a shopping arcade respectively.

After seeing Bob off to join the Royal Navy at Worthing Station, when we were both aged fifteen, the next few years consisted of looking forward to letters and Naval leaves. Later the Second World War started and I remained in Worthing, becoming a GPO telephonist, which was a reserved occupation. Consequently I found myself entertaining various members of HM Forces who were stationed in and around the Worthing area, but I always carried a torch for Bob.

Eventually after eleven years of 'going out together', we had a disagreement which resulted in both of us marrying someone else in 1947, and both had happy marriages, each producing two daughters.

For years we lost touch with each other as he was living in different places all over the world in the Royal Navy and later had emigrated to Canada, but I used to hear news of him and his family from time to time as he was friendly with my brother Vic. Incidentally, years before, Bob had bought a motor-cycle from Vic and so they had a common interest.

I lost my husband after thirty-five years in 1982, and have been living alone for twenty years. In 2001 Bob was also bereaved after fifty-three years and he came to England from Canada to visit old friends and relations. He came to see me and the moment we met again the years between us just rolled away and we felt like teenagers again.

In due course he took me back to Canada for a holiday and to meet his family who made me very welcome. I was swept off my feet and then in October 2001 he made a great sacrifice and disposed of his home in Ontario, left his family and many good friends to come to England, home for good and we are now very happy together and looking forward to our future years. Our early years were spent together and now after knowing each other for sixty-five years we hope to spend the rest of our lives together.

Bob's determination and strength of character shine throughout this book and I am amazed at his memory, all written without keeping a diary.

Joy Street (née Bonsall)
March 2002

Introduction

BEING THE FIRST DAY OF JANUARY 1998 it seems an appropriate time to embark on the project of trying to write one's memoirs. I should start by saying that, in spite of a lot of encouragement from my family, this is a venture which I have always firmly resisted. When asked why, I have never been able to come up with a valid answer – I just knew that I did not want to do it. However, over the past month I have given a lot of thought to this matter and therefore have faced an analysis of the reasons both 'for' and 'against' such an undertaking. So, let us start with the negatives.

(a) It has always seemed that writing one's memoirs was something undertaken by old men re-living their glory days. Nothing wrong with that, but, after a pretty average life, I did not feel that there was a lot to write about anyway.

(b) My knowledge of our family tree is somewhat limited and therefore may prove of little interest, even to my immediate family.

(c) I did not have much of a clue on how to set about it. Just the other day my wife remarked, 'Where will you start?' and (trying to sound confident) I replied, 'I will start at the beginning and see what happens.'

(d) There is obviously a lot of work involved and, on that score alone, I have always procrastinated.

Now for some points in favour:

(a) I felt that if I looked upon this as a hobby rather than a task I might even grow to enjoy it!

(b) One of my big regrets in life is that, in my younger

days, I did not find out more about my family and their lives before I was around. So I would like my own grandchildren to have some idea of how I spent my life – instead of having to ask, 'Well what did Papa do when he was alive?'

(c) In the past 'lack of time' has always been a factor in dismissing the subject but, now that I am retired, I can no longer offer that as an excuse.

(d) Finally, I read somewhere the other day that keeping the brain active will retard the ageing process, so, with the amount of head scratching I shall be doing over the coming year I should be all right.

At this point I should tell you that as to the real reason for changing my mind, the credit must go to Fred and Anne Luken, our friends and neighbours in Pier Twelve, who very kindly loaned me three biographies of their fathers and one grandfather. I must admit I was quite surprised to find them all so interesting – and to me, an outsider.

So, here we go, with the hope that, after all my scribbling, there will be some merit here so that at least my own family will appreciate my efforts.

Part One
Early Years

CHAPTER ONE

The Early Years

ALTHOUGH I CANNOT PERSONALLY vouch for the event, my Certificate of Birth states that Robert Alexander Adams was presented to the world on 5 December 1922. I believe the time was around two a.m. which I know was very inconsiderate of me. The place was a Nursing Home called 'Homefield House' and situated on Homefield Road in Worthing, West Sussex.

I think it might be nice if our memories functioned from birth but, unfortunately, that is not the case and so there is a blank of three or four years before this story can really get started.

Although I was born in Worthing, the first few years of my life were spent in Southwick, which was a small harbour town about halfway between Worthing and Brighton. My recollection of the house is that it was small and rather dark; a terrace house (row house) with a small garden at the rear and it was facing onto the village green.

One incident at Southwick is, and always has been, very clear in my mind. I would have been about four years old and my younger brother, Jack, about 18–20 months. My mother was taking us for a walk one afternoon. Jack was in the pram and I would be walking beside it – that is until I got tired and then I would be hoisted onto a little seat on the end of the pram to face 'astern'. Southwick was, and still is, the harbour entrance for Portslade, which is a non-tidal basin, and therefore all vessels have to pass through a lock both inbound and outbound. In addition to a couple of huge lumberyards, Portslade Basin was also the home of the electricity generating station which supplied most of the power for West Sussex. For this reason, most of the ships visiting the harbour were small colliers from Newcastle with loads of coke for the power station plus a few lumber carriers from Scandinavia – nothing terribly exciting.

Anyway, on the day in question, my mother decided to walk us down to the lock and there happened to be a collier in the lock waiting to enter the basin. To pass the time some of the crew were on the dock kicking a football around and, to my delight, they invited me to join in. The highlight of the afternoon came when somebody kicked the ball into the water beside the ship and they had to fetch a rope and bucket to fish it out.

Many years later, when reflecting on that afternoon, I came to two conclusions. First, that the sailors had less interest in playing football with a four year old boy than with the excuse to strike up a conversation with the attractive young mother accompanying him. Secondly, although the ship was small, dirty and really unimpressive, I think this incident was when the first inkling of going to sea entered my very young mind, because, even in later years, I never wavered from that ambition.

The next event that I can remember pretty clearly, which was certainly a major step in the shaping of my life, was when we moved to Worthing. I have no idea what prompted the move, nor how the decision was made to settle in Worthing, but ever since I have been grateful for that decision. Worthing was, and still is, a delightful place to live or even now, to visit. I guess it would have been in 1928 when I was five years old and Worthing was a rather quiet seaside town with a population around 40,000. I remember hearing many times, that elderly people came to Worthing for their retirement but, because the sea air was so healthy, they never died off! Worthing has a lovely seafront with an excellent, wide promenade running the width of the town and along the top of the beach – which was pebbles; we only had sand when the tide went out. During the 1930s on a calm day one could watch dozens of elderly people in Bath chairs, either being pushed along the promenade or just sitting and looking at the sea. The Bath chair was a strange looking but nevertheless very practical form of conveyance for elderly or infirm people. It originated in the city of Bath, a very famous and popular spa in Victorian times. The body of the chair was made of heavy basket (or wicker) weave and was sort of pear shaped and rather reminiscent of the old time 'hip bath'! The passenger, invariably wrapped in travel rugs, sat in this facing forward i.e. towards the narrow end, where there was a small wheel with a long handle that enabled the passenger to steer. Towards the rear were two large wheels and at the rear was a handle (rather like a perambulator), which allowed the escort to provide motive power.

Ethelred Road, which was to be our new home, was the first of three parallel roads being built just up from West Worthing railway station. The three were named Ethelred, Athelstan and Ethelwulf and I remember thinking, much later of course, that somebody in the Town Planning Department must be a history buff. I remember my first impression of Ethelred Road was the large board on the vacant corner lot which proudly announced 'All Electric Homes, 550 pounds Built by Frank Sandall & son'. We had a look at the homes, which were still under construction, and we all thought how wonderful and modern they were. The term 'All Electric' was not <u>quite</u> true because cooking was on a gas cooker (stove), water heating was achieved with a fat little coke fed boiler in the scullery and the main rooms were heated with coal fires.

The only problem seemed to be the '550 pounds' because,

Baby Billy, 1923.
Oh, wasn't he cute!

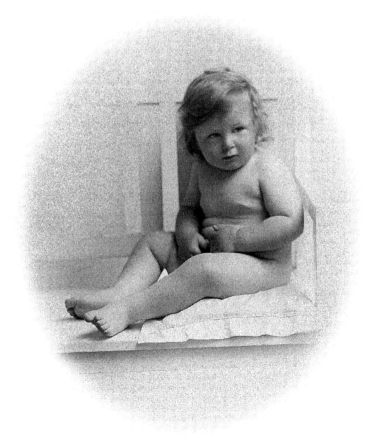

although it sounds like a give-away price today, it was a small fortune then and, of course, my mother had no money anyway. We soon discovered that Frank Sandall had retired and Weller Sandall (the '& son' part of the business) was in charge. I do not remember Weller Sandall but he must have been a reasonable man because my mother charmed him into letting us rent No. 6, which, being the third house in the road, was still being built.

Pretty soon it was moving day and we were all very excited – everything was so new and bright and shiny – all, that is, except the road itself. It was unfinished which meant no pavements (sidewalks), no lighting and the road itself a mass of potholes with either mud or dust, depending on the weather. In those days the builders would build their houses and sell them and then it would be the responsibility of the Council to construct the roads which, of course, would be done when they had the funds to do it. Until then the road would have a sign on it saying 'Un-adopted' – meaning the Council was not responsible for the state it was in.

Mother in fancy dress.

The Family

PERHAPS I SHOULD FILL IN this space with a brief family history – it is brief not from choice but because I deeply re-gret that I know so little about most of my family. In those days children were supposed to be seen and not heard and questions from the younger set (and particularly about 'private affairs') were neither welcomed nor answered. I envy the youngsters of today who, at an early age, want to know all about everything and, as far as I can see, get all the answers they want.

My grandmother was Mary Barnard (who always lived with us) who came from Scotland. She was a lovely, grandmotherly person, short and round with white hair, and, because she did most of the cooking, always seemed to have a smear of flour on her somewhere. I knew my grandfather rather briefly as he died when I was about five or six. My only memory of him was being in bed upstairs (he had a couple of strokes), with visits from the doctor who, I remember, prescribed 'only white meat' which was a little problem because, in those days, poultry was more expensive than beef. After a while he became unmanageable and was transferred to the Sanatorium at Portslade (halfway

Grandmother.

between Worthing and Brighton) where he died shortly afterwards.

My mother was born in 1900 (so it was always easy to figure out how old she was) and was christened Leonora, which I think is a very elegant name but, for some strange reason, was always known as 'Queenie'. During the First World War my mother worked at the Admiralty in the Code and Cipher Department and, after the war, was employed as receptionist at the Stanhoe Hotel, just off the seafront in Worthing. The Stanhoe was a small and private hotel that survived two wars and, when Marks & Spencer came to Worthing, was located between their store and the seafront. I believe it was finally demolished to make way for bigger and better things in the late sixties.

My father was always a mystery, not only to me but also to most of the family, apparently. As I have a younger brother and a sister it will seem slightly astonishing that, to the best of my knowledge, I never knew him nor even met him. Growing up in a single parent family did not seem at all strange and it was not until later years that I even wondered about my father. I think the first time I consciously thought about it was when I was fifteen and applying to join the Royal Navy – then I wondered what my mother wrote on the form – but I never saw it.

In my later years I have heard several different versions of my parentage (some of them strange but nonetheless interesting) and from what I heard, and partly from my own intuition, I formed my own opinion of my parents' circumstances. It is my belief that my parents met at the end of the First War when my mother worked at the Stanhoe Hotel and my father, who was still in the Army, stayed there. Of course, they fell in love but, because they never married, I believe he already had a wife but, nevertheless, they decided that their relationship should continue. Some evidence seems to point to the fact that, in civilian life, he owned a hotel in Bognor Regis, a small seaside town about twenty miles west of Worthing.

It was about this time that I can remember clearly that once a week my mother would have an evening out at the cinema. On these occasions I would be in bed extra early which I objected to because it was still daylight outside (I think it was probably between six and seven p.m.). I can remember lying in bed and watching my mother sitting at the dressing table doing her makeup. Also very clearly

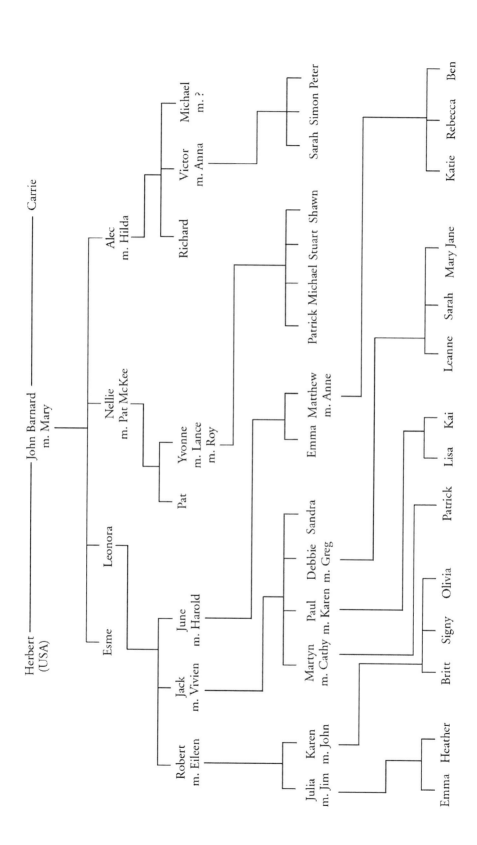

I can see the two framed photographs on the dressing table – on the right was a portrait of my mother in her young days and on the left a portrait of a young man wearing Army captain's uniform (WWI). I remember also that, when I asked who he was, my mother told me, 'just a good friend' – of course, I believe now that he was my father and that mother was going to meet him that evening. The next morning we would linger over breakfast as my mother explained to grandmother all about the film she had seen. My mother was a very conscientious and caring parent and a great homemaker which meant she never seemed to stop working. Even in the evenings, when she

Mother with Aunty Hilda outside Ethelred Road.

should have been relaxing, we would find her in the kitchen, ironing or sewing or cleaning etc. Of course we did not have TV to distract us in those days and an evening's entertainment usually meant listening to a mystery play on the radio.

Because I was only sixteen months old when my brother Jack was born on 13 April 1924, I naturally know very little of the circumstances surrounding that event. However, by the time my sister June was born on 17 July 1929 I was seven years old and I do remember that I was very well aware of her being born. My mother went to the hospital in Brighton for the occasion – I don't know the reason

Bob in his first car.

for this because I am sure there were adequate maternity facilities in Worthing – which made it somewhat inconvenient for visiting. I think she was in the hospital about ten days and, if I remember rightly, Jack and I were taken by our grandmother to visit her (and our new sister) twice during this time. The events were very festive and well remembered; not so much (I regret to say) from the 'visiting' point of view but for all the treats that were involved with these visits. Our grandmother would take Jack and me on the visits which started with walking to West Worthing station to get the train for Brighton but,

Front to back: Jack, Bob, Pat, Yvonne.

before we did so, we would visit Oaklands Dairy (right across the road from the station) and there we would have our first treat – a large glass of very rich, creamy milk. It might seem a strange place to have a dairy but, in those days, it made sense because the milk used to arrive from the farms in huge metal churns on the early train. It was then bottled at the rear of the dairy premises (there was no pasteurisation in those days) and then delivered to customers – all within hours of production. Bear in mind that homes did not have refrigerators then and, even though milk was delivered every morning, it was difficult to keep it fresh in the summer. Also at the front of the dairy premises was a very bright and clean retail shop where all their products (milk, cream, eggs, butter and cheese) could be purchased.

The next part of our day out was the train ride itself which was a big adventure for us. When we arrived in Brighton we had to walk up a very steep hill to the hospital which did not seem very big even then – more like a row of large converted houses. After the hospital we would board a tram at Brighton station to take us to the seafront which was rather exciting because the route was down a steep hill and we always sat on the top (open) deck as near to the front as possible. On the floor of the tram's entrance platform was a metal button which, when trodden on by the driver, would sound a bell – Jack and I could never resist this and it would result in very reproachful looks from the conductor.

Brighton seafront was always a special wonderland for us with its two piers, all kinds of entertainment and stalls selling ice cream, candyfloss and the fishermen selling fresh fish they had just landed. Yet another treat involved a ride on Volk's Electric Railway, which was a small affair that ran from Palace Pier to Black Rock and back, right along the beach.

Aunt Esme

My aunt Esme was the eldest in my mother's family and, perhaps because of this, had definite views on how everyone should behave. At quite an early age she decided to enter the Church and became a nun – I do not know many of the details but I do know it was in France. After some time as a nun she was befriended by a young French woman named Yvonne Chevalier and I think it was her influence that persuaded my aunt to leave the Church.

They were destined to spend the rest of their lives together in the teaching profession and, quite soon, Yvonne became known as 'Aunty Yvonne' although she was not a relative. Eileen still has the gold wedding ring worn by my aunt when she was married to the Church. All this took place before, or shortly after, I was born.

My earliest memory of Aunt Esme was as a teacher at a very exclusive school for boys in Eastbourne and Aunt Yvonne was there also in some administrative capacity. St Bede's was a Catholic boarding school and the students all came from wealthy families and, in one way at least, this was to my advantage.

Aunt Esme did not visit us often but when she did my brother and I would look forward to it with a mixture of pleasure and horror. Being a teacher, my aunt was a strict disciplinarian and I remember a couple of times we were put across her knee and paddled with the back of the clothes brush off the hatstand for some previous misdemeanour (my mother could not bring herself to do this).

The good part was that she always brought for us some expensive toy that had been left at the school by some departing student. We accumulated some good toys this way, notably a steam engine powered by methylated spirit and a large fort with lots of lead soldiers in many uniforms. This was a great advantage because my mother certainly could not find money for many toys.

I remember one summer when we spent a vacation on the Isle of Wight at Totland Bay when Esme and Yvonne rented a cottage there. This was a real treat for us because holidays away from home were unheard of but, because we lived at the seaside, we did not suffer too much.

Just before the war my aunts bought a piece of land at East Dean, just outside Eastbourne, and had a beautiful Sussex cottage built on it surrounded by a large garden which they both tended with much care.

Both aunts lived to a ripe old age although Esme was devastated when Yvonne died first.

Aunt Nellie

I am still not sure whether or not that was her real name; I very much doubt it but, at the same time, I never heard her referred to by any other name. Auntie Nellie was a very easy-going and charming person who was kind and generous to a fault (even though she had nothing to give). She had a tough life because she did not have the support of a husband and, with even less money than we had, bringing up two children was difficult to say the least.

Yvonne (her surname was GILL but I was too young to have known her father) was several years older than me and my earliest memory of her was when she was leaving school at fourteen. She turned into a very glamorous blonde and was never short of partners at the Assembly Hall dances, especially when the war started and the town was swarming with servicemen (mostly Canadians).

Pat, who was three years my senior, was tall and, although outwardly reserved, was a lot of fun to be with – perhaps because he always had something interesting, like roller skates or an air-gun. Pat's father, who was Auntie Nellie's second husband, was, I believe a Canadian soldier, who settled in England after the first war. Unfortunately, they were separated and he lived in London and visited Worthing only occasionally. He seemed to me a pleasant man, perhaps because he gave Jack and me a half-crown each to get lost!

Auntie Nellie always seemed to be one of the more interesting members of the family, principally because she made a habit of moving home frequently (I imagine because the landlord got too pressing) and the move was always to some interesting and unusual accommodation, usually over a store. Not being able to afford a regular removal service Auntie Nellie always recruited us boys (myself, Jack and Pat) to do the job and, I remember, it was always a great adventure for us. On Tarring Road in Worthing there was Bridger's greengrocery store and they owned three tradesmen's barrows which they used to hire out for one shilling a day. They were flat, two-wheeled barrows with two handles for either pushing or pulling as desired and we usually reserved one of these a couple of days before the move.

On the big day – usually a Saturday or after school – we would then transport the McKee household to the new residence that was usually over a store. I remember Railway Approach, above an Estate Agents, and Crescent Road, above Potter Bailey's the grocers, then Park Crescent on Clifton Road. After that probably, because Pat and Yvonne were now working, they moved to a nice, modern house on Congreve Road in Broadwater. Pat was a clerk at Marsh & Ferriman, a solicitor's office in Worthing, and Yvonne now had a steady job as manageress of a rather classy confectioner and tobacconist called 'The Tudors', on Goring Road

After Congreve Road the next move, I believe, was to 'The Bungalow' on St Thomas Road, which was much nearer to us, so we would naturally spend more time there. It had a very large garden and at the end, an old garden shed where the boys would have 'secret meetings' to plan and discuss all sorts of things. Yvonne was popular with us because she had acquired a canoe. It was wooden in construction and carried the name 'Yvonne II'. She kept it on the beach near Grand Avenue and we enjoyed many summer days with it.

Not quite so popular was her other pet, a yappy little terrier called Kim who, although never vicious, did not make friends too easily. Yvonne eventually bought her own home called 'Glentorran' at the end of our road on Peveril Road and also got herself a beautiful Irish Setter called Babs. This was a very friendly dog and we all enjoyed taking her for walks while Kim went into the care of Auntie Nellie.

It was somewhere about now that Auntie Nellie worked as a housekeeper for Major Teal (retired) who I remember as a short, stern and rather pompous man who lived in a large bungalow on Highdown Avenue which was off the Littlehampton Road at the 'Thomas A'Beckett'. He did not have a wife but he did have a daughter, a rather unattractive girl who went by the name of Pinkie. I remember visiting Auntie Nellie at Highdown Avenue – we would be in the kitchen, perhaps having a cup of tea, and she would be chattering away when suddenly she would ask the time and, upon learning it was ten to one, she would leap into action – 'The Major must have his lunch at one o'clock!' Another thing the Major was strict about was his garden, which was large, secluded and very well kept with beautiful fruit trees trained to grow along the high stone walls. One day I could not resist and picked and ate one of his peaches (I had never before seen peaches actually growing) but I think he knew because I believe he took inventory daily.

Auntie Nellie liked to get out in the evening so, once a

week, would visit my mother for a chat; she would arrive about nine o'clock, on her bicycle with Kim (which she had now adopted) in the front basket and then she and my mother would talk and smoke in the kitchen until after midnight. When she finally left it always appeared she did not have a light for her bicycle, and it was the law for bicycles to have front and rear lights after dark. She always seemed to run into the local constable, PC Bluebell, on his beat who, after giving her a stern talking to, would often walk home with her.

Early in the war Yvonne met and married a young RAF fighter pilot named Lance but it was not long before he was shot down and killed over France. Sometime later, Yvonne married an army captain named Roy King whose family lived in Worthing. Unfortunately, it was not a great success (Roy seemed unable to settle into civilian life when the war ended) and they were eventually divorced but not before producing four sons. As youngsters Patrick, Michael, Stuart and Shaun were all lively, happy children and in later years, I only met Michael again – he was a very pleasant young man who was then an officer in Customs and Excise. Stuart, I believe, grew up to be a staunch communist.

At the outbreak of war Pat joined the RAF as a wireless operator and was flying Wellington bombers from a base near Oxford. Shortly afterwards his plane exploded on landing and he was killed.

Uncle Alec

Being the youngest in a family of four I believe that he was rather spoiled as a youngster, not only by his mother but also by three older sisters. When he grew up he went into banking and when I first knew him (about 1930 I believe) he was working in the Streatham branch of Lloyds Bank.

He lived then in a pleasant semi-detached house in nearby Thornton Heath (I think it was Carolina Road). I remember we visited there when we were invited 'up to town' to stay for a few days holiday. We travelled on the Southdown coach for London – I remember it was very exciting for Jack and me and we thought it was the ultimate in luxury

Uncle Alec's wife was Hilda who I remember as a small,

blonde lady who never seemed to get flustered – even with all us kids getting underfoot. About twenty-five years later when Eileen and I were living in Ferring, as was Uncle Alec, we had Julia and Karen at a school which adjoined the rear of our property and Aunt Hilda used to help out with the school lunches there. Naturally she took a special interest in our children and, through them, became very friendly with Eileen. But I am jumping ahead.

Sometime during the war, I think it was, Uncle Alec was promoted to Head Cashier at Lloyds main branch in

Mother with Uncle Alec.

Worthing and consequently the family moved from Thornton Heath and took up residence in Worthing on Peveril Road, which was at the end of Ethelred Road. I remember shortly after the war Uncle Alec, who had never owned a car and always cycled to and from work, suddenly bought a car even though he could not drive. I think this was probably due to Victor's persuasion and I remember seeing Victor enjoying it quite frequently. It was a very beautiful automobile – an Austin Princess – but much too large for normal family use. A few years later Uncle Alec bought a house and moved his family to Ferring, a lovely little village just to the west of Worthing. This was also where Eileen and I chose to live after we were married.

But, going back to my younger days, there was an incident which I have always regretted, not for myself but because I now know it must have caused my aunt and uncle a lot of anxiety. It was during the time Uncle Alec lived at Thornton Heath and he had rented a nice holiday bungalow at Rustington for their summer vacation that year. Very kindly, they invited me to spend a week with them and I remember being very excited about the prospect of spending all our days swimming because the bungalow was very close to the beach. Rustington is another pretty village close to Littlehampton so I suppose it was about six miles from where we lived. We did have great fun swimming and playing in the water, especially as we had an inflated motor inner tube to play with, and I was very happy to be there.

One day the water was pretty rough and the waves were crashing onto the pebble beach but we did not mind – it was just more fun than ever. I was floating in the inner tube when a particularly large wave caught me and threw me onto the beach where the stones took the skin off one elbow.

Auntie Hilda stopped the bleeding and bandaged it up for me but the next day it had turned septic and I was not allowed to swim. So, in the morning, I wandered down to the beach just for something to do. Of course, I do not clearly remember my thoughts that day but I expect I was feeling pretty sorry for myself and wishing I was at home.

Whatever it was, I started walking along the beach towards Worthing and, after covering a considerable distance (it seemed a long way to go back), I just thought I might as well keep on going! Obviously, I did not realize the distance that was still ahead of me and neither did I stop to think of anyone being worried. All I remember is just pressing on, sometimes on the sand, sometimes on the pebble beach and often climbing over huge wooden breakwaters.

I finally reached home at 3.30, totally exhausted and probably looking a sorry sight – I know it was 3.30 because my mother, who nearly had a fit when she saw me, was just leaving to meet my sister June from school at four o'clock.

Much to my surprise (at the time) I did not seem to get into too much trouble for my stupid and inconsiderate adventure.

Bob and sailor Jack.

Uncle Alec and Aunt Hilda had three sons – Victor, Michael and Richard – but I used to see very little of them when I was in the Navy because I was away from home so much. I think Victor and Michael were a couple of years younger than Jack and me and therefore we felt a bit closer. Victor was eventually to follow his father's example and go into banking with Lloyds Bank and, in 1958 I think, was with the main Worthing area branch on South Street in Worthing. I believe he was not too thrilled about his future prospects there and, being young and single, decided to look around for something more exciting. One day he responded to an advertisement in the *Daily Telegraph* for an opening overseas and was subsequently asked to attend an interview in London. The job was in the Trustee Department of the Hong Kong & Shanghai Bank, in Hong Kong, and Victor was offered the position but there were two conditions – he had to be prepared to depart very soon and he had to be married! Not wishing to miss such an opportunity Victor and Anna were soon wed and spent their honeymoon in the luxury of a P&O liner bound for Hong Kong. At that time Eileen and I were living in Hong Kong and this was where we really got to know Victor and Anna – but more about that later.

Michael, I believe, was not too popular with his family when he decided not to complete his education and took a very menial job with a local manufacturing company in Angmering. I did not see him again until 1990 when Eileen and I were in England to attend the wedding of Victor's son Simon. Michael was also there and was now the Managing Director of the same manufacturing company, had a glamorous French wife and a home in France where he spent most of his time.

Richard, who I did not know at all, very sadly died when he was quite young.

CHAPTER TWO

School Days

T HE NEXT MAIN FEATURE of my young life involved the subject of education and the question of where and when it would be started.

I was never quite sure why, but my mother was definitely reluctant for me to start school: was it the transportation problem? Did she want to protect me from the rough old world? Or could she not bear to be parted from me?

It all began when my mother started to get visits from Mr Wallace who was the Department of Education inspector, although his official title was 'the school attendance officer'. For some strange reason he was always known as 'the school board'. It was really bad news to get a visit from him because he wanted to know, very officially, why you had not been attending school! During their conversations at the front door I am sure my mother was finding all sorts of reasons for me not to attend school and Mr Wallace was countering with very good reasons (like the law) as to why I should!

Inevitably, Mr Wallace won the battle and it was agreed, in the summer of 1929 (I was six and a half then), that I should commence school in the autumn. It was arranged for me to start at St Elizabeth's Preparatory School for Boys and Girls on Crescent Road in Worthing. This was a Catholic School run by the nuns from the convent attached to St Mary's Roman Catholic Church where I was to start attending Mass. I do not recall the nuns who taught me as being particularly soft and gentle – to me they were very strict and a bit scary! I don't think they taught me an awful lot during my brief stay there (I left at Christmas after only four months) except perhaps how to be a well behaved, polite little boy; perhaps that was the object? One thing I did find strange was that we always seemed to be singing in French! I have hated *Frère Jacques* ever since. The school was a separate building from the convent and separated from it by beautiful gardens with high stone walls. On the couple of occasions that I was in the convent – the first time was an interview with the Mother Superior prior to my acceptance – I found it extremely impressive and, although rather dark, everything glistened as though it had been polished for a thousand years; and above all the heavy smell of candle wax and floor polish

I would like to digress here for a moment as I remember how religion played a part in my young life. Although my mother and my grandmother were both Catholics they were not churchgoers and I remember the priest knocking on our front door every few weeks to enquire as to when they would be attending Mass. As I said, St Elizabeth's was a Catholic school so, of course, we learned to say prayers and sing a couple of hymns each morning.

It was about this time that it was decided that I should be introduced to the church and accordingly I was sent to Mass one Sunday with my cousin Yvonne who was seven years older. St Mary's is quite a large and beautiful church and this was my first visit; we were standing at the back (because we arrived late) and the priest was at the altar with his head bowed over the chalice. All I could see was this motionless figure in the vestments with the high collar at the back (i.e. no head) so I remember thinking to myself, 'That must be the Holy Ghost'! Little did I know that in the next eight years or so I would spend many, many hours on that altar as an altar boy. I still feel that religion, no matter what the denomination, is an important factor in the forming of a young character.

My next school was St Mary's RC Elementary School (boys and girls) located on Cobden Road and adjoining Victoria Park; and this was where I would spend my next seven years – and that would be the extent of my education in civilian life. Being a Catholic school, the day naturally started with morning prayers followed by the first session (45 minutes) which was always religious instruction. Apart from this, and going to Benediction after school on Wednesdays, religion did not seem to interfere with our other school activities.

St Mary's was a new construction and therefore bright and airy but, although open for only a couple of years, was filled almost to capacity. For instance, what had been designed as the school hall had already been converted into a classroom. The school was the brainchild of our parish priest, Canon C. M. Westlake, who had worked tirelessly to overcome all the obstacles to get it opened and was now bursting with pride at having achieved it. The previous Catholic school was St Joseph's which had been housed in two cramped wood huts located in the rear yard of the church. They were now in use as the Scout hut and a recreation centre.

Canon Westlake, probably in his fifties then, came from a well-off and very religious family and it was not until much later that I found his initials (C.M.) stood for Charles Mary. Basically he was very shy but it was not always evident because he always had a smile and a joke for the children; with adults it was different and I know many thought him stand-offish and perhaps difficult. His bald head and his face were always very red and when he laughed (usually at his own jokes) he seemed to shake like a raspberry jelly – a bit like Sidney Greenstreet except he was not fat. He seemed to take me under his wing and after my First Communion and Confirmation, got me to serve as an altar boy. I remember pacing back and forth in the yard on a summer evening as he coached me in the correct pronunciation of the Latin responses for the Mass. As I got more proficient he called on me more and more for the services so that, before I left school at fourteen, I used to serve on the altar for the eight o'clock Mass each morning and eleven o'clock on Sunday plus Benediction on Wednesday and again on Sunday. I somehow fitted all this in, additional to my newspaper delivery rounds.

Every year there would be two weeks camp in the summer for the older boys and paid for by their parents. Canon Westlake organised this and, knowing that my mother had no money for such extras, took me along on two occasions at no charge. I remember the excitement of shopping with my mother at Walter Bros for the list of required items, including a groundsheet, a grey blanket and half a dozen blanket pins. On 'Camp Day' we were all packed into the back of a lorry, on top of our kit, for a long and rather uncomfortable, but nevertheless exciting, ride to Wonersh, near Guildford in Surrey.

Fortunately for us, Canon Westlake had gone ahead a couple of days before with the 'camp crew' consisting of two or three older boys who would set up the tents, do the cooking and generally supervise the camp activities.

The camp was always on the property of the Catholic Seminary (theological college) where young men were trained for the priesthood. Of course, during one of these visits Canon Westlake let me know that, should I be interested in such a future, he would point me in the right direction – but I decided it was not for me.

The Seminary was a very large property and, in addition to the college itself, included extensive gardens, a lovely chapel and its own farm. Our campsite was located in one of the farm pastures and on top of a steep hill; I could not understand this at first, until somebody explained that when it rained we would not get flooded out. Very logical but, although I don't remember it raining, I do remember we carried an awful lot of buckets of water up that hill from our water supply in the farm at the bottom! I also remember digging what seemed endless latrines and rubbish pits – all designed, I suppose, to make sure we would sleep at night. The other memorable experience about camping was the swimming ... because of the climate there were, understandably, not many outdoor swimming pools in England in those days so, when we heard there was one at the Seminary, we were all excited and keen to use it; although the enthusiasm for swimming waned quite noticeably when we saw the pool. It was located in a wooded area of the property (very private) and had large trees overhanging it so that very little sunshine got through. It was a large oval in shape with a large concrete area on one side and the water appeared quite black because of the weeds in it. In spite of this, the water was very clean and very pure – it should be because it had a natural stream running right through it which, besides purifying the water, also kept it very cold. Nevertheless, we swam every day (I think as a substitute for bathing) and the more reluctant boys were flicked with a wet towel until they finally jumped in.

I think that is enough 'R&R' (in this case 'Religion and Recreation') and time to get back to the business of schooling.

As I said earlier, I was due to start at St Mary's RC Elementary School in early January of 1930, now that I was seven years old, and having completed one term at St Elizabeth's. However, before I could do this, I had to comply with the law which required that every child, before being accepted at a public school, must first have their tonsils removed. Nowadays that may sound like a strange condition but I think in those days it was a precaution against diptheria. Also today, it is a very minor operation but then it was a very traumatic experience – one that I would equate with stomach surgery today!

The operation was done at the Public Health Clinic, a very uninviting building located next to Worthing Town Hall. At 8 a.m. on the appointed day a dozen mothers deposited their young sons and were told to come back for them at 5 p. m. One by one we went into the operating room and I remember very little after that except that the anaesthetic was rather primitive – a bottle of ether dripping onto a gauze pad over the nose and mouth. However, the main problem came in the afternoon when I woke up in a totally darkened basement room, with eleven others, all lying on cots and groaning and ejecting large mouthfuls of blood and vomit into the nearby bowls, As I recall there was nothing sophisticated like IVs or painkillers – just a mug of water if you wanted it. Nobody did because it was too painful to swallow and felt as though your throat had been cut. I learned later that, as a bonus, the surgeon had also removed our adenoids – 'to save trouble later'.

Anyway, enough of the gory details. My mother picked me up at five p.m. and we went home in a taxi – the first taxi ride of my life but I felt too awful to notice it. I must say things got better from then on as my mother kept me in bed and fed me on a diet of ice cream and mashed potato with gravy and quite soon I was fit enough to start school in earnest.

St Mary's School, as I recall, held no terror for me and I seemed to settle in right away. As I entered the school I think the first person I met was a rather short man with bow legs encased in leather gaiters and a very fierce looking waxed moustache. He introduced himself as Mr Hayes, the school's caretaker. He was an ex-Army Sergeant from the First World War, appeared very efficient in his duties, and seemed to control the kids better than some of the teachers – I know all the kids were scared of him. Anyway, I never ran foul of him; just the opposite, in fact, because a few years on his daughter Mary Hayes was in my class and we became quite friendly. I remember the two occasions when I was invited to the house for Mary's birthday party and I was a little surprised to find what a pleasant and easy going family they all were.

The teaching staff at St Mary's were, to my mind at least, a rather varied bunch but, no doubt, all competent teachers and quite pleasant people. Anyway, I am happy to say that I did not have an enemy amongst them although I think I had my share of the cane from some of them.

The Headmaster was Mr Albert E. Joy BA – he was a very large and jolly man who, quite naturally, was known by the nickname of 'Jumbo Joy'. He used to cycle to school (nobody had cars in those days) and it always appeared that his bicycle would collapse under him. Invariably he was in a hurry and, when he came flying along a corridor it was a wise move to flatten against the wall. He was also musically inclined and did a great job as organist at the church.

The second in line was a lady who really fitted her name – Miss Weeds! She was a very tall person and as thin as a rake and, when I was in her class, always very firm but also loved to reminisce about her days at university.

Next came Mr Martin P. Costello who was also tall, very thin and quite grey and always wore glasses. When out of earshot he was always referred to by his nickname of 'Ghandi'. He was a good teacher and I always got on well with him, partly because he was our neighbour, living a few doors away from us on Ethelred Road. This bond of affinity was strengthened when, knowing that I was interested in the Navy, he told me he had been a Wireless Operator in the First World War and had the unpleasant experience of a shell passing right through the W/T Office where he was working. I was very interested in this story, little knowing that, in a few short years, I would find out exactly what it felt like! His wife was May Costello, a very friendly person who appeared to be forever leaping on and off a high frame bicycle as she met people while doing her shopping. This sort of antic reminded us so much of the actress Margaret Rutherford who was so popular at that time. We remained friends of the Costellos for many years after school; in fact until they both died at a very good age.

Mr Kinsella was next and, for some reason, I was never in his class so I did not know him too well. I just remember him as quite young and rather reserved – a man who got on with his job and that was it.

Next was a different story – Miss Pitt was young, attractive and unattached. In addition to being a class teacher, she was in charge of Physical Education (which consisted of exercises in the playground because we did not have a gymnasium) plus she was also in charge of the Wolf Cubs, of which I was a member. Underlying this charming exterior she had quite a temper and could rant and rave with the best of them. One day when I was in her class she took me to the stockroom to replenish the class exercise books and, whilst in this confined space, I took the opportunity and kissed her. I don't recall any conversation at the time and as I didn't get slapped or expelled I guess I got away with it.

Then last but not least was Miss Patterson who, when I started, was in charge of the junior class and, because she later moved up the scale, I twice had the pleasure of being in her class. She was very short, very round, had a moustache and, although I could not verify it personally, was rumoured to have a 'rug'. She was very strict in class and, when roused, had the temperament of a pit bull and, in spite of her size, could wield a wicked cane.

So that was the staff – we did not have any luxuries like school secretaries, nurses or counsellors – and the staff had to cope with everything. Neither did we have school lunches or school buses – nearly everybody seemed to use a bike. Hours were from 8.50 until noon and 1.50 till 4 p.m. In addition to normal classes there were other subjects; on Wednesday morning we would go to Heene Road Baths for swimming where the water, supposedly heated, was still cold. After swimming, when we were on the way back to school, we would visit a nearby baker's shop where, for two pennies, we could buy a whole bag of stale cakes to eat on the journey. The girls had netball and the boys soccer and cricket and Victoria Park, adjoining the school, served as our playing field.

Friday morning was another special experience when we went to a Vocational building on Richmond Road, quite near to the Town Hall. The girls went downstairs to learn cookery and how to be a good housewife, except then it was called Domestic Science. The girls' Instructor was a very matronly lady (I can't remember her name) and I am told she would stand no nonsense. Meanwhile, the boys would be upstairs learning the art of woodworking from Mr Brebner who was our Instructor. He was a very stern man who never seemed to smile but, nevertheless was a very good Instructor who was meticulous about the measurements – and heaven help the boy who was a sixteenth out. He had been a Battery Sergeant Major in the Royal Horse Artillery and I think he looked on us as a bunch of raw recruits. He must have found it very boring, teaching us carpentry, one minute step at a time. Anyway, he always discovered that he had some urgent business to attend to at the Education Offices in the Town Hall and always came back just before noon when we finished. It was not long before we discovered that he was spending the time sinking a couple of pints in the Wheatsheaf across the road. Of course, before he went he would issue dire warnings about what he would do if there was the least noise while he was away, but the result was usually a near riot with bits of wood flying everywhere. This resulted in Mr Brebner being met, on his return, by the 'Chief Cook' from downstairs with a complaint about 'the terrible noise those boys have been making'. We were glad to get out of there in one piece. The total result, after about a year's hard labour, was that I completed a small, plywood letter rack. Well, my mother was proud of it!

I think I should say something now about the other children I remember from my days at school. First of all, the boys – I had three special friends at school and the first one was Peter McCarthy who had an older sister, Eileen. Their parents owned a newsagent's business on Montague Street, down by the seafront. Peter was a bright and lively boy but one who had a tendency to exaggerate. When I was home on leave in 1942 I met him again in my favourite pub the Fountain and he told me that he was a (civilian) aircraft inspector and also how great the pay was – that really made me feel good!

Next was Bert Trussler who lived with his parents at 96 Beckett Road and I would be invited for tea on a Sunday afternoon and then he and I would go off to the early house at the Plaza cinema. His father had been a milk roundsman but was now in charge of operations for Oaklands Dairy. Remember, earlier they were opposite West Worthing station and now, to make way for Caffyn's Garage, they had relocated to the end of Ethelred Road. Mr Trussler worked very hard and very long hours and I don't think he made it to retirement. At the outbreak of war Bert joined the RAF and last I heard of him he was a Flight Sergeant.

I had a firm and long-lasting friendship with a boy in my senior class named Tony Taylor but universally known as 'Spud' Taylor. When I joined the Navy he enlisted as a boy in the Army, to follow in his father's footsteps. He went to the Royal Artillery Depot at Woolwich and was then sent for his Boys Training at Oswestry in Wales. We were fortunate that, until the war started, our leave periods from training would coincide. There were two memorable incidents during our mutual leaves The first, in summer of 1938, we decided to switch uniforms for a day (strictly illegal, of course, but fun all the same). When we went out together and walked all round the town our friends thought they were all going balmy! The second was during the Easter leave 1939 when Spud and I were out together – in our correct uniforms – and were approached by a couple we did not know. They wanted us to act as witnesses for their wedding: so, when we agreed, we all trooped off to the Registry Office which was nearby. After the deed was done they gave us a half-crown each and said goodbye. I hope they didn't have any problems later because it probably wasn't legal (we were only sixteen at the time) although we did not think of that before the event. I am happy to say that Spud survived the war OK and next time I met him (and his wife) was in 1949 when he was the RSM at a base in Germany. I believe he retired a few years ago as a Lieutenant Colonel and went to live on Salisbury Plain – no doubt so that he would feel at home.

Then there were other boys – Frank Kelly, a wiry boy with thick glasses who always had his head in a book and consequently never spoke unless he was spoken to. He lived on High Salvington, which was too far to go home for lunch so he always brought sandwiches and, strangely, I always envied this. He was a good student and always did well in class. At the other end of the scale were the Jones boys who came from a family of gypsies and both were as tough as nails. Bailey Jones was in my class and his younger brother Pongo Jones was in my brother Jack's class – don't ask me where they got those names from. Both boys seemed to have a habit of getting into trouble but never flinched when the cane whacked down on their palms.

In contrast to the Jones boys were the MacNaughtons who came to us from Canada in 1935. I remember the stir one day when we were told to be on our best behaviour because some important visitors would be visiting the school. Mr MacNaughton, a tall, distinguished looking man and his two sons came to inspect the school (and us I suppose) and this in itself was a rare event in those days.

We must have met with their approval because the boys soon joined us: Eddie was in my class and his younger brother was in Jack's class. They were both quiet, reserved boys but they soon fitted in and became popular classmates. I recall they were always immaculately dressed and their shoes were highly polished (perhaps their father was in the Army?).

Then there was Philip Oxendale, a very quiet, tall, well spoken boy and a good student. He made his career with the Southdown Bus Company – started as a conductor, then became a driver and, when I met him after the war, he had just been promoted to Inspector.

Two other interesting friends I had were Dennis Garrett and 'Soapy' Watson. Dennis was interesting, not so much for himself but for where he lived – in a semi-detached house in agricultural land in an area of Tarring as yet undeveloped. In the other half of the house was a family of diddicoys who made a living door to door selling handmade clothes pegs and clothes props. Near Dennis's house was a large hollow tree where we used to climb inside, light a fire and sit until the smoke drove us out for some air.

'Soapy' was not really remarkable but he did live close by on Ethelwulf Road. I remember one Easter Sunday I was on my way to Mass, all dressed up and feeling very smart, when I met 'Soapy' at the end of our road. We were having a chat when he suddenly decided to reach out and mess up my hair – well, I didn't appreciate that and reacted instinctively – I punched him and, unfortunately, connected with his nose and made it bleed. I went off to church but he went to my house and told the story of what I had done; my mother sympathised, bathed his nose and gave him tea and hot cross buns. Of course, when I got home I was really in the doghouse for being such a bully!

The last one, but by far the most memorable (and for very good reason) was Michael Cooney. Mick, as he was known to everybody, was a well built, good looking, golden haired boy (in every way). He was an excellent swimmer and always seemed to win the West Sussex Diving Championships; plus he had the most beautiful voice and always sang solo in the church choir. He came from a very poor, hard working family who lived in a small, terraced cottage on Clifton Road, just around the corner from the school. His father was disabled (blinded by a gas attack in Flanders in the First World War) and eked out a living by making baskets, after being trained by St Dunstan's Institute for the Blind. Mick joined the Navy when war broke out and was a Leading Seaman serving as Coxswain of an MTB when they took part in the Commando raid on the French port of St Nazaire on 27 March 1942. The object was to disable the dry dock there, the only one on the Atlantic coast capable of taking a German pocket battleship, thus denying its use for the *Tirpitz*. This was to be done by loading one of the old, ex-US, destroyers, HMS *Campbeltown* with explosives and ramming the dock gates. Anyway, Mick's MTB was one of those badly shot up and with a lot of casualties, including both officers, but somehow Mick managed to get the vessel back to Plymouth.

For this he was awarded the Conspicuous Gallantry Medal. I don't know, but I can only hope that his father was still alive for this event.

Some of our favourite activities while at school might be frowned on today. One of these was to get into a very large, old building on Henty Road. It was three or four stories high and had been a school for girls but was then totally empty and deserted. About six of us would get in and, pretending the school was haunted, try to scare each other by hiding in cupboards and closets; but the best attraction was a 'dumb waiter' which went to all floors.

There always seemed to be different activities at school (and always changing – almost as if they were seasonal) and, as they changed, the boys would rush off to the nearest store to spend their pocket money on whatever the latest craze was. There would be cap guns and potato guns which were my favourite – they required you to carry a potato in your pocket and you would stick the gun into the potato, which would produce a small pellet, and when it hit you in the back of the neck really made you jump. Another was little 'aerial bombs' which comprised two pieces of lead on a piece of string and, when loaded with caps and tossed in the air, would explode on landing. There were glass 'alleys', which we used to play along the road on the way home or in the playground. Then there was the 'conker' season, which didn't cost us anything – in the autumn we would collect bags of horse chestnuts and then the best ones would be threaded with a piece of string and then we could try to break our opponent's conker and be the proud owner of a 'fiver' or more. Another playground favourite I think was called 'drawbridge', where two teams of five or six would compete. With an 'anchor' against the wall, one team would bend down, one behind another, and the opposing team had to leapfrog from the end of the line, reaching as far as they could along the line – the object being to cause the line to collapse. Sounds a bit dangerous now but I don't recall anybody getting seriously hurt.

Now, a few words about some of the girls I remember from my schooldays. First were the 'convent girls' – these were a group of girls (probably six or seven) who, for one reason or another, were being raised by the nuns and would attend our school daily. They all seemed to be bright, diligent students but it was difficult to know them as they were very reserved and did not take part in activities outside the classroom. There were two in my class, Joyce and Cora Kent, and I always felt so sorry for them because they did not have any fun in their lives and had to wear rather long and drab uniforms.

An attractive girl in my class was Gladys Addlesea, who was always the centre of attention for my friend Spud Taylor. She did go out with him for a time while at school but years later when he proposed he was unlucky. I remember reading in the local paper that she had died of a stroke at the early age of 56.

Another pretty girl in my class was Peggy Mason and we were good friends for quite a while. This mainly involved walking her home from school (she lived on Howard Street which was not too far out of my way) and a couple of birthday parties. Little did I know then that I was destined to meet her again much later in my life – but we will come back to that later on.

Speaking of birthday parties – there was a particularly lively one given by Doreen Hudspeth who lived on Pavilion Road.

One of my special friends was Vera Brunton, a quiet and polite girl whose parents owned a greengrocery business on North Street, just opposite the Town Hall and Rivoli cinema. We used to spend hours on the seafront in winter but it was always a rush to get home because her parents were rather strict about her being home at nine o'clock and, as the Town Hall clock was both loud and illuminated, there could be no excuse.

Mary Moore was a tall, slim, girl with classical features who lived on the corner of Tarring Road and Shakespeare Road. This friendship was brief and doomed from the start because her parents would be in the corner of the living room, listening and watching, as we discussed our respective stamp collections.

Lily Hourigan was a nice girl from a large, Irish family who lived on Pavilion Road. After I went into the Navy she caused quite a stir by marrying Mr Turner, one of the teachers then at St Mary's School.

Almost a neighbour of mine was Yvonne Bowden, a pretty, well spoken girl who lived behind us on Athelstan Road.

A girl in my class who later made a name for herself as an opera singer was Maria Pirelli who broadcast on BBC radio many times. She was, of course, Italian and her parents owned a large ice cream parlour on Worthing seafront so, needless to say, her birthday parties were a huge success and helped to make her very popular.

Also, for a while before leaving school, I had a girlfriend from another school which, in itself, was rather unusual because there were not many opportunities for meeting. I think we met because Muriel Wright lived on Reigate Road which was not far from West Worthing station and attended 'The Davison School for Girls' which was then located on Chapel Road opposite the New Town Hall. Muriel was a pleasant girl but for some reason which I never knew, had been saddled with the nickname 'Murky' Wright.

On the day I finished school for good, in December 1936, something happened which was both unusual and significant. As we trooped out of the school gates (free at last!) Spud Taylor and I were met by three girls from Worthing High School, with their bicycles, who were waiting for us by the gates of Victoria Park. Until then we knew them only by sight but soon discovered they were Joyce Bonsall, Peggy Watkins and Doreen Baker. The five of us, plus two more later, were to form a lasting friendship and, for Joyce and me especially, it would last many years. The two additional members of 'our gang' were to be Bert Trussler, who I mentioned earlier, and Ken Gill (always known as 'Gillie'), a very pleasant boy who had left school and was working at Morton's the butcher opposite Tarring railway crossing. I think his father was the manager there because they lived in the flat over the shop. During the coming year (1937) the seven of us were almost inseparable and spent all our free time together. Of course, the three girls who were at the High School still had two years of schooling ahead of them while the four boys were gainfully employed. Spud had got a job at Khong's, the tea and coffee merchants right in the centre of Worthing, where they used to roast the coffee beans right in the open store window and so this gorgeous smell used to permeate the whole area.

Looking back on it, 1937 was a very carefree year when the threat of war had not yet overtaken us.

We were young and healthy, we never had any money but we did have bicycles which we used to ride all over West Sussex. In the spring it would be trips to Goring Woods where we would come home with huge bunches of wild primroses and bluebells. In the summer we would be swimming in the sea off the beach at Grand Avenue and in the autumn and winter we would hike for miles on the South Downs to Cissbury Ring and Chanctonbury Ring.

St Mary's RC School, Worthing, Senior Class 1936.
Back row: Dick Baldwin, Fred Greavat, Arthur Harris, Pat Tierney, Bob, unknown.
Front row: Joyce Kent, Mary Hayes, Mary Moore, Maureen Murphy, unknown.

In addition to all this we would meet every evening at Tarring Recreation Ground, known to everybody as 'Tarring Rec'. It did not qualify as a park because there were no flowers or shrubs and it was not big but it did provide some equipment (maypole, swings, parallel bars and a swing plank). In other words, a great place to let off steam – sometimes a ball game but more often just playing 'tag' or fooling on the equipment. The gates to the Rec. were locked at dusk, no bikes or dogs were allowed and all activities were strictly supervised by the park-keeper. 'Old Bill', as he was known to everybody, was a veteran of the First War –he had a gammy leg and needed a large cane to walk, had an empty sleeve where his right arm should be, and the right side of his face was badly disfigured. In spite of all his disabilities he was a tall, straight man (well over 6ft) who would stand no nonsense and could strike terror into the heart of an offender. When we caught him in a good mood he would tell us gory stories of life in the trenches in Flanders.

The following year, in the January of 1938, Spud and I left to join the Army and the Navy respectively and the next year, when the war started, Bert and Gillie both went into the RAF. By then the girls had left school – Peg went to work as a bookkeeper at Sultan's the butchers, on the corner of Beckett Road, where she stayed for a great many years and, as far as I know, did not marry. Joyce went as a switchboard operator with the GPO who, at that time, operated the telephone system in Britain. Gillie, after the war, married and for some years owned a hardware store on the corner of Ethelwulf Road but was stricken terribly with arthritis, spent many years in a wheelchair unable to do anything for himself and, tragically, died at a very early age.

CHAPTER THREE

Joining the Work Force

B Y THE TIME I HAD REACHED my thirteenth birthday
I had made the decision that I would go into the Royal
Navy. From there on I spent a lot of time in finding out
all I could about how to go about it and conditions of
service etc.

During this year I had obtained a recruiting booklet for
the Navy – I found it on the counter at Tarring Post
Office (the Post Office being a government department).
Of course, it presented the life of a sailor in the best
possible light – it almost sounded like a world cruise.

At the same time it told me all the essential things that
I wanted to know – how to join, where to apply, rates of
pay plus a list of all the various branches of the Service
and where the appropriate training for these branches
would be carried out. I treasured this booklet, read and
re-read it until I knew it by heart.

On my fourteenth birthday I sent off my application to
join the Royal Navy, even though I knew that the minimum age for acceptance was fifteen. I couldn't wait to get
started and hoped that I could enter the Service immediately after leaving school. Of course, they replied promptly
enough – telling me to re-apply when I was fifteen. Although expected, the reply was, nevertheless, rather a
disappointment. This was in December 1936. I had just
left school upon reaching my fourteenth birthday (quite
normal then), and was destined to become an office boy
with a firm of estate agents – something I had hoped to
avoid.

About this time (i.e. during 1937) I had three other
sources of information on my future career. The first was
Harold Bonsall, who was my girlfriend Joyce's half brother,
who had made a career in the Navy and was now a Petty
Officer. I met him a couple of times when he came home
on leave (he and his wife Violet lived quite close by), and
although he was very interested in the fact that I wanted
to join I cannot remember asking him too many questions.

The second source was the current lodger at my mother's house. His name was Ron Paige and he was an ex-Navy man (a Leading Stoker if I remember rightly) who was now employed as a lineman with GPO Telephones. He was a friendly, easy going, sort of man who seemed to be ideally suited to the work he was doing. This was when the GPO was getting rid of all overhead wires and telephone poles in the town and putting in underground cables.

I can just see Mr Paige and a couple of co-workers down a large manhole along Tarring Broadway (the new local shopping area). The hole would have a little portable fence around it with a couple of red flags and a sign stating 'Danger Men at Work'. Whenever I called to see him, on my way home from work or school, he was either just brewing, or drinking, a mug of tea. I didn't know much about the work ethic of the British worker in those days so it didn't seem strange to me that they managed to stay in one hole for three or four days and then move a hundred yards along to the next one. Mr Paige had served in the Navy on what the Service called (with tongue in cheek?) 'a Short Service engagement', which meant seven years active service followed by five years on the Reserve. Therefore, now a civilian, he was quite a young man – certainly

Mother, Uncle Alec, Hilda, Jack, Michael, June, Granny, Victor and Bob. Worthing 1937.

young enough to appreciate the view, from his work-hole, of the legs of all the young female shop assistants in the area. Although not a great drinker, he also enjoyed a pint of beer. One evening, in the summer of 1937, he took me to see a show (summer variety type of thing) at the Pier Pavilion in Worthing. When we got off the bus downtown he asked me, quite casually, if I would like a drink before the show. I replied, just as casually, that I would – even though I had never been in a pub before. So we went into the Marine Hotel and he ordered two pints and, at the tender age of fourteen, I sank my first beer.

My third source of information on the Navy occurred about the same time and was a boy called Michael Good-hugh. My headmaster, Mr Joy, introduced me to him, and we met at church on a couple of Sundays in August 1937 when he was home on leave from the Boys Training Establishment at Shotley. He was a little older than myself (probably sixteen), a well spoken boy who had been educated at Worthing High School and came from a very respectable family with a nice home in Offington. I soon discovered that everything he had to tell me was bad news. He absolutely hated being at Shotley and everything about it. His one ambition in life was to get out of the Navy somehow and, shortly after we met, his father achieved this by 'buying him out' – what the Navy terms 'Discharge by Purchase'. I soon realised what the problem was: he was a nervous boy and, even at that age, appeared to be a chain smoker. Of course, smoking by boys in the Navy was considered a serious crime and the punishment for offenders was really quite severe. For a first offence the culprit was brought before the Captain and, having been found guilty, was sentenced to 'six cuts'. This involved the boy, clad only in white duck trousers and stretched across a boxhorse while the Master at Arms would apply a stout, bamboo cane across his backside. It was a painful procedure and was designed as an instant cure for smoking – not only the culprit but other boys in the Mess who would view the very red tramlines on his backside. Unfortunately, many of the hardened smokers (and Michael was among them) did not learn the lesson and found, on their second appearance at Defaulters Table, that the punishment for further offences was 'twelve cuts'.

I considered myself fortunate, both at this stage and also later in life, that I had never had the desire to smoke –

and never did. This always seemed rather strange because my mother 'smoked like a chimney' as the saying goes, and yet neither I, nor my brother and sister, ever took up the habit.

Michael also told me other horror stories about life at Shotley: the harsh discipline and punishments; the cruel Instructors; the terrible winter weather; of course, none of the comforts of home. Although these were not what I wanted to hear, strangely, they did not make me want to alter my decision while I still had the chance. Quite the opposite, they made me more determined than ever to go ahead and join.

Of course, when questioned by my mother and Mr Joy about the outcome of our conversations I was deliberately reticent about what we had discussed. To this day I still wonder whether or not there was some conspiracy between my mother and Mr Joy with the idea of dissuading me from joining.

The sad postscript to this tale is that Michael's father was successful in 'buying him out' of the Navy (I don't know on what grounds) but, when the war began, he was called up for Army service and was subsequently killed at Dunkirk.

Apart from this, 1937 was also an eventful year for me because, as I mentioned earlier, I had now left school. At only fourteen years of age I was faced with the prospect of earning a living – at least until I could get into the Navy. Apart from the Navy, I had very little idea of what I wanted to do, and even less on how to set about it. By 1937 the job market did not seem too bad, especially following the terrible years of the Depression which lasted throughout the early thirties.

I can still remember the awful plight of workers in the North of England, suddenly unemployed through no fault of their own, setting out on a 'hunger march' from Jarrow (on the Tyne) to London, hoping to get some relief for their families.

Although I did not have to face such horrors there were not a lot of openings for a boy of fourteen leaving Elementary School with no skills. Furthermore, there seemed to be no such thing as counselling as there is today – then you were completely on your own – I can remember also some of the openings that were available to a boy like myself:

(a)   a *Telegraph Boy* for the GPO. I had a couple of friends who seemed to be happy enough delivering telegrams – wearing a uniform with a pillbox hat and riding a red bicycle all year. Poor pay and, after a couple of years, the chance of becoming a postman.

(b)   an *Errand Boy* delivering products from a retail store to their customers' homes – poorly paid, out in all weathers and poor prospects with the possibility of becoming a shop assistant.

(c)   an *Apprentice Gas Fitter*. I remember these chaps, parking their equipment on the road outside the premises they were working at. They would make a big performance of measuring a length of gas pipe, then cut it, and perhaps bend it, then pipe thread it. This was not my style.

(d)   an *Office Boy* in some stuffy solicitor's office – poor pay (and you had to wear a suit and tie) and even poorer prospects for advancement.

So these were just a few of the golden opportunities available in those days. However, the matter was decided for me by my friendly headmaster, Mr Joy, who towards the end of my final year (and knowing that I liked drawing), presented me with some sort of book on architecture and told me to copy the drawings therein.

They were floor plans of various buildings and I thought, 'Great, I am going to be an architect!' But the dream was short-lived. Having completed quite a few of these drawings, in Indian ink and on special drawing paper, over hours of painstaking work, I took them to the headmaster for approval. After close examination, he said they were very good – and then said he was sending me for a job interview with my drawings.

One evening, clutching my drawings with a good reference from Mr Joy, I had to go to the house of Mr C. E. Marr on Offington Avenue, a smart residential area of Worthing. His wife opened the door and, rather coolly I thought, directed me to the study where Mr Marr waited for me behind his big desk. When I saw him I immediately thought of that famous film actor Sidney Greenstreet (remember *The Maltese Falcon*) who always played the quiet-spoken, and ominous villain – a very large man who shook like a jelly when he gave his famous characteristic laugh. The only difference, which I soon noticed, was that Mr Marr did not laugh – in fact, I don't think he even smiled! Anyway, after firing a lot of questions at me and closely scrutinising my drawings with the aid of a slide rule he announced his verdict: 'These drawings are not exactly to scale!' In spite of this crime, I got the job, and after completing my school term on the next Friday I was told to report at 9 a.m. on the following Monday.

Eydman, Street and Bridge were an old established estate agent's with premises on Chapel Road – the heart of Worthing. The office was stuffy, cramped and was as large as a small corner store (which is what it was intended for). In addition to myself there were three others in the main office – two agents and a secretary who, it seemed, never stopped pounding her typewriter. Of course, Mr Marr, being the Manager, had his private office at the back and very seldom showed his face out front – for which I was grateful. My duties as office boy were soon explained to me and were threefold:

(a)   I was in charge of the postage, which went something like this. I was given a float of ten shillings (which I signed for) and would purchase stamps from the GPO, just up the road (I think the rate was a penny-ha'penny, i.e. one and a halfpence for a letter at that time). I was then responsible for weighing all the outgoing mail, sticking on the correct postage and then recording in a ledger the name and address of each letter and the amount of postage applied to each one. I always felt this was rather a waste of effort for the price of a stamp but then, who was I to query such procedure? Especially when Mr Marr diligently checked the postage book every week to see if there were any fiddles going on.

(b)   My next and, I believe, equally important function was to provide refreshment for the staff – tea was served (by me) at 11 a.m. and 4 p.m. In the afternoon we were allowed a biscuit with our 'cuppa' and, regularly every week, I was sent across the road to Sainsbury's for a new packet of biscuits. I can't swear to it but I think somebody counted them every week.

(c) My other function was to act as 'general dogsbody' for everyone else which usually meant helping the agents with the installation of their signs 'To be Sold' and 'To Let' etc.

Being situated on the comer of Chatsworth Road we had access to a yard at the rear of the office where a supply of these signs were stored, as well as the two office toilets.

Jack Spratt was one of the agents – a rather superior young man who thought he was 'the cat's whiskers' because he drove a small, sporty car and played the saxophone in a small dance band which sometimes appeared at the Pier Pavilion. He seemed to enjoy telling me to 'get a To Let sign, put it in my car and let me know when we are ready to go'. We would then drive to the property and I would be instructed on how to install the sign (usually by wiring it to a gatepost or something).

Well, as you might imagine, I was not too thrilled with all these activities and therefore it was not too long before we parted company. Mr Marr politely said I should find more suitable employment and, after a rather brief career of six weeks, I was happy to go.

I still believe that if a person does not gain some pleasure or satisfaction from the work they are doing then they will not do a good job. I know it was certainly true in my case. Although the terms of employment were not out of line for those days, I did find my working life very tedious. We worked what were normal office hours for those days which meant we started at 9 a.m., had a break for lunch from 1 to 2 p.m. and finished at 5.30. On Saturdays we finished at 1 p.m. Retail shops in those days would all close for lunch daily, had a half day on Wednesday but, of course, worked a full day on Saturday. For my efforts I was paid the princely sum of ten shillings and sixpence.

With my next job I was fortunate in many ways – I found it on my own, I started right away, I enjoyed the work and I doubled my salary overnight. Marshall's was a family owned retail newsagent and tobacconist in the Tarring area where I lived. When the father retired he left to his two sons, two very modern and, I think, prosperous stores. The eldest son had the one at the Thomas a' Beckett (Offington) which was about 15 minutes bike ride away and the other was at Tarring Crossing (West Worthing station) which was only three minutes away from my home.

I had heard through the grapevine that the store closest to me was looking for a fulltime employee so I wasted no time in getting in to see the boss and asking for the job. Doug Marshall was a very pleasant young man and we got on well from the word go – he was hardworking, conscientious and dedicated to making a success of the business. The same could be said of his sole assistant, Miss Grevatt, who put in long hours and was very efficient. She always wore a pale green smock to work, wore glasses,

Bob, 1938.

smoked heavily and, though probably only about thirty, appeared older because she seemed to have a permanent hunched back condition. All the time I was there I never knew either of them taking a day off – but then, neither did I!

Anyway, when Doug Marshall offered to take me on, at twenty shillings a week, I jumped at it. I think I was successful because I could boast of previous experience in the business – I had been delivering newspapers for the past four years.

In those days the requirements to be accepted for a newspaper round were:

(a)　To be at least ten years old;

(b)　To have your parents' permission;

(c)　To own a bicycle;

(d)　To know your way around Worthing.

Of course, it goes without saying that you had to be prepared to get up very early – and in all weathers. The rewards were not great (sixpence per day) but at least it provided some pocket money which our parents could not find. I had worked for two other newsagents in the area – Sillence, opposite West Worthing station, and Betts at Heene Road.

I soon found that, at Marshall's, I was earning my twenty shillings a week – I was always on the go and it was seven days a week, although my hours were staggered to meet the requirements of the business. A typical day would be that the morning papers would be dropped at the shop by the wholesaler's truck before we opened at 6 a.m. We would set up two long trestle tables so that we could sort and mark up the papers for each customer. When this was done the young delivery boys would be sent out on their respective rounds, usually by 6.30. It was then my time to go out – being a full time employee and therefore not being required to get back in time for school, I had the largest, and furthest, route to cover. I would start at Reigate Road, Wallace Avenue and then all along Goring Road, including Sea Lane (and all its offshoots), Shaftesbury Avenue, Robson Road, the farm cottages at the end of

Goring Road and then down Sea Lane, Ferring and finishing at Goring station. All this took about two hours, getting home about 8.30–8.45 after cycling about seven miles. Fridays were a little bit different because I had to collect money from all the customers, which added another 45 minutes to my time.

After breakfast I would be back at the shop and I remember my first duty was always to polish the cigarette vending machine at the front of the store. It was a recent addition and was Doug Marshall's pride and joy. It dispensed about a dozen different brands and gave change and the front panel was chrome plated which used to

Vivien with baby Martyn.

tarnish a bit, especially with the damp weather. I was only allowed to use a dry chamois leather to clean it (no polish of any sort) and this entailed an awful lot of elbow grease.

Here I must digress for a moment to recall two rather memorable events on my morning rounds. The first involved a house on Robson Road – a very nice house with very nice people but with a rather unpleasant little dog (a white Scottie). One day he decided to take a bite out of my leg – and succeeded! Strangely, when I think of it now, I did not complain to anybody – I guess I thought 'it goes with the territory'. When my mother saw it she was horrified and sent me off to 'Boots the Chemist' where the manager/pharmacist was a very stern looking gentleman. He took one look at it and pronounced, 'I will have to cauterise it' – which didn't mean much to me but I remember it hurt like hell.

The second incident was less painful and involved a customer on Goring Road. Most of my customers lived in small to medium size houses but this one lived at Courtlands Estate – a huge mansion lost in its own grounds with a very long driveway from the road. I used to cycle in, park my bicycle against one of the huge pillars and then knock at the front door, which was about twenty feet high. After a while this huge door swung open and there stood the butler, in full uniform, to receive the paper (nothing so common as a mailbox)!

On the Friday before Christmas, when I had to collect the one shilling and sixpence for the week's papers, he ceremoniously handed me an extra shilling for my 'Xmas Box'. I never knew who lived there because I only ever saw the butler. I believe the property was taken over by the Army during the war and afterwards was ultimately demolished to make way for another housing project.

I think I did quite well at Christmas (my only one in that job) when my customers gave me just over two pounds altogether – quite a sum in those days.

Anyway, to get back to my routine. A couple of mornings a week I would cycle into town to pick up our order from Collis & Co, the tobacco wholesalers, who were located on Montague Place. I would go home to lunch at noon and would then be free until four o'clock when I returned to the shop for the evening papers. Quite often I would find Doug and Miss Grevatt enjoying a quiet cup of tea in the lull before the evening rush. I liked this because

Jack, aged 15, in the Worthing Air Cadets.

they would offer me a cup of tea and, best of all, send me across the road to Collins the bakers for three delicious cream cakes.

At 4.30 I had to be at Carey's, the newspaper wholesalers, which was located in store premises right opposite Worthing Central rail station. I don't know how many there were, but every newsagent in Worthing sent a boy to Carey's to pick up their evening papers, so you can perhaps imagine it was a bit rowdy and, in addition, Carey's employed about ten men who worked like demons to get the papers sorted and on their way as fast as possible. In the middle of this circus was the ringmaster, Mr Carey himself – he was a small, wiry man with white hair and moustache. I think he even hated his mother because he certainly seemed to dislike everybody else. I never saw him smile and he was always yelling – at his men 'to speed it up' and at the boys 'to shut it up'. That was on a normal day – heaven help us when the London train (and the papers) were delayed because then he really went mad. But he always got the job done.

Evening deliveries, once we got them going, were a bit more relaxed than the morning – except Wednesday when the *Worthing Gazette* was published. Evenings were usually the time when I might pick up a new customer – I would always knock on the door when I saw that a house was newly occupied – and each one was an extra shilling for me.

When I gave my notice of leaving in December I know I was quite sorry to go, and I think my employers felt the same, although they had known for months that I planned to go into the Navy. All in all I had enjoyed the retail newsagent business – I had found it interesting and competitive and I particularly enjoyed the freedom of being outdoors all the time.

Part Two
The Navy

B.—234 (Established—July, 1931.)

R.N. & R.M. RECRUITING OFFICE,

....

[oval stamp: R.N. & R.M. RECRUITING OFFICE, 6 – JAN 1938, 191, KING'S ROAD ARCHES, BRIGHTON]

Date.............................

Mr. *R. A. Adams,*

6 Ettelbrad Road,

West Worthing.

With reference to your application to enter the Royal Navy as
a *Boy II class. C.S.*......, I have to inform you that you should
report at *the R.N. Recruiting Office at Portsmouth*......at *9*....a.m. on
MONDAY 10/1/38......and, subject to your being found in all respects
fit on being Medically re-examined, you will be forwarded for entry
in H.M.S. "*Ganges*" on the same day.

It is to be clearly understood that your entry will be subject to
final approval at *Portsmouth*......................

*A Railway Warrant, together with instructions regarding
travelling, is attached.

A. B. C. Woodhouse
Cmd. Sergt. R.M.

..................iting Staff Officer, R.N. and R.M.

......................rant is not issued.

...........5/8994 7m 4/34 S.E.R. Ltd. **Gp. 602.**

From:— R.N. & R.M. RECRUITING OFFICE,
191, KINGS RD, ARCHES,
BRIGHTON.

To:— *Master Robert Adams,*
6 Ettelbrad Road, West Worthing.

Please attend this Office for the preliminary examination at *9.45am*
on *WEDNESDAY 8.4.47* or *FRIDAY 10.4.5* at *2.45pm.*
This Office is situated on the Sea Front near the Bottom of West
Street, a direct route from Brighton Station to the Sea.
YOU ARE WARNED NOT TO THROW UP YOUR EMPLOYMENT ON THE OFF CHANCE
OF BEING ACCEPTED.
Railway Warrant is enclosed. This is to be handed to the Booking
Clerk at the Station when a RETURN TICKET will be issued in exchange.
If you are unable to attend for any reason, please RETURN THE
WARRANT AT ONCE with an explanation. *Please bring your Birth Certificate & two School Reports.*
Please call here on WEDNESDAY for preference but NOT on Saturday.
If it is impossible to call on Wednesday please be sure to return the Railway Warrant at once with an explanation!

A. B. C. Woodhouse Cmd Sgt R.M.
for Recruiting Staff Officer,
Royal Navy & Royal Marines.

[oval stamp: R.N. & R.M. RECRUITING OFFICE, 7 – DEC 1937, 191, KING'S ROAD ARCHES, BRIGHTON]

CHAPTER FOUR

Royal Navy

*There is not so helpless and pitiable an object in the world
as a landsman beginning a sailor life.*

Richard Henry Dana
Two Years before the Mast

REMEMBERING MY UNSUCCESSFUL APPLICATION of
the previous year which was rejected for being below
the acceptable age, I now took the Navy's advice and sent
a new application on my fifteenth birthday. I remember
having it all completed and ready to mail well before my
birthday; so, on 5 December 1937 it was posted to the RN
Recruiting Office in Brighton.

With today's fast paced life where everything is very high
tech and automated it always surprises me how long it
takes to achieve anything.

Compare it, if you will, with 'The old days' (1937)

(i) I mailed my application on Sunday 5 December

(ii) A reply was mailed to me at 4 p.m. on Tuesday 7
December

(iii) That reply was delivered to me early on Wednesday
8 December

(iv) p.m. the same day I was in Brighton (with my mother
in tow) to attend an interview at 2.45 p.m.

And subsequently:

(v) A notice was mailed to me on Thursday 6 January
telling me to report for service on Monday 10 January.

If nothing else, I think the foregoing illustrates how efficiently the situation was handled and, above all, is a great

example of how expeditious the Royal Mail was in those days and could always be trusted to deliver on time. What a pity we can't do it now.

When we (my mother and I) arrived at the Brighton Recruiting Office it was all locked up because I think we were a little early for my 2.45 appointment. The office was located at Kings Road Arches which is a rather pretentious name for a long row of cubbyholes (rather like caves) underneath the promenade. Nowadays, of course, they have large and spacious premises, with several staff, located on Brighton's main street. In 1937 though, it all seemed to be handled by one man and he was Colour Sergeant Woodhouse, Royal Marines. When he returned from his (late) lunch we got down to work, filling in forms and answering questions etc. I know he checked me over physically, just to make sure all parts were working normally.

He explained the conditions of service and the two types of engagement available to me (which, of course, I knew already):

(a) A Short Service engagement of seven years active service and the five years on the Reserve

(b) A Continuous Service engagement of twelve years active service (from the age of 18) followed by optional re-engagement for a further ten years to qualify for pension. Both of the engagements would not start counting until I reached my eighteenth birthday because, in the Navy, 'Boys Service' did not count as 'time served'.

Of course, I chose the latter option.

As I am starting to write this chapter it is another important date in my memory and marks a very significant milestone in my life. Today is 10 January 1998 and exactly sixty years ago on this date in 1938 was when I left home to be trained as a sailor in His Majesty's Navy.

Early on the Monday morning we all trooped down to West Worthing station – myself, my mother, Jack, June and my girlfriend Joyce. It was a rather tearful parting as I boarded the 7 a.m. train to Portsmouth. Once on the way I found I was sharing a compartment with a young man of similar age and we soon established that we were both headed for the same future. His name was Ron Maskell and he was from Brighton so we naturally became good friends during our training. Unfortunately, he was killed when the *Ashanti* (one of our Tribal class destroyers) was torpedoed and sunk.

When we arrived at Portsmouth Town station we made our way, rather apprehensively I admit, to the Royal Naval Recruiting Office on Edinburgh Road where we were due to report at 9 a.m. Once there, along with boys from other areas, we were given a medical examination and after signing some more papers and accepting *The King's Shilling* we were officially enrolled in the Royal Navy. *The King's Shilling* was a traditional bounty (now discontinued) which was paid by recruiters to enlisting men and, once accepted, there was no turning back.

About noon we were all marched (I use the term loosely at this point) back to Portsmouth station, having been issued with railway warrants to Harwich plus a meal voucher valid for a sausage roll or sandwich and a cup of tea in the railway buffet. We were put on a train to Waterloo with instructions to report on arrival to the Naval RTO.

Having achieved this, we were loaded (under the direction of the said Rail Transport Officer) into the back of a 3-ton lorry which took us on a trip across London to Liverpool Street station. Here we were off-loaded (under the supervision of another RTO) and we then boarded a very slow train destined for Harwich, on the East Coast. After a very uneventful, but slow and tedious, journey we finally arrived at Harwich Town about 5 p.m. where we were met by a stern-faced Petty Officer who managed to sort us out and 'march' us down to the harbour. There we were embarked on a steam picket boat (rather like a small tug) for the trip across to HMS *Ganges* at Shotley Point. I recall to this day how bitterly cold it was crossing the water but poor, unsuspecting souls that we were, we had no idea of the 'warm welcome' awaiting us upon reaching 'the Stone Frigate'.

CHAPTER FIVE

HMS Ganges

THE ORIGINAL HMS *Ganges* (the ship) was a teak-built sail training ship and, in 1895, had sailed around the coast from the harbour of Falmouth to anchor in Harwich Harbour. Ten years later, in 1905, the boys came ashore to establish HMS *Ganges*, the stone frigate, and, shortly after, the ship was taken to Chatham, re-named and used as a tender to RN Barracks. She was ultimately towed to Plymouth and broken up – an ignominious end for a vessel who, in her seagoing days, had the distinction of being the last wooden ship in the Royal Navy to carry an Admiral and acted as the Flagship of the Channel Fleet.

Geographically, the stone frigate *Ganges* was ideally situated for its purpose: it was located on the point of land where the two great rivers of Suffolk, the Stour and the Orwell, joined to form a huge delta where they flowed into the North Sea. On the northern tip of the estuary was the seaside town of Felixstowe with a Royal Air Force base from which they operated Sunderland flying boats. On the south side of the estuary was the busy port of Harwich which was the headquarters of Trinity House, the organisation responsible for the care and maintenance of all lighthouses, lightships and navigational marks around the coasts of Britain. All the famous lightships, so familiar in shipping forecasts (Goodwin, Dogger, Humber, North Foreland), would be towed in, one at a time, for repainting and repairs. Harwich was, and still is, famous as a North Sea port for ferries to Europe and Scandinavia. The Parkeston Ferry Terminal, with its long quays and sheds, was just to the west of Harwich and therefore immediately opposite Shotley.

So much for the geography lesson. Now on to my first impressions of life in the RN and of HMS *Ganges* in particular.

As we arrived at Shotley Pier it was cold, wet and dark and the only human being was the civilian 'piermaster' in his little cubbyhole at the end of the long pier. As we disembarked on to this enormous wooden structure there was an eerie feeling as we saw row upon row of grey boats (whalers and cutters) secured for the night on their davits like lines of grey ghosts, resting after an exhausting day on the water.

To reach the main establishment we had to climb three flights of large, stone stairs. When we reached the top we were all out of puff, even though it had been in slow time. We were soon to learn that these stairs were known among the boys as 'Faith, Hope & Charity' and were held in great respect. Instructors who felt their class had performed poorly in their boat work instruction would 'double' them up the steps (and sometimes down again).

Upon arriving on the Quarter Deck we were fallen in and inspected by the Officer of the Day and then checked in by the duty Regulating Petty Officer. We were informed that whenever coming on to the Quarter Deck we would salute and then double across it (to quick march or walk were considered loitering and therefore not allowed).

I now know that my overall impression of HMS *Ganges* was being overwhelmed by the sheer immensity of the place; the property and the buildings, The Mast and, not least of all, the population. Of course, in the dark and wet of 10 January 1938 very little of this was visible, but I do remember staring up at The Mast, disappearing up into the night sky, and wondering what it would be like 'up there'. Of the population there was virtually no sign – they were all on their Mess Decks enjoying supper (it was now 6.30).

Next, our Petty Officer marched us out of the Main Gate, past the huge figurehead of the old *Ganges* and, about a quarter of a mile along the road we entered through another gateway – a little less impressive this time. We were now in 'The Annexe' or the New Entries Barracks, which was to be our home for the next six weeks. This was a fairly recent construction with grey, corrugated iron buildings forming a square around the parade ground. On two opposite sides were the Boys' Messes, on the third the Mess Hall, stores and offices and on the fourth (alongside the road) was the Instructors' quarters and the Annexe main gate.

Our Instructor now introduced himself as Petty Officer Weaver (he was grey-haired and with an unsmiling face) and told us that for the next six weeks he would be our mentor, guide and mother – or, as he more eloquently put it, our wet-nurse! In six weeks he promised to lick us into shape so that we would not disgrace the uniform or ourselves when we moved into the Main Barracks with the 'old hands'.

Before being allowed to get our supper (everyone else had long gone) we were issued with 'temporary clothing' for use until our 'full' kits were issued the next day. Whilst clean (it had been washed but not pressed) this temporary clothing issue had obviously belonged to somebody else and was therefore not a particularly good fit – we must have looked a real mess but by now we didn't care; we just wanted a hot supper and a warm bed. But that was not to be – at least not yet – because first we had to strip off our civilian clothes, which were then parcelled up and, with an accompanying letter, and using a label written by us, despatched to our parents.

We then had to take a shower and, after donning our temporary clothing, were finally allowed into the Mess Hall for supper. It was now almost eight o'clock and the Duty Cook had not done a great job of keeping our food hot; and so it was that we sat down to nearly-cold Irish Stew and dumplings with a slice of bread and a mug of tea. After eating and clearing up we went to our own Mess Decks where each boy was allocated a bed – a basic iron frame with a mattress, two blankets and a pillow. We slept in a garment rather like a flannel nightshirt with a square neck trimmed in navy blue – not unreasonably this article was known as a 'flannel'. Sheets and pyjamas were not introduced into the Royal Navy until after the war. The bugle sounded 'Lights Out' at 9 p.m. and so ended my first day in the Navy – the first of very many.

The next few days were sometimes dreary, sometimes interesting and sometimes painful but invariably hectic and tiring for us 'Nozzers' – the rather derogatory name used by the 'old hands' when referring to New Entries like us. During the first week we went to the Barber Shop where we parted company with most of our hair; then to the Sick Bay for yet another medical and a couple of injections for good measure; to a rather large and busy Dental Surgery where Naval Dental Officers prodded and poked in our mouths while muttering all sorts of dire predictions about future treatment. I am sure they were very competent dentists but they were not big on sympathy and were very reluctant to waste time and money on injections.

During this time we were also introduced to the enormous gymnasium where immaculate Physical Training Instructors with apparently boundless energy put the boys through all the rigors of PT – graduating from regular exercises to parallel bars, springboards, box horse jumping and rope climbing. We also went to the Olympic size swimming pool where more PTIs put us through our paces and, before we could qualify as a swimmer, we were required to jump from the top board(I think it was 32ft.), swim the length of the pool and then stay afloat for three minutes. The only drawback was that we were required to do all this whilst wearing a uniform duck suit of jumper and bellbottoms. Anyone who failed would be known as a 'backward swimmer' and would have to attend special classes, always at inconvenient times.

Then came the first of many tests to see if we were made of suitable material to become sailors – i.e. The Mast – and this proved to be the most frightening experience of my life, until I had got used to being up there with the birds!

The Mast, which stood at the end of the parade ground, was from an old sailing ship and was a very impressive landmark, rising to 152 ft. with another eighteen feet buried in the concrete. The 'rig of the day' for The Mast was sports rig – i.e. sports' shirt, shorts and gym shoes – very draughty in the winter!

Our Instructor would line us up, six abreast, facing the rigging and, on the command 'Way Aloft', the first six would clamber up the rigging as fast as they could go, to be followed by the next six, and so on. The Mast had two yard-arms – the first had what was known in the Navy as 'The Devil's Elbow' which entailed leaning backwards in space, while hanging mostly by the hands, until you could pull yourself up to the next set of rigging. For somebody like myself who had never been higher than the top of a double-decker bus, this was a rather hairy experience. There was an opening (known as 'The Lubber's Hole') against the mast where one could get onto the platform of The Devil's Elbow in reasonable comfort and safety, but of course we were forbidden to use it! After The Elbow the second set of rigging narrowed as it went up to the top yard so that, on reaching the yard-arm, it was necessary to haul oneself up until you were standing on it and then wriggle around to the opposite side of the mast for the downward journey on the other side. Going down was a lot less nerve-racking, even though one still had to negotiate The Devil's Elbow from above, and reaching the ground still in one piece was the answer to a lot of prayers.

Quite naturally, on the first time up, many boys just froze when they got forty or fifty feet up with 'The Elbow' jutting out above them. If the Instructor's shouted insults, threats and encouragement failed to shift them a senior boy would be sent up to coax them. Many boys got to love The Mast, many more hated it, but almost all of them conquered it. The few who didn't make it were generally discharged back to civilian life.

As New Entries this mast climbing was scheduled for us every morning until we had achieved the required standard of three minutes for the whole class; after that we reverted to once a week for the rest of our training. Because I started in January it was not a very comfortable time for this activity – sometimes with a bit of ice on the rigging it required extra care but, like all activities at HMS *Ganges*, the season or the weather did not make any difference; they went ahead as scheduled.

Safety on The Mast did not seem to be a major factor and inevitably there was an occasional accident. There was a rope safety net at the base of the mast, eight feet above the concrete, but there was always the possibility of bouncing off. Instructors loved to tell their classes, 'It is impossible to fall off The Mast – no chance whatsoever!' and then some young lad, thinking the Instructor knew something he didn't, would innocently ask, 'Why is that, sir?' and the reply, of course, was, 'Because you will be hanging on too b—— tight!'

The next major project in our New Entry training was very important – getting issued with our kit. This took a full day to complete and, like everything else at Shotley, went very smoothly and efficiently, obviously from long practice. We were marched to the Clothing Store where we lined up patiently as we filed through, in alphabetical order, which was great for me. As we reached the counter an elderly (to us anyway) and very experienced civilian storekeeper would take one look and yell out 'size eight' (or whatever) and then we would be bombarded with every imaginable piece of kit. There were blue serge suits, white duck suits, footwear, underwear, sports gear, brushes (for hair, clothes, boots, teeth) and finally two books – a Manual of Seamanship and a Prayer Book (both of these I still have). But this was not the end of it because, before leaving the store, every item of kit (including the prayer book) had to be marked with the boy's name. This was quite a fascinating process. First the 'hard' items like boots and wooden brush handles, were stamped with a set of alphabetical punches and a hammer. We were then issued with an item called a 'type' – this was a piece of wood with our names carved along one edge in letters a quarter inch high. I guess it was done by a machine because they were all perfect.

The marking process itself was quite critical because every item had to be stamped so that every name was showing when it was laid out for kit inspection. The navy blue items were marked first with white paint, followed by the white items, using black paint.

After returning to the New Entry Annexe with our lovely new kit (we just couldn't wait to get rid of the second hand stuff we had been using!) the bad news hit us – every piece of clothing had to have the owner's name SEWN IN to it!

One item we had been issued was called a 'housewife' – it was a roll-up sewing kit and contained skeins of red and black silks; the red for sewing navy blue items and the black for white ones. At the time this sewing of names seemed an impossible task because firstly, we could not sew, and secondly, because it had to be completed before we could leave the New Entry barracks. I soon realised I was lucky to have a name like Adams; the boys called Worthington or Featherstone really had a problem.

Now came the experience of kit inspections which happened once a week in New Entries and every second Saturday in the main barracks; once a month by the Divisional Officer and once a month by the Captain. We soon learned all the tricks of laying out kit but, no matter how hard we tried, the Inspecting Officer usually managed to find some fault. When we had received our kit it had included several bundles of thin cord, about twelve inches long, called 'clothes stops' and we soon learned that these were an essential part of a kit muster.

Every item of clothing had to be tightly rolled, to match exactly the width of the Seamanship Manual, and then tied with two clothes stops (using a reef knot of course) located exactly the thickness of the Seamanship Manual from each end of the garment. On leaving the training establishment it was a relief to find that kit musters were behind us; they were only handed out as a form of punishment for sloppy appearance – and that was very rare.

During our six weeks in the New Entry Division we were all rated as a 'Boy Seaman' and it was not until we had completed many tests (educational, aptitude etc.) that we were segregated into different Instructional Courses when we moved to the main establishment to begin our professional training. Based on the test results, the top half of the New Entries class were routed into either the Communications Branch, which involved a fifteen month course, or the Advanced Course (Seaman) which was a twelve month course. The lower half were put into the General Course (Seaman) which was a nine month training. Even before joining I had decided I wanted to be in the V/S (Visual Signals) Branch so I was very pleased to find that I was in a position to choose this.

Therefore, our six weeks as New Entries comprised a lot of basic training, mostly parade ground drill, schoolwork, physical training and sports. In our spare time there was an awful lot of sewing to be done!

One incident in the second week allowed me to see the other side of Petty Officer Weaver, our rather strict Instructor. One day I developed a fever and, by suppertime, was feeling terrible so I went to the Instructors' Block and asked to see PO Weaver. I did not know what sort of reception to expect – would he send me to the Sick Bay, or would he be angry because I had disturbed his off-duty time?

To my surprise he took me into his cabin and told me to sit down, took my temperature and then told me to sit quietly. I guess I was there for an hour or more, not daring to cough even.

During all this time my Instructor was sitting at his desk, obviously writing a letter to his wife. Just before 'Lights Out' he sent me back to my Mess and told me to report to the Sick Bay in the morning. Of course, by the morning I felt a lot better but went to the Sick Bay anyway and when I came out I could see my class on the parade ground so decided I had better join them, even if I was late. So I trotted over and joined on the end of the rear rank – and then I heard a roar from PO Weaver to report to him. I doubled to the front of the class and received a terrific blast for 'joining a formation without first asking permission' – I never made that mistake again.

Finally the big day came when we were to move to the main establishment – our first step up the ladder but, more importantly, leaving behind all the square bashing, sewing, kit inspections and the ignominy of being a 'Nozzer'.

HMS *Ganges* was a very efficient training establishment which seemed to run like clockwork and it did not take long to realise that there were four things (at least) making it that way. The Instructors were efficient and dedicated Petty Officers and Chief Petty Officers, the well-tried daily routines were rigidly adhered to, discipline was very strict and for offenders (known as 'defaulters') punishments were harsh.

HMS *Ganges* was a little bit overwhelming, if nothing else, for its tremendous size and also the size of the population living there. It accommodated two thousand boys and over one hundred Instructors and perhaps fifty officers. All these were organised into eight Divisions (Benbow, Collingwood, Drake, Grenville, Blake, Rodney, Anson and Hawke). Each Division was in the care of a Lieutenant with a Warrant Officer to assist. Our division was to be Collingwood and our Divisional Officer was Lieutenant Johns and his assistant Mr Price. My class was to be #278 V/S Class which was instructed by Yeoman of Signals Fuller and our corresponding W/T (Wireless Telegraphy) class was instructed by Petty Officer Telegraphist Meadows. Both classes were to be accommodated in 36 Mess. PO Meadows was a small man and Yeo Fuller was a large one, inevitably known as 'Tiny'; and both proved to be first class Instructors.

In addition to all this there was a small army of administrative personnel, some naval and some civilian. There were storekeepers for the large clothing and victualling stores, many cooks for the huge galley and bakery, medical and dental staff in the small hospital plus a detachment of Royal Marines (mostly Corporals) who performed sentry and regulating duties, and not forgetting the large Royal Marine Band.

There were, of course, many diverse buildings; in addition to the Boys' Messes there were a huge Chiefs and

Petty Officers accommodation block, a Wardroom for the Officers, a Signal School, a Gunnery School, a Seamanship School and, of course, a 'school' School.

There was also a very large Laundry – not one where you sent your shirts and they came back clean, but where you took your 'dirties' and scrubbed them yourself! This was known in the Navy as 'dhobying' and was believed to be taken from the Hindu word *dhobi*, meaning to wash clothes. We had, of course, been introduced to this very important feature of Shotley life very soon after our arrival and would return there for the frequent *dhobi* sessions that appeared on our class routine. It was generally first thing in the morning and the Duty Instructor would get us out of bed half an hour before Reveille so that we could get back in time for breakfast. On arrival at the laundry we would strip off to our under-shorts, put our clothes in huge, galvanised tubs filled with hot water (two boys to each tub) then, on hands and knees, scrub our clothes on the floor.

There was no detergent in those days and we used a large bar of hard yellow soap; this was known as *Pusser's Hard*. Everything that came from naval resources was known as *Pusser's* which was the Navy adaptation of the word Purser – the man who, in the Merchant Navy, is the Supply Officer. After scrubbing, our clothes were rinsed in a huge communal tub and then put into the 'spinner' which was an enormous and noisy version of the modern spindrier. After this we would hang our clothes on huge racks in the heated drying room and would come back for them in the afternoon. We were then free to take a shower and get dressed.

As I remember, there were three unpleasant things about the Laundry; first, there was 'Laundry Joe', the man in charge of the place – a really grumpy ex-Marine who always had a rope's end (known as a 'stonnicky') handy to lay across the backside of any boy who was caught skylarking. I don't think he had a home because he was always in the Laundry. Secondly, the intense, heat and steam of the place almost overcame you and it was always a pleasure to get away from this. Thirdly, like many buildings at Shotley, the Laundry was built on the side of a hill (the steepest one) and so the roadway outside was a favourite location (like Faith, Hope & Charity) for any Instructor to discipline a class that got a bit too boisterous.

As I have said, discipline was strict and any boy brought before the Captain or Commander as a defaulter was almost certain to collect a period of *Jankers*. Normal Naval punishment is stoppage of leave and pay but, at Shotley, we had so little of either that *Jankers* was the alternative. This involved attending the parade ground every afternoon where the duty Gunnery Instructor would put the defaulters through their paces, usually double march around the parade perimeter whilst holding a rifle above their heads.

Food at *Ganges* was, I suppose, plain wholesome and adequate. Although personally I was always starving (I thought)! this could not be true because I put on weight while I was there, partly due to growing up, accelerated by the large doses of physical activity and fresh air. Partly also, I suppose, because my mother used to regularly send me a parcel which contained home baking. In order to claim a parcel one had to attend the Mail Office where a stern-faced Royal Marine Colour Sergeant would examine the contents, looking for cigarettes and money, before handing it over.

The Communications course I had chosen, and had been accepted for, was of 64 weeks duration. This was composed of six weeks New Entry training, six weeks Seasonal Leave (two weeks each at Easter, Summer and Christmas) and fifty-two weeks of professional training. The latter included: the art of sending and receiving messages by flashing (Morse lamp), Semaphore and Morse flag; the recognition and knowing the meaning of all naval signal flags (as well as the International Code); learning a dozen or more signalling instruction manuals, including codes and cyphers.

There would be examinations every twelve weeks to qualify at higher speeds and standards and those who failed would be 'back-classed' to the following course – this was the ultimate disgrace.

Then there was school and, in Boys Training, education was taken very seriously – a fact that I have always appreciated because I know that I learned more from my naval schooling than anywhere else. Shotley had its own school (which looked just like a typical grammar school) and was staffed by approximately twenty teachers serving as regular officers in the RN, wearing a distinctive blue stripe below their gold rings. Their title was Instructor Officer and any boys who thought that they might be the least bit soft soon found out to their cost that this was not true. The Instructor Commander was a particularly fierce man who, when classes fell in to march away, would not hesitate, if he caught a boy talking or moving around, to have the whole class double up and down School Hill.

The subjects we were taking were a little different – in addition to the usual Mathematics, History, English and Geography we had to learn Magnetism & Electricity (always abbreviated to 'Mag and Elec'), Navigation and General Knowledge, the last two being my favourites. School was also an area where, if one did not pass the regular examinations, one would be 'back-classed' and, because school qualifications also affected future promotion prospects, it was something that was to be taken seriously.

In addition to all these activities we also spent a lot of time on the water, both sailing and boat pulling, known collectively as 'Boatwork'. For every session the boats had to be lowered to the water, rigged for sailing or pulling and, on completion, hoisted on the davits and secured. To us youngsters the 32ft cutters, and even the 28ft whalers, always seemed heavy and ungainly, so that in our early days we all suffered from blisters from the ropes and oars. An added discomfort was that the Boatwork was always done in 'Sports Rig' (i.e. shorts and rugby shirt) both winter and summer, although in winter we were allowed to wear a woollen sea jersey. If it was raining we were also allowed to wear our black oilskin coats but these only hampered our movements and tended to chafe the neck and wrists.

The 32ft cutters (which were in the majority) were rather unpleasant, both for pulling and sailing. When pulling, the 20ft oars were heavy and cumbersome, making it difficult not to catch the occasional 'crab', thus incurring the displeasure of the Instructor. For sailing they were not a lot better because they had an awkward rig called the 'dipping lug' which made *coming about* a strenuous manoeuvre.

HMS *Ganges* had a tremendous advantage in the enormous, land locked area of water available in the mouth of the two great rivers. Although, virtually, surrounded by land on all sides, it was such a wide, open, expanse of water that it could get quite choppy in the frequent NE winds that swept in from the North Sea. It always surprised me that there were not more cracked skulls from a mast being dropped when rigging or unrigging a boat in these sorts of conditions.

A very familiar sight on the waters of this area were the solid and majestic Thames sailing barges as they made their way steadily up and down the Stour and Orwell. Today, unfortunately, these beautiful vessels are long gone from service and only a very few, privately owned and restored to former glory, are used in the Thames Barge Race, held annually on the River Thames.

In view of the prevailing weather conditions at Shotley, especially in the winter months, coupled with two thousand boys living in close quarters, it would always surprise me that we did not suffer from more illnesses. Although our health was guaranteed by a well-equipped and staffed Sick Bay (small hospital to be accurate), I believe our physical fitness was due mainly to activities in the fresh air in all weathers.

However, there was one occasion when I was on the Sick List for about a week. In the winter of 1938–39 there was an outbreak of impetigo which is a particularly unpleasant skin disease that is highly contagious. It consists of a mass of small blisters which burst and form sores. In those days, the treatment was painting the area with a purple liquid; nowadays, of course, it would be treated with something simple like antibiotics. Anyway, I caught it and it spread over one shoulder and armpit; because it was not responding to treatment I was classified as 'Light Duty – Sick Bay'. This meant that I was confined to the Sick Bay and, because I was not confined to bed, could perform light duties there. I would sleep in a cot in the hospital, see the doctor every morning and, twice daily, get the purple painting job.

My 'Light Duties' were mostly twofold. The man in charge was the Chief Sick Berth Petty Officer, who occupied an office with a fireplace. The office had to be dusted, the fireplace cleared out and the fire burning brightly when he arrived for duty at eight a.m. My second duty was unofficial because the Sick Bay cook didn't like washing up and would get me to do it whenever possible. I did not mind this because I always got rewarded with extra food, but the Chief objected to this situation and, whenever he caught me washing up, would yell at the cook and take me off it.

Anyway, one evening, with the Sick Bay deserted, I was

getting my treatment from the duty Sick Berth Attendant (he was a Leading Hand and obviously had some experience) when he asked me if the infliction was improving. When I shook my head he said, 'It never will with that useless purple stuff.' He then told me that he could cure it for me but there were two problems – first, it would be painful and second, he would be in serious trouble if anyone found out what he had done.

It didn't take long to decide because I was missing valuable instruction time and, with exams approaching, I would hate to be 'back classed' through no fault of my own. He soon appeared with a large bottle in one hand and cotton wool in the other and then proceeded to wash my shoulder and underarm – I nearly shot through the roof with the agony – he was using neat Methylated Spirits! A couple of days later the doctor was congratulating himself on having cured me and I was allowed to rejoin my class. Nobody ever knew what really happened but I was eternally grateful to the man who had caused me so much pain!

A lot of time was also used in learning other aspects of Seamanship such as knots, splices, anchors, cables, mooring and securing ships; also the various types of rope, wire and canvas used by the Navy. We also received instruction in the use of a rifle – how to handle it, clean it and fire it. In addition to a lot of parade ground drill with rifles there was also a rifle range where we had target practice. In those days it was the Short Lee Enfield .303.

I think the biggest single activity at Shotley was recreational sports, and *Ganges* was certainly well equipped for it. There were enormous green playing fields where we were coached in cricket, field hockey, rugby and soccer. In the huge gymnasium we trained in gymnastics, rope climbing and boxing. The Olympic size swimming pool gave us swimming, diving and water polo.

All these activities, plus boatwork, took place in the afternoon. At 12.15 every day, after a long morning in various classrooms, the pipe was 'Hands to dinner and clean into sports rig', and at 13.15 we would commence whatever activity had been prearranged for our class. Then at 4 p.m. it was 'Hands to tea and clean into Night Clothing' – tea was always a mug of tea with bread and jam (a slice of fruitcake on Sundays) and 'Night Clothing' did not mean pyjamas! It was a blue serge suit (as opposed to the white duck suit worn in the forenoons). We were assembled for 'Evening Quarters' at 4.45 p.m. and then marched off for more classroom instruction until supper-time. We were never allowed to be idle and I think this was what kept us so healthy and certainly made us ready for 'Lights Out' at 9 p.m.

The only exceptions to this p.m. routine was on Wednesday, which was our big day because, not only was it pay day, but we also had a cinema show in the gymnasium after Evening Quarters. I think now that the films were carefully selected and considered morally uplifting for young boys, but we enjoyed them nevertheless! On one Wednesday evening, instead of getting a cinema show, we were given a lecture and slide show by Admiral Evans on his expedition, as a junior officer, to the South Pole with Captain Scott. Evans was famous for his daring exploits, being known throughout the Navy as 'Evans of the *Broke*'. During the First War, he was Captain of the destroyer HMS *Broke* which led the daring, but costly, raid on Zeebrugge. In the gymnasium on either side of the huge stage (where the cinema screen was located) was a large board on which was reproduced the famous poem by Rudyard Kipling, *If* – a morale booster if ever there was one!

Nowadays it is difficult to relate present day wages, etc., to what it was in those pre-war days; but it is, I think, interesting to look back to those times.

When I first entered the Royal Navy my rating was 'Boy 2nd class' and the pay for that was five shillings and three pence per week (i.e. ninepence per day) and, out of that, I would receive one shilling each pay day, with the rest

Heavy gun battery.

being held in my account until I reached the age of eighteen. After six months at *Ganges*, and passing the necessary examinations, I was rated 'Boy 1st class (Probationary Signal Boy)' and my pay jumped to eight shillings and ninepence per week (i.e. fifteen pence per day) but I still only received one shilling and sixpence per week as pocket money and the balance continued as a credit to my account.

The only comparison I can make now is that I believe the US dollar in those days was worth six shillings and eight pence (i.e. three dollars to the pound).

The system of holding back a good portion of our pay meant that, in my case, my mother got a nice present when it was finally released. As regards to the small amount of pocket money, it should be borne in mind that there was virtually nothing to spend it on. There was a canteen, of course, and on Wednesday afternoon it would be crowded with boys eager to 'blow' their shilling. Mine soon went, usually on the same items, i.e. one postage stamp (for my weekly letter home), one chocolate bar (to be consumed at the cinema show), one bottle of pop and one 'Charlie'! A 'Charlie' was a sort of baked concoction which came in a huge tray, which was cut into three-inch squares which cost threepence each. The top and bottom layers were some sort of pastry and in the middle was bread pudding with sultanas – delicious – but I am sure it was not good for the digestion!

At *Ganges* there was no such thing as local leave except on Sunday afternoon when we were allowed to walk out between 1 p.m. and 6 p.m. Having done this once you probably would not bother again because, once outside the main gates, there was nothing to see and nowhere to go except to walk along a country road and back. The tiny village of Shotley boasted one pub and one small general store, both of them strictly forbidden to sell cigarettes or beer to any *Ganges* boy. Of course, the smokers usually got round this by getting a couple of local girls, who were usually hanging around, to purchase them for them – but then they generally got caught trying to smuggle them in – which inevitably meant 'six cuts' (or more). Sunday afternoon leave was also popular with any boy who had decided to desert and wanted to 'do a runner' – it gave them five hours start before they would be missed. I don't know how many tried but I don't think any of them ever made it – the local police were pretty watchful and usually picked them up at Ipswich railway station or, if they were more adventurous, across the river at Parkeston Quay, the ferry terminal.

When my class (thankfully) moved to our new Mess in the main establishment it was coming near to the end of February 1938, so Easter leave could not be far away – but it did seem likes ages at the time. The main topic of conversation at Shotley was always, 'How many Charlies to leave?' – and every boy always knew the answer to that one!

This was not the same Charlie that was consumed in the canteen. This one was the sound of the bugle at Reveille, the first bugle call of the day and which was known as Charlie because the notes of the bugle had the same rhythm as the words 'Charlie, Charlie get out of bed'. Eventually, of course, the magic day came when we would be going home, in our best uniforms, for our very first leave – and the excitement was intense. The previous day we had been issued our brand new overcoats and dress shoes – these were kept in storage from one leave to the next as they were not worn during training. I don't think any boy waited for that final 'Charlie' – they were all up at four or five o'clock, making doubly sure everything was ready for going home on leave.

After breakfast we were assembled on the parade ground and detailed for the red double-decker buses that would take us the ten miles to Ipswich. The train journey to London and then on to Worthing was exciting and, on arrival, it was wonderful to be back with my family again,

Boatwork instruction.

even if it was only for a brief two weeks. My leave was even more enjoyable because Spud Taylor, my friend from school, was also home on leave from the Army. At the same time as I had joined the Navy, Spud went into the Royal Artillery as a Boy Soldier and had been training at a depot in Oswestry, on the border of Wales.

There were two more leave periods for me from HMS *Ganges* – summer 1938 and Christmas 1938. But between Easter and Summer of that year there were two major events in our lives. First, the Munich Crisis was the big news and it appeared at the time that war was imminent. As a result, the boys of Shotley were diverted from our afternoon sporting activities and put to work, with pick and shovel, to dig trenches all around the playing fields in case of air raids. Of course, they were never used while I was there and when Mr Chamberlain came home smiling we stopped digging and went back to our normal routine.

The second event in that period was the King's Birthday Review which was held, every year, on the Sovereign's Official Birthday on 10 June. This was a very complex ceremony involving the full Ship's Company and, with the Royal Marine Band, included drill, marching, field gun drill and a Royal Salute. The final portion was a march past of all classes, in line abreast, with the Captain taking the salute. Of course, at this point, there were many critical eyes watching the performance of every class – and woe betide any class who embarrassed their Instructor by not putting on a good show.

As the weeks and months of training dragged by (very

Digging air-raid trenches, 1938.

slowly it seemed) we gradually became more proficient in our technical skills so that, early in 1939, we began to dream about 'going to sea'. This was the term to describe leaving the training establishment and joining the Fleet, with all the endless possibilities in our minds of what type of ship and in what part of the world we would find ourselves when this happened.

Finally, our big day came, on 24 March 1939, when I and the rest of my class said farewell, for the last time, to HMS *Ganges*. We had passed our examinations and were now rated 'Signal Boy' (the 'Probationary' was dropped) and to all intent and purpose we were ready to 'go to sea' and, I might add, very eager to do so.

I know also, speaking personally, that there was, in addition to the eager anticipation, a feeling of sadness at leaving the place that had been my home for the past fifteen months. Whatever our experiences there – we had been through homesickness, loneliness, triumphs and failures, pleasure and pain – the final moment had come and I remember the overall feeling was pride that we had eventually made it. I was very conscious of the reputation that Shotley carried throughout the Navy of those days – HMS *Ganges* takes in boys and turns out men – (even if we were only sixteen).

Although we were leaving *Ganges* behind, probably never

HMS *Ganges* 278 Class Senior Flag Hoisting Champions, 1939.

Bob Adams, Ron
Maskell and Ron Smith.

to return, I knew that our training there would serve us well and that this would be a period we would remember for the rest of our lives.

The Legend of HMS *Ganges*

There's a village they call Shotley to the east of Ipswich town,
The port of Felixstowe across the way.
There's a stone-built frigate, *Ganges*, near the Orwell flowing

down,
And skirted by the shores of Harwich Bay.
Well, we joined as Nozzers new, the 'sailor boys' in blue:
And punched our oppo's teeth out in the gym.
We marched and doubled-fast! Then we climbed that b——y
    Mast:
The Foreign Legion <u>never</u> was as grim!

Eight Divisions – Admirals all – parade ground – Nelson Hall,
And Nozzer's Lane tucked out of sight away.
There was Collingwood and Blake, there was Benbow, Hawke
    and Drake;
And Grenville – down the long, long covered Way.
The 'dabtoes' learned to sail a boat, correct a starboard list,
And take evasive action from the bombs,
They could 'bend' and 'splice' and 'hitch', they could knot a
    Monkey's Fist,
There was semaphore and flashing for the 'Comms'.

Down Laundry Hill on jankers, tin hat shades the sweating
    frown
And bayonet bangin' 'ard against the thigh.
Rifles chafed our collar bones, the hot sun scorching down,
From inverted bowl of blue, the summer sky.
'Do just as you are told, lad, make do with what you got,
Obey the orders, boy! No *ifs* or *buts!*'
The discipline was *hot*, and some went *on the trot*,
But they dragged 'em back and lashed 'em with twelve cuts.

We had Faith and we had Hope, we had Charity as well;
But these were not just virtues – as you know!
We stumbled and we fell, – on those concrete steps to Hell,
Our souls were signed to *Ganges* – be it so.
What Faith? What Hope? What Charity? Was there really no
    comparity?
As we staggered up those steps with muscle pain,
Well, we knew we'd had enough – but assumed that we were
    tough –
So they made us double up and down again!

Ganges motto states at length, that 'Wisdom, it is strength'
Is there one of you who wouldn't go again?
Though they flogged us and they flayed us, by the living God
    what made us;
You took us on as boys – and made us men!

If

If you can keep your head when all about you,
Are losing theirs and blaming it on you;
If you can trust yourself when all men doubt you,
But make allowances for their doubting too;
If you can wait and not be tired by waiting,
Or being lied about, don't deal in lies,
Or being hated, don't give way to hating;
And yet don't look too good, or talk too wise.

If you can dream – and not make dreams your master;
If you can think – and not make thoughts your aim;
If you can meet with Triumph and Disaster,
And treat those two impostors just the same;
If you can bear to hear the truth you've spoken,
Twisted by knaves to make a trap for fools,
Or watch the things you gave your life to, broken,
And stoop and build 'em up with worn out tools.

If you can make one heap of all your winnings
And risk it on one turn of pitch-and-toss,
And lose, and start again at your beginnings,
And never breathe a word about your loss.
If you can force your heart and nerve and sinew,
To serve your turn long after they are gone,
And so hold on when there is nothing in you
Except the Will which says to them 'Hold on!'

If you can talk with crowds and keep your virtue,
Or walk with Kings – nor lose the common touch
If neither foes nor loving friends can hurt you,
If all men count with you, but none too much;
If you can fill the unforgiving minute
With sixty seconds worth of distance run.
Yours is the Earth, and everything that's in it,
And – which is more – you'll be a Man, my son!

Rudyard Kipling

CHAPTER SIX

HMS *Victory*

O N 24 MARCH 1939, having been drafted from HMS *Ganges* to HMS *Victory*, I travelled by train with my kitbag and hammock, to Portsmouth which was to be my home depot for the rest of my time in the Navy. The choice had been between Portsmouth, Chatham and Devonport and, because Portsmouth was only thirty-five miles from my home in Worthing, the choice was not difficult.

HMS *Victory* was, like *Ganges*, another Stone Frigate and was, in fact, the Royal Naval Barracks, Portsmouth – the latter being the name normally used so as not to be confused with Nelson's old flagship HMS *Victory* which was in drydock in Portsmouth Dockyard and usually addressed as *Victory* (Ship). Nelson's old ship was still in commission with a small crew who kept it in shape and acted as guides for parties of visitors.

RN Barracks Portsmouth was not a particularly inspiring place for a boy who only wanted to be on a ship but the atmosphere was exciting, just to be among all the real sailors. The buildings were a collection of tall, red brick, Victorian-era accommodation blocks. One of these was the Signal School where we were to be housed – we did not settle in because we knew it was only temporary, although we did not know for how long nor where we would be going next.

My brief stay in the Barracks was memorable for one event which was to give me many a laugh in years to come. Although we ate in the Signal School Mess there was a problem when it came to sleeping because boys were not normally accommodated in the Barracks and so there was no separate Boys' Mess. We were told to sling our hammocks in the Insructional area of the block 'KK Room', as it was designated, which was, in fact, a very large classroom (probably 90′ × 30′) with the Admin offices off to one side.

The outstanding feature of this room was its cleanliness –

the floor of wood strip was highly polished and looked like burnished gold. The many tables and benches were scrubbed pure white and, about eight feet above them were the hammock rails for slinging hammocks. Because we had slept in beds at Shotley this was to be our first experience of sleeping in a hammock. Before leaving Shotley we had returned the bedding we had been using (a mattress, two blankets and a pillow) and were issued with two hammocks, one hammock mattress, one blanket and a set of clews and lashings.

Although we had been shown how to sling a hammock and how to lash it up in the morning (it had to be seven turns, no more, no less) our first night in one was not the greatest success. In the morning we got up at Reveille, carefully folded our new blankets and lashed them up in our new hammocks. We then washed, dressed and went to breakfast but when we returned all hell had broken loose and we couldn't understand why we were suddenly so unpopular.

Then it was pointed out to us – the whole room, and especially the highly waxed floor, was covered in a thick layer of white blanket dust, not to mention fibres from the heavy canvas of the hammocks and the sisal lashings!

Needless to say, we spent the rest of that forenoon restoring KK Room to its former glory.

There were about twelve or fifteen boys in my draft from Shotley and on the following day we were told that we would all be going to HMS *Iron Duke* to complete three months Sea Training.

CHAPTER SEVEN

HMS *Iron Duke*

O N 28 MARCH 1939 my group from Shotley left RN Barracks Portsmouth and were on our way to join our first ship, berthed in HM Dockyard, Portsmouth.

HMS *Iron Duke* was a battleship of World War I vintage and had seen a lot of active service in her younger days but was now well past her prime and, in 1939, was serving a dual purpose as the Navy's Gunnery Training Ship and Boys' Sea Training Ship.

Iron Duke was completed in 1914 after building in Portsmouth Dockyard and served as Flagship of Admiral Jellicoe, Commander-in-Chief, Grand Fleet, from 1914 to 1916, including the *Battle of Jutland* on 31 May 1916.

In 1931 came the London Naval Treaty which attempted

Iron Duke boys in camp at Fort Fareham, June 1939 (Bob, fourth from left in rear rank).

to equalise the Navies of the world and, because the Royal Navy was the most powerful, several vessels had to be sacrificed to what was known as 'DeMiltarisation'. *Iron Duke* was one of those chosen and suffered the indignity of having two of her four main armament turrets removed. This, coupled with the fact that she was the last coal-burning ship in the RN, now made her an ugly duckling.

On our route through Portsmouth Dockyard we passed the battle cruiser *Renown* (a beautiful ship) in dry dock preparing for the Royal Tour of South Africa that summer. I remember thinking, 'I wish I was joining that one.'

We found the *Iron Duke* in her regular berth at North Corner Jetty which was the coaling berth and, besides the mountains of coal nearby, had the added disadvantage of being the furthest point from the Dockyard Main Gate. We joined the ship and were soon settled in, having discovered that *Iron Duke* carried two hundred and fifty boys. We were accommodated in a large mess deck of our own and the two Petty Officers who were the Boys Instructors were in an enclosed mess adjoining ours.

Our routine was somewhat similar to *Ganges* with the emphasis on school, PT and Departmental Training (Communications for me) except the atmosphere was more relaxed in the environment of a ship afloat. One thing I didn't like much was that the Boys Division was called half-an-hour earlier than the remainder of the ship's company. We mustered on the upper deck and then the Signal Boys were sent to scrub the Bridge and Flag Deck while the 'dabtoes' (Seamen Boys) scrubbed the upper deck.

A couple of days after joining we made our first trip to sea for a Gunnery Practice where gunnery personnel fired the big guns at a BPT (Battle Practice Target) towed by a Navy tug. I don't know whether the tug's crew got danger pay but I always felt they deserved it!

In late May we sailed further than usual on a courtesy visit to Torquay – I think it was Regatta Week – but I was not able to enjoy the local attractions owing to having my arm in a sling with a busted left hand – some boy sat on a mess bench while my hand was underneath securing it.

At the beginning of June the *Iron Duke* was due for docking and boiler cleaning so the opportunity was taken to send the entire Boys Division off to camp for two weeks. The location was to be Fort Fareham, just off the Fareham to Gosport road, one of the tremendous fortifications built to protect Portsmouth during the Napoleonic Wars.

We lived in huge cave-like rooms built into the enormous earthworks around a large central area which included a parade ground. I really enjoyed that time – the weather was perfect (just as well because we were always outside), and the routine was different with lots of sports, PT, route marches and rifle drills. We were under the command of Lieutenant Commander Lichfield-Speer who was the Boys Divisional Officer on *Iron Duke*. He was a rather aristocratic gentleman and amazed us boys by leading our route marches mounted on his own huge horse! I also remember he delighted us one evening by giving his own cinema show of film he had taken on his previous appointment in HMS *Malaya* in the Mediterranean. Black and white of course and no sound, only his commentary, but nevertheless it was exciting for us novices to get a view of a real Fleet at sea on manoeuvres.

I must digress for a moment to relate an incident that occurred while I was serving on *Iron Duke* but I was not aware of it until much later. My brother Jack, now at home and just turned 15, had an odd hobby of digging large holes, sometimes to a depth of five or six feet, in the back garden. My mother used to worry about him getting buried and, whenever she could, got someone to fill them in when Jack was not around. Anyway, at this time he found, in his diggings, a very small wooden barrel and, when he cleaned it, discovered a tiny plate on it saying, 'From the teak of HMS *Iron Duke* Admiral Jellicoe's Flagship Jutland 1916.' True or not, I thought it was a remarkable coincidence that he would discover it while I was serving in HMS *Iron Duke*.

Soon after returning from camp we learned that all of my Shotley group of Communications Boys were to be drafted back to RN Barracks 'for disposal'. So, very shortly, we found ourselves with a large group of other communications ratings fallen-in outside the Signal School as we listened to a Chief Petty Officer reading off two lists of names. It appeared that there were two capital ships due to re-commission – HMS *Hood* in the Home Fleet and HMS *Eagle* on the China Station. I think my group was split about half each and I was in the half to go to *Eagle*. I had secretly been hoping to get the *Hood*, the pride of the Royal Navy but, if I had got it, I would not be writing this now because, two years later, she was sunk in a battle with the *Bismarck* with the loss of fifteen hundred men (all but three of her complement). There were only three survivors; one Midshipman, a Stoker and a young Signalman, Ted Briggs, a friend of mine who survived the war and retired as a Lieutenant. He was also interviewed on TV for the *Bismarck* programme. HMS *Iron Duke* was bombed in Scapa Flow in 1940 but was beached before she sank and served the rest of the war as Fleet Depot Ship in Scapa. She was subsequently scrapped in 1946.

CHAPTER EIGHT

HMT Dilwara

AFTER BEING ISSUED WITH our tropical kit, suffering a couple of injections and having enjoyed ten days Embarkation Leave we returned for our final day at RN Barracks, Portsmouth. The day was spent doing our 'Drafting Routine' which involved going to all the administrative offices (Pay, Records, Victualling etc.) to make sure they knew you were leaving and, as proof of your visit, you were required to collect all the departmental stamps on a form to be handed in to the Regulating Office on completion. Therefore it was customary to see any number of sailors, with a piece of paper in hand, walking all around the parade ground perimeter. The reason for this (instead of the shorter route <u>across</u> the parade ground) was soon learned, even by youngsters like me; the rule being that anybody on the parade ground was required to move at the double. To enforce this, the Chief Gunnery Instructor

was stationed in the centre of this enormous area and woe
betide any unwary man who did not notice him – two
steps and they would hear a bellow – 'That man – report
to me at the double.'

In those days it was normal for a ship to be commissioned for two and a half years, whether in the Home
Fleet or on a foreign station. So, knowing that the *Eagle*
was on the China Station, we realised that we were going
to be away for a long time – and also that it would take
a long time to get there. So now we had a full crew of
900 officers and men travelling to Hong Kong to relieve
the existing crew who would return to England for a well
earned leave.

Air travel was in its infancy, even for civilians, and service
personnel were invariably moved by train in mainland
Britain and by troopship overseas.

So, early on 1 July 1939 there was a special train waiting
for us on a siding within the barracks which would take
us to Southampton where we were to embark in HM
Troopship *Dilwara*. As the description implies, troopships
were operated and run by the Army and so it was a strange
feeling for us sailors to be at sea and under the jurisdiction
of the Army. The Naval Draft, comprising 900 officers
and men, was about one third of the total on board –
there was a small contingent of RAF and the rest were men
of the County regiments (I think it was the East Yorkshire)
going to join the Hong Kong garrison. Unfortunately, it
would prove to be a one-way journey for most of them.

All troopships were chartered by the War Department
from the British India Steam Navigation Company, a
subsidiary of P&O; BISN had been transporting British
soldiers to and from India for a hundred years. These ships
had British officers, a Lascar crew and Indian stewards.
The *Dilwara*, and her sister ship *Dunera*, were modern
ships, purpose built for the job of troop carrying and
therefore well equipped and comparatively comfortable
although there was, inevitably, a feeling of overcrowding.

We had arrived at Southampton and embarked in
Dilwara and, being early arrivals, had settled into our
messdecks when the majority of the troops arrived. By
afternoon the *Dilwara* had swallowed over two thousand
bodies and a mountain of equipment and baggage; we
were about to start on our long and, for me at least, very
exciting voyage.

POST CARD

Correspondence   Address

Dearest Mather & Gran

Just a card to let you know I am O.K. & I will write later. We left "Iron Duke" 7, AM Friday & went to R.H.

POST CARD

Correspondence   Address

Barracks for our tropical kit, left there today & have just embarked on "Dilwara." Sail 2.30 PM this afternoon. Have met lot of "Ganges" pals on here also going to China.

lots of love
Billy

POST CARD

Correspondence   Address

Postcard mailed from *Dilwara* at Southampton, 1 July 1939.

I can still remember the feeling of wonder and excitement as we sailed down the Solent, past the Isle of Wight and on down the Channel. It is also easy to recall the feeling next day as we entered the Bay of Biscay – the weather changed and the sun came out; the seas got more aggressive and the ship took on a steady pitch and roll – all this told us that we were really going abroad. I think there were a few green faces, but not too many.

The routine on board was not too bad, even for us boys. We had about thirty Boys going to *Eagle* (6 V/S, 6 W/T and the rest were Seamen Boys), and the Boys' Mess would be roused half an hour early so that we could do PT on the boatdeck. After breakfast and then cleaning and scrubbing the messdeck, most of the forenoon was spent at school classes with the 'Schoolie', who was also bound for *Eagle*. The rest of the day was our own and would be spent reading, sleeping, sunbathing, dhobying or swimming. The ship did not have a pool proper, but, after passing Gibraltar, the crew rigged a large canvas pool (about 10′ × 10′) on the afterdeck and this was filled daily with seawater – quite cool, but a lot of fun.

As we sailed through the Mediterranean, the sea got bluer and calmer and the sun got warmer – all of which made life very pleasant. This was just as well because it was going to be a very long voyage and there would be no opportunity of shore leave – in fact, we only made two stops, for re-fuelling, at Port Said and Singapore. I remember being disappointed that we did not see more places, such as Gibraltar and Malta, but, as we ploughed on our way without even a glimpse of them, we were made to realise that we were *not* on a pleasure cruise.

Our first stop was at Port Said and this was for two reasons – first, to refuel and, second, to await our turn to transit the Suez Canal. I will never forget my first impression as we approached the Egyptian coastline – it was the almost over-powering smell – and this was something that never changed in later years. Although not totally pleasant, it was so strong and so different that it aroused excitement because, undoubtedly, you were entering a foreign land – a sensation especially powerful when experienced for the first time. Port Said was a very busy place, both with shipping and also on shore but, interesting though it was, the heat was so oppressive that we were not sorry to be on the move again. By then (late afternoon), many of the troops had made purchases (mostly of leather or cotton goods) from the Arab dealers who swarmed alongside the ship. They were a humorous and interesting bunch who very obviously had a lot of experience in dealing with British troops, because they all sported unlikely names such as 'Jock MacGregor', 'Jaudy Wells', 'Taffy Evans', and so on.

Our journey through the Suez Canal was very interesting and I think everyone was on deck for it – the camels, the local population and the ingenious irrigation systems to cultivate a green field amid so much sand. It was also very impressive when we passed another ship that was homeward bound. After dropping our Canal Pilot at Suez we were southbound again and it was not too long before we were in the Red Sea.

It was here that a tragedy occurred which cast a shadow over the whole ship for many days to come. A young soldier disobeyed a very strict rule and was sitting on the ship's rail when he lost his balance and went overboard. Of course, the ship was stopped and a boat was lowered but we watched helplessly as before it could reach him the sharks got him.

After clearing the Red Sea we made a very brief stop at Aden to disembark a small contingent of RAF personnel. Even though I did not go ashore at that time I did not envy those RAF men because I thought then, and still do now, that Aden was one of the most unattractive places in the world.

Then followed a long and uneventful voyage through the Indian Ocean, finishing with a few hours stop at Singapore to refuel. Singapore looked (and smelled) interesting because we called at the very busy commercial harbour close to the city – the Naval Base, which I would later know quite well, lies to the north on the far side of Singapore Island.

Soon we were away again on the final leg of our voyage and, five weeks after leaving Southampton, we arrived in the Colony of Hong Kong. Hong Kong has a very large and very busy harbour and it is most impressive when you see it for the first time – merchant ships unloading their cargoes from all over the world, a few warships and dozens of Chinese junks and sampans.

We docked alongside at the P&O pier in Kowloon, on the mainland side, and already berthed on the other side of the same pier was HMS *Eagle*. Both vessels rigged two gangways each and so we, the new commission crew, went down the gangway from *Dilwara* and up the opposite one to *Eagle*. Simultaneously, the old commission crew left *Eagle* and joined *Dilwara* for the return trip to the UK.

It was a well-organised and smoothly run operation that was completed in a matter of hours.

CHAPTER NINE

HMS *Eagle*

T HE *Eagle* was, by any standards, an old ship but still very serviceable and still a very proud ship, fulfilling a very useful role in the Navy.

Aircraft carriers were a rarity and the Royal Navy only had four of them in service – *Eagle*, *Furious*, *Glorious* and *Argus* – and all of them were old and had been converted from other types. *Eagle* was the youngest, having been built in 1923 and originally intended as a battleship (the *Almirante Cochrane*) for the Chilean Navy. For some reason the deal did not go through and she was converted to an aircraft carrier for the Royal Navy.

Now, sixteen years later, as she rode at her moorings in Hong Kong harbour, with the sun glistening on her immaculate paintwork, her decks scrubbed white and her brasswork gleaming, she was an impressive sight.

Having embarked in *Eagle* and sorted ourselves out a bit, we soon moved the ship away from the P&O berth out to our regular mooring in the centre of the anchorage. I found it exciting to be on board and knowing that I was now a member of the ship's company (and not just a boy under training) was a special source of pride. The feeling of excitement was added to by the fact of being in the middle of the Hong Kong environment. The harbour itself is very impressive, being one of the largest natural harbours in the world and also one of the busiest.

Of course, at this point, I did not know exactly what my duties would be but by that same afternoon we found out. My first job was to be on the Quarterdeck as 'Boatman' of the forenoon watch next day. I should point out that the Quarterdeck in a warship is hallowed ground and every officer and man coming on board will face aft and salute the Quarterdeck.

The White Ensign is flown on the ensign staff right on the stern; the after gangway (for officers only) is on the Quarterdeck and it is the place of duty for the Officer of the Watch and his staff of Quartermaster, Boatswain's Mate and Bugler. Of course, all this activity is only while the ship is in harbour – at sea the Quarterdeck is deserted.

In the tropics the 'rig of the day' was white shorts and shirt but the Quarterdeck staff (including the Boatman) were required to wear No. 6 dress which was full white uniform. With a pair of binoculars round my neck it was my duty as Boatman to keep a very sharp lookout for all naval boats moving around the harbour and to report to the OOW any important ones that were approaching or passing close to the ship. At first this job seemed over-whelming for me but, as I began to recognise the various boats around the harbour – C-in-C's barge (green), Admiral's barge (blue), Captain's gig, Officer of the Guard's boat, the Despatch Boat and the various duty boats and liberty boats – it got less intimidating.

I was also responsible for hailing any approaching boats by the call 'Boat Ahoy' – then, if the officer concerned was in the boat, the reply would be 'Aye Aye'. This had to be reported to the OOW pretty quickly so that he could arrange the correct ceremonial salute that was required.

I also found that I had two other special duties – one for entering/leaving harbour and the other for flying operations. For the first, I would be stationed on the forecastle with a set of numeral flags on staves that I would hold up to indicate to the Captain the number of shackles of anchor cable that was out. For the flying operations I would be stationed, in a netting, at the edge of the flight deck opposite the bridge where the senior air officer (Commander 'F') would indicate the identity letter of the next aircraft he wanted to land-on. It was then my job to select the appropriate flag and hoist it out on a small, horizontal mast jutting out level with the flight deck. Sometimes he would give me a thrill – this would be when he wanted an aircraft, in the process of landing, to abort the touchdown for some reason or other. In this case he would wave a small, red hand flag at me and I would race across the flight deck, pulling a long rope with a huge red flag attached. I would be holding my breath and hoping the pilot would see it in time! I know very well that all this sounds like a ludicrous method of communicating with aircraft but, bear in mind, we had no VHF or UHF for Voice Radio communication – and, anyway, the top speed of our aircraft was 200 mph.

Living on board was not a comfortable experience for several reasons; the main problem was the tropical heat – a steel box like a ship became very hot below decks, especially when in harbour. Air conditioning was unheard of and although ventilation fans would work overtime they could not cope with the temperature. For this reason, many of the crew, including myself, chose to sleep on the upper deck – a bit hard at first but one got used to it. Also, the Boys' Mess was a couple of decks down in the centre of the ship and was a bit cramped. I always remember the Boys' Bathroom which was one deck lower and therefore right on the waterline – there was an ongoing problem with the sump pump and, when at sea, the bathroom was continually flooded, knee deep, with seawater.

HMS *Eagle* in Hong Kong Harbour, July 1939.

In Hong Kong there was a very good Fleet Club where the older men were able to eat, drink and sleep when they had overnight leave. For us youngsters our leave expired at 6 p.m. and, having very little money in our pockets, our 'run ashore' was limited to walking around the town.

We were soon at sea for the first time in *Eagle*, mainly to embark our aircraft that had been stationed at Kai Tak airport during the changeover. We had two squadrons of Fairey Swordfish – known throughout the Navy as 'Stringbags' for their appearance of being held together by bits of wire – but, in spite of their looks, they were to prove, during the war, that they could take a lot of punishment. They had a three-man crew of Pilot, Observer and Telegraphist/Air Gunner (the first two being officers) and their primary function was as Torpedo Bombers.

They all landed on safely and so *Eagle* was now ready to resume her regular peacetime duties on the China Station which, apart from exercises and drills, mostly involved air searches for local pirates. There was, and always has been, considerable pirate activity on the China coast where they prey upon their victims, mostly small steamers who were plying their trade along the coastal ports. These pirates were not easy to find – they did not go around flying 'The Jolly Roger' and were embarked in apparently harmless looking junks – and this was where our aircraft proved their worth.

Each August it was customary for all ships of the China Station to congregate at Wei Hai Wei, ostensibly for combined exercises, but also to get a welcome break from steamy Hong Kong. Wei Hai Wei was a great natural harbour to the north along the China coast and because of its more temperate climate was the location of the Summer Palace for the Emperors of old China.

It was shortly after this visit that we learned, on 3 September 1939, that we were now at war with Germany. Before leaving England the summer of 1939 had seemed very peaceful and, after the Munich Crisis of the previous year, nobody seemed to be talking about the possibility of an imminent war. Although not entirely unexpected it was a bit of a shock and took a little while to sink in. We were steaming along on a calm, blue sea and everything was so peaceful – <u>and normal</u> – that it was impossible to even imagine how much our lives would be changed by this war. Nobody could visualize that this war was going to last for six long years, or that millions of lives would be lost during that time. We now knew that Britain and Germany were the first combatants in these hostilities, but no one thought that it would spread into a truly global conflict.

I must not get into a history of the war so I will try to contain my remarks to specific situations as they affected me personally. Even now I find it hard to believe that I survived the entire war without a scratch from enemy action; and this I attribute to two things. First, I think I must have had some feline ancestors because I certainly enjoyed the protection of the proverbial 'nine lives of the cat' – and I know I used up eight of them! Secondly, without even trying, I seemed to develop the fortunate habit of leaving each ship shortly before it was sunk!

Now that we were so far from Europe our first thoughts were, 'How could a war with Germany affect us in China?' It was not very long before we found out because, almost immediately, we received orders transferring us to the Indian Ocean where our task would be to search for enemy surface raiders. It was expected that Germany would not waste any time in getting these ships into action – both warships and armed merchant cruisers – to intercept and sink British shipping to and from the Far East. At this time there was no threat from Japan (even Italy was not yet in the war) so there was no reason for us to remain in China.

HMS *Eagle* –
Flying Operations
China Station, August
1939.

Our new base was to be Ceylon (now Sri Lanka) and we operated from Colombo which was the capital and had a large commercial harbour. I never liked Colombo much – it was expensive, the population was passive but never friendly and there was very little to amuse a sailor on shore leave. Ceylon was (and still is) famous for its tea plantations and, although we were never welcomed by the English plantation owners, I do remember visiting the local Maharaja's palace where we were given a tour and entertained with tea and lemonade. Speaking of tea, I recall a couple of times when I purchased some local tea, about 2 lbs, packed in a neat little wooden box, to send home to my mother to help with the rationing.

Anyway, our change of station to the East Indies soon lost its initial attraction and life, when we were in harbour, became boring.

Also, after a time, our seagoing operations lost their promise of action and excitement and just became long and tedious periods of ploughing across the Indian Ocean searching for something that did not seem to be there. To assist us in these operations – and also to provide some firepower with her 8-inch guns in the event of a surface action – we were accompanied by a County Class cruiser HMS *Cornwall*, who had also come from Hong Kong. These operations, through repetition, soon became a familiar routine and, because they did not produce any dramatic results, were very unexciting.

We would sail from Colombo in company with *Cornwall* and then separate for our search pattern, with *Cornwall* out of sight over the horizon but in touch by radio. We would operate air searches, usually by four *Swordfish*, from dawn 'till dusk. Occasionally, when an aircraft sighted a ship, there was a flurry of interest but it soon went flat again when *Cornwall* had established that it was a neutral vessel. This routine was followed for about twelve days and then we would be back in Colombo for a couple of days to refuel etc.

I should mention that life at sea in a warship operating in war conditions is very different from the peacetime version. All kinds of aggravations and inconveniences are introduced: like all watertight doors and scuttles (portholes in the Merchant Navy) have to remain closed; 'darken ship' at night when not a chink of light must be seen; meals and sleep are taken when the situation permits;

additional watches for everybody because the ship is at 'Defence Stations' (a constant state of readiness). In peace-time Boys are 'Daymen' which means they are employed from dawn 'till dusk but do not keep night watches. With the war this all changed and we Boys were incorporated into the watch-keeping organisation.

After a couple of months of these operations we began getting reports of a German surface raider operating in the South Atlantic where several British merchantmen had been sunk – and interest perked up again.

On 15 November 1939, things really livened up and it was then that, for me at least, the war began in earnest.

On the night in question I was part of the Middle Watch (i.e. from midnight until 4 a.m.) when an Emergency-Secret signal was received. After it had been de-coded by the Duty Cypher Officer I was handed a sealed envelope and told 'go down and shake the Commander with this'. Being very young and very inexperienced I did exactly what I was told – I entered the Commander's cabin, grabbed him by the shoulder and shook him awake! Well, when he stopped yelling at me, threatening me with a court martial for assaulting an officer, I handed him the signal and left. Next morning I did not get court martialled but I did get a lecture from the Signal Bosun (Warrant Officer) on the correct procedure to be used to 'arouse' an officer (i.e. DO NOT shake!).

There ended the funny side of this story; the serious side came next day when we learned that we had been ordered to proceed at full speed to intercept an armed German raider who had, the previous day, sunk a small British tanker, the *Africa Shell*, off the coast of Madagascar. Of course, by the time we got there (from the middle of the vast Indian Ocean) there was nothing to be found and, after a fruitless search, we were ordered into Durban, South Africa.

It was only later that we learned the elusive attacker was the *Graf Spee* – a German 'pocket battleship' designed and built during the 1930s specifically for the purpose of hunting and destroying Allied merchant shipping on the outbreak of war. The Germans built three of these vessels which they called *Panzerschiffe* (meaning 'armoured vessel') and they were undeniably the most powerful and well equipped warships afloat at that time. The rest of the world coined the name 'pocket battleship' because they were about three quarters of the size of a contemporary battle-ship but, in spite of this, at 25,000 tons they were a formidable enemy with six 11-inch guns and their modem diesel engines giving them 28 knots and a range of 21,500 miles.

The *Graf Spee* had left Germany before the war started with orders to attack merchant shipping south of the Equator. The *Graf Spee* sunk a couple of British ships off the coast of Brazil, but, even so, the pickings were not plentiful. This was coupled with the fact that the Royal Navy were mounting a huge search for him in the South Atlantic so Captain Langsdorff decided to go round the Cape of Good Hope and try his luck in the Indian Ocean. Thus he met the *Africa Shell* off the coast of Madagascar and, after allowing the crew to escape ashore and taking the Captain prisoner in *Graf Spee*, he sank the vessel. Captain Langsdorff was a very compassionate man and, before sinking his victims, would take the entire crew on board his own ship, to be transferred later to his supply ship, the infamous *Altmark* (but more about that later).

So, it was here that *Eagle* came into the picture – we spent three weeks searching for *Graf Spee* on the eastern seaboard of South Africa, not knowing that she had reversed course and returned to the South Atlantic. Very soon she was to meet the Navy's South Atlantic Squadron which resulted in the Battle of the River Plate. The cruisers *Ajax*, *Achilles* and *Exeter*, outgunned by the 11-inch guns of *Graf Spee*, managed, after suffering heavy casualties, to inflict enough damage to force the *Graf Spee* to seek shelter in neutral Montevideo.

On 17 December she sailed again, but only as far as the Plate Estuary where she was scuttled. Two days later Captain Langsdorff shot himself in his hotel room

This dramatic closure to the *Graf Spee* operation left us, in *Eagle*, free to enjoy a welcome, and very pleasant spell in Durban for Christmas. Durban struck me as the nicest city I had seen and the people were definitely the friendliest and most welcoming in the world. Every afternoon there would be a long line of cars alongside the ship with local families anxious to entertain a couple of sailor boys; perhaps a tour of the city or a drive in the countryside of Natal and very often a home cooked meal with the family. During our time in South Africa we also visited Newcastle,

Port Elizabeth and Cape Town and the reception was always the same.

While serving in the Indian Ocean we also visited Madagascar, the Maldives, the Seychelles (they have the unconfirmed reputation of being the original Garden of Eden) and finally a spell in Bombay. India was truly memorable for its sights, sounds and smells but mostly for its teeming population.

After eight months of service on the East Indies Station we had covered an awful lot of ocean, our aircraft and our aircrews had done a tremendous amount of flying and, most important, *Eagle* was overdue for a refit. To accomplish this we were ordered to Singapore to go into dry dock for a spell, and for everybody on board this was very welcome news. On the day prior to arrival all our aircraft were flown off to Seletar, the RAF base at Singapore. I was on the Flag Deck with the afternoon watch (12.30 to 4 p.m.) and, as was customary at Stand Easy, I was sent down to the Signalmen's Mess to brew a jug of tea for the watch. Sounds simple enough but it was here that I expended the first of my 'cat's nine lives'. I had made the tea, had just stepped out of the mess onto the upper deck and was on the ladder to the flight deck when there was a muffled rumble and the ship seemed to tremble – and then there were calls for Fire and Damage Control Parties. When I got to the Flag Deck we all thought we had taken a torpedo or struck a mine although both seemed unlikely because of the area we were in. The truth was that, in preparation for docking, the Air Armourers were 'striking down' the aircraft bombs (defusing and returning them to the Bomb Magazine in the bowels of the ship). Something went wrong and there was an explosion which, of course, eliminated everyone on the Magazine Deck (one officer and nine men) and the blast came up the ammunition shaft and out of the open door on to the Signalmen's and Royal Marine Band Mess deck. Leading Signalman Puckey and Signalman Robinson, who had done the Middle watch, were asleep in the Mess – Puckey and two Bandsmen were killed instantly and Robinson died in hospital three days later. Had I lingered in their Mess just two minutes longer I would no doubt have joined them – but my guardian angel was watching over me! It was not immediately known if more explosions would follow and a Lieutenant Comdr RNVR (Lord Curzon) volunteered to go down and report. Of course, there was nothing left – he got the DSC and everyone felt he earned it.

This tragedy put a real damper on our return to Singapore and we were all so glad that the entire crew was to be accommodated ashore during our refit.

This was possible because the Navy had built, just outside the Dockyard, a large complex known as the Fleet Shore Accommodation for this very purpose. It had been completed only recently and we were to be the first occupants. It consisted of large, airy dormitories with overhead fans and mosquito nets, a Mess Hall, a Canteen and even an outdoor swimming pool.

This period in the Fleet Shore Accommodation, Singapore (I think it was about 3–4 weeks) was one of the most relaxed and pleasant interludes of the war for me. The *Eagle* was in dry dock and each day, after breakfast, we would be taken by buses to the Dockyard (about ten minutes ride) to work on board for the rest of the day. Because we were on 'Tropical Routine' which meant starting at seven and finishing at one and after lunch (or dinner as it was known then), we would be free for the rest of the day.

Shore leave allowed us to go to Singapore City to see the sights but, after a couple of trips, I gave up on this – it was a bit expensive for my pocket and was also a long bus ride.

Besides working on the ship, Communications men had to operate a Main Signal Office in the FSA but I was excused these duties by what I considered a piece of luck. The Signal Bosun, Mr Tom Godden, was the Warrant Officer in charge of the V/S Department and he 'asked' me if I would like to take on his laundry whilst we were in the FSA. It was an offer I could not (and did not want to) refuse. He provided the cash for all the soap powder, Robin Starch and Reckitt's Blue that I could possibly use and I would spend a quiet afternoon dhobying (his and mine). In the evening, I would starch and iron all his white uniforms – shirts and shorts for the day and white monkey jackets and evening shirts for dinner in the Wardroom.

After some more searching of the huge Indian Ocean, all with negative results, we were all quite relieved to learn that we had been ordered to yet another station – this time the Mediterranean. In early May 1940 I was again in the Suez Canal, but this time northbound. It was shortly after this that our lives changed dramatically – our 'quiet war' in the tropics was over and we were facing a very active role with the Mediterranean Fleet whose Commander-in-Chief was Admiral A. B. Cunningham flying his flag in the battleship *Warspite*. Cunningham was an extremely competent and aggressive sailor who, not without reason, had earned himself the title of 'The Fighting Admiral'.

'A.B.C.' (as he was known for short) had just moved his Mediterranean Fleet from its precarious location in Malta to its new base in Alexandria when Mussolini started making warlike noises in May 1940. It was here that *Eagle* joined the rest of the Fleet in Alexandria's splendid harbour. On 10 June 1940 'the balloon went up' when Mussolini declared war on Britain and France. Less than twenty-four hours later, on the morning of 11 June, the Mediterranean Fleet sailed from Alexandria to look for the Italian Fleet. We had the battleships *Warspite* and *Malaya* followed by *Eagle* and supported by two cruisers and a flotilla of nine destroyers.

Eagle's aircraft carried out searches ahead of the Fleet until nightfall but there was no sign of the Italian Navy. That night came the first sign when the cruiser *Calypso* was sunk by a torpedo from an Italian submarine – she went down slowly and only lost 39 men. Next day we actually saw the enemy but it was not the Italian Navy, but the Air Force, which attacked us. I can still remember sighting those planes, a huge bunch of high level bombers at about twelve thousand feet and, even more fascinating, when we watched clusters of bombs falling from them. We soon realised this was not a game or an exercise when they began exploding all around us – this was an experience to be repeated many times and somebody who kept score eventually reported over two hundred bombs dropped on *Eagle* alone. Although many were extremely close, we were never hit – mainly due to Captain Bridge who, while lying on his back, would order evasive action as he calculated where the bombs would land! This became a routine event – it was what we expected (and usually got) every time we left Alexandria.

Another very tense situation arose in Alexandria when France was overrun by the Germans in June 1940 and the Vichy government capitulated. Under the terms of surrender all ships of the French Navy were supposed to be interned in ports under Nazi control and, in return, the Germans promised not to operate French warships for their own use. In view of Hitler's history of broken agreements, this was taken with a pinch of salt and Britain decided not to take any chances. In Alexandria we had a squadron of French warships (cruisers and destroyers) under the command of the French Admiral Godfroy who, up to this point, had been operating in conjunction with us. The British government, mistrusting the German agreement, gave orders that the French were to be immobilised. Cunningham gave Godfroy three choices: 1. to take his ships to sea and scuttle them; 2. to have his crews repatriated to Vichy France; 3. to discharge all fuel and ammunition.

It was known that the choice was not easy and, alert to the possibility of other action such as attempts to escape or opening fire on our ships, we were kept at Action Stations with our searchlights trained on the French squadron throughout the night of 3–4 July. Everyone breathed a sigh of relief the next morning when we saw French tankers unloading the fuel from the French warships. The majority of the French crews elected to return to France and this was arranged, leaving skeleton crews behind to live on the immobilised ships for the duration of the war. We had little contact with the men who remained because their shore leave was arranged not to coincide with ours. One of their main relaxations seemed to be playing water polo alongside their ships and we did arrange a few water polo matches with them – we usually got beaten because they had become such experts.

On 4 June 1940, having gained the necessary educational qualification and been recommended, I was promoted to the dizzy heights of 'Ordinary Signalman'. This would normally happen at age eighteen but, because of the two factors above, I was entitled to 'Accelerated Advancement' as it was called. This was very welcome because it meant drawing a man's pay and also leaving the Boys' Mess deck forever.

The Mediterranean proved to be an ongoing battle for the ships of the Royal Navy who were continually harassed by attacks from the Italian Air Force whenever they put to sea. The Mediterranean Sea is large (over two thousand miles from east to west) but is comparatively narrow which enabled Italy's land-based, high-level bombers to locate and attack without difficulty. The *Eagle* had now been equipped with two Gloster Gladiator fighters – not by any means very modern, being single engine biplanes – but they were certainly better than nothing. Somebody had found them, packed in crates marked for the Royal Air Force, and after a lot of negotiating, persuaded the RAF they didn't really need them because they were now equipped with Hurricanes.

Almost in the centre of the Mediterranean was the island of Malta and both sides recognised that it was the key to the operation of the campaign being fought in North Africa and, ultimately, the whole of the war in the Middle East. Therefore, the sea war was primarily the protection of convoys (from Gibraltar and from Port Said) to supply and maintain, at all costs, the fortress of Malta.

The Italian Navy was also faced with the task of protecting their own convoys to North Africa but, apart from this duty, it was difficult to entice the Italian Navy to leave harbour, let alone fight a sea battle.

Early in July 1940 the Fleet (including *Eagle*) left Alexandria to escort an important convoy to Malta and the following day we received a report from one of our submarines of a strong Italian Navy force at sea and covering a convoy to North Africa. We flew off our own aircraft to locate and shadow them and they reported there were two battleships, six cruisers and seven destroyers. It was also reported they were turning north which meant they were heading home again. Later that day we flew off a strike of Swordfish armed with torpedoes and Cunningham tried to cut them off before they could reach Taranto. Twenty four hours later we were coming close to them although by now the Italians had been reinforced by another six cruisers and thirteen destroyers. By the afternoon we had caught up with them and there was a brisk exchange of gunfire – the Italian fire was accurate but we did not suffer any damage. The *Warspite* firing her fifteen-inch guns, at a range of fifteen miles, scored a hit on the Italian flagship just before they disappeared into a heavy smokescreen. We did not get away unscathed – an Italian bomb had hit the cruiser *Gloucester* on the bridge, killing the Captain and seventeen others (including half of her signalmen). The action came to be known as the Battle of Cape Calabria.

Shortly after this the Mediterranean Fleet, which was seriously outnumbered by Italian ships, was to receive badly needed reinforcements. These were the new aircraft carrier *Illustrious*, the battleship *Valiant* and two anti-aircraft cruisers – all were most welcome but, most importantly, the *Valiant* was equipped with radar.

On 9 September 1940 I was drafted from *Eagle* to join HMS *Gloucester* who had now completed repairs to the bomb damaged bridge and was seaworthy again.

HMS *Eagle* was sunk on 11 August 1942, off Tunisia, by four torpedoes from the German U73. 161 men went down with her.

CHAPTER TEN

HMS *Gloucester*

A TOWN CLASS CRUISER of 10,000 tons, *Gloucester* had been built in 1937 and had a main armament of six-inch guns, was 600ft long and carried a complement of 700 men. But, most important, she had a top speed of 32 knots.

Although I was only to be on board for six months it proved to be a very active period. In addition to the usual convoy protection there were bombardments of Italian positions on the coast of North Africa and then, in November 1940, came the brilliant raid on the Italian Fleet in its home port of Taranto. *Gloucester* was part of the force which included the two carriers *Illustrious* and *Eagle* who provided a strike of thirty *Swordfish* torpedo bombers to attack the enemy at night. The raid was a total success – 2 battleships, 3 cruisers and 2 destroyers were sunk and the rest of the Italian Fleet retired north to Naples. It was also a great boost for British morale which was sorely

HMS *Gloucester*.

needed at this part of the war and provided a rather triumphant end to 1940.

However, this uplifting situation was very short-lived because, at the turn of the year, a new enemy arrived to make life unpleasant again. The Italian operations, both at sea and on land in North Africa, had not been highly successful and the Germans now arrived in the Mediterranean areas.

This involved German submarines at sea, Panzer Divisions in North Africa and, in the air, the formidable Stuka dive bombers. In January 1941 we met them in earnest when we were involved in a ferocious air battle off Sicily. We were escorting a very important convoy which had come through Gibraltar heading for Alexandria. This was unusual because they normally came round the Cape to Suez but, because the Middle East situation was getting desperate, it was decided to accept the danger of a faster route through the Mediterranean.

We had been under air attack for a day and a half when, on the afternoon of the second day, I lost the second of my 'cat's nine lives'! I was on watch alone in the Main Signal Office which was located one deck below the bridge. I could certainly hear the din outside but, of course, could not see anything so it was a nasty shock when a bomb went by me, from above, and disappeared through the deck. Yeoman McInnes was asleep on a camp bed in the office (he had done the middle and forenoon watches) and as the bomb passed through it hit his right arm and badly mangled it. I was wondering what had happened to the

Ship's mascot, 'The Jeep'.

bomb when I was ordered to evacuate the office and went up to the Flag Deck.

They say that lightning never strikes the same place twice but I know that to be a fallacy. Six months previously when the first bomb hit *Gloucester* it passed through the Gunnery Control Tower, seriously injuring the Director Officer before exploding on the Bridge and killing eighteen people.

The young RNVR officer had recovered in hospital and had requested to rejoin *Gloucester*. This time (my bomb) had struck exactly the same spot but this time he was not so lucky because he was killed instantly. The bomb passed through four decks without exploding and came to rest in a huge soup kettle in the galley. It was soon disposed of over the side but, in the attack, we had lost nine killed and fourteen wounded. This was relatively light punishment because, shortly afterwards, our sister ship the *Southampton* who was in company with us was critically damaged by bombs and had to be sunk with our own torpedoes. We had been rejoining the main body of the Fleet after escorting a bomb damaged destroyer *Gallant* into Malta. We took off *Southampton*'s survivors but most of the officers and Chief and Petty Officers were lost because the two bombs had hit their Messes.

However, when we did rejoin the Fleet we found that, in the same operation, we had suffered a real disaster when, during two days of almost continuous air attacks, we virtually lost our new aircraft carrier *Illustrious* who was hit by six bombs and severely damaged. Her steering gear had been smashed and, with fires in the hangar and her flight deck badly damaged, she was not able to operate aircraft and so those that were airborne had to land on Malta. The decision was made (a risky one at best) to get her into Malta for emergency repairs and so the entire Fleet shepherded her in (she was steering by engines only).

Of course, the Germans knew where the *Illustrious* was, and why she was there, so her stay in Malta was subject to frequent air attacks and it was a race by the Dockyard to get her sufficiently repaired before more damage was inflicted. This was achieved and, two weeks later, the *Illustrious* was safely back in Alexandria and *en route* to Norfolk Navy Yard in the US for permanent repair.

After *Gloucester*'s safe return to Alexandria it was obvious she would be out of action while repairs were completed and so I was on the move once more – this time to a destroyer – HMS *Hasty*.

HMS *Gloucester* was subsequently sunk on 22 May 1941 during the Battle for Crete.

CHAPTER ELEVEN

HMS *Hasty*

SERVING IN A DESTROYER was to be a new, and certainly exciting, experience for me. When I joined HMS *Hasty* on 1 February 1941 as a replacement for a signalman who had been hospitalised it was a time when the war was about to change drastically for the Mediterranean Fleet – and not for the better.

Hasty was relatively modern, having been built in 1936, and was a typical destroyer of that time – she was 1,400 tons, 320 ft long and had a top speed of 36 knots. Destroyers were known as the 'greyhounds of the ocean' and therefore presented an image of glamour and excitement. In truth they were overworked and, because they took a beating in a rough sea, were not very comfortable living spaces. In a larger ship it was easy to get warm and dry after a wet four hours on the bridge but, in a destroyer, it was often difficult to achieve this. It was for this reason that men serving in destroyers were paid an extra sixpence per day – known as 'hard-lying money' – little enough but it was something! Before the war Lady Astor, who was a prominent member of the British Government, spent a day at sea in a Home Fleet destroyer and, because it was calm and sunny, tried to get 'hard-lying money' cancelled but, fortunately, the motion was soundly defeated.

We had eight torpedo tubes, four 4.7" dual purpose guns and depth charges but, like all destroyers, our biggest asset was Asdic, used for detecting submarines and, because of this, destroyers at sea with the Fleet would be used as a protective anti-sub screen for the main body.

Hasty also had a crew of 150 men so it was a very close-knit family because each depended so much on the others. In the V/S Department we had a Yeoman of Signals, a Leading Signalman and three Signalmen, including myself, so we were kept pretty busy. Our Captain was Lieutenant Commander Tyrrhet – a pleasant man and a good skipper but with an awful problem – he got violently sick if it was a bit rough – but somehow he never let it get the better of him; he just kept his bucket in a corner of the bridge! As I never did get seasick perhaps I did not appreciate fully the discomfort of this ailment but, nevertheless, I always felt sorry for him.

As I said, it was here that the Mediterranean War changed – the Med. Fleet had always had its hands full coping with the Italians and then the Germans and now the action spread to Greece. For some time the British Government had wanted to send troops to Greece to safeguard against a possible attack but the Greeks had refused because of their neutrality. It seemed at first that Hitler would ignore Greece in his rush to get into Russia but Mussolini, seeing his chance of an easy victory, invaded Greece through Albania, though it turned into a flop for the Italians because they met stiff resistance from the Greeks and the Italian columns got bogged down in the mountains in winter.

In early spring Hitler once more came to the rescue of his ally and the Germans poured in through Albania and this was a different proposition for the Greeks who could not hold them. British troops from the Western Desert were rushed to support them but, of course, it was 'too little, too late'!

HMS *Hasty* at Suda Bay, Crete 1941.

So it was that one of my first operations in *Hasty* was escorting a troop convoy to Piraeus, the port of Athens. The troops having safely disembarked, we were allowed a couple of days break and took the opportunity to see Athens and the Acropolis. At this point, apart from the many uniforms to be seen, there was no sign of the war and the people of Athens welcomed us. I do remember our favourite hangout in Athens was a bar called *La Petite Trianon* – I always thought it strange to have a French name in Greece – but the ouzo and Metaxas brandy made up for that.

After this trip, instead of going all the way back to Alexandria, we refuelled and then anchored in Suda Bay on the north coast of Crete. It was here that I witnessed, at close range, one of the most audacious attacks of the war. We were due to sail early and I was on the Bridge as dawn was breaking (probably about 5 a.m.) when two high speed motor boats came streaking across the bay, passed *Hasty*, and slammed into the cruiser *York* and our Fleet tanker. After terrific explosions both ships sank and settled in shallow water. The two attackers were Italian, in specially designed boats packed with explosives – the 'pilot' would lock the steering and then eject, backwards, into the water and wait to be picked up (and captured).

The *York* lost fifty men in the explosion and the rest of the crew were distributed throughout the Fleet as required.

The next operation for *Hasty* was the Battle of Cape Matapan when the British and Italian Fleets were to meet, presenting a rare opportunity for a real sea battle. This was brought about by luring the Italian Fleet out of harbour to attack a lightly escorted British troop convoy to Greece and, prodded by the Germans, the Italians took the bait. The Italian Fleet consisted of the new battleship *Vittorio Veneto*, six heavy cruisers, two light cruisers and a dozen destroyers. The British Fleet, after careful surveillance of the Italians by a force of four cruisers and four destroyers (including *Hasty*) slipped out of Alexandria at night to intercept. In *Hasty* the first part of the battle was rather uncomfortable because the Italians, who were ahead of us, opened fire with their eight inch guns and were straddling our ships while the six inch guns of our own cruisers were unable to reach them. When the *Vittorio Veneto* opened fire with her fifteen inch guns it was decided that discretion was the better part of valour and we retired to join our own Fleet who were coming up astern. The *Formidable* launched torpedo bomber strikes and this achieved a hit on the Itahan battleship. The day turned to night and Cunningham would not give up the chase and it was here that *Valiant*'s radar proved invaluable. To cut a long story short, we caught up with the enemy about ten p.m. and, apparently undetected, switched on searchlights at the same time as we opened fire. The Italians were caught unawares (their guns were trained fore and aft) and it took a while for them to open fire.

The big cruisers *Fiume* and *Zara* were soon ablaze and later sank as did the destroyer *Altieri*. Also, later that night, we came upon the heavy cruiser *Pola* and she was sunk as was another destroyer when they made a torpedo attack.

Next morning, we cruised through the rafts and wreckage picking up Italian survivors (we got 900 of them before we were attacked by German planes and had to call it off). We radioed for an Italian hospital ship and they got a couple of hundred more. In the final count Italy had lost three big cruisers and two destroyers plus 2,400 men – our losses were one *Swordfish* aircraft and its crew of three.

However, our triumph was short-lived because very shortly after this our troops in Greece were being overrun by the Germans and the only way to save them was for the Navy to pull off another Dunkirk. This time though, the enemy would be in full command of the air because the Luftwaffe vastly outnumbered the RAF.

This evacuation took place from beaches on the southern coast of Greece over a period of one week at the end of April. We would go in after dark, load as many troops as possible and get well away before dawn (and the dive bombers) came. We raced to Crete (about fifty miles away) and repeated this every night. In the end I think we got 50,000 men off – but about 10,000 were left behind.

Once again there was only a brief respite because, three weeks later, Hitler decided to invade the island of Crete, using a massive air assault of glider and parachute troops. These would be supported by large convoys of regular troops embarked in caiques (a twin-mast Greek sailing vessel). It was here that Cunningham made his 'Nelson type' signal which said, 'The Navy must not let the Army down, No enemy forces must reach Crete by sea.'

Therefore the Fleet, was committed to patrolling the coasts of Crete without the benefit of any protection from the air and, in consequence, was badly mauled by the fierce dive bomber attacks. The first to be lost was the destroyer *Greyhound*. The cruiser *Gloucester* was detached to pick up survivors and, when she was stopped by a bomb in the engine room, the cruiser *Fiji* was ordered to give anti-aircraft support. When the *Gloucester* and *Fiji* both ran out of AA ammunition they were sitting ducks and were both sunk. We did not know until much later that some of the *Gloucester*'s crew made it to shore and were taken prisoner – meanwhile our destroyers, at night, managed to pick up about 500 of the *Fiji*'s men. We also lost the destroyers *Juno*, *Kashmir* and *Kelly* (Lord Mountbatten's ship) and, two days later, the *Formidable* and destroyer *Nubian* were badly damaged by bombs. But this operation was not totally one-sided because at night, when the German land forces arrived off Crete, we were waiting for them and it was a total disaster for the enemy. There were about two thousand men, embarked in Greek caiques and escorted by an Italian destroyer. The wooden sailing vessels caught fire and sank very easily when hit and about half of the German troops were drowned while less than fifty (on life rafts) made it to shore. The Italian destroyer *Lupo* was brave and aggressive but, badly damaged, retired to Greece with the surviving caiques.

Ultimately, of course, the British troops on Crete were finally overwhelmed, due mostly to the sheer volume of the German airborne invasion which was highly successful in the absence of any Allied air support. The next move was obvious – we would have to attempt the evacuation of as many troops as possible in the face of heavy enemy air attacks. It was not a happy prospect and, in view of the heavy Naval losses so far, many felt it could not be done. The decision to try it was made by Cunningham with his second famous signal – 'It takes the Navy three years to build a ship. It would take three hundred years to rebuild a tradition.'

The *Hasty* and four other destroyers were given the task of attempting the job at Sphakia, a very small port on the south-west coast of Crete.

It was now the end of May and, over a period of four nights, we would creep in to the jetty at midnight with no lights and no noise as the Germans were close to the harbour. After we had embarked the maximum troops (about 700–800 each, which meant we were jam-packed) we would slip out again (about 2.30) and then, still under cover of darkness, transfer the bulk of the soldiers to our cruisers waiting offshore before racing for home.

In total the Navy managed to pluck 16,000 troops off Crete but, unfortunately, twice that number remained behind. Even worse, many of those evacuated did not make it back because, when the Germans woke up to the situation, our ships were fiercely attacked by the *Stukas*, like a bunch of angry hornets … It is one thing for a warship to suffer an internal explosion but when those same messdecks are packed tight with soldiers, it is horrific.

Shortly after the debacle in Greece and Crete, *Hasty* had got back to Alexandria and the welcome arrival of some mail. Next thing I knew the Captain had sent for me to come to his cabin. This in itself was pretty unusual but, when I saw him, he was obviously not pleased to see me. He accused me of not writing home often enough and then explained that the Admiralty, when the *Gloucester* had been sunk, had sent a telegram to my mother saying, 'Missing, believed killed in action.' Of course, this was devastating news for my family and, I am told, there was much weeping and wailing at No. 6 Ethelred Road and prayers were offered for me in Church. It was six weeks before my mother received a letter from me in *Hasty* and suddenly realised I had not gone down with the *Gloucester*. I did try, very tentatively, to suggest to the Captain that if the official mail (notifying my transfer) did not get through then how could mine? – but he did not agree!

Anyway, *Hasty* survived all this, I am glad to say, and our next operation was to be part of the Inshore Patrol. This involved a pair of destroyers patrolling close to the North African coast, past Benghazi, Sidi Barrani, Bardia, Sollum and Tobruk. The object of this was to intercept and attack enemy convoys, E-Boats or submarines in the area – there were a few night skirmishes which produced the odd moment of excitement but the biggest one came at Tobruk – and this cost me the third of my 'cat's nine lives'.

We had been patrolling in company with HMS *Dainty*, a destroyer similar to *Hasty*, and put into Tobruk to refuel and then, at dusk, we sailed again to resume patrol. We had just cleared the harbour when one of Tobruk's frequent air raids developed while we were steaming east in the swept channel, which ran parallel to the coastline. Seeing all those Stukas diving on Tobruk harbour, we opened fire on them – had we not done so they probably would not have noticed us because it was getting dark. Anyway, a group of dive bombers decided two destroyers made a better target and switched their attention to us – one bomb hitting *Dainty*'s stern which stopped her dead. With their bombs expended, the planes went home and we went alongside *Dainty* to take off survivors.

As there was no signalling to be done, I went down the bridge ladder to the upper deck to lend a hand but, as I reached the waist, there was an enormous explosion as *Dainty*'s after magazine went up. The blast sent me through the mess deck door where I woke up with a large lump on my head but otherwise in one piece.

We had saved about one hundred of *Dainty*'s crew (including the ship's pet monkey) and then headed back to Alexandria.

After just less than six months in *Hasty* I was surprised to find that I was to be drafted to the aircraft-carrier *Formidable*.

HMS *Hasty* was subsequently sunk after being torpedoed by a German E-Boat on 15 June 1942.

CHAPTER TWELVE

HMS *Formidable*

AT THE BEGINNING OF JUNE 1941 HMS *Formidable* was still undergoing emergency repairs in Alexandria after taking six bombs during the evacuation of Crete.

When I joined *Formidable* on 10 June 1941 she was preparing to sail for Norfolk Navy Yard in the US for a complete refit and, I must admit, I was looking forward to that prospect. However, my dreams in that direction were short-lived and my service in *Formidable* was destined to be the shortest ever. The normal complement of 1,500 men was being rapidly reduced by drafting them around the Fleet as replacements or reinforcements. At the same time a few like myself who had been away from the UK for more than two years were sent to join for the trip home. Unfortunately for me, the Signal Bosun of this ship was determined to hold on to a young signalman who was his best typist and so, when a draft order arrived for that young man, the name on it somehow got changed to Adams!

HMS *Formidable* – Mediterranean 1941.

Therefore, after barely a month in *Formidable*, I was on the move again and this time to HMS *Stag* (K. Div.). This in itself was intriguing because nobody seemed to know where or what it was – except that it certainly was not a seagoing ship. After a lot of questions I eventually discovered that HMS *Stag* was simply a pool (for pay and records purposes) of 'unattached' naval personnel in the Middle East. I then found that the 'K. Div.' part was to indicate Kabret, a place near Suez, where the Navy had a large camp (tents), in the middle of the desert to train oddball types like parachutists and demolition people. I began to wonder, 'What am I getting into now?'

HMS *Formidable* was repaired to fight again, survived the war and was scrapped in 1956.

CHAPTER THIRTEEN

TLC 17

B<small>Y THE TIME I LEFT</small> *Formidable* on the morning of 10 July 1941 I knew that I was not headed for the naval camp at Kabret but instead was being diverted to Port Said to join a strange new vessel called a 'Tank Landing Craft'.

Initially I came ashore in Alexandria and went to the Naval Shore Headquarters at Ras El Tin. This was a wonderful property, right on the point of land next to the lighthouse and overlooking the entire harbour. Before the war this was the summer palace of the famous King Farouk of Egypt and was spacious and airy with beautiful grounds. However, I did not have time to appreciate all this because I was only there for twenty four hours.

Early next morning I was at Alexandria railway station and boarding a train for Port Said. It reminded me that when I was a young boy, somewhat interested in railways, I had always thought that Egyptian railways must be among the best in the world – simply because they seemed to have the largest and most powerful looking locomotives. In truth, they were terribly slow and even more uncomfortable.

Finally we arrived at Port Said in the early evening and I was taken to the small Naval Barracks there. After supper I went to the Canteen to learn what I could about local conditions and any information on my future home.

The following morning I took the ferry across the harbour (in fact, the Suez Canal) and made my way to the dockyard at Port Fouad where *TLC 17* was fitting out. It was certainly a strange sight for me, and not only me but the whole Navy, who had never seen this type of vessel before. It was a flat-bottomed barge with a flat, drop-down door at the bow and, at the stern, a small wheelhouse and bridge above.

What I found interesting was that this type was a British invention and No. 17 was one of the first batch produced in the United States. Because they were not ocean going

Some of the crew (Bob on the right) at Port Said, 1941.

vessels they had been fabricated in three sections and shipped out to Suez as deck cargo on large freighters.

When I joined *TLC 17* she had just been welded into one piece, the engines installed and was in the final stages of preparing for service. We had by then received eighteen of these craft in the Eastern Mediterranean and most of them were already in operation. I think the Admiralty, not having any invasion plans for the near future, sent them to the Med. to see: (a) how they would perform and (b) if they could prove valuable in the Desert Campaign.

We had mostly a young crew who worked well together and I would say we were a happy ship. I think I was the youngest member of the crew but, strangely, I seemed to get a lot of respect from the others because of the fact that, apart from the Cox'n, I was the only Regular Navy man on board and therefore had already seen a lot more active service than the others.

We had a total complement of thirteen but nobody seemed to pay any attention to the 'unlucky' bit. Our Cox'n was a Leading Seaman, although it was a Petty Officer's job, and he was proud of the fact that he was the only Leading Seaman Cox'n in the Flotilla. Leading Seaman Markey had been dis-rated from Petty Officer in his previous ship owing to a rather aggressive argument with an Officer. He was a Londoner, spoke in a loud voice and would stand no nonsense. In addition to myself there were seven Able Seamen and two Engine Room ratings – a Petty Officer (Motor Mechanic) and a Leading Stoker.

We had two officers and they were two totally opposite characters. The Captain was a young Sub-Lieutenant RNVR, was South African and very inexperienced but took his position and his duties very seriously. The second-in-command was an ex-Grimsby trawlerman who had done an officer's course and held the wartime rank of Skipper, Royal Naval Reserve; a strange title but it fitted the personnel absorbed into the RN from the fishing Fleets. They were a great asset because they were very experienced seamen and most were now employed on minesweepers. Not surprisingly, he was a complete contrast to our Captain – he was cheerful, brash, tough, hated regulations and was probably what would now be called 'a free spirit'. He was a great drinker and enjoyed a good 'run ashore' but, one night, got a bit too boisterous and was arrested by MPs for firing his revolver outside the house of the Naval Officer in Charge, Port Said.

We spent two happy weeks, working by day and enjoying the advantages of Port Said at night – the restaurants were reasonable and the food and beer were good. This was especially appreciated because, whilst at Port Fouad, we were accommodated in a nearby Army Transit Camp and the food there was not the greatest.

Finally, we were ready for sea and we set off for Alexandria, where we would refuel, and then on to Mersa Matruh on Egypt's western border with Libya, These early *TLC*s (they later became '*LC*(T)' – standing for Landing Craft (Tank) – were fitted with twin V-eight Packard automobile engines and, of course, ran on gasoline. The problem here was that we were floating around with our fuel tanks loaded with several thousand gallons of petroleum and we expected to go up in a puff of smoke. Because of a lumpy sea we had to reduce speed but we made it to Alexandria, where we topped up at an Army fuel depot. During the process we were admiring a nice 14 ft dinghy belonging to the RASC and thinking how nice it would be for fishing when we got to our destination. When we left harbour at dusk, a couple of us got the dinghy and secured it, planning to tow it astern on the next leg of our trip. The next morning the Captain couldn't understand why we had not yet reached Mersa Matruh, but when daylight came we all saw the reason – our lovely dinghy had filled up with water and was acting as a sea-anchor, reducing our speed from ten knots to about six.

Of course, we were forced to abandon our prize!

Mersa Matruh was an enormous armed camp which was the main base for the entire Western Desert campaign and, as such, supplied the Army with everything from toothbrushes to tanks. We soon learned that our role was to transport this stuff to the beleaguered garrison at Tobruk which was under constant seige and therefore the only way in, or out, was by sea. This was not an endearing prospect because, for us 'slow pokes' with a top speed of ten knots, the *TLC*s were easy prey for everything from seagulls to submarines. By the time we had joined the rest of the Flotilla at Mersa Matruh several of them had already been lost – one by a submarine on the surface, three by air attack and two, on their initial run from Port Said, just filled up with water and sank when the sea got a bit too rough.

These craft, although not entirely suitable for the purpose, certainly filled a valuable role when they were urgently needed but it was equally obvious that they were expendable; it was a lot less costly to lose a landing craft than a destroyer.

The destroyers were used for night runs into Tobruk, taking in reinforcements and bringing wounded out. With their high speed, these vessels could be in and out in a couple of hours, all under cover of darkness. One of these destroyers saved our bacon one night when we were attacked by a surfaced submarine as we tried to creep into Tobruk in the darkness. Just in time a destroyer left harbour, heading for Alexandria, and our unfriendly submarine disappeared.

Unlike the destroyers, our trips to Tobruk were long and slow and often hairy, Our sailings were dependant on the Desert Air Force being able to provide fighter cover for us during daylight hours. Our trip to Tobruk would take two nights and one day and that meant twelve hours when we were open to enemy air attack. We would sail at dusk one night and arrive at dawn of the second night. Sometimes the RAF had to cancel which could prove tricky if we had already sailed.

I found Tobruk itself to be an interesting and exciting place although, owing to frequent air raids and land bombardment, there were very few buildings still in one piece. The harbour itself was cluttered with half sunken wrecks, including the Italian cruiser *San Giorgio*.

Our usual routine was to run up the beach at dawn and then we would leave the unloading of our cargo (usually barbed wire, food and ammunition etc.) to the Army (usually Indian troops) while we found a nearby cave and tried to catch up on some sleep before sailing again after dark.

On one of these occasions I had the unfortunate experience of being arrested by the MPs as we left the ship. The Major in charge was very agitated and was threatening me with all kinds of unpleasant things when I was rescued by our First Lieutenant (the Skipper RNR) who got equally excited and told the Major, in no uncertain terms, that if any charges were pressed, the Army would have to take care of its own shipping problems. In this case, the problem was that the sandbag of rations I was carrying also included a bottle of Scotch originally destined for the Army Officers Mess in Tobruk!

Early on, we had discovered that our cargo always included a plentiful supply of this stuff and so, somehow, an odd case had found its way under the engine room footplates – to be used as required for medicinal purposes!

At this point we all agreed not to borrow any more of their Scotch and they let me go – but I do remember having the most awful hangover when we sailed that night.

On another occasion, at the same beach, three of us decided to walk around the harbour to the town on the other side with the object of scrounging some fresh bread. Of course, it proved to be much further than it appeared and, because the terrain was so rough and our footwear so unsuitable, our feet suffered badly and we never volunteered for that again.

One of the interesting things about the desert was the enormous amount of equipment that was abandoned and

Italian Cruiser *San Giorgio*, Tobruk Harbour 1941.

available to anyone that was interested. I remember I settled for an Army tin hat (apparently nobody thought we needed them) and a brand new sleeveless leather jacket. Our Leading Stoker was a bit more ambitious and salvaged for himself a nice looking Norton motorcycle but, after returning to Mersa Matruh, I think the Army confiscated it back again.

Of course, there was a permanent Naval contingent in Tobruk, mostly Communications people, and I used to visit their Mess sometimes to scrounge a meal which was always tinned corned beef and dehydrated potatoes.

Our food in the desert invariably came out of tins – mostly Spam, corned beef, beans, potatoes, bacon and, of course, the usual dehydrated eggs and potatoes. Apart from the monotony of this sort of diet it was not particularly healthy and the absence of fresh fruit and vegetables resulted in everybody developing 'sand sores'. These were horrible, weeping blemishes, usually on the arms and legs, but were not particularly serious unless they became in-fected, usually by the local flies – of which there were swarms.

Of course, I had my share of these and initially I was sent ashore to the Army Field Hospital for treatment but, after walking a mile and a half and waiting half a day, was only told, 'What do you expect us to do? Everybody has got them!' After that I just kept them bandaged and it wasn't too bad; until one developed on my back, close to my left shoulder and, because I could not reach it, it became quite badly infected.

The First Lieutenant (our Skipper RNR) noticed the swelling and decided to do something about it. He pro-duced a scalpel and a bottle of Scotch (I thought the Scotch was for him but he did pour a few gulps into me!) and, with me face down on the mess table, and two of the crew on top of me, went to work. In spite of the Scotch it was quite painful but it did heal up – and I still have the scar to prove it! I couldn't help laughing afterwards as I thought it was just like the movies.

After about three months of this wild existence it became obvious we were coming to the end of our combined tether; some nerves were shattered and our original Flotilla of eighteen was now down to two (No. 14 and No. 17). Our next run, which proved to be our final one, was also the worst one of all.

It started off badly when our scheduled sailing was delayed two or three times due to lack of any fighter cover. This in itself was problem enough but this time, apart from the frustration, was the added difficulty of a very perishable cargo – potatoes! I do not know where these potatoes originated but they arrived in several Army trucks and were loaded, as usual, by the Pioneer Corps. Had we been able to sail on schedule I am sure the boys in Tobruk would have welcomed and enjoyed this rarity – fresh vegetables. I am not sure what the useful life of a potato is normally, but I do know that by the time we finally got away from Mersa Matruh our load of potatoes was well past its 'sell by' date. By the time we reached Tobruk, thirty-six hours later, they were rapidly becoming a stinking, oozing sludge after sitting in the hot sun for so long. We all felt bad about this but we had no control over the situation; it was just a feeling that the Army had been let down – even though it was not our fault. Of course, in addition to the potatoes, there was other vital cargo (ammunition, canned food, barbed wire and blankets) so our trip was not wasted but, what made it memorable to me was that, before we got back, I was to lose two more of my 'cat's nine lives'.

The first problem was the RAF who, for three consecutive days, had been unable to promise any sort of fighter cover for us; we used to curse them but, at the same time, knew they were short of planes and certainly had their hands full in the Western Desert. Finally, because air cover was promised for the next day, we sailed at sunset and I recall a feeling of relief that we were finally getting on with it. Next day, under a clear blue sky, we spotted a lone reconnaissance plane and, a couple of hours later, came the dive bombers – but our fighter cover had failed to show. A whole squadron of JU 87B Stukas came screaming down on us, strafing as they came, and their aim was pretty good. For anti-aircraft protection we had two single 20mm Bofors and a Lewis gun – not very effective in the circumstances. The bombs fell all around us and some were so close that we were soaked with black water from the explosions. Fortunately, our bridge was protected by good old fashioned sandbags which stopped the hail of shrapnel. When it was all over we were amazed to find that, in spite of a lot of holes in the steel plating, we were still afloat and, even more incredible, we did not have any casualties except – it was goodbye to 'cat's life number four'.

In the early evening, there was, as expected, a second attack but, thank goodness, not as violent as the first although by now we were all praying for darkness.

After an uneventful night, we got into Tobruk about five a.m. but, instead of our usual beaching, we made our way through the wrecks to the end of the harbour and secured alongside a stone jetty where we were to be unloaded. About four hours later, the job was done – the troops had unloaded our cargo, including the stinky potatoes and, as usual, we were preparing to go ashore to get some rest. However, because of the garbage remaining in the hold, one AB and I were detailed to clean it up before going ashore.

Everyone else left and we had just got started when the air raid warning sounded. Looking up from the bottom of the hold but seeing clear sky we decided it was another reconnaissance flight and therefore carried on with our work.

We soon heard the unmistakable scream of the Stukas and, before we could move, the bombs were exploding; one of them was a direct hit on our jetty and demolished it. We were not wearing tin hats so we held our shovels over our heads to protect them from the shower of flying concrete that was raining on us – goodbye to 'cat's life number five'!

When we finished our clean-up we went ashore and, being on the town side of the harbour, we decided to sleep in the huge underground caves below the town. Before the war, the Italians had constructed an enormous complex of these caverns in the rock and now they housed the hospital, the kitchens, the cold storage rooms, in fact, every item that enabled the garrison to live whilst under constant attack. The wide passageways (you could drive a truck through them) were filled with wounded men on stretchers awaiting evacuation that night so we just grabbed a blanket, lay down beside them and were soon asleep. Of course, the temperature in there was much lower than outside; it felt very comfortable at first but when we woke up we felt like frozen beef!

We were glad to get back to Mersa Matruh after that particular run, even though it did not have very much to offer. Mersa Matruh was a typical North African town (more like a village really) which was just a collection of flat, stone buildings. It was important however, for two things; it was the railhead from Egypt and Suez and it had a nice harbour – not big enough or deep enough for normal shipping but ideal for TLCs. It was really a big, natural lagoon with one entrance from the sea. The lagoon was edged with sandy beaches so that the TLCs were able to run straight up them, after dropping a kedge anchor which would be used to pull them off again. Because we never bothered going ashore – there was nothing to see or do – we used to spend our free time swimming or fishing in the clear blue water. Fishing was done by means of tossing a lighted stick of gelignite into the water and then diving in to collect the fish killed by the explosion.

Shortly after our return to Mersa Matruh we received sailing orders, not to Tobruk this time, but to Kabret on the Great Bitter Lakes, via Alexandria and Port Said. During our brief stop at Port Said we were all interviewed by a Naval psychiatrist and I guess we all passed. When we reached Kabret TLC 17 was immediately put to work unloading a large freighter anchored in the Lake. It was tedious day and night work and, after a week, we were glad it was over. We then left the TLC and were accommodated ashore in a single group of cabins on the shore of the Lake and I was sent to work at the local Suez Canal Company Signal Station. This was a very quiet job as there was not a lot of shipping transiting the Canal at that time, but for me, it was not a very happy experience because the local operators, who were French, were not at all friendly and were jealously guarding their jobs. Back at our own little camp the rest of the crew was employed in teaching Indian troops how to handle boats.

When we had lived on board TLC 17 it had been the practice for all the ABs and myself to take turns at being 'Cook'. I quite enjoyed this but, of course, what we served up was not ambitious owing to the limited supplies available. This improved at Kabret and I remember one day we were issued with a large piece of beef and, as we had no proper cooking facilities, I cooked a roast beef dinner in an oil drum, lying on its side, with a fire underneath. Not very good oven temperature control but a great success and we all enjoyed it including our two officers who used to eat with us.

At the beginning of December 1941 I was moving on

once more; this time I was being sent back to Alexandria 'for disposal' which meant that, until they found a permanent slot for me, I would be accommodated in the Naval Transit Camp. This was located in Sidi Bish, a seaside suburb of Alexandria which was a wealthy and pleasant area, but life in the Camp was boring and the food wasn't the greatest. I was almost glad when, after a few days there, I felt sick and the MO said I had caught 'yellow jaundice' and would have to go to hospital which meant the British Military Hospital, Alexandria which proved to be a pleasant enough place and very civilised. I remember the feeling of relief as I climbed in between clean, white sheets but I also thought it wasn't the greatest way to spend my nineteenth birthday.

After ten days in hospital I had recovered and was discharged back to the Transit Camp at Sidi Bish. I was now expecting to be sent to another ship but Christmas came and went and nothing happened for me. My friend Signalman Potter (from TLC 14) told me one day about a couple of people he knew who were being sent home to England. Less than hopefully, I went along to see the Drafting Office (in a tent) and, when they heard I had been abroad for two and a half years said, much to my surprise, that I was to be sent back to the UK.

So it came about that over New Year 1941–42 I was on another train, south through the desert past Kabret, and bound for the Port of Suez where I was to embark in the *Mauretania*.

CHAPTER FOURTEEN

Mauretania and Scythia

THE *Mauretania* was a very large and beautiful ocean liner, owned by Cunard, and was now serving her time as a troopship in a coat of drab, grey paint. When I joined her at Suez I could not believe how lucky I was to be making the journey home in such a fine ship. Once aboard, this dream was shattered, when we discovered the *Mauretania* was only doing the run from Suez to Durban and back.

We were a very small Naval Draft – about 20 or 25 – a few of those were South Africans who would be leaving us at Durban; and even the rest of the ship was almost deserted. She normally carried POWs from the desert in this direction. As a result there was plenty of room for us to spread out and none of the usual aggravations of service life, such as line-ups for meals, canteen etc. We spent most of the ten days voyage playing cards for *tickies* – the name for the South African threepenny pieces.

This carefree existence came to an end when we reached Durban. We were all very happy to be there, especially those of us who had visited Durban previously, but when we disembarked from *Mauretania* it was as if everyone had disowned us because there was no onward shipping, or even shore accommodation, arranged for us. There we were, twenty of us with a pile of kitbags and hammocks, in a dockside warehouse, with nowhere to go and no money in our pockets! There was a Petty Officer in charge of us (no officers) and he ran himself ragged in an effort to get us fixed up with money, accommodation or, better still, a homeward bound troopship. After his first unsuccessful morning he came back with the news that nothing could be arranged for us until tomorrow and that we were free to go ashore. That was not exactly bad news but, to go ashore, we needed money so back he went and finally managed to get us an advance of pay. We did not know it but this sort of gypsy existence was to last for the next three weeks and, in that time, we would be put on (and off) nine different troopships. I don't recall all their names but two of the more famous ones were the *Andes* and the *Stratheden*.

On our second day we were told that a convoy from England was due in next day and that we would be going back in the *Highland Monarch*. Sure enough the convoy arrived and disembarked troops of the 51st Highland Division and, late in the afternoon, we took our baggage on board, prepared to remain there until she sailed again for UK. However, when we saw the troop deck allocated to us there was a near mutiny because it was such a disgusting sight – littered with garbage and incredibly filthy. We had quite a 'discussion' with our Petty Officer (we could not blame him for it) with words like 'why should we have to clean up after somebody else?' and 'we are not going to live in this pigsty!'

Our friendly PO came back with one of the ship's officers who wasn't terribly sympathetic. He said, 'If you don't want to live in it like that you had better clean it up.' We finally agreed to do this provided we would be granted shore leave that night and, after two hours vigorous work we had it spotless and then went ashore, in the knowledge that we would return to a clean mess deck in the morning. Well, when we returned on board next morning we were greeted with the news that *Highland Monarch* had been diverted elsewhere – and so we were on the beach again.

Finally, we were told to board the *Scythia* and, to our great relief, were still on her when she sailed for England. *Scythia* was not a glamorous ship. She was quite an old, medium size, Cunard liner but that did not matter – we were on our way at last. We called in at Cape Town and then it was 'next stop Liverpool' and, because we were sailing independently (not in convoy), this meant a large sweep out into the South Atlantic to avoid the U-boats lurking along the African seaboard.

We were not overcrowded because the accommodation was not full and our duties were easy – I was sent to keep watches on the bridge and life was very peaceful. There was only one incident and that happened in the Bay of Biscay when a lookout reported a periscope; although I was on the bridge, I did not see it. We took evasive action and the gun's crew fired a couple of shots for good measure.

After another large detour to take us around Northern Ireland to avoid the U-boats known to be in the Irish Sea we finally made it into Liverpool. Needless to say, we were very happy when we got on a train to London and then, finally to Portsmouth Barracks.

I remember reporting in at the Signal School Block in the afternoon and, when I asked to go on leave, the Regulating Chief told me I would have to wait until tomorrow. Fortunately, the Divisional Officer was listening and, when he found I had just arrived from the Mediterranean after nearly three years, he told the Chief to 'get that man on leave tonight.' Within an hour I was on the train to Worthing and in my pocket was all my back pay, a ration book and a leave pass for six weeks. My mother nearly had kittens when I knocked on the door of No. 6 because she did not know I was in England, It was now 24 March 1942.

It was a glorious six weeks leave and a small part of my life that was truly memorable. The sheer exhilaration of being nineteen years old, home and safe, with my family and friends again. Even the weather was beautiful as only a perfect English spring can be, even in wartime.

It took a little while for me to adjust to the changes the war had brought to England while I had been away. First, the blackout (and it really was black) – no street lamps, no lighted shop windows, trains and railway stations 'dimmed out', tiny headlamps on vehicles and, at home, all our doors and windows covered in heavy, black material. Then, in our front room, the dining table had been replaced by a contraption known as a 'Morrison Shelter'.

About 30 inches high and about 5ft × 7ft it had four HD angles on the corners, a half inch steel plate on top and wire mesh on the sides. This was a household air raid shelter and all the family had to squeeze in there when the air raid warning sounded. Many people, I know. slept in them permanently but, because air raids in Worthing were not a frequent event since the Battle of Britain we did not bother. However, one morning during my leave I was enjoying a lie-in at about 9 a.m. when the siren sounded but I did not bother to get out of bed until I saw a Messerschmitt racing past my window very low – on his way to bomb the local gasworks as it turned out.

My family also were changed after three years – my mother and grandmother were looking a bit older and both Jack and June were growing up rapidly. Jack was now seventeen and heavily into anything to do with aircraft, was a keen member of the Worthing Air Cadets and frequently spent the night on fire watching duty at the Town Hall. Jack was also busy keeping chickens in the back garden to help with the family rations. June was then an attractive twelve-year old and was showing signs of becoming a real tomboy.

After more than four years of life in the Navy where food was sometimes uninteresting but seldom in short supply, especially on basics like tea, sugar and milk (tinned), it was a bit of a shock to see how meagre the civilian rations were. When I was offered sugar for my first cup of tea I lied and said, 'I don't take sugar' – and have never taken it since.

Of course, being reunited with my girlfriend Joyce was great and we spent an awful lot of time together, usually walking on the South Downs or cycling through pretty villages in the West Sussex countryside. Of course, all our South Coast was covered in barbed wire and minefields and, in the country, all the signposts had been removed to confuse an invading army. Also, large tracts of the Downs were closed off as Army training areas. I do remember one incident that I found a bit embarrassing at the time but laughed about later. I was walking with Joyce on the Downs on a warm, sunny, day and we stopped for a rest beside a rough cart track across the hillside. We were lying on the grass (very innocently I might add) when suddenly there appeared a large Army truck loaded with Italian POWs – and guarded by one soldier with his rifle casually slung on his shoulder. Well, the Italians got quite excited about seeing an English matelot, in uniform, with his girlfriend lying in the grass (however innocently) and were cheering and shouting and laughing.

Later on I wondered whether any of those Italians had been plucked from the Mediterranean a year ago by the Navy – if not they probably came from the Western Desert campaign. Wherever they came from, I thought what pleasant peaceful lives they were leading now, working on English farms. I believe the records show that only one POW (a German) was successful in escaping from Britain during the war but I am not sure whether this fact was due to the tight security or perhaps lack of effort on the part of the POWs.

Another incident during one of the walks on the Downs was to have a very far reaching effect on my future life. I mentioned earlier that, at the same time as I left for Hong Kong, the Synnott family had moved into No. 8 next door and therefore I did not know them when I returned home at the end of March 1942. One day, a cold and blustery one, Joyce and I with two friends were going to walk across the Downs and invited Jack, and Eileen from next door, to join us. I knew Jack was rather keen on Eileen and used to spend some time with her but, until now, I had not met her. Eileen was then sixteen and, at that time of my life, seemed much younger than myself. As we walked I tried chatting to her to make her feel more comfortable but I formed the idea that she was rather shy and reserved. That evening, the six of us went to the Rivoli cinema in Worthing although I don't know what film we saw.

Little did I know, as that day ended, that one day Eileen and I would be married and that she would be my wife for more than fifty years. I did not see Eileen again until she was de-mobbed from the ATS in November 1946.

I also remember visiting Joyce and her family at their home at 50 Loxwood Avenue where I was always made very welcome. Joyce had two older brothers whom I got to know fairly well. The eldest one was Eric, who was still in the Army (an officer) and the other was Vic who had been invalided out of the Army after a very nasty motorcycle accident when he was a despatch rider escorting a convoy of trucks at night. But it was not all bad because Vic had the good sense to marry the very attractive Irish nurse who had cared for him while he was in hospital. Vic and Paddy are still very good friends of ours and we always see them when we visit England.

Joyce was employed as a telephone switchboard operator (no automatic dialling in those days) and worked at the General Post Office building on the main street in Worthing and sometimes at the local exchange in Durrington. While on leave I used to go and meet her when she finished her shift at ten p.m.

There was one thing I could not understand about my leave and that was how I managed to complete all six weeks of it without being recalled. I was always hearing about 'so and so' who had had his leave cut short by a recall. This was quite normal in wartime when circumstances would change so rapidly. Every day I expected to receive a telegram, but it never came and I and my family were very grateful for this. So finally, my wonderful leave came to an end early in May. When I reported to the Royal Naval Barracks, Portsmouth I found that I (and a lot of others) were being drafted, that same day, to join a new ship just being completed in Scotland.

CHAPTER FIFTEEN

HMS Howe

T HE JOURNEY TO SCOTLAND to join HMS *Howe* was, as might be expected in wartime, long and tedious. We were on a special troop train with personnel of all services who were *en route* to Scotland for one reason or another. The normal overnight train to Scotland left Kings Cross about 10.30 and would arrive in Glasgow around 6.30 a.m. But, because ours was a 'special', we were often sidetracked to allow other trains to pass. Consequently, our journey took from early afternoon until 8 a.m. the following morning.

I found that I was part of a group of 200–250 ratings of all branches who were the 'Advance Party' being sent to prepare the ship for the Commissioning Ceremony, when the balance of the ship's company would join, on 1 June 1942. This date was well chosen by the Admiralty for the commissioning of their newest battleship. The ship's name and the commissioning date were no coincidence – they were to commemorate the defeat of the French by Admiral Lord Howe on 'The Glorious First of June' – and also known as 'Lord Howe Day'. The *Howe* was a ship of the *King George V* class – a battleship with a displacement of forty thousand tons, 700ft long, 103ft beam and capable of thirty knots.

Her main armament was ten 14-inch guns and a secondary armament of 5.25 inch dual purpose guns but, best of all, she was fully equipped with radar. Of course, a vessel like this was not built overnight – she was laid down in 1937, launched in 1940 and completed in 1942. Her full complement was to be 1,650 officers and men. She had been built at Fairfield's Shipbuilding Yard at Govan, one of Clydebank's biggest shipbuilders.

When we arrived at Glasgow Central station at eight in the morning we were tired, scruffy and hungry after our long and uncomfortable journey. We were pleased to find a fleet of red, double-decker buses waiting for us; better still, they stopped on the way at a Salvation Army hostel where we were given time for a wash and brush up followed by a really good cooked breakfast. We were feeling a lot better when we arrived at Govan, a suburb of Glasgow, and drove into Fairfield's Yard and, as we went up the gangway, I remember thinking, 'What will the future hold for me now?' Apart from the tremendous size, my first impression was, 'How do we ever get this ready for sea in three weeks?' Everything on the upper deck was wet and very dirty and the entire ship seemed to be trapped in a huge spider's web – there were an incredible number of ropes, wires, pipes and hoses connecting the ship to the shore. Not only that, the entire ship was swarming with shipyard workers (and most of them did not seem to be doing a lot of work).

When we got on board we realised just how large this ship was. Our living space on the Communications Mess deck was comfortable, but not luxurious; the Flag Deck was huge and, for a while at least, it was not difficult to get lost when trying to find a particular compartment. Of course, with only the Advance Party on board everything appeared more spacious than it would later, when the full complement arrived.

Whilst in the shipbuilder's yard our only means of communication was by telephone so my duties entailed keeping watches in the Main Signal Office, handling 'in' and 'out' signal traffic by means of the phone. It was by no means arduous and I enjoyed keeping regular watches because it meant that our off-duty time was assured and we were allowed ashore during the day when all the 'daymen' were working.

Our on board telephone was, of course, an extension from the telephone exchange in Fairfield's main office. I was soon intrigued by the pleasant female voice with the Scottish accent coming from the switchboard operator so, after a couple of days, I found an excuse to go ashore on duty to visit the switchboard. I took a friend, 'Knocker' White with me (we were in the same duty watch) for moral support and as we strolled through the huge office complex we only attracted a few curious glances but later, when this became a regular occurrence, we got some very knowing looks, and a few comments, as we passed the rows of draughtsmen. In the telephone exchange we found two very nice young ladies who, although somewhat surprised at being approached, while on duty, by two strange sailors, soon relaxed and we all became very good friends. I was immediately in love with Helen who was a tall, slim girl with light brown corkscrew curls and twinkly eyes. Her partner on the switchboard was Jean who, although a bit more cuddly, was a very attractive girl and certainly my friend 'Knocker' found her so because he eventually married her.

Helen and I found we enjoyed each other's company and spent all our free time together. Probably because we did not drink in those days, our activities together would be a lot less sophisticated – an occasional cinema show, a visit to the zoo, but, more often, long walks on the very green hills on the banks of the Clyde. Sometimes these outings would involve the four of us and sometimes not. Very often I would be invited to come home to tea and sometimes dinner on Sunday and Mr and Mrs Munro were always very hospitable. Helen's father, like most men in the area, worked at the shipyard – he didn't drink and they always went to church on Sunday. Once I was persuaded to join them and, although it was a new experience for me, I did not care much for the Presbyterian service. Helen and Jean both belonged to a 'walking club' organised by the Fairfield workers and one Sunday 'Knocker' and I accompanied them on a hike over the hills to Loch Lomond. When we eventually got there we all had tea and I was very pleased to learn that the return journey would be by train.

After about two and a half months of this very pleasant existence the *Howe* was ready to move out and begin sea trials prior to the final acceptance from the shipyard.

On a beautiful summer day at the end of July the ship was moved slowly from her berth by four tugs and edged carefully out into the Clyde. For this operation the entire shipyard workforce turned out, waving and cheering, somewhat wistfully I thought because they were losing not only their pride and joy but also the source of several years' job security. As the *Howe* moved slowly and majestically down the Clyde I know she was an impressive sight, with a crisp, new White Ensign on the stern, the Royal Marine Band on the Quarterdeck playing lively naval tunes, our Signal Letters flying at the yardarm and the crew lining the rails for leaving harbour. On the banks of the Clyde I think the entire local population turned out, waving and cheering, as though saying farewell to a favourite son. So much for wartime secrecy of ship's movements!

After several hours we arrived, and anchored, at Greenock which is an enormous expanse of water at the mouth of the Clyde and was famous as the assembly and jumping off point for trans-Atlantic convoys. We soon learned that we were to be based there for three or four weeks whilst carrying out 'acceptance trials'. This involved testing every piece of equipment on board – sometimes in harbour and sometimes at sea for speed trials, manoeuvrability trials, gunnery trials etc. For this purpose we still carried senior shipyard representatives on board until the Captain was assured that everything was working as it should – and then he would sign acceptance papers, on behalf of the Admiralty, for a very large piece of steel called HMS *Howe*.

For me, this was another very pleasant period because it meant that when 'Knocker' and I were off duty we could go ashore and get a train to Glasgow to see our girlfriends – it was about forty-five minutes each way. Of course, the girls worked during the day so, when 'Knocker' and I were off we would stay in Glasgow to check out the city. One day we were walking past Glasgow Central Station when two Army officers came towards us and, of course, we automatically saluted. Then one of them shouted, 'Hey Bob.' When I looked round I was amazed to find it was

Engine Trials off Scapa Flow, October 1942.

Joyce's eldest brother, Eric – he was about to ship out to the Mediterranean for the Italian campaign. Of course, I was pleased to see him and we had a long chat about everything – at the same time I was glad it was not Helen walking beside me!

Finally, all was pronounced well, the Captain signed off and were on our way. As we cleared the Clyde we picked up our destroyer escort and headed out into the Atlantic – our destination was to be Rosyth, on the Firth of Forth. Rosyth is only an hour and a half by bus from Glasgow but our journey would be much longer; we would detour out into the Atlantic and then turn north and pass above the Orkney Islands and the top of Scotland, finally coming down the east coast to the Forth. This took us the best part of two days and we were not sorry to see the famous Forth Bridge and slip into our berth in Rosyth Naval Dockyard which lies in the shadow of the bridge. We found that we expected to be there for about a month whilst the dockyard undertook the list of 'Alterations and Additions' that had been found necessary. This was encouraging news and we all looked forward to some good runs ashore in Edinburgh and nearby Dunfermline.

In our V/S Branch we had a Yeoman of Signals (Petty Officer) named Tony Setford and we had become quite good friends in spite of the difference in rank (I was still a Signalman) and mostly because we both came from Worthing. Tony was still quite young (early twenties) and had done well to make Yeoman so soon – he was always clean and smart and claimed that there was nothing he could not do. For this reason he was nicknamed 'The Wizard' (plus another one that I'd rather not mention).

At the seaward entrance to the dockyard was the Dockyard Signal Station and, as it was only two hundred yards from our berth, Tony and I decided to walk along there to have a chat with the guys and see if there was anyone we knew. We had not been in touch with them (apart from making our identity on arrival) because we were again connected to the shore telephone and had closed down V/S watch on the Flag Deck. The entrance door on the ground level said 'No Visitors Allowed' but we went in anyway and, when we got to the Signal Deck we found it was manned by Signal Wrens! It was at this point that I fell madly in love with Sylvia – Sylvia Fearn, a dark vivacious girl, was one of the dozen Signal Wrens operating the station which was a busy place. Their accommodation was adjoining the station and they were under the command of a Wren Officer, whom we took care not to meet. The Wrens we did meet all expressed an interest in the huge battleship so close to them – so Tony and I resolved to do something about it. We managed to get permission to bring the Wrens on board, and give them a tour of the ship followed by tea in the Petty Officers' Mess – it all went smoothly and I believe everybody enjoyed it. And so began an enjoyable few weeks in Rosyth, with visits to Edinburgh, which I thought was a beautiful and interesting city, sometimes a visit to the cinema in Dunfermline and, inevitably, some long walks in the lovely countryside.

All too soon our happy time was over and we sailed from Rosyth, on our way to join the Home Fleet at Scapa Flow in the Orkney Islands. Scapa Flow is a vast area of water inside a ring of islands and, with only two entrances, made a secure anchorage in wartime. The entrance used by destroyers was at Lyness and the 'big ship' entrance was beside the island of Flotta and, of course, both were protected by anti-submarine nets in wartime. Scapa Flow is probably the most desolate and inhospitable place I have visited. On land the only visible habitation was the Signal Station on the top of Flotta and the only inhabitants appeared to be sheep. There are two small towns in the Orkneys, Kirkwall and Stromness, but both are too remote from the anchorage for anybody to visit. Not that we had much time for shore leave anyway – we were kept busy on 'working up trials'. This involved both sea and harbour drills where not only the equipment but also the men were brought to peak efficiency.

At the end of September, we left Scapa Flow for a very secret destination and, for once, there were not even rumours as to what we were doing. We arrived at a very remote, and almost unknown, Scottish loch on the north-west coast. It was even more uninviting than Scapa Flow – there was not a single building there and even the sheep were missing.

We were still not told why we were there and speculation ran wild when a small submarine depot ship arrived and work crews began surrounding the *Howe* with protective anti-submarine nets. Subsequently one of our larger submarines entered harbour but had an unusual outline – on the deck casing behind the conning tower was an unusual structure that appeared to be an enormous, corrugated steel, oil drum.

I was on watch on the Flag Deck at the time and while we were still trying to guess what it might contain, a friend of mine, Ted Andrews, who was also the Leading Hand of my watch, decided to find out for himself. With an Aldis lamp, he called up the submarine and passed a message 'for the watch on deck' which meant that, normally, this would not be reported to the Captain. Unfortunately for 'Andy' the Captain of the submarine did get to see it and, as a result, wrote quite a strong letter on the subject of security to the Captain of the *Howe*. The outcome was that Andy was brought before the Captain and was ordered to lose his Good Conduct Badge and to spend the next six days in the cells! By then we knew it was a two-man midget submarine in the 'oil drum' and it would be practising underwater night attacks on the *Howe*. Joining the 'fun' would be four teams of two frogmen who would be mounted astride a torpedo for the attacks – they were known as 'charioteers'. Although these weapons were new to the Royal Navy they had been used, very successfully, by the Italian Navy when they attacked the Mediterranean Fleet in Alexandria in December of the previous year. Our training exercises lasted for six weeks as the frogmen and the mini-sub would attack *Howe* every night, at any time between dusk and midnight, while the watch on deck would try to spot them and, if that happened, we would illuminate them with a ten-inch signalling projector. Unfortunately, we lost a couple of frogmen who became caught in the anti-submarine nets.

Towards the end of November when we got back to Scapa Flow it was a real boost when we found that leave would be granted for Christmas 1942. Obviously, the entire crew could not all go at the same time so volunteers were called for to form an Advance Leave Party, who would go at the beginning of December and be back on board during the Christmas period while the main body were away. In the V/S Department, Tony Setford and I volunteered (along with a couple of others) to go on leave early, partly because it meant that I would have my twentieth birthday at home (but not Christmas).

Our journey home from Scapa was quite horrendous – we left the *Howe* in the ship's drifter at eight a.m. and went to a depot ship, the *Dunluce Castle*, where we were kept hanging about until late morning. Finally, we got on the mainland ferry which took us across the Pentland Firth to a small town called Thurso which is the most northerly point on the Scottish mainland. I remember we had about six hours to kill before we could catch the night train to Edinburgh at ten o'clock. Because we had not been ashore for three months it was nice to stretch our legs on dry land once more but, even so, we were hungry by now and went to a small hotel where we had an excellent cooked meal.

Afterwards we had a couple of beers to fortify us on our journey – we almost had to fight for them because of the terrific crowd of people from all services who were going on the same train. The night train left Thurso at ten p.m. and got us into Edinburgh at eight the next morning. After breakfast we were on the day train to London where we arrived about eight p.m. on our second evening of travel. After getting across town, we managed to catch the last train for Brighton out of Victoria but, when we reached Brighton just after eleven p.m. we were stuck because there was no way of getting to Worthing, even though it was only ten miles further. There was no choice but to spend the night drinking coffee in a rather dingy café outside Brighton station. When we finally arrived home the next morning, after forty-eight hours of travelling, we were well and truly ready for our leave.

I know it was a very enjoyable leave, although all too short, but there was one incident which has stuck in my mind all these years. On my birthday, four of us went out for an evening celebration – myself, Joyce Bonsall, her friend Paula and Tony Setford. We finished up at closing time (I think it was 10.30 in those days) in a bar of the Albion Hotel on Montague Street in the centre of Worthing. As we left it was drizzling rain and, of course, very black. We tripped over something on the pavement – as I reached down to see what it was I touched fur and thought, 'It's a dead dog.' But when we looked closer it proved to be an elderly lady in a fur coat, which by then was pretty wet. It took a while to hoist her up and get any sense out of her – she was, as they say, 'completely legless'! We finally got an address out of her so we decided to take her home – half carrying her and trying to keep her awake. It was not too far out of our way and when we found the house it was in darkness and took a while to rouse a young man who came to the door. When he saw the picture he said, 'Oh no, not again'. It turned out that there were four local policemen sharing the house and our happy companion was their housekeeper.

As the New Year of 1943 dawned we found that our activities and our lives were about to change once again as we were well and truly thrust back into the war. The first significant event was that *Howe* received orders to leave Scapa Flow and take up station in Iceland and, although any change was welcome, the idea of spending winter in and around Iceland was not my idea of fun. We were issued with quantities of woollen gear (gloves, scarves, sweaters and balaclavas etc.) which some good ladies somewhere had knitted for the sailor boys. The object of this move was threefold – we were well placed to cover the increasing number of very important troop convoys coming from America; we could also go north and east to cover the convoys to Russia; finally, we were able to cover the Denmark Strait to prevent another breakout by the German Navy as the *Bismarck* had done. Iceland was well populated by men of the US Air Force who had taken over the island in 1942 and were busy setting up radar stations and airfields. The *Howe* was based in Reykjavik, a fair sized town on the shore of a huge bay which made a great natural harbour. It was not an unpleasant place except for the fact that there was almost nothing to do. After visiting the hot, underground geysers, which were something to see in the midst of all the ice and snow, and purchasing a natural sheepskin, that was about it.

There was a large Services Canteen run by the Yanks but it was not a big enough attraction in itself. The climate, as was to be expected in the Arctic Circle, was pretty awful with lots of rough seas, gales and blizzards. In addition, at this time of year, it was almost continually dark – we used to get about one hour of twilight in the afternoon. The highlight of our existence in these less than ideal conditions was getting back to Reykjavik after a convoy and looking forward to mail, dry clothes and a steady deck under our feet. Because *Howe* was a big ship it was not all that bad but she could still roll pretty heavily. I used to feel sorry for the escorting destroyers because they certainly took a pounding in those weather conditions.

It was about this time that the Admiralty introduced new rules for the promotion of Communications personnel and, because I took advantage of the scheme, I was rapidly promoted from Signalman, through Leading Signalman to Yeoman of Signals when I left the *Howe* – this was quite remarkable and, in peacetime would have been impossible. Under normal procedure it was necessary to attend the Signal School to undergo a long instructional course and examination in order to qualify for higher rating in the Signal Branch. However, after three years into the war, the Admiralty realised that men could not be spared from ships to attend courses and therefore, senior ratings in the Branch were becoming very scarce. The new rules allowed for men who were qualified educationally to sit a written and oral examination, supervised by a qualified Signal Officer in a capital ship, to qualify for Leading Signalman and Yeoman of Signals. The successful candidates could then be promoted to the appropriate rate with the suffix 'Temporary' added to it. This meant getting paid for the job and the (Temp) would be removed on successful completion of the appropriate course in the Signal School. Under this scheme (with a lot of coaching and persuading by Tony Setford) I was rated Leading Signalman (Temporary) on 1 December 1942 and Yeoman of Signals (Temporary) a year later. So, early in 1943, I started to pester the *Howe*'s Signal Officer for a transfer to a destroyer where I thought life would be more exciting than in a battleship. I felt sure there must be a destroyer somewhere who would welcome a keen, young Leading Signalman – but no luck!

After three months in the frozen north, *Howe* was ordered back to Rosyth where, after a brief period in dock, we sailed again for an unknown destination but having been issued with tropical gear we were not too worried – at least it would be warm. By the time we passed eastwards through the Straits of Gibraltar we knew it was to be the Mediterranean only this time it would be the central and western end. We finished up based in Algiers, which has a large harbour with plenty of room for a couple of battleships. We were kept pretty busy at first as the situation in Tunisia, Sicily and Italy was changing all the time. Algiers turned out to be not our favourite place for a run ashore – I suppose it was a typical French Colonial city – the population were not over friendly and there was very little to do because all the buildings seemed to be shuttered, both day and night. My favourite occupation here was

His Majesty King George VI with Captain C.H.L. Woodhouse
inspecting HMS *Howe* at Algiers, June 1943.

swimming in the sea any afternoon that I was free and it was here that I met a boy I had been at school with in Worthing.

His name was Derek Denyer and he was then a Yeoman of Signals in HMS *Penelope* (better known as 'the pepper-pot' because of the incredible number of shrapnel holes in the hull from bomb attacks during the operations in Crete). Derek was a pleasant, quiet young man and we enjoyed each other's company whenever we could.

Sometime in June, I suppose as a boost for the forth-coming invasions of Sicily and Italy, we were honoured by a visit to Algiers by HM King George VI who came on board HMS *Howe* and inspected the ship's company at Sunday Divisions and spoke to many of the men.

A couple of weeks later, also at Sunday Divisions, the Signal Officer came up to me and said, rather smugly I thought, 'Adams, you are always asking me for a destroyer – well, I have got one for you.' Great news I thought, but when I asked him which one, I got the bad news – 'She will be entering harbour at five p.m. today – and she is French!' It turned out that I was to be part of the Com-munications Liaison Team which consisted of one Leading Signalman (myself), two Signalmen, one Leading Tele-graphist and two Telegraphists, all under the command of a young Sub Lieutenant RNVR, and at five p.m. we were all on the gangway, with all our kit and ready to go. Right on time, two very impressive looking destroyers glided into the harbour and anchored not far away and our boat took us to embark in the nearest one.

To all intents and purposes, this is where my story of HMS *Howe* will end because, although I was lucky enough to rejoin her when she returned to the United Kingdom at the end of the year it was only for passage – but I shall come to that later.

HMS *Howe* survived the war and was scrapped in 1958.

CHAPTER SIXTEEN

FS Le Fantasque

THE TWO FRENCH DESTROYERS that entered harbour in Algiers on that Sunday evening in July 1943 were *Le Fantasque* and her sister ship *Le Terrible*, arriving to reinforce the Mediterranean Fleet after escaping from Toulon following the fall of France in 1942. They had since been in the United States for an extensive six months refit where they had been fitted with modern anti-aircraft guns, anti-submarine equipment and some radar. They were also quite modern vessels, having been built in Lorient in 1936 and, with their rakish lines, they certainly looked what they were – very large and extremely fast destroyers, capable of 40–43 knots. This was faster than any ships in the Royal Navy except the fast minelayers of the Abdiel class. French naval designers seemed to go for big vessels (at the beginning of the war they even had a huge submarine – the *Surcouf* – which could carry a seaplane). These destroyers were 435ft long with a 40ft beam and carried a complement of 210.

As we went on board *Fantasque* we were met by the French Officer of the Watch and the French Communications Officer. At this point we were naturally wondering how we would like being in the French Navy and what would be in store for us when we got settled in – but nothing prepared us for the shock that lay ahead.

A couple of their Signalmen were sent for to show us to the Communications Mess deck and to arrange for our supper. They were friendly enough and, in fact, quite pleased to see us. However, when we reached the mess deck we could not believe what we were seeing and smelling – the ship was in a filthy, foul-smelling condition, unlike anything we had ever experienced before. A couple of us had served in our own destroyers and knew what a rough spell at sea could do but, even allowing for the fact that they had been at sea for three weeks with a slow convoy from the US, this was for us disgusting, although it did not seem to bother the French matelots at all. Then they offered us supper – they were eating some sort of stew – but, when we asked about eating utensils, one of them who spoke some English explained that we needed to get an empty can (beans or fruit etc) to use as a dish and we would substitute a seaman's work knife for cutlery. It appeared that crockery and cutlery were unknown in the French Navy! The crew's bathroom was an awful place and the heads (toilets) were even worse. Their idea of cleaning these places was to hit them with a fire hose when they became unbearable.

Our Liaison Team had a quick council of war and, having made our decision, we wasted no time in seeking out our unfortunate Sub Lieutenant. Without actually attacking him we made him understand that these living conditions could not be accepted and, unless alternative arrangements could be made, we would have to take the matter higher. Well, he was not a bad chap and he did do his best for us – he promised to take us ashore next day to the Naval Stores and draw whatever we wanted like cutlery, cups, plates etc. As far as sleeping went we agreed, because there was no accommodation other than the mess deck, to sling our hammocks and sleep in 'B' gun shelter on the upper deck.

Of course, this was not a very auspicious start to our liaison operation and, naturally, made us a bit unpopular with a lot of the Frenchmen but, having made our stand, we did not let it interfere with doing our job.

It took us a little while to get used to the French diet, which was nothing like we had known before. Reveille was at six and then half an hour later we lined up at the galley for our breakfast which was always the same – a cup of black coffee and a Cadbury's chocolate bar. This was a novelty at first but we soon found we were pretty hungry by midday. Lunch (at 12.30) and supper (at 18.30) were both cooked meals and were not too bad (I had never experienced steak in the RN) and both meals included a good measure of sharp, red wine. This also was a novelty but it was not long before we longed to trade the wine for a good cup of tea, something we never got.

Another oddity of the French Navy, which took a while to get used to, was that everybody (officers and men) would shake hands and say 'good morning' when meeting for the first time each day.

The ship had been refitting in Boston Navy Yard for six

months and so there were quite a few lovesick matelots pining for their girlfriends in the US. I remember one young French Signalman, who spoke a little bit of English, who would ask me to translate his letters from Boston which was not too bad but then I had to compose a suitable reply for him to send.

We soon began exercising with RN destroyers to see how we would fit in with them. It was soon realised that, while the extremely high speed of the two French ships was a big advantage, their extra size represented an equally big disadvantage in that it gave them a very large turning circle which made them unsuitable for normal destroyer work as an anti-submarine screen. It was therefore decided that, for Fleet operations, the two ships should be classed as 'light cruisers' and, as such, we were to spend a lot of time acting independently of the main Fleet. We spent a lot of time escorting convoys to Sicily, night high-speed searches for enemy shipping off the Tunisian coast and, of course, we got highly involved in the invasion of Sicily on 10 July 1943.

Shortly afterwards we were back in Algiers and, having been accepted, we were taking our turn as 'Emergency Destroyer' which meant keeping up steam and being ready to go anywhere at a moment's notice. In our case it entailed lying alongside a damaged merchant ship, anchored in the outer harbour, which was burning steadily. We had to keep our fire hoses playing on the cargo of phosphates in an effort to control the fire. This was a duty for twenty-four hours, changing over at eight a.m. daily. We had just been relieved by HMS *Daring*, an RN destroyer, had slipped our lines and were moving away when there was a deafening explosion as the merchant ship blew apart and went to the bottom, taking the *Daring* and most of her crew with her. We picked up a few survivors and, as we did so, I thought, 'There goes cat's life No. 6!'

The weeks went by and we were kept busy with our Communications but we did not see any more of the *Howe* until September when we were both at the landings at Salerno on the Italian mainland. The vicious air attacks on shipping, for which the Med. had become famous, were now lessened for us because the Luftwaffe had their hands full with invasion landings and evacuating the remains of the Afrika Korps from Tunisia.

Towards the end of October *Fantasque* and *Terrible* were

NATIONAL NAVY.

GENERAL STAFF

OFFICIAL MESSAGE OF SATISFACTION.

Rear Admiral LEMONNIER, Chief of the Naval Staff, addresses a collective message of satisfaction to Capitaine de Vaisseau PERZO(C.Y.F.M.) Commanding LE FANTASQUE and to the Staff and Crew of that ship for

"Having brought to a successful conclusion within an extremely short time a particularly delicate operation"

I certify that Leading Signalman R.A.ADAMS, P/JX.156474 was on board LE FANTASQUE during this operation.

ORAN.   12th October 1943.

F. DU TERTRE
for CAPITAINE DE VAISSEAU PERZO
COMMANDING OFFICER, LE FANTASQUE

ordered to a small place called Philipville on the Tunisian coast and when we got there we found, waiting to embark, a large crowd of very fierce looking French Commandos.

NATIONAL NAVY

GENERAL STAFF

NAVAL ORDERS OF THE DAY. TO THE DESTROYER LE FANTASQUE.

"For his effective participation under the command of Capitaine de Vaisseau PERZO(C.Y.F.M.) in important war operations in the Western Mediterranean during the months of August and September 1943 and for the magnificent bearing of his staff and crew during these operations"

LE FANTASQUE and LE TERRIBLE with the submarine CASABIANCA were the first ships to enter AJACCIObringing, by this dashing stroke, the first contingent of troops which made sure the liberation of CORSICA.

I certify that Leading Signalman R.A.ADAMS, R.N.,P/JX.156474 was on board during these operations.

F. DU TERTRE
SECOND IN COMMAND
for CAPITAINE DE VAISSEAU PERZO,
COMMANDING OFFICER LE FANTASQUE

When we got them on board and cleared the harbour we found that we were on our own little invasion to liberate some French territory – Corsica. Our sailing was timed so that, travelling at high speed, we would arrive at Ajaccio on the west coast at midnight. All the way there the Commandos were very busy preparing their weapons – cleaning, polishing and oiling their automatic weapons and sharpening some very dangerous looking knives.

As we approached Ajaccio the ship was completely blacked-out and absolutely silent. The Germans were believed to be in, or close to, the town. On shore, the only thing to be seen was a few fires burning outside the town. However, as we slid silently into the harbour, we all looked at each other in amazement because we could now hear the sound of singing and we soon found out why – the entire population was assembled on the harbour wall and singing *The Marseillaise*. I think the French national anthem is one of the most stirring anyway but to hear it under these conditions in the stillness of that night it was very inspiring and quite heart stirring.

But so much for invasion security!

We got alongside all right – there were plenty of willing hands to take our lines – and then we began unloading. The troops were no problem but, of course, they had a mountain of ammunition and supplies. The word had been passed among the crew that nobody was to leave the ship but, feeling adventurous, the Leading Telegraphist and I picked up a box of ammunition each and walked down the gangway – nobody even noticed as we disappeared in the darkness. We were walking through the town and, as we passed the Hotel d'Étranger we were joking about going in for a beer. Suddenly a woman's voice from an upstairs window called, 'Are you English?' and, getting an affirmative came down and invited us in. She was English and her husband, who owned the hotel, was French and they were delighted to see us, especially under the circumstances of our arrival. Of course, we enjoyed a long chat (and a couple of beers) before we decided we should get back to the ship. It appeared the German Staff had been billeted at the hotel and had pulled out only that day.

We did one more Commando run to Ajaccio without incident but on the third run we were not so lucky.

Ajaccio has two half-moon bays – the first one is the harbour and the second one is the seaplane base. Well, our Navigating Officer pulled a boo-boo, missed the first entrance and entered the second with the unfortunate result that we ran straight up the beach! We got the troops ashore OK although they didn't seem to appreciate having to jump in the water first. Then, however hard we tried, we could not get the ship afloat again – we were stuck hard and fast in the soft sand but, fortunately there was no apparent damage – except perhaps to a couple of naval careers. There were no vessels in Ajaccio to help so there was no choice except to radio for a tug from Malta – and then wait.

Not unexpectedly, when daylight came so did an enemy reconnaissance plane – and then we did not have too long to wait before the arrival of some Stuka dive bombers, always a formidable sight with their 'gull' wings and screaming sirens as they dived. I expect they were delighted to find such a juicy target waiting for them, motionless in the sand like a beached whale. They certainly pressed home several attacks during daylight on that day but, miraculously it seemed, we did not take a direct hit although the beach all around us was churned up with dozens of bomb craters.

The French gunners certainly gave a good account of themselves but, as darkness fell, everyone breathed a sigh of relief although, after the experience of that day, there were not too many who felt we could survive another one like it.

Thankfully, the tug from Malta arrived next day and made pretty fast work of towing us off the beach – with a lot of cheering from the ship's company. *Fantasque* did not seem to be too much the worse for the grounding although I am sure there must have been a lot of dents and wrinkles in the bottom which should not be there. We did not waste any time hanging around and headed for home at best possible speed. This time though it was not to be Algiers – we had been ordered to Oran for inspection in dry dock which showed that fairly extensive repairs were required and so *Fantasque* would be out of action for some time. This meant that our liaison job was finished and we were being sent back to Algiers to rejoin the *Howe*. We caught the train early next morning but, besides being hot and uncomfortable, we found it was just as slow as the Egyptian trains – Oran to Algiers is only a couple of hundred miles but the journey took all day. We were met at Algiers station and taken to a small naval barracks in the city where we got the news that

Howe had sailed two hours earlier for Gibraltar and the UK.

This was not the happy ending we had all been looking forward to but, next morning, our depression was eased a bit when we were told that a corvette, HMS *Poppy*, would be calling at Algiers that day to refuel and that passage to Gibraltar would be arranged for us. The question in our minds was 'would we get there before *Howe* left?' These little Flower class corvettes, much smaller than a destroyer, were very seaworthy vessels but had a reputation that 'they would roll on damp grass' – and it was true. The passage to Gibraltar was exceptionally rough for the Mediterranean and this slowed us down a bit so consequently nerves were a bit frayed as we approached Gibraltar. But, as we rounded The Rock, there was a sigh of relief as we saw the familiar bulk of the *Howe* still in the harbour. It was a great feeling to be on board again and we were welcomed back like Prodigal Sons.

We sailed next morning for England and, after an uneventful voyage, arrived in Plymouth on the evening of 4 December 1943.

The following day was a very significant one for me because: first of all it was my twenty-first birthday; secondly I had to see the Captain (as a 'requestman') to receive my first Good Conduct Badge (for three years of 'man's service') and also to be rated Yeoman of Signals (even if it was 'Acting Temporary'); thirdly I was discharged from the ship to join HMS *Mercury* on completion of leave.

The long train journey home did not bother me at all because I was on top of the world.

As for the *Fantasque* – she eventually survived the war, which I found rather surprising because of her construction. She was a beautiful ship but her extreme speed had only been achieved because they had sacrificed watertight security.

In other words, her huge engine rooms and boiler rooms were all in one huge compartment which meant that a single hit in that compartment would, almost certainly, send her to the bottom.

After being employed by the French during the trouble in French Indo-China, she was finally scrapped in 1955.

CHAPTER SEVENTEEN

HMS *Mercury*

I THINK IT GOES WITHOUT SAYING that I thoroughly enjoyed getting home to my family again and I know we all celebrated a wonderful Christmas, in spite of all the wartime shortages and restrictions. Of course, I did not know it then but this was to be my only Christmas at home during the years 1939–45.

Towards the end of December when my leave was completed I went to join HMS *Mercury* which I knew was the new Signal School which was located outside Portsmouth, near the town of Petersfield in Hampshire. The old Signal School Block in the Royal Naval Barracks at Portsmouth had soon proved totally inadequate to handle the volume of courses required for what were then modern communications. At that time a lady called Beatrice Lille, who was a very famous British stage actress, agreed to make her country home available to the Admiralty for the purpose of establishing a Signal School. At the end of 1943 when I joined *Mercury* I knew very little about it and had only a vague idea where it was. It was, in fact, a very beautiful country home property called 'Leydene' and comprised a very large house with a sweeping driveway and large forecourt (which made an excellent parade ground). This was surrounded by some formal terraces and gardens but, most impressive of all, there were acres and acres of natural estate which included lawns, woodland and huge, grassy broadwalks. Doesn't sound much like a Naval establishment but then, those were the early days.

When I got to HMS *Mercury* for the first time I was happy to find that I was scheduled to take a Yeoman of Signals course, starting at the beginning of January 1944 and lasting two months. The instructional course was, naturally, very exacting with lots of evening swotting required but living at the new Signal School was very pleasant – not least because a lot of the staff were now Wrens. We were accommodated in Nissen huts, which were scattered around the grounds and, at first, all the cooking and eating was done in the Main House. Later the Main House was reserved for Officers as Messes and Galleys etc. were provided 'for the troops'.

Naturally, in later years (after the war) I was destined to spend many periods at *Mercury*, sometimes taking a course, sometimes instructing a course and quite often just waiting for a draft to the next ship. They were all happy and pleasant times because, although the training and routines were rigorous, the beautiful surroundings made life so much better than being in a regular barracks. However, this first visit of mine was to be the most impressive because it involved so much of things I had not expected in the Navy. Another attraction of that period was the Wren who worked in the Master at Arms office – her name was Betty Tierney and she was the sister of a boy I had been at school with. Her brother Pat was now a Sergeant in the Royal Marines somewhere. The family lived on Newlands Road and so we used to travel home on weekends together.

Finally I had completed the course, and passed, so I could get rid of all the 'Temporary' stuff – but I still retained the 'Acting' bit until completing a year in the Petty Officer rate. This was required by the Navy to prove that you were suitable for the job before they incurred the expense of you changing from a bell bottom outfit to a peaked cap – or, as it was generally known, 'changing from round rig to square rig'.

Although Petersfield was the nearest town it was not usually the place chosen when we were going on shore leave, unless going to the cinema or (on rare occasions) to eat in a restaurant. The most interesting (and therefore most popular) places to visit were the country pubs in all the little villages surrounding Leydene. Of these, I think the most favourite was the Bat & Ball which adjoined the local cricket pitch where the great W. G. Grace was reputed to have played – and it also had the advantage of being within walking distance (when sober, that is).

But all good things come to an end and as soon as my course was finished they wasted no time in drafting me out to my next ship,

So, on 29 February 1944 (Leap Year) I left *Mercury* to travel to the United States to join my next ship which was HMS *Indomitable*, another aircraft carrier.

CHAPTER EIGHTEEN

HMS *Indomitable*

O N 1 MARCH 1944 I found myself on a large troopship sailing out of Liverpool and bound for New York and, because it was a fast ship, we were routed independently (i.e. not in convoy). The weather in the Atlantic was not the greatest but aside from that our voyage to the United States was fast and uneventful and soon we found ourselves passing the Statue of Liberty and berthing alongside in New York harbour.

Pier 92 on the New York waterfront was one of the huge warehouse complexes where the pre-war transatlantic passenger liners used to dock, but which, in 1944, had been converted to US Navy barracks. After disembarking we found that we were to be accommodated at Pier 92 for a few days before transferring to Norfolk, Virginia to join the *Indomitable*. I never knew the reason for this but just welcomed the opportunity to see something of New York City before joining our ship. I was rather surprised to find that as a brand new Petty Officer, I was in charge of a draft of 30–40 Communications ratings. Understandably the US Navy was not particularly interested in us and, apart from providing food and shelter, left us to our own devices. I especially remember my first breakfast with the Yanks – there was juice, rolls, eggs (prepared how you desired), sausages and huge piles of pancakes, but most of all pure, white, freshly sliced bread which tasted like cake to us after the British 'National Loaf' which was a bit grey and not very interesting.

We were free to go ashore at noon every day and were not to be back 'on board' until eight the next morning which gave us plenty of time to explore the city. The United States (and especially New York) was a real culture shock to us because, after nearly five years of wartime restrictions and shortages in Britain we were suddenly in a land where, apart from the many uniforms to be seen, there was no sign of a war. The city was a blaze of light, food and drink were plentiful and cheap, there was no petrol rationing and everybody seemed to be well-dressed and enjoying life. For us, our few days there were spent seeing famous places – Broadway, Central Park, Fifth Avenue, the Empire State Building and many more. We were delighted to find there was a theatre ticket booth in Times Square where we could obtain tickets for tonight's show at very reduced rates. I particularly remember an evening at the Radio City Music Hall where we saw the famous Rockettes, a movie and an excellent stage show. We even walked up the stairs of the Empire State Building, just to prove it could be done! Like the rest of New York City, I don't think we slept very much and I remember crawling into bed at 4.30 to catch a couple of hours before Reveille.

We travelled by train from New York City to Norfolk, Virginia and, although it seemed a long way, we were fascinated by all that we saw along the way, especially the huge expanse of the waters of Chesapeake Bay.

Our first impression of Norfolk was the huge, sprawling dockyard (or 'Navy Yard' as they call it in the States). We found HMS *Indomitable* berthed at one of the piers, and on the other side of the pier was the USS *Randolph* which was nearing completion of repairs of bomb damage suffered

HMS *Indomitable*, Pacific Operations, 1945.

in the Pacific. The flight deck on the *Indomitable* and all British carriers was armour plated and it was, therefore, a surprise to see that the *Randolph* (as with other US carriers of that time) had a wooden flight deck. This proved to be fatal for, after returning to the Pacific, she again suffered severe bomb damage and was sunk. On the other hand, *Indomitable* (and her five sister ships) were all hit by *kamikaze* attacks whilst in the Pacific but, thanks to their armoured flight decks, were back in operation a couple of hours later.

The Navy Yard was filled with ships of all shapes and sizes, either under construction or being repaired. For us 'Limeys' the most overwhelming feature of the Yard was the PX (abbreviation of the US term 'Post Exchange') which sold goods of all descriptions at special prices well below the normal retail value. Of course, we needed a special pass to entitle us to shop there and we spent everything we had at the Commissary (another US term for a base supermarket) where US Navy men and their dependents were allowed to shop. I remember stocking up on beautiful boxes of chocolates and nylons – both of which were unobtainable in the UK.

Unlike the *Howe*, when I had been part of the Advance

HMS *Indomitable*,
Pacific Operations,
1945.

Communications draft, I was now one of the final crew members to join *Indomitable* who, while refitting had only retained a skeleton communications staff. In a couple of weeks we were again ready for sea and, before heading back across the Atlantic, we had to load up with aircraft which proved to be quite a novel experience in itself. From where we berthed alongside in the Navy Yard we were able to look straight along the length of the main street of Norfolk. On the day in question the police had cleared all the traffic so that our planes, with their wings folded and engines roaring, were able to taxi all the way down the main street until they were alongside *Indomitable* – a truly amazing sight! As they arrived, they were hoisted onto the flight deck by crane. Because we were not yet operational we were ferrying as many aircraft to Britain as we could carry but here we ran into a problem, which was ultimately solved by more American ingenuity. Some of the aircraft were the Corsair fighters – a wonderful plane with gull wings which, when they were folded, stuck straight up in the air, and therefore made the plane too tall to go into *Indomitable*'s hangar. But this was soon resolved when somebody suggested letting the air out of the plane's tyres.

Indomitable was a modern carrier (one of a class of six)

Indomitable leading *King George V* and *Victorious*.

and was laid down in 1937 at Vickers Armstrong in Barrow and completed in 1941. She was modified from the original design by adding a second aircraft hangar which reduced the hangar height and therefore caused the problem with the Corsairs. *Indomitable* was 30,000 tons and 750ft long with a beam of 100ft and was capable of 30.5 knots – she carried a complement of 1,600. She was a large ship, with a large crew, but, because she was my third aircraft carrier it was not long before I felt at home.

Another Yeoman of Signals on *Indomitable* was Ted Bragg and we became very good friends until well after the war ended. He had been stationed at Asbury Park which was the Naval Communications Centre in Washington and he was reluctant to leave there due to a strong affiliation with one of the secretaries.

Our passage home to the UK was uneventful and after off-loading all the ferried aircraft we went through a 'working up' period and were once again ready to roll. After a brief embarkation leave we were once again issued with tropical kit and were soon on our way out to the East Indies Station. Of course, before leaving we embarked our own squadrons of aircraft, which, at this time, were Albacore torpedo bombers and Firefly fighters. The Firefly was a modern fighter but the Albacore was a later version of the old Swordfish. Thanks to the hangar modification, we were able to operate forty-eight aircraft and, on the passage east, we were kept busy with all kinds of aircraft operations.

Prior to leaving England I had discovered that Sylvia Fearn, my Wren girlfriend from Rosyth, was now stationed at Ras El Tin Signal Station in Alexandria so, on arrival there, I wasted no time in getting in touch with her which was rather a surprise for her because she had no idea where I was serving. We had a brief but happy reunion but that was it – she was now engaged to a soldier in the Western Desert.

So, onwards through the Suez Canal again and down to my old stamping ground of Colombo in Ceylon. We spent about six months operating from Ceylon, sometimes from Colombo but mostly from Trincomalee which was now a naval base at the northern end of the island. We spent a lot of time at sea carrying out attacks against the Japanese airfields and installations in the Nicobar Islands and the Andaman Islands which run parallel to the west coast of Malaya. It was a bit of a 'cat and mouse' game

— we tried to hit the airfields before the Japanese torpedo bombers could hit us.

After several months of these operations the *Indomitable* needed to go into dock and was sent north to Bombay for this purpose. While the ship was in dry dock the crew were given a break from living on board when we were sent ashore, in two batches, for one week each in a tented camp for rest and recreation. In the camp itself there was little to do except eat and sleep — and drink endless mugs of tea, purchased from the 'cha wallah' on his frequent trips around the camp. Our favourite occupation was to rent a taxi for the day and drive to one of the beautiful beaches away from the city. The taxis were interesting — large, open touring cars (American gangster type) of early thirties vintage and were kept in immaculate condition by their owners. The heat in Bombay was very oppressive and we felt overwhelmed by the throngs of humanity milling everywhere.

During this period there were two incidents worthy of mention here. The first was when we received a new squadron of aircraft — they were Fairey Barracudas (a type we had never seen before) and were designed for a dual role as torpedo bombers and also dive bombers.

We soon learned there were two problems with this aircraft. The first was that, when in a steep dive, the wings tended to fall off — so they soon forgot about the dive bombing bit! The second problem was not quite as serious — the Barracuda was fitted with a three bladed wooden propeller which, upon hitting the 'crash barrier', would shatter and fly in all directions — which was a bit discouraging to say the least. Anyway, one afternoon when I was on watch on the Flag Deck a Barracuda came in to land, made a poor touchdown, which meant he missed the arrester wires, and so ran into the crash barrier. I was watching all this as I leant over the side of the Flag Deck and, as the propeller shattered, I threw myself on the deck just as the airscrew put a large dent in the steel right where I had been standing. I thought at the time 'that could have been my head' — so I felt that episode qualified as losing 'cat's life number seven'!

The second incident was a little more light-hearted and involved my friend from the *Howe*, Yeoman of Signals Tony Setford. He was now the Yeoman of a Fleet destroyer, HMS *Raider*, which happened to be in dry dock during one of our rare visits to Colombo. It was the birthday of one of *Indomitable*'s Yeomen – Oscar Fleming – so Ted Bragg and I decided to give him a little celebration and also invited Tony Setford to join us for the evening. We had both been saving our daily tot of neat rum (strictly illegal of course) and the two bottles meant that nobody was feeling any pain at the end of the evening. Tony went away happy and later wanted to repay our generous hospitality but couldn't get his hands on enough booze for us all. He tried to wheedle some out of his Captain's steward but without any luck. He then had a brainwave – he cut his Yeoman's badge (crossed flags and crown) off his jacket, borrowed a boat and visited all the merchant ships in the harbour, explaining to each Captain that he was the Captain's steward from *Raider* and that his Captain was giving a cocktail party that evening but, unfortunately, was short of a bottle of scotch and a bottle of gin!

I am not sure how many ships he visited before he finally found a sympathetic Captain who generously provided the requisite two bottles. The fun did not end there – we were supposed to meet him at 4.30 on the landing pier but, when we got there, he was not to be found. A friendly policeman finally told us he was 'in the Customs House answering a few questions'. I am not sure what answers he gave but they must have been convincing because the Customs Officers finally released him and, even more to our surprise, the two bottles as well! Inevitably, it turned out to be a very good evening and we all had a few good laughs at Tony's expense.

At the end of the year (1944) the war in the Pacific was approaching a climax and we were ordered out there to join the newly formed British Pacific Fleet. The war in other areas had slackened as far as the Navy was concerned and so maximum effort was directed towards the Pacific area which involved not only a huge number of ships and men but also a whole new way of thinking because we would be operating with the American Fifth Fleet. On the passage from Ceylon to Australia we would be required to carry out aggressive air attacks, from dawn to dusk daily, as we sailed through the Japanese held areas of Indonesia, Sumatra and Borneo. Of course, the Japanese did not take this lying down and we in turn were attacked by all types of enemy aircraft.

During one of the skirmishes with a large force of

torpedo bombers there was an unfortunate and tragic accident as a result of 'friendly fire'. During all this time our 'chummy ship' had been our sister carrier *Victorious,* who we now had difficulty communicating with on completion of the action. We knew she had not been struck by a torpedo and it was a shock when we finally learnt that her entire compass platform and all personnel there including the Captain, Navigation Officer, Officer of the Watch and Chief Yeoman of Signals had been wiped out by a shell exploding. The subsequent Board of Enquiry established that, in the heat of battle, a shell from the anti-aircraft guns of *Indomitable* had been responsible. Of course, everyone in *Indomitable* felt terrible about this and it certainly put a damper on celebrating an otherwise successful period of operations.

The day of our arrival in Australia was one of the most memorable in my life for the simple reason that I felt Sydney Harbour was the most spectacular and beautiful harbour I had ever been to. Although it was summer in Australia, the ocean outside the harbour was rough and windy until we passed through Sydney Heads (which is the name for the twin headlands which form the entrance to the harbour). As we passed through everything changed dramatically – there was a gentle breeze, the water was calm and blue and stretched for miles to the magnificent sight of the Sydney Harbour Bridge. On either side were the beautiful green bays, each with its own residential community and usually, a private yacht club as well. This dramatic change of scenery reminded me of an old pre-war film *Shangri-la* (I think it was a young Gary Cooper) when the weary travellers emerge from a stormy mountain pass into this beautiful sunlit paradise of Shangri-la. As the Fleet steamed majestically up the harbour we were treated to a traditional Aussie welcome: dozens of small boats escorting us and the occupants shouting, 'Welcome.'

We entered harbour at eight a.m. *Indomitable* was allocated a berth alongside at Woollamaloo, which is the main passenger ship terminal close to the ferry terminal at Circular Quay and therefore closest to the town. We were very fortunate in this and really appreciated it for the ease of going ashore and returning.

By noon we were allowed ashore and the three off-duty Yeomen (myself, Ted and Oscar) wasted no time in checking out this beautiful, modern city. After walking around in the sunshine we got a bit thirsty and decided to investigate one of the local taverns which just happened to be the Tatler Hotel located on the main thoroughfare. I can remember it looked very respectable outside and, as we entered, it was very nicely fitted with carpeting and furniture. There were two bars – a beer bar on the ground level and, on the first floor, a cocktail lounge where ladies were permitted so, naturally, the choice was not difficult and we went upstairs. The lounge was quite plush and very respectable with quite a few female customers and so it was not too long before we were good friends with three of them. I remember when we left the hotel in their company we went and purchased some food and wine and went back to one of their homes for supper.

Ted Bragg became very attached to his companion whom we knew as 'Blondie' and he never had a moment's peace whenever the ship was in harbour – she was always the first person on the telephone asking for him.

There is an amusing sequel to this little story. Some time ago, a couple of years after Karen and John were married, they were going on a trip to Australia which included an ocean cruise out of Sydney. Before leaving Canada, John questioned me closely about places and conditions in Australia and, when they returned, he really kidded me about the Tatler Hotel. They had found it and not only visited it but had also taken photographs of it which showed it now to be a very seedy and rundown joint! I can only reiterate that it was very different when I was there.

Needless to say, we all loved everything about Australia and had a great time there – the people were friendly and many of them had relatives in Britain, the climate was great and there were so many lovely places to visit. This usually involved a trip to one of the famous beaches (Manley or Bondi) for a day's swimming. Although the atmosphere of Australia was peaceful and fun-loving, the people there never forgot about the war – many of them had sons or husbands away in the Forces. Australian troops had fought long and hard in the Western Desert and had then returned to protect their homeland from the Japanese so that many were still engaged in the jungle fighting in New Guinea.

For *Indomitable* (and the rest of the Fleet) we were not allowed to get too cosy and soon realised why we were

HMS *Indomitable* –
Flight Deck crashes.

HMS *Indomitable* –
Kamikaze attacks.

really there as we became involved in many changes. We loaded maximum quantities of fuel, ammunition and food, we had a complete new complement of aircraft which were now the American Avenger torpedo bombers and the Hellcat fighters, both of which proved to be excellent planes – sturdy, reliable and able to take (and give) a lot of punishment. We even had a new Admiral flying his flag in *Indomitable*. He was Vice Admiral Sir Philip Vian and was in command of the First Aircraft Carrier Squadron (at the start of the British Pacific Fleet we had four aircraft carriers, two battleships, twenty-two destroyers and an assortment of support vessels). Admiral Vian was a tall, stern and unsmiling man – very aggressive and, because of this, had the reputation of being a 'Fighting Admiral' in the Navy. He had become famous earlier in the war when, as Captain of the destroyer *Cossack*, he carried out the daring rescue of British merchant ship crews whose ships had been sunk by *Bismarck* and were prisoners on the German supply ship *Altmark*. He took the *Cossack* alongside in Narvik harbour and his armed boarding parties shouted the never-to-be-forgotten phrase: 'The Navy's here'. Until he retired as an Admiral of the Fleet he was known throughout the Navy as 'Vian of the *Cossack*'. Our Captain in *Indomitable* was Captain J. A. S. Eccles who was a very competent man who coped with the worst situations without any fuss.

It was not long before we found ourselves at sea again and heading north into the Pacific where we were destined to become part of the US Fifth Fleet and to operate as Task Force 57. Although placed under the overall command of the US Navy, tactical command of the British Pacific Fleet was retained by Admiral Rawlings who was the second in command of the BPF and flying his flag in the battleship *King George V*. The Commander in Chief of the BPF was Admiral Sir Bruce Fraser who had his own headquarters in Sydney. This organisation seemed to work very well and I think we did a good job because, at the end, we received high praise from the US Naval Command.

Because the Pacific Ocean is so vast and our targets so remote from any Allied base it was necessary to operate as a Fleet in a manner that was completely new to us. The US Fleet had been doing this for some time and had proved it very effective. Our objective was the enemy airfields on the Japanese Ryukyu Islands which stretch for

750 miles to Taiwan. Included in this group is the island of Okinawa that later proved to be the most fiercely fought battle in the Pacific and cost 1,500 lives to capture it. Our operating procedure was to go in close and, for four consecutive days, carry out dawn to dusk strikes against the Japanese airfields. The enemy would retaliate fiercely and therefore it was necessary to maintain a continuous Combat Air Patrol for the protection of the Fleet. This meant we werc very busy for those four days (mostly at 'Action Stations') with launching and recovering aircraft besides defending against enemy air attacks. After these four hectic days the Fleet would retire approximately two hundred miles to make a rendezvous with our supply ships which were now known collectively as the Fleet Train. For three days it was more peaceful, but still very hectic, as all ships had to be refuelled, ammunition and bombs replenished, repairs made good, replacement aircraft and personnel embarked – and sometimes we even got mail transferred to us. Once fully replenished and operational we would go back for another four-day bash at the Japanese airfields. All this made for an eventful, exciting life, but it was also very hard on men and machinery so that occasionally a ship had to be detached for docking or repairs – sometimes back to Sydney and sometimes to the American Fleet bases at Manus or Truk. The *Indomitable* made one such trip to Sydney for some repairs after *kamikaze* attacks.

The Japanese initiated the *kamikaze* ('Divine Wind') attacks when they were running short of aircraft, but mostly short of well-trained pilots. The idea was simple – take a young pilot, straight out of basic training, put him in a plane loaded with a large bomb, have another plane guide a group of these suicide planes to the target and then let them dive onto the deck of their selected target. It proved to be quite an effective, and quite frightening, form of attack – if they hit a destroyer it would probably sink but, fortunately, the aircraft carriers, being the primary targets, were able to withstand most of these attacks.

It was during this period that I was, once again, grateful for my 'cat's nine lives'.

I was on the Flag Deck for the Morning Watch (4–8 a.m.) and as dawn was breaking there was a warning from our radar of approaching enemy aircraft. The Fleet went to Action Stations as a matter of routine, even though the intruder was expected to be an early morning 'prowler' looking for us. The radar blip was getting nearer, it was approaching from directly astern and flying very low. I rested my telescope on top of the flag locker and looked in that direction and very soon I could see the approaching plane – not only that, but I could see little red dots ahead of it and coming fast. I quickly realised that they were tracer ammunition, I yelled at my signalmen to hit the deck and did so myself. There was now a hole in the flag locker – right where I had been standing – turning round, I saw that the cannon shell had also passed through the half inch steel plate behind me. Unfortunately, behind that partition was the Radar Petty Officer who, at that very moment, had stepped out of the radar compartment to see the plane he had been tracking on the screen. The bullet hit him in the stomach and he died a couple of hours later. Jack Fish was a good friend of mine – a very pleasant young man who had recently received news that he was a proud father. There was a saying during the war that you would never hear the bomb or shell that had your name on it – well, I did not hear that one but thank goodness I saw it coming! So, here I scratched off 'cat's life number eight' and I was really happy when the war finished soon after – whilst I still had one in reserve!

On 14 August 1945 when Japan surrendered and six years of war was finally over, the *Indomitable* was in Sydney, having just got out of dry dock. The whole of Sydney went wild with hooters blasting, all ships in the harbour sounding their sirens, and even some fireworks. I remember it was difficult to grasp the fact that all the tensions and hardships of the war were now at an end. I also remember we all thought, 'This is great – now we won't have to leave Sydney,' and we couldn't wait to get ashore to celebrate the fact with all the families and girlfriends we had become closely associated with. However, these dreams were in vain – we were not even allowed off the ship because we had received immediate sailing orders 'to proceed with all despatch to Hong Kong to accept the surrender of the Japanese garrison there.'

As we raced north once more I remember thinking how ironic it was that the war, for me, had started in Hong Kong and now was also going to finish there.

As we approached the Colony it was decided to send one of our planes in to bring back on board the Japanese commander and also the Senior British Officer of all the POWs. Accordingly, we flew off an Avenger with only a pilot (so as to leave two seats for his passengers on the return). Unfortunately, we lost radio contact with him and, for several hours, there was some concern as to what might have happened. As it later turned out he had some engine trouble and had to make a forced landing somewhere but we eventually got him back safely. In the meantime a second plane was despatched and this one got back with the two VIPs and we were all interested to see a small, docile Japanese officer with a large sword but we were shocked to see the British officer accompanying him – he was tall and looked like a walking skeleton. We soon learned there were many more ashore in the same condition and it was obvious they were our priority. Fortunately, we managed to get a hospital ship in very quickly to take care of them.

When *Indomitable* reached the harbour it was soon found that the Colony was in a sorry state. The Japanese had been in control there since Christmas Day 1941 and obviously care and maintenance not been high on their priority list. There was no electricity because there was no fuel for the generators, the water supply was almost non-existent, garbage collection the same and the whole place was stinking and decrepit. For the first week the only people allowed ashore were repair parties and working parties. After that we were granted limited shore leave but there was not a lot to do and it was all depressing. Strangely enough, the worst thing was just being in harbour (something I had never thought we would complain about) because being there in the excessive heat the temperature inside the ship was almost unbearable and we longed to be moving to blow some fresh breezes through the ship. However, this was not to be – for me at least – because I was never to go to sea in the *Indomitable* again.

At the end of August 1945, *Indomitable* was ordered to return to the United Kingdom, which normally would have been very welcome and exciting news for us but what was different now was for those of us who had ties back in Australia and our ambition was to return to Sydney. Because of this, Ted Bragg and I looked for a way to achieve this and eventually found the answer in the Admiralty Regulations. The Navy would allow two ratings, of equivalent rate and good character, to exchange ships subject to the approval of both Captains. This was the first step and then Ted and I spent some time sending morselamp messages to all the ships in Hong Kong, asking if there might be two Yeomen who would like to exchange ships with us. Of course, the clincher was that the *Indomitable* was soon to be heading for England. We eventually found two Yeomen who were very anxious to be going home. The other ship was HMS *Euryalus* – a light cruiser – which suited us fine but the wonderful bonus for us was the fact that she was due to return to Sydney for a two-month refit. Accordingly requests to the Captain were entered in both ships (and thankfully approved). On 12 September 1945 a boat left *Indomitable* with Ted Bragg and myself headed for *Euryalus*, returning with two Yeomen for *Indomitable*.

The following morning, when *Indomitable* left Hong Kong for England, Ted and I watched her, perhaps with a few mixed feelings, but the following day when *Euryalus* sailed for Sydney we certainly had no regrets.

This was the end of my association with *Indomitable* but, before going on, I should relate the sequel to our exchange situation. This happened when *Indomitable* stopped at her first port of call, Singapore. The Admiralty realised that it would be foolish to send her home empty (her aircraft had been left at Kai Tak in Hong Kong) so, to ease the desperate shortage of troop transports, *Indomitable* was converted to a temporary troopship and embarked ex-POWs and other personnel (of all Services) due home for demobilisation. Unfortunately for our two exchange Yeomen it meant that they were put ashore in Singapore to make room for ratings who had been abroad longer (they had only been out a year). Although we had never met the two, Ted and I could not help feeling a bit sorry for them, although I must admit the story raised a few good laughs in *Euryalus*!

CHAPTER NINETEEN

HMS Euryalus

O N 12 SEPTEMBER 1945 when I joined HMS *Euryalus* in Hong Kong harbour the future looked very promising – the war was over, we were due to return to Sydney for a two-month refit, I was now confirmed in my Petty Officer's rate and who knew what might lie ahead in the peacetime Navy. I am happy to say that I was not to be disappointed because the year I was to spend in *Euryalus* proved to be a very happy one for me.

Euryalus was a Light Cruiser of the Dido class which were laid down at the beginning of the war and launched in 1942. They had very efficient anti-aircraft armament and these ships were a great asset wherever they served during the war. They were about 7,000 tons, had a complement of 500 and were capable of 32 knots.

HMS *Euryalus*, Sydney, 1946.

We were due to leave Hong Kong for our trip to Sydney but, before this could happen, we were ordered to sea unexpectedly to search for a Navy plane that had gone missing. After two fruitless days of searching the ocean it was decided to call off the search and, instead of returning immediately to Hong Kong, the Captain decided to anchor for the night in a sheltered bay of a supposedly deserted island off the Chinese coast. It was already dark when we anchored and, before leaving the bridge to go below for supper, I was idly scanning the shoreline through my binoculars when I spotted a faint flicker of light. After watching it for a while I decided that I could make out the letters 'SOS' and I responded with an Aldis lamp but could not read anything further because the light was getting fainter. When I reported this to the Officer of the Watch and then to the Commander they all thought I had been imagining it but nevertheless decided to send a boat inshore to investigate. To provide communication with the ship I volunteered to go in with the landing party. By now everybody in the ship knew the situation and, of course, there were all sorts of speculation as to what it was all about – but not one of them guessed correctly. In the boat, as we approached the shore there was some apprehension because we did not know what lay ahead.

When we landed on the beach we were met by half a dozen men who were in a very dishevelled and scruffy condition but from their voices they were soon identified as English. They proved to be a squad of Royal Marine Commandos who had been using the anchorage as a base for their anti-pirate patrols of the area. Unfortunately, a couple of weeks earlier they had run into trouble – their main vessel (a 53ft gunboat) had developed serious engine problems which they had been unable to fix and, as a result, their radio also failed. They had been unable to raise anybody on the portable radio and their rations had run out a week ago so, in desperation, two of them had set out in their small motorboat but, apparently, never made it to civilisation. Their fresh water supply also dried up two days ago and so they were in pretty rough condition and we could imagine their relief when they made contact with a British warship with their last flashlight battery!

The Captain offered them passage back to Hong Kong but they insisted on staying where they were so we left them with a small mountain of food and water, medical supplies and flashlight batteries and, of course, radioed their situation back to naval headquarters.

Before we started on our voyage to Australia, I went ashore once more and, on Nathan Road in Kowloon, found an Indian shop that still had some decent dress fabric. I bought what he had in a pale blue Indian silk which I was sure my girlfriend in Sydney would really appreciate because she was a keen dressmaker and worked in a big fashion house in Sydney. Nancy Crocker was an attractive girl, tall, slim and vivacious. By now our relationship was becoming quite serious even though she was only seventeen. It had started about six months previously when Ted Bragg and I had first made the acquaintance of the Smith and Crocker families, which had happened like this. Ted and I were enjoying a quiet afternoon, sipping 'schooners' of Aussie beer in a bar located in Concord, which is a suburb of Sydney. We got into conversation with two men who came in for a quick beer – they were Bill Smith, an elderly man who owned a small brass foundry across the road, and Bill Crocker who was his foreman. The latter had recently been discharged from the Australian Army after serving in New Guinea. A couple of days later we were invited to visit the foundry to see the work they did there. Ted and I found it very interesting and were fascinated by the beautiful moulds that were made with sand and then the liquid metal poured in to form the product. After we got to know them better we were invited to dinner one Sunday at Bill Smith's house and that was how it all started. Each family had one attractive daughter and so Ted and I were accepted and fitted in very well. As time went by we came to spend more and more time at the two homes until eventually I spent all my off-duty time at the Crockers' home. Both families were extremely hospitable, welcomed us into their houses and made us feel at home.

I should, perhaps, explain a little about the strange drinking habits in New South Wales at that time, due to the existing liquor licensing laws of that period. Bars would open at ten a.m. but had to close at six p.m. Because factories and offices closed for the day at five p.m., the final drinking hour was bedlam. The Aussies had two beers ('New' and 'Old') and both were pretty strong, especially when drunk very quickly. This resulted in a great many husbands arriving home in no condition for anything except sleeping it off. Apart from this final hour, bars were pretty quiet for most of the day even though they used to put free food on the bar to attract the lunchtime crowd. This was very popular with the customers but unpopular with restaurants who rightly complained the bars were stealing their trade. Before we got used to the strange drinking customs we could not understand why the bar-men, at 4.30, started pulling innumerable 'schooners' and lining them up on the counter. It was for their regulars (four for this one and five for that one) because there would not be time to do it in the big rush and it would be unheard of to keep a thirsty customer waiting.

Needless to say our two months spent in Sydney was a very happy and pleasant time for us and, of course, passed much too quickly.

As we neared the end of our stay we were due for a day at sea for post refit trials and for this occasion Ted and I put in a special request to the Captain to have Bill Smith come on board for the day. In naval ships it is generally acceptable to have visitors on board whilst in harbour but very unusual for them to be allowed when at sea. However, in this case the Captain relaxed the rule and our request was granted.

In the forenoon we gave Bill a complete tour of the ship, including gun turrets and the engine room, and then he had lunch with us (including his own tot of rum) in the Petty Officers' Mess. In the afternoon he was on the bridge, chatting with the Captain and other bridge per-sonnel and when he left the ship he could not have been happier. We found out later that, during his chat with the Captain, he had asked if there was something he could do for the ship to return the favour and the result was that he agreed to make a set of 'Tompins' (a ship's crest, in metal, mounted on a wooden plug and used in the muzzle of the guns in peacetime). Because *Euryalus* was a wartime construction vessel she was lacking in some of the peace-time trappings that would normally be provided for a warship. These were duly made in the brass foundry – in fact, Ted and I watched them being poured. There were fourteen of them – one for each main armament gun, one each for the Captain, Commander and Engineer Officer – and, of course, one each for Ted and me.

On the night before we sailed from Sydney Ted and I were given a fantastic farewell party by Bill Smith – he hired one of the Sydney Harbour passenger ferries for the night and filled it with friends, food and drinks. On completion, we said our goodbyes at Circular Quay and then Ted and I caught the last liberty boat out to *Euryalus*, tied to a buoy under the Harbour Bridge. The only problem was that we were also carrying two canvas bags containing fourteen brass 'tompins', which seemed to weigh about a hundred pounds each. The Officer of the Watch must have thought we were drunk when he saw us staggering up the gangway with our heavy load – even when he saw what we had in the bags it took a bit of explaining to convince him why we were carrying so much brass!

As we left Sydney at the end of November and once more headed north into the Pacific – now very peaceful and different from the one we had come to know, but old habits die hard, especially those concerned with self preservation and learned under wartime conditions. I was on the bridge as Yeoman of the Morning Watch (4–8 a.m.) and just as the dawn started to break, with the sky turning from black to grey, the Officer of the Watch suddenly shouted, 'Mine ahead – hard a'starboard.' I looked through my binoculars and, sure enough, right ahead of us was this black blob but strangely, as the bow started swinging to the right, this 'thing' remained directly ahead of the ship and then I realised what it was. It was not a mine but the large crown on the top of the jack staff which was mounted right in the bow. During six years of war the jack staff (and ensign staff on the stern) were always removed immediately on leaving harbour because they would obviously interfere with the operation of the guns – but in peacetime they could remain in position while at sea without causing any problem. I seem to remember the OOW had a little difficulty explaining this to the Captain when he came rushing to the bridge in his pyjamas!

We were now embarking on a goodwill cruise (known as 'showing the flag') to all the British colonies in the South Pacific. Whilst on passage to our first call I celebrated my twenty-third birthday on 5 December 1945 and, of course, this required the naval tradition of being offered 'sippers' (a sip of their rum tot) by every member of the Mess. This was much appreciated by yours truly and then, during the night the ship crossed the International Date Line that runs north and south through the Pacific. This line is actually the 180 degree meridian which is exactly halfway round the world from the Greenwich meridian which is 0 degrees. The Date Line is the point where the time zones of the world meet – either twelve hours behind when travelling west or twelve hours ahead when travelling east so that crossing the Date Line involves either gaining a day or losing a day, depending on the direction of travel. Well, fortunately for me, we were going east so, of course, the following day was also the 5 December (and my birthday again) but when I suggested this to the Mess at tot-time I nearly got mobbed but, after producing my Paybook to prove it and getting a lot of ribbing, it was accepted that I was entitled to two birthdays (and 'sippers') that year.

The first port of call on our South Pacific cruise was to be Tonga which, at that time was a British protectorate but gained independence in 1970. Tonga consists of about 150 islands, most of them very small and uninhabited, spread over an area of almost three hundred square miles. The Polynesian population are famous for two things – being fat and being friendly – and it was easy to see why Captain Cook, who discovered the islands in 1770, christened them 'The Friendly Islands'. In 1945 Tonga was ruled by Queen Salote, who was certainly fat and friendly, and who endeared herself to the rest of the world when she attended the coronation of Queen Elizabeth in 1953. Tonga today is ruled by her son who has the reputation of being the world's heaviest monarch – he weighs in at 440 lbs. Our visit involved a very unusual, delicate and amusing situation. A man of war when arriving in a foreign country is required to fire a gun salute to the head of state and, in the case of Tonga, this called for a Royal Salute of 21 guns. Protocol also requires that such a salute must also be returned, gun for gun but when our visit was arranged it was realised that Tonga did not possess a gun with which to fire a salute. The problem was solved when *Euryalus* arrived and promptly sent a boat inshore with our Ordnance Artificer, a Shipwright, several bags of cement and a three-pounder saluting gun. The gun was duly mounted on the beach in front of the Royal Palace and *Euryalus* returned next day when the cement was dry and, as we began firing the Royal Salute, our boat was racing in-shore again with a gun's crew to return it! Queen Salote was very appreciative of this gesture. That night we were entertained at a typical Polynesian feast with a couple of young pigs roasted in the ground and complete with Hawaiian dancers. The following night we matched our PTI against the local champion in a boxing contest which proved very popular – I don't think the performance was particularly skilful but they allowed us the courtesy of winning the bout. We also visited the Royal Palace and met Queen Salote and, on the Sunday, the Catholics among our crew were invited to Mass in the local church. About twenty per cent of the population are Catholic and there was a good turnout for us. After Mass, each of us was presented with the gift of a very nice rosary – I still have mine. When the time came for us to leave Tonga we did so with many happy memories of our visit.

Local policemen in Fiji 1946,

From Tonga we headed north-west for the island of Fiji and soon arrived in Suva, the capital of the Fiji Island. We found it to be a delightful place to visit – the locals were very welcoming with their famous trademark of a very broad grin. We enjoyed the lovely beaches, the tropical palm trees and the beautiful temperate climate but I think the most lasting impression we took away with us was the local policemen – very large, very black, with a big grin, a white skirt and bare feet. It was here that I obtained a natural tortoise shell with the idea of polishing it to a smooth, shiny and colourful finish – but after several weeks of unrewarding labour I think it went over the side. While I was in Fiji – so remote and on the other side of the world from Britain – I could have no idea that one day my daughter would be spending her honeymoon there.

Upon leaving Fiji we then set a northerly course for Western

Samoa which was to be the final call on our cruise. We found Samoa to be a real tropical paradise though with not a lot of civilisation but, nevertheless, we were made very welcome. My most vivid memory of Samoa was playing in a soccer match against the local team on a blazing hot afternoon – it was a bit embarrassing because the locals played in bare feet and beat us.

After Samoa we headed back to Sydney but it was only to be a brief spell as we were soon on our way north again, this time to Hong Kong where we had a short stop for refuelling. Then we were into the Yangtze River and on our way to Shanghai where we were required to 'show the flag' for a different reason – not as a sign of friendship but as a sign of authority. In the 1930s Shanghai had grown rapidly into a large and prosperous city with international interests from all over the world having a finger in the pie. Now, in the post-war re-establishment of these interests, there was unrest in the area and *Euryalus* was there to protect British interests and, if the pot boiled over, to evacuate British nationals. We lay in the river, in company with a French cruiser and a couple of US ships, in a state of alertness, for two or three weeks until things simmered down.

When we left Shanghai it was back to Hong Kong where we stayed for several weeks and we were pleased to find that the Colony had almost returned to normal.

I enjoyed one final visit to Sydney before I was to bid farewell to Australia for good. Whilst in *Euryalus* I visited several other Australian ports – Darwin on the north coast which was a very remote and uninteresting place. Townsville, on the north-east coast – not much there either. Then to Brisbane which I thought was a lovely city – very lush and green and quite tropical. At the end of the final visit to Sydney, *Euryalus* was to sail on a visit to New Zealand but I was not to be on board because, on 1 July 1946 I was posted ashore to HMS *Golden Hind* which was the Navy's shore base in Sydney. There I was to wait for passage arrangements to be made for me to return to England, which happened a couple of weeks later. I was to take passage home in the cruiser HMS *Swiftsure* which would be sailing from Perth in Western Australia a week later and this involved a long and tedious overland journey from the east coast to the west coast.

After some sad farewells with Nancy and all my other

friends I left Sydney one evening in a troop train on the first leg of a journey that was to take three days and nights. One problem was that we had to change trains three times because the gauge of railway track differed in each State. There was no sleeping accommodation so we did the best we could and catering involved the train being stopped for an hour or so, in the outback, while Army cooks brewed up some sort of stew in a huge cauldron over an open fire. This at least gave us a chance to stretch our legs a bit – but making sure not to stray too far from the train. Our final stop was at Kalgoorlie in Western Australia, a mining town a couple of hundred miles from anywhere. We were set free for a couple of hours so we set out to find a cold beer – the 'hotel' was just like a western saloon out of a cowboy movie set and was complete with swing doors and sawdust on the floor.

We were very relieved when the train pulled into Fremantle, which is the port of Perth, and even more relieved when we were on board *Swiftsure* and able to enjoy a good shower, a change of clothes and a good meal.

Two days later we sailed for England and, four weeks later, after a pleasant and uneventful passage we arrived at Portsmouth in the early evening of 23 August 1946 but, much to our disgust, we were to anchor at Spithead for the night and go alongside in Portsmouth Dockyard the following morning. It was disappointing but at least it allowed all the Customs formalities to be cleared away before entering harbour.

When we did get in there were a great many relatives waiting on the dockside and among them I found my Mother and Joyce who, apparently, had not forgotten me. As I left the ship and joined them I had in my pocket a leave pass for seven weeks leave which I knew I was going to enjoy.

CHAPTER TWENTY

HMS Dolphin

WHEN I ARRIVED BACK IN ENGLAND on 24 August 1946 my life, and everything connected with it, seemed to be just perfect. I could look forward to spending seven weeks Foreign Service Leave at home with my family after being absent for most of the war. England itself, after so long away, struck me as wonderful. Always green, it was now brilliant in the late summer sunshine and everything about it was new and exciting for me. Although there were many scars of war to be seen in places like Portsmouth and London, the bombed-out buildings were starting to be cleared although reconstruction appeared to be slow at the time. The population appeared to be happy and looking forward to a peaceful future and, although there were many families grieving the loss of loved ones, there was a positive atmosphere of 'thank God it is over – let's get on with our lives'. As a direct result of the war many things were still in short supply and I was a bit surprised to find that we were still using Ration Books for many of them.

I was now twenty-three years old and, although I could not know it at the time, the next couple of years were to produce some significant changes in my life. For a start, being reunited with Joyce was unplanned but, nevertheless, very pleasant and, as time went by and we spent more and more time together we inevitably became very close. Just as inevitably my correspondence with Australia became less and less until, finally, it ceased altogether. About this time many people were expecting Joyce and me to announce our engagement but, before this could happen, Joyce and I had a disagreement and, owing to my youthful stubbornness, we could not reconcile and so our separation was final this time. Not too long afterwards there was an announcement of Joyce's engagement to Jack Street – I knew Jack, who had recently left the Air Force and I also knew that he had been attracted to Joyce for a long time. They were subsequently married in the following March.

My own family had changed quite considerably in my absence. As was to be expected, Jack and June had grown up rapidly. June, having left school at fourteen (which was normal then), was now seventeen and working as a sales-girl at Boots the Chemists. I know my mother thought she needed looking after and asked me to keep an eye on her but, of course, there was little I could do – she was quite mature and certainly never seemed short of male admirers. Jack, being only fourteen months younger than myself was busy shaping his own life but, at the time, my mother could not see where it was going. During the war Jack had been prevented from joining the Forces due to a bout of tuberculosis, which it was thought he contracted from his friend who lived next door. He had always been (and still is) extremely keen on anything connected with aircraft and had been a member of Worthing Air Cadets, a Fire Watcher and Aircraft Spotter. He now had a very close friend who was soon introduced to me as Dave Price, a handsome and well built young man who appeared to have the ability to charm the birds out of the trees.

Dave came from a very respectable home (his father was a local banker) and, although I don't know the details, I believe Dave had spent a short time in the Parachute Regiment. When I met him he seemed to be engaged in all sorts of schemes; some of them not quite within the law and therefore he was on speaking terms with the local constabulary. I guess he was what used to be described as a 'charming rogue'! He and Jack had established their own business which was patriotically called 'HMS' which stood for 'Household Maintenance Service'. They used to drive around in a very small, very old car with a sign on top proclaiming their business. Because 'Do it yourself' had not yet become popular and there was also a severe shortage of most building materials they seemed to pick up quite a few jobs. I never liked to ask, or even think, about their finished work in view of their lack of experience in the building trade. Their most auspicious undertaking was the total renovation of the clubhouse at nearby Shoreham Airport which, during the war, had been occupied by the RAF. Because of their joint interest in aircraft, Dave and Jack used to spend some time hanging around the airport and so got to know the Chief Flying Instructor there. I think his name was Pascoe. He had been a First World War pilot and was now anxious to get Shoreham up and running again as a flying club. Typically, Dave and Jack struck a deal with him – they would renovate the clubhouse and, in lieu of cash payment, would each accept flying lessons from him. Later they got to know a local man, a keen horse fancier, who used to travel to all the race meetings and 'the terrible two' somehow managed to persuade him that, instead of all that road and rail travel, it would be so much better to go by air! Accordingly, they bought an ex-RAF Auster plane – at that time there were masses of 'war surplus' material available – for a very nominal sum, which I believe, was one hundred pounds – and so their friend travelled in style. The most interesting feature of this situation though was the illicit carpet trade they engaged in with their new toy.

They would take the plane across the Channel to Belgium and buy a load of cheap carpets and, to avoid any embarrassment with the Customs, make the return trip after dark. The trouble was they were not too great on navigation at night and sometimes followed the wrong railway track; and once even landed and then discovered that they were on an RAF airfield. Surprisingly, the air boys were very hospitable to the smugglers!

Towards the end of my leave and just when I was beginning to wonder what might be in store for me next, I received notification from the Navy that I was to join HMS *Dolphin* at Gosport on 16 October 1946. Of course, I already knew that *Dolphin* was the Navy's principal Submarine Base and I also knew that I was not to be employed in submarines so, when I made further enquiries, I found that I was to be in the Main Signal Office there. Because *Dolphin* was also the headquarters of Flag Officer, Submarines this told me that it would be a busy and interesting time for me. I was to be Yeoman of the Watch and we worked in four watches which were arranged so that we virtually worked for two days and then had forty-eight hours off. This was an ideal arrangement and suited me perfectly because, with Worthing only one hour by train, it meant that instead of living in the Mess at *Dolphin* I would be living at home – I would only have to put my uniform on to go to work. This idyllic situation lasted for nearly two years and was a very happy and much appreciated time for me.

My work at *Dolphin* MSO was not hard or stressful and, although we did have some anxious moments while I was there, we never had a submarine disaster. The subs would spend a lot of time on training and diving exercises and the most important feature of this was for them to signal when they were 'Diving' and, even more vital, to report that they had 'Surfaced'. There were some nail-biting sessions when we did not get the 'Surfaced' signal at the expected time but, thankfully, all ended well. Due to the drastic reduction of the Navy to its peacetime strength, most of the people I worked with at *Dolphin* were civilians, invariably ex-naval communications personnel, and we all worked well together.

When I first arrived home at the end of August '46, Jack and Dave were not yet into their 'HMS' scheme and seemed to spend a lot of time dashing around the town on a couple of old motor-bikes they owned. I soon learned that it was best not to ask where they got all their petrol from – at that time it was still strictly rationed.

I believe their favourite source of supply was the gasoline powered generator at an exclusive girls' school on Warren Road. I soon realised that one of their favourite habits was to head into town every morning for coffee and, at first, I could not understand their dedication to this product – not until I was invited to join them one day (I was on the pillion of Jack's 1929 Raleigh). We went into Worthing to visit Smith's Coffee Shop, located above Smith's Books on the corner of Montague Street and South Street in the centre of town. It was a traditional 'Olde Worlde' sort of place and typical of the times and catered to the ladies of Worthing on their shopping trips. I soon realised that coffee was not the main attraction – it was the very young and very attractive waitress who served us. I was introduced to Vivien, who was sixteen at that time and obviously the light of Jack's life. Just over three years later they were married and, happily, remain so to this day.

Another introduction for me at this time was to the Synnotts, our 'new' neighbours next door. Just before the war Dr Synnott had bought No. 8 Ethelred and he and his family had moved in at the beginning of July 1939 but, because I had sailed for Hong Kong on 1 July, I had not previously met the family. I had met Eileen very briefly during my leave in 1942 but she was now away serving in the ATS. Her younger brother Nicky was also away from home and was a student at St Xavier's College in Brighton. Therefore it was Mrs Synnott that I got to know first and we would often chat when we met on Ethelred Road as she was shopping or else at church on Sunday. She was a very pleasant lady and I found it easy to talk to her, especially as she was very interested in all my activities, past and present. Mrs Synnott was a keen organiser of the Catholic Youth Club attached to our church and would always try to encourage me to attend the evenings and I did go once or twice but, I must admit, I was more interested in a pint at the pub. Most evenings I would go out (there was no television at this time) and, almost invariably, I would finish up at the Fountain Hotel on Chapel Road which had always been my favourite watering hole. The landlord and his wife were pleasant, the beer was good and the lounge was very comfortable with a large open fireplace – most of all though, they had a new and very pleasant barmaid. Philomena was young, Irish, and very attractive.

My happy association with Philomena lasted until mid-February the following year – until one evening when I walked to Tarring Post Office to post a letter (probably my Vernon's football coupon) and I found Eileen Synnott coming out of the phone box with tears pouring down her cheek and obviously very distressed. I soon found that her mother had died in hospital that day and she was phoning Brighton for the college to inform Nicky of the fact. At that point I did not know Eileen very well. I had met her at the end of November when she was discharged from the ATS – she came up the road, carrying her kitbag, and I remember thinking what a slim, trim, and attractive Corporal she was. Now, in February, I was trying my best to console her and I know it finished up with a rather tearful kiss. But perhaps I am getting ahead of myself here and I should backtrack a bit. I think it best if I reprint here an essay that I wrote a few years ago on the subject of 'How'd You Meet Your Mate?' – I felt quite proud of my effort and I felt sure I would win – but, no cigar!

I Met Her at the Pig Bin

In wartime Britain food was severely rationed. Even so, the Government had difficulty in maintaining sufficient imports to feed the population and therefore promoted 'home production' in every way it could.

Every piece of ground was turned into a 'Victory Garden'

to provide extra vegetables and, to maintain the meat ration, pig breeding was encouraged in a big way. Of course, pigs have to be fed and so the population was called upon to conserve all their food scraps, mainly vegetable peelings, for this purpose. This was regularly collected from 'pig bins' supplied specifically for such food waste, and placed one on each street.

Towards the end of 1946 I returned home after spending two and a half years on an aircraft carrier in the Pacific and, during my leave, became the proud owner of a Triumph Tiger 80 motorcycle. This, I am sure, caused some dismay among my immediate neighbours because I always enjoyed a final burst of throttle before stopping outside my house. After a while, I could not help but notice this very attractive young lady who frequently attended the pig bin which happened to be situated immediately opposite my mother's house. I soon learned from my brother that this lovely creature was the grown up version of the skinny little thirteen-year-old who had moved next door whilst I was away at the beginning of the war.

It never dawned on me to question the impeccable timing (she always managed to reach the pig bin just as I stopped my motorcycle outside my house). It also never occurred to me to wonder how she could always, no matter what time of day, be so immaculately dressed, with high heels and perfect make-up and hairdo. Well, of course, it started with exchanging a shy smile, then a wave and, finally, a chat each day as we met at the pig bin.

Shortly after, answering a knock at my front door, I found this lovely young lady asking if I could provide a shilling to replenish her gas meter. In those days everybody made sure they had a single shilling in their change for this purpose, otherwise they would go to the store to get one. But this was Wednesday afternoon and all the shops were closed for Early Closing Day. Well, I happened to know one store that remained open and said that I would be happy to take her there if she would accompany me on my motorbike. As soon as she was on the pillion, with her arms firmly clasped around me, I knew there would be no turning back.

We were married a year later, on her birthday, and the local paper headed our wedding photograph with the caption 'She Marries The Boy Next Door'.

Forty-seven years later we are still living happily ever after. (Valentine's Day 1994)

The winter of 1946/47 was quite severe by Southern England standards and I remember we had a fair bit of snow. In late February, when the neighbours saw me help Eileen to clear the snow from the sidewalk in front of her house, the cat was out of the bag and, from then on, we were the centre of attention in the neighbourhood.

We were married on Monday 15 December 1947 (Eileen's 22nd birthday) at St Mary of the Angels RC Church on Crescent Road in Worthing. It was a small affair with just our immediate families present. The ceremony was performed by Father Dunning and Mr Joy (my old headmaster) played the organ for us. Jack was best man and Eileen was walked up the aisle by her older brother John who was then a Sergeant in the Royal Marines. Eileen's father, Dr Synnott, was much too ill to attend and, in fact, died on that very night. We had a four-day honeymoon at Bournemouth, unaware of the tragedy, and returned in time for the funeral.

The motorcycle mentioned in the above essay was my constant pride and joy. Ever since my first ride on Jack's old Raleigh I had desperately wanted a motorbike so, when I heard that Vic Bonsall (Joyce's brother) was selling his machine, I knew that I had to have it. I think he was asking seventy pounds for it (a ridiculous figure now) and I was fortunate that, about the same time, I received from

Eileen showing Bob how to ride BSA B32 Comp. 1949.

the Navy my Post War Credit which was one hundred pounds. At the outbreak of war Vic and his brother Eric were both in the Territorial Army and so were among the first to be shipped over to France as Despatch Riders. The interesting thing was that, owing to the shortage of equipment, Vic had to take his own motorcycle with him! I mentioned earlier that Vic had married Paddy who had nursed him in hospital after his motorcycle accident and I had met Paddy when I was on leave in 1942 and we are all very good friends to this time. Anyway, Paddy and Vic now had a daughter, Maureen, and therefore they needed more than a solo motorcycle for transport so it was then that Vic sold me his Tiger 80 and bought a beautiful new Triumph Speed Twin complete with matching sidecar.

Vic had always been a keen member of The Worthing Eagles which was the local motorcycle club and so, when I got his Tiger 80 I was also invited to join the club. This I did and really enjoyed my membership and have many happy memories of outings with them. It was not a large club and had a varied membership – there were those who were interested in competitive events (for which it was mandatory to belong to a club), some who enjoyed the social activities and many more who just enjoyed riding in company on our weekend outings. I think I qualified for all three categories but whatever their interests the members were a very pleasant and sociable crowd and, perhaps I should add, they were all very civilised people and bore no resemblance to present day 'bikers'. Every Sunday there would be a club outing which always started at Broadwater Green – there would be different activities such as Treasure Hunts, Time Trials (road), attending various motorcycle competitions (Road Racing, Trials or Scrambles) or, if nothing else was available, a ride through the Sussex countryside and tea in a little village teahouse. The most prominent member of The Worthing Eagles was Basil Keyes who was quite good (although I don't remember him winning anything) at motorcycle road racing and, as such, qualified as Worthing's 'Sports Celebrity'. He owned a Manx Norton for racing only and, each year, would enter in the TT Motorcycle Races held on the Isle of Man and also raced in events held at Brands Hatch or Blandford. He always got a big write-up in the *Worthing Gazette* by their Sports Reporter Freddie Feest. Basil was about seven years older than I, was married with one son and always attended outings in a small, red MG. His wife Gladys was short and round, quite outgoing and reminiscent of 'Mrs Boo-kay' of *Keeping Up Appearances* because her favourite occupation was showing off her home and its contents,

Herbert Keyes was Basil's brother but it took a while to recognise this because they only had two things in common – their overwhelming interest in motorcycles and the fact that they were both small in stature. When I first knew him Herbert operated a motorcycle repair business in a courtyard garage off Rowlands Road. He was a great mechanic but he was also slow, calm and methodical – so much so that I used to wonder how he made a living from the business, even if it was single handed. He used to ride a big, old motorbike and sidecar and I was good friends

June – late 1940s.

with him and his wife Pauline for a long time. Ultimately Basil and Herbert took the logical step of joining forces and opened a motorcycle business together

Other club members that I remember very well were Joe Boxall, an ex-Navy man from Storrington, Jack Burchett, single with an eye for June, John Hubbard and his wife and, last but not least, was Cliff Hoath whom I got to know very well and who almost became part of the family. Cliff was a tall and pleasant young man (about my age) but very quiet, serious and reserved. His whole life was concerned with motorcycles; he worked as a motorcycle mechanic at Gray & Rowsell, a large dealership at Bury Hill which was just outside Arundel. He rode a beautiful Triumph Tiger 100 and also owned a bike which he had built himself especially for Trials. He was an unusual combination, I thought, because besides being very competent with his hands, he was also highly intelligent. He had served in the RAF during the war, maintaining the chain of radar stations along the South Downs. He was particularly interested in 'outer space' (this was before *Star Wars* had been thought of), was a member of the British Inter-Planetary Society and was keen to travel to the moon!

Meanwhile, my own competitive motorcycling continued and, with a view to improvement, in August 1947 I traded-in my Tiger 80 for a brand new BSA Competition B32. This had many improvements such as telescopic front forks, large rear tyre and higher ground clearance, all designed specifically for competition. It was a beautiful machine and I really loved it – but, three months later when Eileen and I decided to marry, it looked as though my bike and I were going to part company. However, Eileen would not hear of such a thing, insisting that she did not mind waiting for an engagement ring. In lieu of having a ring though, she did persuade me to teach her to ride the bike! Of course, she never had a licence but did do very well in handling the machine on the road and, later, 'off-road' when I was practising for trials.

The motorbike gave us a tremendous amount of fun and excitement but, I regret to say, it also brought us sorrow. It was April 1948, I was on leave and we were going to stay with Eileen's Aunties in Lydney, near Gloucester. This was to be the first of many visits for me and, of course, we would be travelling by motorcycle. It was a long journey then (about four and a half hours on the road) because, before the advent of motorways, it was necessary to cut across country from one 'A' road to the next. It was also the only time we crossed the River Severn by ferry from Aust to Beachley because, after waiting an hour and a half for the tide to come in, it would have been quicker by road, even if it did mean another fifty miles through Gloucester. Anyway, the next day Eileen wasn't feeling well and it was a miscarriage and everyone said it was too long bumping around on my pillion seat. This was to be the first of several such problems and it would be some time before we were blessed with our first child – but then that is another story.

My happy existence at HMS *Dolphin* was drawing to a close and, that summer, I received orders to join HMS *Sirius* at Portsmouth on 22 July 1948.

CHAPTER TWENTY-ONE

HMS Sirus

WHEN I JOINED HMS *Sirius* in Portsmouth Dockyard on 22 July 1948 I felt quite at home because I was on familiar territory. HMS *Sirius* was a cruiser of the same class as *Euryalus* and so I fitted in immediately. By now I knew that mine was an individual draft to make up the complement because, owing to post war shortages, she had been operating with only two Yeomen instead of the three allowed by complement. I soon found the reason for the increase was that she was due to sail on an Autumn Cruise and would be operating with the entire Home Fleet. I received this news with mixed feelings because, whilst I welcomed the opportunity to see the West Indies which I had never previously visited, I was reluctant to be leaving Eileen at home for the two months we would be away.

It was customary for the Home Fleet to congregate for two major events every year which were known as the Spring Cruise and the Autumn Cruise. In the spring it would involve a period of intense exercises and training, usually at Invergordon or Scapa Flow, both of them remote and uninteresting but ideal for the purpose involved. On completion they would split up for short visits to Scandinavian or European ports. In the autumn of 1948 we were scheduled to have ten days of combined exercises in the Atlantic and then split up for visits to the various islands of the Caribbean and Bahamas. I was quite excited about the prospect of these visits because I had always envied anybody who got drafted to the West Indies Station and I was even more pleased when I learned the places *Sirius* had drawn.

We sailed from Portsmouth at the end of August 1948 and, by the time we had cleared the English Channel, we had collected many ships from other ports and so it was quite an impressive Fleet that sailed into the Atlantic to carry out the 'working' part of our voyage. There was one memorable incident on the outward leg and it happened as we got further south and the weather was warmer and calmer. At 4.30 one hot afternoon the Admiral signalled for the Fleet to stop and pipe 'Hands to Bathe' which meant swimming over the side. It was a very welcome order and many of the crews took advantage of it; I could not because I was Yeoman of the Watch and could not leave the bridge. Unfortunately, many of those who jumped or dived into the ocean landed in a large school of poisonous jellyfish, known as 'Portuguese Men of War' because they have a little jelly 'sail' which moves them along the surface. Of course, everybody came out even quicker than they went in but not before many men had been stung. Fortunately there were no fatalities but a great many were in the Sick Bay for a couple of days until they had recovered.

The exercises finished and we moved onto phase two – the courtesy visits to West Indies ports.

After the Fleet split up the first port of call for *Sirius* was Caracas, Venezuela. We did not see much of the city itself because we were berthed at La Guira, which is the port. I remember it was very hot there and so we spent most of our time on the beautiful white sand beaches outside the town and were able to do this in comfort because one of the local 'oil barons' had put a large black limousine (and a large black driver) at the disposal of the Petty Officers' Mess during our stay.

By now I had got to know most of the ship's company and I had three particular friends in the POs' Mess; the other two Yeomen, Pete Foster and Ed Gurton and also PO (Cook) Mitchell. 'Mitch' was a real character and very popular with everybody; he was quite tubby and, for some reason, had almost no hair and looked more like an out-of-condition prizefighter. He would do anything for anybody and for his friends, always seemed to have a spare 'tot' in his bottle.

The next visit for *Sirius* was Belize in what was then British Honduras although since 1981 it has been independent. This is another place where I remember the population being friendly and hospitable, but most memorable were the beautiful beaches. Our next stop was to be Jamaica and here we would have a double visit – first at the capital, Kingston, and then to the opposite side of the island for a few days in Montego Bay which of course was, and still is, the very popular tourist region of the island. Jamaica has a very hot climate, very white beaches and very black local population. Kingston was not a terribly attractive place and, with a very high rate of violent crime, it did not inspire a feeling of being safe. I did not encounter any such problem but it was a feeling I did not experience in any other part of the Caribbean. On the other hand Montego Bay was very beautiful and very peaceful. Apart from a few large hotels, there was not much development there and so we would spend our days sailing and swimming among the coral reefs of Doctor's Cove.

From Jamaica we headed to Trinidad and Tobago which were both interesting and delightful places to visit. They are not far off the coast of Venezuela and consequently are truly tropical islands – in fact, the land of calypso, cricket, carnivals and steel bands (not to mention the rum). There was not so much poverty as Jamaica because, in addition to the normal exports such as coffee, cocoa, sugar and fruits, they boasted a couple of oil refineries and were also the world's largest producer of asphalt. At that time, of course, they were part of the British Commonwealth but became independent in 1962. *Sirius* berthed alongside in Port of Spain, the capital, and once again enjoyed the use of a large black limousine offered by a local oil king (I could never understand why they all favoured black for their cars). My friends and I took advantage of it one day to visit the large US base on the other side of Trinidad – leased to them during the war. The road was not the greatest and we seemed to be in continual danger of falling off it! We then sailed to the neighbouring island of Tobago for a few days – it was tropical, tranquil and beautiful but there was not a lot to do there although I believe it is now a very popular tourist destination.

After a brief and uneventful stop at the island of St Kitts in the Leeward Islands, our next visit was to be Bermuda, which for me, at least, was to be the most memorable. Before our arrival in Bermuda I had received a letter from my mother with an interesting piece of news. At that time there was a young man named Roy who was lodging in her house and when she told him that I was on a ship in the West Indies and would soon be visiting Bermuda he said, 'Tell him to call on my older brother at the Mid-Ocean Club.'

Because Eileen and I lived next door at No. 8 I had, of course, met him casually but knew nothing about him or his family and so the letter added interest to our forthcoming visit. It was a beautiful morning when we reached Bermuda and as we steamed along the length of the island we were escorted by several small boats all shouting, 'Welcome to Bermuda.' I remember the scenery was gorgeous with the pink sand beaches and the multi-coloured houses with red tile roofs set among the lush green trees. When we entered Hamilton Harbour, it was equally impressive, with lots of little ferry boats dashing across the large expanse of water. In those days there was still a Royal Navy dockyard there but *Sirius* was given the privilege of securing alongside in downtown Hamilton in what is now the berth for visiting cruise ships.

On the first day of our visit, at 5 p.m., I went ashore, accompanied by my friend Mitch (the PO Chef), with the sole intention of looking up Roy's brother Bill at the Mid-Ocean Club. We got a taxi and told the driver where we wanted to go and were a bit surprised when he gave us a funny look and said, 'Are you sure that's where you want to go?' We explained that we had just arrived, didn't know anything about the Club (not even where it was) but that we had to meet someone there. So off we went on a long and picturesque ride to the other end of the island and, after negotiating a long and winding driveway, arrived in front of a very impressive building that looked as though it was out of *Gone With The Wind*.

We knew from the sign at the entrance that we had found The Mid-Ocean Golf & Country Club (Members Only). Nevertheless, we paid our taxi and marched up the steps and through the very grand doors to find ourselves in an enormous reception hall that was completely deserted except for one lonely reception desk. After a while a very dignified young lady appeared and asked, rather coolly I thought, 'How can I help you?' I had the feeling that she was wondering if it would be necessary to call Security to get rid of these two unwelcome *matelots* – even though we were smartly dressed in our best white uniforms. Undaunted, however, I asked to see —— (I can't remember his name) but she insisted that she had never heard of him and wondered if we were in the right place but when I explained the circumstances she did go to her desk and consult the Club membership list. When this was unsuccessful she did condescend to make a phone call and then, pointing to some wide stone stairs in the corner, said, 'If you go down there you will find Mr ——, he is the Head

Chef of this Club.' Wondering what to expect next, Mitch and I went down the stairs and were met by Roy's brother, in his chef's uniform and complete with big hat. Bill was delighted to see us, having been warned by his brother that we would be coming to see him, and he made us very welcome.

Of course, the first order of business was to show us round his place of work and to introduce us to the remainder of his staff

I can remember this enormous underground kitchen (reminiscent of a movie about Henry VIII) with half-a-dozen assistant chefs rushing around preparing meals, and along one wall were four large black ladies washing up endless pots and pans. After we had done the tour Bill asked us if we would like something to eat and, having missed supper on board (it was now about 7.30), we readily agreed. I can't remember exactly what we asked for but I know he reeled off a long list of choices – roast beef, lamb, pork, turkey or pheasant plus many more I cannot remember. We then retired to his private dining room and were served a delicious meal, including wine, by members of his staff. I remember thinking that being a chef was not a bad profession after all and I know that Mitch was also very impressed.

During the conversation we soon learned that Bill was married, they had a brand new baby and they lived in a nice bungalow in the grounds of the Club. He invited us to join him there for the following evening where he, once again, arranged for a delicious dinner to be served to us in his bungalow. After a very pleasant evening, he told us that the following day was his day off and he had arranged to take us by taxi on a tour of the island. Of course, we had seen very little of Bermuda so far and we really appreciated this gesture. We soon learned that, to see the island properly and to learn something of its history, there is no better way than to do it by taxi because the taxi drivers are very knowledgeable and ours was certainly pleasant and friendly. I remember one high-point of our tour was when we stopped to visit a local perfume manufacturer who specialised in scent made from the local flowers. It was a strange place because it was built into the rock face on a beautiful beach and, to our dismay, it was a terrible smell as we toured through these caves until we reached the final process and then we were treated to samples of this wonderful floral perfume.

Unfortunately 'all good things come to an end', and all too soon we were saying goodbye to Bill and his wife as we prepared to leave Bermuda. I thought it was a beautiful island and certainly one that I would want to re-visit; in fact, I told Eileen when I got home that I would take her there on vacation one day. I am sorry to say we have not made it so far.

The next, and final, visit of our Autumn Cruise was to be Nassau, in the Bahamas. Our arrival in the harbour of Nassau was not memorable and neither was our initial view of the town and surrounding area but this was mostly because we had to anchor in the middle of the harbour and it was not until we went ashore that we found what a truly attractive place it is. On the first day of arrival in a new port there is usually a list of invitations to certain local events and always challenges by local teams to take part in any sporting events. Nassau was no exception and a couple of these occasions in which I participated were very interesting and well remembered. The first concerned the Nassau Police Force who challenged *Sirius* to a shooting match (.303 rifles) on their own rifle range. I had always been keen on target shooting and was selected as one of the team to represent *Sirius*. We were picked up early in the morning by a couple of police vans and driven to the far side of New Providence Island. When we reached the rifle range we all had a good laugh, including the police who said they had not been there for some time, because the very coarse grass had grown to shoulder height.

Fortunately, we were able to see the targets from the firing points and we spent a very enjoyable forenoon on the range. It was early afternoon when we packed up (I cannot remember who won the match) and we were amazed when a small pick-up truck arrived – the back was completely filled with ice and countless bottles of very cold beer – it was the most welcome sight I have seen.

Paradise Island in Nassau was the second occasion. Nowadays Paradise Island is densely populated with high-rise hotels and is one of the most popular and attractive holiday destinations in the world. In 1948 however, it was quite primitive and undeveloped and privately owned by Mr Billy Butlin, the originator of Holiday Camps in Britain, who had made a fortune in the process.

He very generously invited our ship's company to make use of Paradise Island during our stay in Nassau. Normally Paradise Island is reached by a private bridge from the town of Nassau but, for our purposes, a ship's boat would simply drop us on one of the beaches.

Another unusual situation arose in Nassau when Pete Foster and I were refreshing ourselves in a local bar and got into conversation with a young man doing likewise. He invited us on board his 'yacht' that was tied up at the pier – it sounded very grand, but in fact it was a small (26ft) sailboat that looked as though it could use a good scrub. However, we went on board with him and he cruised lazily around the harbour and, after he found a bottle of rum in one of the lockers, told us his life story. He was the only son of the local bank manager but did not seem able to fit in with his own home and family and therefore spent most of his time on, or around, the boat. He told us it was a change to have a couple of sailors on board because normally he only entertained a couple of local girls. Finally, we felt we ought to return his hospitality, so invited him back to the ship with us. I think the Officer of the Watch must have wondered what was going on when he saw a civilian sailboat tying up to the boom and two Petty Officers, followed by a civilian, about to climb the Jacob's Ladder. Anyway, we gave him a tour of the ship which was followed by a tot in the POs' Mess and then sent him on his way.

Nassau, like Bermuda, was a place that I desired to visit again and later, I would do so. Eileen and I went there on our first vacation after moving to Canada; we will come to that later on.

After we arrived back in Portsmouth there was a big Ship's Dance arranged to take place in one of the local dance halls and most of the ship's company and their families attended. Pete Foster and his wife Pat had just had a new baby, a beautiful little girl, and were very proud parents. They lived in a gorgeous old country cottage with a thatched roof that they rented in the village of Frogmore, close to East Meon in the beautiful Meon valley. It was very convenient for Pete because it was close to the Signal School at Leydene and also Portsmouth Harbour, the two places he would be likely to spend a lot of time in.

I left *Sirius* on 1 June 1949 when the ship was 'paid off' and went into the reserve Fleet.

Immediately after this Pete and I were detailed to take a large draft of communication ratings, both male and female, to Londonderry, in Northern Ireland, for the annual 'Submarine Summer War Exercise'. We were to man the Communications Headquarters for the exercises which lasted two or three weeks and, for me, it was a very pleasant time. There was some tension there, which meant you had to be careful what you said, but there was no violence at that time. I remember it was a long journey – we took the train to Scotland and got the ferry from Stranraer across the Irish Sea to Larne – only about forty miles but it seems more because it is invariably rough.

After this I went back to *Mercury* for a short spell which included summer leave and, when I returned, I was told that I would be going abroad again. This meant I was entitled to another ten days 'embarkation leave' and it was during this time (late August) that things got a bit hectic. I was being sent to the Naval Headquarters in Malta (which meant two and a half years) and, because it was a 'shore' posting, I would be allowed to have Eileen with me. This was a big relief for both of us and we were really looking forward to it but it also meant that a lot of arrangements had to be made before I left. First of all, we had to rent out our house and to do this we engaged the services of Jordan & Cook who were Worthing's largest Estate Agents and they soon came up with suitable tenants for us. I remember the day we interviewed them at the house – the husband was a local police constable who had also been a Petty Officer in the Navy and his wife was a nurse at the hospital. In addition, there was the mother who was a charming lady with furs and a small dog and obviously not short of a few bob. References supplied to Jordan & Cook were impeccable and we considered ourselves very lucky to find them. Next we had to pack up all our spare belongings (i.e. stuff we would not be taking to Malta) and for this I went to a warehouse on Chatsworth Road and bought half a dozen tea chests. When these were filled, we stowed them in the loft and filled a couple more with what we would need in Malta and arranged to have them shipped out by sea. Then the time had come for me to sell my beloved motorcycle – I had to do this to raise the airfare for Eileen to join me in Malta. The Navy required that I travel by sea to Malta and, when I had found suitable accommodation and had it approved by the Naval Welfare

Officer in Valletta, I could then arrange for my wife to join me by air. So it came about that, when I sailed for Malta, Eileen had to go and stay with her friend Hilda on Haynes Road because the new tenants had moved into our house.

The other major event at this time (end of August 1949) was the wedding of Jack and Vivien. We all knew they had been thinking of tying the knot for some time and I was so glad they did so before I left. I was best man and the reception was held at the Norfolk Hotel, close to Broadwater Bridge.

Finally, after all this excitement, it was early September 1949 and time, once again, for me to say goodbye to my family at West Worthing station as I caught the train to Southampton. It was very reminiscent of the first time (ten years ago) when I headed to Hong Kong because I now knew that I would again be embarked in *Dilwara* for the voyage to Malta.

CHAPTER TWENTY-TWO

Malta

THE THREE YEARS THAT Eileen and I spent together in Malta was a very pleasant and happy experience for us but was made most memorable by three events that occurred whilst we were living there. First and foremost, our eldest daughter, Julia, was born; secondly, Eileen's brother John and his family were also stationed in Malta at that time; and thirdly, we bought our first car in Malta.

On 6 September 1949 when the train steamed into Southampton Docks I saw a very familiar sight – the troopship *Dilwara* which had taken me, at age sixteen, to Hong Kong more than ten years earlier. This time, on the passage to Malta, the routine for me was very relaxed and I was pleased when we arrived there a week later.

Initially, I joined HMS *Camarata* which was the Naval Barracks in Valletta and was situated close to Fort St Elmo. This was where I would be accommodated until such time as I had found suitable accommodation and Eileen could then join me. *Camarata* was quite a small barracks where 'unaccompanied' personnel were accommodated and therefore not very interesting or exciting – I remember the Petty Officers' Mess there was like a bachelors' club.

My job was to be Yeoman of the Watch at the *Lascaris* Naval Head-quarters, just off Castille Square which was the heart of Valletta. *Lascaris* was a large building which accommodated two Admirals and their staff – Admiral Grantham who was Commander-in-Chief, Mediterranean Fleet and also the smaller staff of Flag Officer Malta who was in charge of naval administration on the island. The Communications Centre occupied the entire top floor of the building and comprised a large Wireless Telegraphy room, a Phone Centre, a Teleprinter Room, a Code & Cipher Room, the Message Centre and the Main Signal Office and, on the roof, a Harbour Signal Station. There was a Chief Yeoman (in the Message Centre) in charge of each watch – on my watch, it was Bill Dickinson who was a likeable Cockney who was never without a foul-smelling, curly pipe. The Phone Centre was manned by a Leading Signalman – on my watch his name was Eric Burton, universally known by the nickname 'Blood' because of his thick, black beard which gave him the appearance of a pirate. He and I became good friends, initially because we both played field hockey, which was a very popular sport in Malta; we played in many matches together. The Code & Cipher Department was manned by Signal Wrens (a couple of whom I had trained at *Mercury*) under the charge of a Second Officer WRNS. My particular job was in charge of the Main Signal Office where I had three civilian female typists, two civilian males for processing and two messengers.

I soon settled into the organisation and found the work quite pleasant but, most enjoyable was the watch-keeping routine which was somewhat similar to *Dolphin* – being two days and nights of work and then forty-eight hours off duty.

The island of Malta is not large – 122 square miles – and one can drive all the way round its coast in an afternoon – but, because of its location in the centre of the Mediterranean, it has always been of great strategic importance. In the times of ancient Greece it was known as 'The Navel of the Inland Sea' and has always been the objective of marauding nations. It has been invaded by the Phoenicians, Moors, Turks, French, Spanish, Carthaginians and the Romans.

All this has left a definite mark, not only in the island's history, but also on its culture and, not least of all, the unique Maltese language which has developed from those times. The Maltese people have evolved as very independent, hard working, devoutly Catholic and very proud of their heritage. The two outstanding moments in Malta's history are the award of the George Cross for withstanding the brutal punishment of the German and Italian Air Forces in the Second World War and, very much earlier, when it withstood the Turks in the Great Siege of 1565. It was then that the Knights of St John took over and re-designed and rebuilt the capital of Valletta and remained there until the British arrived in 1800. The British pulled out in 1964 when the island became independent and finally became a republic in 1974. Here ends the history lesson of Malta.

For me, the first two months in Malta were both tedious

and frustrating. Whilst I quite enjoyed my working hours (which were always busy and interesting) it was my off-duty time that was the problem. Anxious to have Eileen join me as soon as possible, the first (and only) thing I could do was to find a suitable apartment – and this was where the problem arose. Living accommodation of any sort was in very short supply, due mainly to the huge number of buildings destroyed by the wartime bombing. In addition, whatever apartment I might find had to be approved by the Naval Welfare Office before I could even apply for Eileen to leave England. The standards they set were not, in themselves, unreasonable but they did nothing to make the search easier. They required the building to be clean and respectable, with a self-contained entrance and, under no circumstances, any sharing of kitchen or bathroom facilities. Every day I would search the classified ads in the *Times of Malta* but, of course, there was not much to see and anything that sounded even a little suitable I would make an appointment to view. Finally I came to rely more on getting word from other men whose families were with them, of any possible vacancies in the area where they lived.

After about a month I learned from another Yeoman at *Lascaris* that there was a possibility for me in the village of Birzebbuga, a little seaside village at the southern end of the island where he lived with his wife. Bill Heath and his wife Babs were from the North of England and were kind and generous to me in my hour of need, as it were. They would invite me to their apartment for meals and, occasionally, for a sleepover. I was not too impressed with their apartment because it was a strange set-up but they seemed happy enough and stayed there for their whole tour of duty in Malta. The building was designed and built as a cinema by an enterprising local businessman after the war but, to ease the severe accommodation shortage, the local government passed a law that forced him to turn it into living space.

This was done by providing partition walls (but no ceilings) to convert the place into five or six separate apartments which were all occupied by British servicemen and their families – adequate perhaps but not a place where one could get too boisterous. The cinema show was held in the parking lot at the rear of the building – except when it rained. Bill also had a small car – a little Standard with a soft top – and he showed me a lot of the island before Eileen arrived.

When I saw 'our' apartment I considered myself lucky to have found it and had no hesitation in signing up for it. It was, in fact, one half of a new house being built by a local man who, although he spoke only a few words of English, proved to be a good landlord and good friend to us while we lived there. The house was just outside the village on the road to Kalafrana and Hal-Far where the Naval Air Station was located and a Petty Officer from there was already installed in the adjoining apartment which was separated from ours by a double connecting door. Reg and his wife Maxie were from Scotland and had one little boy. In our half of the house we had a decent sized kitchen which opened onto an enclosed backyard with a well for the water supply and each day Joe would come to pump the water up to a tank on the roof so that we always had water available to us. Coming in the front door there was a hallway which was to become our living room and at the top of a staircase was a bedroom and a small dressing room with a hand washbasin.

Living in Malta in those days would seem primitive by today's standards – and I suppose it was. There was electricity on the island but it was only available in Valletta; in outlying areas like ours the lighting was provided by a single Tilley lamp (like those used for camping today) – it had a mantle and ran on paraffin which had to be pumped up to pressure and then made a loud hissing noise whilst alight. Nor was there any gas and so cooking was done on a small, portable stove with two burners that also used paraffin. Houses and apartments had no heating or cooling because, with a temperature range of twenty-five degrees (75–85°F in summer and 50–55°F in winter) it was not considered necessary. On 'bath' nights the water would be heated in saucepans on the cooking stove and we would sit in a large tin bath on the kitchen floor. All this may seem like huge obstacles but we soon adapted to it and were soon enjoying it all.

When I found that a naval family was already living in the building I knew that I would have no trouble getting Naval Welfare approval and, sure enough, a couple of weeks later Eileen was ready to join me. This was to be a big adventure for her – leaving England for the first time and travelling all alone – and she was still only twenty-three. On the day before her flight she left for London by train and was seen off at West Worthing station by her friends the Smith family with whom she had been staying. That night she had a reservation at a small hotel and, early next morning, got a taxi to the West London Air Terminal and checked in for the British European Airways flight to Malta. Meanwhile, in Malta, I had the afternoon watch and came off duty at 7 p.m. when Bill Heath took me in his car to Luqa Airport to meet Eileen's flight, which was due in at 8 p.m. It was now early November and we were into the stormy, wet season and, sure enough, that night we got the works – torrential rain, wind and lots of thunder and lightning.

It was a couple of hours before I learned that Eileen's plane had been diverted because of the storm and that she would be spending the night in Rome and arriving in Malta the following afternoon. This in itself was a bit disconcerting but at least I would be off duty in the afternoon and able to collect her at Luqa; the problem was that I would be on watch all that night and so I arranged with Bill and his wife to put her up for the night, thinking it would be preferable to spending the first night alone in a strange apartment and in a strange country – but I was wrong!

Eileen soon settled in and adapted very well to our new life in Malta, finding that, in addition to the disadvantages, there were also many advantages to be enjoyed. For instance – swimming in the blue Mediterranean from the many wonderful beaches, making new friends and enjoying the abundance of foods which had not been available in England. There were unlimited supplies of chocolate and confectionery, biscuits, tinned fruit and fresh fruit – in fact, there did not seem to be a shortage of anything and there was no rationing. Each week we would do our shopping at the huge NAAFI commissary located in Castille Square in Valletta – they sold everything from Scotch to tennis racquets and their prices were generally a bit lower than in the local stores. Fresh meat and vegetables we would purchase in the huge market on Merchant Street in Valletta. We did not have a refrigerator so the iceman would call once a week with a huge block of ice which went into an icebox about 18″ × 24″ and somehow we managed with that. Generally, I suppose, the cost of living was on a par with England but I know we never seemed to have any money to spare but, nevertheless, we lived very well. We were delighted to be together in Malta and secure in the knowledge that it would be for two and a half years. Our social life whilst in Birzebbuga was rather limited and usually consisted of visiting our friends, mostly for a meal which in England was known as 'high tea', such as ham salad. We became friends with one couple who also lived in Birzebbuga – Eddie Leigh was a PO Telegraphist in my watch and so our off duty time coincided. His wife Margaret was an insomniac when Eddie was on duty and used to spend half the night baking cakes and pies. We used to visit them about once a week to play Monopoly and we usually finished about three a.m. I remember we used to take with us a bottle of Marsala which was the local red wine and, at a cost of one shilling and threepence a bottle, was about what we could afford then.

I think it is worth saying something about transport in Malta. Apart from Valletta, the Maltese roads were not great – they were mostly narrow and twisty country roads – but it was not a great problem because traffic was very light. There were commercial vehicles and buses for public transport but the local population were not into automobiles for pleasure. There were some taxis and hire cars but most private cars were owned by the English population and therefore, on a drive outside the city, one would only meet donkey carts and buses. It was the buses, and their operation, that was most remarkable. Every bus started its journey from Castille Square and, depending upon its destination, would be painted a distinctive colour so, at any time of the day, there would be a dozen or more buses in Castille Square (red, blue, green, brown etc) waiting to set off on their journey. They were single deck vehicles, clean and cheap but I am sure they had square wheels!

The Maltese buses were all fitted with huge motor horns and the driver, before starting and throughout the journey, would constantly squeeze the large rubber bulb, emitting a loud blast so that everyone knew they were coming. This, coupled with the fact that they never got out of second gear, ensured that nobody ever missed the bus. Without exception, every bus had a miniature statue of the Virgin Mary mounted just above the driver; it would be surrounded by a Rosary and decorated with tiny lights and artificial flowers. Prior to setting off, the driver would make the sign of the cross, as would every Maltese passenger when getting on and off the bus. As far as I was concerned the only hazard when travelling by bus was getting too close to any of the 'country' passengers (mostly farmers) who seemed to live on a diet of garlic!

I found the Maltese people generally to be honest, hard-working and easygoing but, inevitably, there were a few bad eggs so Malta had a police force but not a modern one. Apart from a few constables scattered around the countryside they were mostly concentrated in Valletta and seemed to be in the sole charge of a very large, intimidating man who was the RSM of the Malta Police. He used to drive around in their only police vehicle (a small, beaten-up Ford) and he was also the only qualified Driving Examiner on the island. One day an Englishman was leaving for work and found his nice car sitting on blocks and the wheels missing. He called the police and 'the CID' came but, when he returned from work, the doors were also missing! They told him they were needed for fingerprint evidence.

The Maltese population were mostly simple folk who lived by very strict rules, dictated by the church. Outside the city they were mostly farmers and goat-herders (the source of local milk) and the women used to wear voluminous black dresses and black headscarves. On a hot summer's day I remember seeing them bathing in the sea – still wearing their full-length black petticoats. Soon after Eileen's arrival we went into Valletta for some shopping and I left her looking at something while I wandered further on, but she soon caught me and was all upset because a couple of Maltese women had been following her and hissing at her. We later realised that it was because she was wearing slacks!

In the following year (1950) we decided that we needed our own transport and therefore invested in a second-hand car to get us around. It was rather a nice looking car – a 1937 Standard Nine, four-door saloon in beige and black and looked to be in good shape. However, I soon became disillusioned with it when I found that the steering was, to say the least, not reliable. By now I had seen our dream car in the showroom of Mizzi's who were the largest car dealers in Malta – it was the first of the new Morris Minors – a 1951 black, two-door convertible with a beige soft-top.

We both fell in love with it and decided we had to have it, but, of course, we did not have the four hundred and fourteen pounds needed to buy it. But, after a lot of dickering, we traded in the old one and, by using some of the rent money from the house in England, we managed it.

Shortly before this happened we were delighted to welcome Eileen's brother John to the island when he arrived there in a troopship to take up his new appointment as the Regimental Sergeant Major, Royal Marines, of the Mediterranean Fleet. As such he was to be based at the Royal Marine Training Centre at Ghajn Tuffieha on the northwest coast of the island. We were also happy to learn that his family (Margery and two boys, Terry and Brian) would soon be joining him because a house was awaiting them at the RMTC. When they did arrive (also by troopship) Eileen and I were at the docks to meet them and then drive them to Ghajn Tuffieha – about an hour's drive from Valletta – in our old car. John and Margery were very fortunate to have a very nice house provided for them – it was quite new, detached, fairly spacious and furnished and, because it stood on a hill at the end of the camp, was called 'The House on the Hill'.

Not too long afterwards I learned from my friend 'Blood' Burton that there was a possibility of an apartment being

Julia, Bob, Eileen, John, Margery, Terry and Brian, 1951.

available in Mosta where he and Joan lived. I did not particularly want to live in Mosta (a small town almost in the centre of the island) and we were quite happy with our apartment in Birzebugga. However, Mosta did have the advantage of being about halfway between Valletta, where I worked, and Ghajn Tuffieha, where we were already spending most of our off-duty time. So I made an appointment to look at it and was very pleased that I did because I was immediately impressed by it. I found it on the main street of Mosta (Constitution Street) and it was one of four units on the side of a brand new cinema (not yet completed). There was only one apartment still available (the 2nd floor) and I took it without hesitation because it was spacious and airy, with large windows, a balcony back and front and, of course, the typical marble floors and, being new, had all new furniture – not luxurious but adequate. Just like Birzebbuga the cinema was only permitted because the owner had also provided adequate living accommodation but here the owner was smart and included it all in one building. The owner (Sam) spoke very little English but one of his daughters was fluent because all the youngsters were now taught it at school. Sam was a quiet and pleasant man as were his wife and daughters, and proved himself to be a good friend as well as landlord. He soon told me that, as soon as the cinema opened, we would be welcome to see the show as often as we liked – at no charge!

A month later, when we moved in, we found that the ground floor apartment was occupied by Ted Banham (a Flight Sergeant in the RAF), his wife Dorrie and a small son. The unit above us was the home of Tony and Nan Chapman, also with a small son – Tony was a Leading Signalman on HMS *Forth* which was a Submarine Depot Ship in Sliema Creek. We kept in touch with the Chapmans after returning to England and we met them again when they came to Worthing on a Caravan (House Trailer) Rally which was then their hobby. The top floor apartment was then occupied by a couple we never got to know very well. He was a civilian and employed as a representative by Hopleaf which was one of the two local breweries. He had a tough job and, as a result, usually seemed to be a bit unwell. When they moved out the unit was taken by Reg who was a Chief ERA and his wife Mona who were a quiet and pleasant couple whom we enjoyed being with.

There is one oddity which I feel I should explain. I have described our apartment as being on the 2nd floor because this is the Canadian way of doing it and it makes sense. However, in Malta, our apartment was described as being on the 1st floor, simply because that was the English way of doing it – i.e. the next above the ground floor being the 1st, and so on up. This illustrates just one of the strange usages of the English language and phraseology.

After moving in we were able to watch the daily progress, from our rear balcony, of the construction work to complete the cinema. At first it seemed slow but, bearing in mind the type of work, it really went remarkably well. From slabs of local rock the men would cut sandstone building blocks (approx. 12″ × 12″ × 24″) using a hand tool called an adze – rather like a long handled axe. These were hoisted into position – not by crane but using a system of ropes and pulleys. It was fascinating to see how accurately these blocks were cut, simply by chipping away by hand.

Mosta was quite a small town – there was no shopping centre or anything like that. We did have a chemist (small drugstore), a couple of small general stores and, inevitably, several bars, the most popular being Johnie's Bar located in the town square right opposite the Church. The Maltese were not drinkers but, during the day, the men liked to sit in the bars sipping on a glass of tea. The Church was the most outstanding feature and also what made Mosta famous because not only was it a large church but it also boasted the second largest unsupported dome in the world. It was a miracle that the church had somehow survived the wartime bombing – one bomb had pierced the dome but had failed to explode in the church.

When we moved to Mosta we had not long taken delivery of our new Morris Minor and I was very reluctant to leave it parked on the street, but there did not seem to be a spare spot anywhere else. Almost next-door was a small garage for auto repairs so I sought out the owner to see if he had any ideas. Charlie spoke excellent English and soon told me that he knew everything about cars, but I also got the idea that his interests lay elsewhere because he was always dreaming up odd schemes to make money. Anyway, he did provide me with indoor parking in a large garage which he owned, right opposite to us. Also opposite to us was a row of houses and in one of them lived Charlie's parents and sisters. The daughters were very glamorous and every evening the mother and four girls would bring their chairs out to the street and sit in front of their house doing their knitting and chatting to their friends which was the Maltese custom. The father owned a herd of goats and at the end of the day, after completing his 'milk round', would arrive home, open the front door and drive his goats through the house to where they lived in the backyard! Actually, they were not true goats because the Maltese had developed a hybrid animal – part sheep to provide meat and part goat to provide milk – so naturally they were known as 'shoats'. This was something I had to bear in mind when I went shopping in the Valletta market for our weekend roast, which was usually a leg of lamb. I had to be sure of seeing the 'New Zealand' stamp in case the butcher tried to sell a piece of local 'shoat' meat – nothing wrong with it but it had a sweet flavour.

John and Margery were extremely hospitable and we soon found that we were spending most of our off duty time at Ghajn Tuffieha where we even had our own room at 'The House on the Hill' and were able to use all the facilities at the camp. There were not a lot but they did have a tennis court which we used and adjoining the camp was the finest beach on the island, and on days when we felt energetic we would pack a picnic and a bottle of wine and hike a mile and a half through the rocks to Dorey Harbour. This was part of the camp and was where the Marines stored their Doreys used for training purposes. It was here that we would swim and, with homemade spear guns, dive among the rocks looking for small octopi – I don't think we ever caught any but it was great fun. We were also made very welcome in the Sergeants' Mess and spent many an evening there playing cards or dice with the Instructors and they, of course, appreciated the additional revenue for the bar.

Another big feature at the RMTC was 'the obstacle course' – not for recreational purposes but for training of the Royal Marine courses held there. Nevertheless, when the camp was deserted on weekends John and I could not resist having a go and, after a while, became quite proficient. There were all the usual obstacles – swinging by rope over a water-filled ditch, climbing a brick wall, climbing over the scrambling nets and, most daunting, the swinging bridge. The latter was a very heavy plank, about ten feet long and suspended at four points above a ditch and, of course, the objective was to get across without landing in the ditch. To achieve this one had to take it at the run, touching down only twice before leaping off the other end. We had done this successfully many times but one day (perhaps over confident) I hit the bridge while it was still swinging after John and, as a result, I was thrown off balance. Of course, I went in the ditch but, unfortunately, as I fell the bridge swung back and caught me in mid-air and a large black bolt protruding from the plank hit me just below my right knee and made a nasty looking hole. We went back to the house and did some first aid, after which I was prepared to leave it until I could attend the Sick Bay at *Camarata* the following day. However, by the evening John did not like the look of it and called out the Camp's duty Sick Berth Attendant who, when he saw it (we were all in the Sick Bay now) decided he would have to call out the Camp's Medical Officer (a Naval Surgeon Lieutenant). When he arrived I got the feeling he was a bit ticked off because he had been called out of the Sunday evening cinema show. In any case, he decided the hole needed some stitches but as he put five stitches in my leg he 'forgot' to give me an injection or any anaesthetic – I remember it as being very painful and I thought he would never finish the job.

We were delighted with our new car and I was never happier than when I was driving it. We enjoyed being able to take John and Margery with us sometimes because, being out in the wilds, they were dependent on public or service transport. However, there were a couple of incidents with our car that did not, at the time, seem very funny. The first one was when John and I were on our way to visit Eileen who was in Bighi Naval Hospital which was on the south side of Grand Harbour. Eileen was suffering from a bad outbreak of eczema on her hands due, according to the doctors, from an overdose of chocolate, candies, cookies and canned fruit.

Anyway, John and I were almost there when I had a problem with the car – the gearshift lever came off in my hand! Unable to find any suitable assistance where we were it was decided to leave the car at the nearest Naval establishment which happened to be the Naval Detention Centre at Corradino where John knew some of the Royal Marine Sergeants stationed there. To get there I had to drive the car, <u>in reverse</u> for five or six miles and, although we got a few funny looks, nobody asked us why we were doing such a dumb thing. The second incident was a bit more serious and occurred when the four of us attended the RM Sergeants' Mess at St George's Barracks (on the east coast) for the Annual Ball of the 4th Royal Marine Commando who were stationed there. It was quite an elaborate affair and we all enjoyed a very pleasant evening until it came time to go home, probably about 1 a.m. It was the height of summer so we had the car top down and although John and I were wearing jackets, our wives were just in evening dresses. As soon as I got the car rolling I knew we had a problem and, sure enough, we had a flat rear tyre! As I opened the trunk to get the jack and spare I suppose our voices were carrying a bit because the next thing we knew was when a deluge of water hit us – somebody had emptied a fire bucket on us from the top floor of the barrack block. Well, of course, John (being the RSM) just blew his top and, as I followed him into the building, he was yelling for everybody to 'turn out and stand by your beds' and then, unable to locate the culprit, left them standing there while he went and turned out the Duty Officer in the Guardhouse. Meanwhile, I went back and changed the wheel (quietly) and, although we gave Margery and Eileen our jackets, they had rather a damp ride home. The Officer Commanding and the Sergeants' Mess apologised profusely for their guests being treated in such a way but they were unable to identify the guilty party, in spite of the troops being confined to barracks for a week. The outcome was that we both received a letter of apology from the Colonel and, once we got over it, we had many a laugh about the incident.

Early in 1951 we were all delighted to find that, at last, Eileen was pregnant and, this time, would remain so, thanks mostly to the young Surgeon Lieutenant RNVR who was serving as the Families Medical Officer in Malta. At last the big day came and Julia was born on the morning of 8 August at the British Military Hospital at MTARFA. I was on the forenoon watch when I got the telephone call and could not wait to get out there to see our new daughter. Eileen remained in hospital for ten days, which was normal then, and, on the very day she was released, we drove out to Ghajn Tuffieha to show off our beautiful baby to John and Margery. Julia must have been a very good baby because I know we continued to visit the Sergeants' Mess at RMTC in the evenings – Julia would be asleep in her Kari-cot in the corner and all these big, burly Sergeants would be smiling and cooing at her.

Previous to Julia's birth though (in the spring of 1951) Eileen and I had an unhappy surprise when, quite unexpectedly, I was ordered to sea for temporary duty. It was because of the Spring Cruise and Exercises for the Mediterranean Fleet and, because Admiral Grantham was personally taking part, extra communication personnel were required to be embarked in the Flagship, HMS *Gambia*, a Colony class cruiser.

Of course, I was very reluctant to leave Eileen alone at this stage but, unfortunately, I had no choice in the matter and therefore went off for 6–8 weeks, hoping there would be no complications while I was away. After completion of the exercise programme the Fleet split up and headed for their appropriate destinations for the cruise. In *Gambia* I visited Venice and Trieste – both of them interesting places but my heart was not in it and I was relieved when we got back to Malta and I could resume normal duties.

At the end of 1951 my normal tour of duty was nearing completion and I had to decide whether to accept returning to England in the usual way (which would be early spring of '52) or whether to request an extension of my foreign service in Malta. We chose the latter for several reasons – our house in England was still rented out, we were still paying for our car and, most of all, because we were greatly enjoying our life in Malta. Under the rules I was allowed to request, and was approved, for an extension of up to one year and we were very grateful when it was settled.

However, in the summer of 1952, there was a very interesting development when we received a letter from my mother telling us about a lot of police activity at our house which, of course, was next door to her. It was quite a while before we found out the whole story – and then it was difficult to believe. Our tenant, who was a constable with the West Sussex Police and stationed in Worthing, had been livening up the long nights when he was on patrol by breaking into shops and helping himself to a lot of merchandise. I do not know how long this had been happening but he must have been quite successful because the police eventually took away a couple of truckloads of stolen goods from our house. Unfortunately, in their zeal they also took away our six cases of effects which had been stored in the attic but, once they had been examined, they did bring them back. I believe the goods recovered included portable typewriters, radios, women's lingerie just to mention a few. I never knew whether he sold any or how he intended to dispose of them – I got the feeling that he took the stuff just for the excitement of doing it. Of course, he came unstuck when the police found a pattern to these burglaries and, having set a trap for him, caught him red-handed when he broke into the garage refilling station on the Findon Road at Offington. I found it difficult to understand how his wife and mother, who were also in the house, could be unaware of what was going on but, because they were never implicated, I guess he managed to hide the stuff pretty well. The outcome was that he was charged and finished up in prison for quite a spell but, as far as we were concerned, it was 'business as usual' i.e. the wife and mother continued to pay the rent and stayed in the house until shortly before we returned to England.

During our time in Malta there were several very distinguished personalities, either living there or just visiting, whom we had the opportunity to see, or sometimes to meet. Prince Philip, who had married Princess Elizabeth just three weeks before our own wedding, was now a Lieutenant RN and serving as Commanding Officer of HMS *Magpie*, a sloop currently based in Malta. He was quite often seen around Valletta but Princess Elizabeth, unlike other naval wives, was not able to join him because of her royal duties in England.

However, she did manage to visit him a couple of times during his time in Malta and in the summer of 1950 Eileen and I saw her when we were on the beach at Ghajn Tuffieha. She was being landed from a destroyer to inspect the RMTC but, because the launch could not get in close enough, she had to 'walk the plank' to get on dry land. As we watched this Eileen was holding her breath because Elizabeth was very obviously pregnant with Anne, but she made it without getting her feet wet. During these visits they would stay with his uncle, Lord Louis Mountbatten, and his family at their lovely house called Casa Mdina, just outside Valletta. Lord Mountbatten's family, his wife Edwina and daughters Pamela and Patricia, were very well known and liked in Malta because they had owned a home there for many years. Lord Louis was now a Vice-Admiral and was commanding the First Cruiser Squadron which was based in Malta. Mountbatten was, and always had been, a very outgoing, personable and sometimes flamboyant man but, nonetheless, very well liked because he knew what he wanted and how to get it but, most of all, because he was a born leader. As a young officer he had distinguished himself by coming top of his class to qualify as a Signal Officer when Wireless Telegraphy was first introduced and, ever since, had been considered the RN's No. 1 Communications Officer.

Probably because of this reputation and coupled with the fact that he would soon be leaving the Mediterranean for another appointment it came about that the first Annual Communications Ball was arranged in the summer of 1952 and the guest of honour was to be Admiral Mountbatten. Of course, this was a very big event and was to be held at the Phoenicia which was the largest and most exclusive hotel in Malta and we had arranged for John and Margery to be our guests. So far, so good, but on the big day I made one of the major mistakes of my life – I came off night-duty in the morning and, after some shopping at the market, decided to get a haircut to spruce up for the evening. That was OK but, while in the chair, I told the barber to remove the rather splendid beard I had cultivated over the past year and, when it was gone, I thought I looked quite sharp. However, when I got home, it was a different story because Eileen was just horrified at my appearance and, for a while at least, even refused to go to the Ball with me!

In the latter half of 1952 we began to think more and more about returning to England and, sure enough, I received word that we were to return to the UK on 11 November but the most exciting part was that we would be travelling by air. For about a year now the Navy had been using exclusive air charter flights (two or three per week) to move families and personnel between UK and Malta. The scheme had proved to be efficient and also cost-effective because of the time and inconvenience saved. Of course, by today's standards, the planes were small and slow but the main thing was they did get there. They were operated by a small and relatively unknown charter company called *Dan Air* who are now one of the largest and most successful charter holiday companies.

Before we actually left Malta though, there were a couple

of significant events. One day we received a letter from Eileen's younger brother Nicky who had joined the RAF and was soon to complete his pilot's training in Kenya. He was to travel home by RAF transport and would be stopping in Malta for a few hours to refuel. It was a very happy reunion but much too short.

The other event concerned our car which had been causing me a headache for some time because the paint-work was not standing up to the Maltese sunshine and was showing very distinct 'orange peel' effect on the hood and trunk (that's 'bonnet' and 'boot' for you English people!). After a lot of moaning at the dealer he had finally got the manufacturer to agree it was their problem (mine was not the only one) and they authorised a complete paint job and, happily, this was done just prior to our departure from Malta. The other good news concerning the car was that I had been able to arrange with the Naval Dockyard people to have my car shipped back to England in a Naval Store ship, just prior to our own departure and at no cost! This was wonderful news and all I had to do was deliver it to the Dockyard in Malta and, a month later, pick it up at the Dockyard in Plymouth.

I remember it was a very sad time as we packed up our home and said goodbye to our friends and the beautiful lifestyle we had enjoyed for over three years. Of course, this was offset by the anticipation of returning to family and friends in England and being able to show off our beautiful daughter Julia. Inevitably, at the back of my mind was the thought of what the Navy might have awaiting me and, although we did not talk of it, I felt sure we would be facing a period of separation on completion of my leave.

Finally the big day came and I think I was a little surprised at how smoothly all the travel arrangements worked out. On the day before our flight we had to report to the 'Families Transit Camp' at Luqa Airport. After checking in and handing over our luggage, we were shown to a cabin that was clean and comfortable and, after a pleasant supper in the dining hall, we turned in for an early night because we had to be up at 6 a.m. The following morning, after breakfast, we boarded our flight – due to take off at 8.30. It was what would now be called a small plane – a twin-engine Vickers Viking but we did not care as long as it got us home. They served tea, coffee and lunch on the plane. It was a long day because, after a stop at Nice to refuel (we were there about an hour and were allowed to stretch our legs), we flew over the Alps, which I thought very impressive, finally landing at Stanstead Airport at about 5 p.m. Stanstead is now a major airport and second to Heathrow but in 1952 it was a very minor operation. We were then taken by motor coach into London and I very well remember the feeling – it was getting dark when we landed and now, driving through London, looking at all the lights and the feel of fog and frost in the air – we were definitely back in an English November. We went to Goodge Street Underground Station which was being used as a rallying point for families returning. From there we made our own way to Victoria Station where we were met by June and my mother. After lots of hugs and kisses and a meal in the station buffet we caught the train for Worthing and arrived home exhausted but very happy and thrilled by the prospect of ten weeks leave. I was entitled to two days for every month spent abroad. I know it was wonderful for us all to be reunited again and there was many an hour chatting over tea. Of course, Christmas came in the middle of my leave and I know it was very special. The only black spot was that Jack could not be with us – he was in Margate, convalescing from a bad bout of tuberculosis. Margate, in Kent, is not easy to reach from Worthing (it was 'cross-country') and I was pleased when I got my car and we could take Vivien to visit Jack more often.

Finally the New Year of 1953 was upon us and I was beginning to wonder what the Navy might have in store for me when, in the middle of January, I received notice to report to HMS *Mercury*, the Signal School at Petersfield, on completion of my leave.

CHAPTER TWENTY-THREE

Signal School

TOWARDS THE END OF JANUARY 1953 as I travelled by
train to Petersfield to join HMS *Mercury* there were
two feelings uppermost in my mind. First, a feeling of
pleasure and anticipation because I was rejoining an establishment which I already knew and liked – besides pleasant
memories of Leydene I looked forward to meeting previous
shipmates who would be there on courses or as Instructors.
The second feeling was a nagging thought that my stay
there would be short-lived – after enjoying the luxury of
a three-year 'Accompanied' posting I felt sure there would
be a draft to another ship and involving a period of
separation from my family.

When I reported in I found out just how perverse the
Navy could be because, instead of a seagoing ship as I
expected, I was told that I had been enrolled in an eight-
week Instructor's Course due to start at the beginning of
February. After a rapid calculation I knew that I would be
safe until April and that I could probably look forward to
a couple of weeks leave for Easter. The course, naturally,
covered all aspects of Naval Communications and, although demanding, it was good to feel 'up to date' on all
subjects again. In addition to refreshing us on professional
subjects there were also some sessions specifically designed
to teach us the art of instructing. I well remember one of
those occasions when the course syllabus was deliberately
vague and, as we entered the classroom, we had no idea
what was in store for us. The Course Officer explained
that the object was to teach us to 'think and talk on our
feet' and that each student would select a random piece
of paper with the subject written on it and would then be
required to lecture the remainder of the class, on that
subject, for not less than twenty minutes. Everybody's face
dropped a couple of notches but mine especially because,
being Adams, I was first on the list again. It did not help
when I drew my piece of paper and found that my subject
was 'Euthanasia' – even the Course Officer seemed a bit

shocked and offered to let me pick again but I was determined to press on. I managed an introduction, a case for and against, a few examples and, finally, a summary of the subject and it was well-received but, more important, I had passed. Eventually the course was completed; I had qualified and was able to relax and enjoy my Easter leave which we spent with Eileen's Aunts Gertie and Eve in Lydney.

When I returned from leave the main topic of conversation was the forthcoming Coronation of Queen Elizabeth which was scheduled to take place on 2 June 1953. Because all ships and establishments of the Royal Navy were to be represented at this huge event *Mercury* was limited to sending two Chief or Petty Officers and thirty other ratings. I thought this would be something memorable to do so I put my name forward as a volunteer and I was selected to be in charge of 'the Naval street-lining platoon'. I soon found there was a lot more to the job than putting on a best uniform and going to London to see the Queen.

Because *Mercury* was sharing this requirement with one other establishment I found that I was to take fourteen ratings with me to HMS *Dryad* who would be providing a like number and we would all be required to undergo six weeks intensive training prior to the event. HMS *Dryad* was the naval Radar School and was located at Southwick (Hants) which was a pretty little village nestled at the back of the South Downs in the beautiful Hampshire countryside. *Dryad* was similar to *Mercury* in that it was a naval establishment, built during the war and centred round a large country house and estate and, in this case, it was Southwick House.

As soon as we had settled in, no time was lost in getting started on the training programme which involved all day, every day, from 8 a.m. to 4 p.m. On the first morning (and every morning thereafter) we were pounced on by the Physical Training Instructor. After a period of physical exercises on the parade ground, he took us for a cross-country run through the surrounding woods. Until now I had thought of myself as reasonably fit but already I was feeling the strain with aching muscles that I did not even know I had. After a shower and back into uniform we spent the rest of the day on the parade ground, doing rifle and marching drills and being introduced into the art of holding a rifle and standing completely still for long periods without fainting, or even twitching. All this training seemed a bit excessive at first but we soon learned how necessary it was. In charge as the Chief Gunnery Instructor was Charlie Carse from *Mercury*. Charlie was a likeable fellow but a typical Chief GI – rough, tough and no sympathy as he put us through our paces – but in the end we were all grateful to him for the tortures he put us through. Each day the screws were tightened as the training intensified – the cross-country runs got longer, we were involved in long distance route marches and, most of all, the periods of standing at attention without moving a muscle were stretched every day.

This was during May and, that year, the weather was beautiful – sunny and warm every day – but, because of our activities, we did not always appreciate it. As the days and weeks went by we were obviously getting fitter, feeling very confident, and not suffering the earlier strain we had known. We soon had a chance to use these to good advantage as, towards the end of May, the *Dryad* Annual Sports Day was approaching and we were looking forward to taking part but we were told that the *Dryad* ratings in our platoon could only participate with their own Division, and that *Mercury* ratings were not eligible to compete. Well, this was a big disappointment and we all kicked up such a fuss that, in the end, it was allowed that the Coronation Platoon could take part as a separate entity. This was fine with us, even though it meant that two POs and thirty men would be competing against Divisions many times that size. Anyway, the big day came and, because we were all keen, we had managed to have entries in every event, even though it meant us all taking part in two or three events each. Well, the benefits of our training paid off when we won, or were placed, in every event and, of course, walked away with the trophy for the 'Best Overall Division'. Well, we were on top of the world and that night, when we went to the village pub to celebrate, it was a night to remember.

The big day came when our training was finished and we were going to be on our way to London. It started when the *Mercury*/*Dryad* platoon was taken by bus to Portsmouth Town Station where we joined hundreds of others from the Portsmouth area and boarded a special train bound for Waterloo. When we arrived in London there was a whole fleet of red, double-decker buses to take us to our destination which was Clapham Common. We were to be accommodated in Clapham South Deep Shelter which was the London Underground Station which had been a famous air raid shelter during the war. It was not uncomfortable there except for the fact that the two thousand sailors there were to be fed in mess tents on Clapham Common, serviced by an Army Field Kitchen, and this involved climbing a couple of hundred stairs every mealtime because there were no lifts or escalators in operation.

The big day we had all been waiting for finally arrived and, at 6 a.m., the entire Naval Battalion was paraded on Clapham Common and, after inspection, we again boarded London Transport buses to take us to our various assembly points in the City. The destination for my group was the Victoria Embankment where we disembarked, were fallen in and again inspected before we marched from the Embankment, up through Northumberland Avenue to Trafalgar Square. As we took up our positions for lining the royal route it was about 8.30 and already there were hundreds of people on the sidewalks, most of them having spent the night there. We settled down for a long wait until the Royal Procession would be going past on its way to the Abbey but, in the meantime, there was all sorts of activity (including a shower of rain) so the time passed not too badly.

Finally, we 'presented arms' as the Royal Procession passed our location and I will always remember how gorgeous and dignified the Queen looked as she sat in the Golden State Coach with Prince Philip beside her. Then, of course, we had another blank patch until it was time for the return procession from the Abbey to Buckingham Palace and, by now, the crowd behind us was really going mad with excitement. When it was all over, we formed up and marched back to our buses for the return to Clapham Common – I will never forget how good it was once again to stretch arms and legs which had stood still for so long.

After we had been fed and had returned our rifles and other gear, we were free for the rest of the day so I and the other PO (from *Dryad*) went back into the City and joined the thousands of people who were milling around in front of the Palace. We waited to see the several appearances of the Queen and the royal party on the Palace balcony.

The following morning it was all over and we dispersed back to our own establishments (*Mercury* and *Dryad*) and on return I found that I had been awarded the Queen's Coronation Medal for my part in the ceremonies. There was one little tail-ender which I always thought amusing – Charlie Carse (the Chief GI who trained us) was told at the last minute that he was not required in London and would not travel with us. Charlie was very upset by this and said there was no way he would let us go without him. True to his word, he managed to bluff his way through somehow and I know he was behind us on Coronation Day.

While all this activity was going on I had taken Eileen and Julia (who was now nearly two) to stay with her aunts in Gloucestershire until the Coronation was over. But they did not miss it all because a relation in Lydney had a new television set and they were invited to join the watchers – this was Eileen's first experience of TV (B&W then).

Another major milestone in my life, and totally unconnected with the Royal Navy, came in the summer of 1953 when Eileen and I bought and moved into our first new home. We had now been married over five years and most of that time we had been living in Malta. Although No. 8 Ethelred was (and still is) a very nice house in a good area of Worthing it never really felt like <u>our</u> home because we had inherited it from Eileen's parents. So, in the spring of that year we started looking but the task was not made a lot easier by the fact that we had little idea of what we wanted, or even where we wanted it. I do remember that we both rather fancied ourselves in a bungalow but when we had looked at a few re-sales that all looked like little boxes we began to realise that No. 8 was really quite a spacious house. Some of these bungalows were in Lancing and some just off the Findon Road – in other words in the general area of Worthing – and I think this slowed us down for a while until in the early summer, I was driving the Morris Minor and came along a road I did not normally use. It was Goring Way and ran west from the village of Goring – half of this had been developed with bungalows pre-war and now was to be extended, with new bungalows, all the way to Ferring. I was quite excited when I read the board, and even more so when I found out the price – two thousand eight hundred and fifty pounds – which seemed reasonable and, best of all, within our budget. We wasted no time in getting our name down for one and putting Ethelred Road up for sale and it, fortunately sold very quickly.

The ensuing weeks were very exciting for us as we watched our future home being built and also in selecting some new furniture and fixtures to go in it. This included three items which we had never experienced before – a refrigerator, a television and a telephone. We did consider ourselves fortunate in owning a washing machine – it was the first Hoover spin-drier machine (about eighteen inches square and thirty inches high) which we had bought in Malta and, when we got it home, had to change the motor to suit UK cycles. Finally, it was time to move in and, once we were installed, we were certainly not disappointed with anything. We lived there until I left the Navy at the end of 1962 and it was a very happy period in our lives.

When I returned to *Mercury* after the Coronation I found that I had been assigned as an Instructor with 'C' Section – the designation for the Cryptographic Dept. of the Signal School. This suited me fine because I knew it was an endlessly interesting subject and also one that I enjoyed teaching. After a couple of weeks in the Section – spent in getting to know the people and also brushing up on course materials – I found that I had been appointed as Crypto Instructor for a new class of Signal Wrens which would be starting shortly. This was good news because it was a twenty-six week course so that, with summer & Christmas leaves, it would take me well into the New Year of 1954.

These girls were new recruits who had completed their basic training elsewhere and were now sent to *Mercury* to learn the intricacies of Communications in the Royal Navy and ultimately to qualify as Signal Wrens. There were about thirty in the class and they were all good students because they were interested in what they were learning, even though it was probably a bit complicated to start with. I enjoyed teaching them and, of course, was very gratified when they all passed their final examinations.

After my Wrens class, the next one I got was a very different proposition – they were a group of young men who were categorised as 'Coder (Ed)s'. They had been recruited from universities as linguists who were fluent in Russian (remember, this was the period of the cold war) and would be employed translating intercepted Soviet messages. Of course, to do this they also had to be proficient in Cryptography – which was where I came in – but, in the end, I felt I learned as much from them as they did from me!

Finally, it was time for me to move on again when I received notice that I was to be drafted, on 21 May 1954, to join HMS *Glasgow* in Portsmouth Dockyard.

CHAPTER TWENTY-FOUR

HMS *Glasgow*

O N 20th MAY 1954 when I joined HMS *Glasgow* (along with 700 other men) I knew that we were making naval history because *Glasgow* was the first RN ship to undertake what the Admiralty had designated a 'General Service Commission'. For as long as anyone could remember British warships had been put into service on the basis of a two-and-a-half years commission which meant that the ship's company would remain in that ship until she 'paid off' at the end of her commission. This would apply no matter what area the ship was to serve in – it could be Home Fleet, or Mediterranean, or Far East – and, for those on foreign service, it meant an awfully long time absent from home and families and this obviously put a strain on certain relationships. I believe approaches had been made to the Admiralty to come up with a more fair and acceptable system of sea service and, as a result, the Lords of the Admiralty, in their post-war improvements to naval service, had devised the General Service Commission. In theory it sounded most acceptable because it decreed that every warship would now be in commission for a total of eighteen months but, more importantly, that nine of those months would be spent on foreign service and the other nine months in the Home Fleet. That was the idea anyway!

Glasgow was to be the guinea pig for this scheme and so 700 men (and myself) who commissioned the ship, were feeling that the future for us was not to be too bad. It was planned that *Glasgow* would spend the first period in the Mediterranean and the second half in the Home Fleet.

Meanwhile, back at the ranch as they say, life had been going very smoothly for Eileen and me. We were extremely happy with our new home and by now were well settled at 261 Goring Way. Julia was growing up quickly and, when we learned that we would have a new baby at the beginning of August, our life seemed almost perfect. Until

I received the news of joining *Glasgow*, when suddenly the future looked very unhappy, for not only would I be absent for the birth but I could not expect to see the new baby until he, or she, was six months old. After fifteen years in the Navy I had got used to saying goodbye but, when I finally had to leave Eileen, I could not believe how difficult it was and still think it was one of the most difficult steps I have ever had to take.

HMS *Glasgow* was a familiar type of ship for me because I had served in her sister ship, HMS *Gloucester*, early in the war. She was a Town Class cruiser of 10,000 tons, built pre-war at Greenock on the Clyde and, in her new coat of paint (Med. Grey) she was a very smart and impressive looking warship. Which was no less than appropriate because we were headed for the Mediterranean to resume duties as the Flagship of the Commander-in-Chief, Mediterranean.

Admiral The Earl Mountbatten of Burma had been the C-in-C Med. since 1951 and *Glasgow* had been his Flagship during her previous commission – she had returned to Portsmouth in May 1954 and, in a very hectic two-week period, she had paid off and we (the new commission) had taken over. We had sailed on 28 May and, after spending a few days in Gibraltar, where we changed into tropical rig, had arrived in Malta on 7 June 1954 and very

HMS *Glasgow*, Grand Harbour, Valletta, 1954.

soon Admiral Mountbatten and his Staff were re-embarked and settled in.

It so happened that we not only had a famous Admiral but also our Commanding Officer was very distinguished – he was Captain Peter Dawnay who was not only a cousin of the Queen but was also well known in the Navy as a very competent Signal Officer. In fact, until he joined *Glasgow* he had been Captain of the Signal School, HMS *Mercury*, so he was a very familiar face to me. He was tall, distinguished looking, quite stern and did not seem to smile very much but he clearly knew how to handle a ship. Also to join the ship from *Mercury* were all the senior rates in the V/S Department so we all knew each other from the word go. Bill Giddings was the Chief Yeoman, a very likeable and easy-going man and therefore popular with everybody. The four Yeomen were myself, Hank Brown, Alf Songhurst and Andy Edge. We got on well together so it made for a happy and efficient Department. Hank Brown was in charge of 'the books' (all of the communication publications on board) – keeping them up to date and promulgating any significant changes. Alf Songhurst was in charge of Instruction (for the junior rates) and Andy Edge was in charge of the Main Signal Office. Which left me as the Senior Yeoman in charge of the 'Daymen' – a group of about six young signalmen who were not required as watch keepers but would work, as required, during daylight hours. Their principal responsibility was the care and maintenance of all V/S equipment, such as signalling projectors, flags. etc. and also the cleanliness of the Department One of my main jobs was to see that all Ensigns, Admiral's flags and signalling flags and pendants were clean and in good repair. Naval flags and ensigns are made of bunting which is a woollen material, very hard wearing but when they become frayed or torn they have to be repaired on a sewing machine. Thus I became very proficient in the use of the sewing machine and spent many hours working with it.

Before sailing from Portsmouth I found that I was faced with a mammoth task in having to make a new set of 'dressing lines'. These are lines of signal flags used for any ceremonial occasions and stretch from the Jackstaff to the top of the foremast, then from the foremast to the mainmast and finally from the mainmast down to the Ensign Staff. As the *Glasgow* was 600 feet long this would involve almost 750 feet of lines and require a total of about two hundred flags and pendants – and each one has to be sewn onto the one-inch wire, using a marlin spike to separate the strands and a sailmaker's needle to sew. This was not a normal 'on board' job because dressing lines were normally supplied to warships, ready made by the dockyard sail loft but, in our case, the old dressing lines had mysteriously gone missing and, in the hectic two-week turnaround, the dockyard could not come through for us. Therefore, it was a job for us.

After drawing the necessary wire and flags from the dockyard stores I got the Bosun's party to cut and splice the lines to the correct length and then my half dozen daymen were set to work on attaching the flags. To a non-naval person it would appear that the flags and pendants are just randomly attached but, in fact, they must be in a very specific sequence. There was no time to spare because the lines had to be available by the time we reached Malta and, fortunately, the weather was good while we were on passage so we were able to spend every day on the forecastle until the work was completed.

Our arrival in Malta was splendidly memorable and, as we secured to the Flagship buoys in Grand Harbour, I know we all felt very proud of our ship and also the fact that we were to carry such a famous C-in-C as Admiral Mountbatten. Once embarked, the Admiral wasted no time in getting us on the move and we soon realised that Louis Mountbatten was not a man who was prepared to spend a lot of time swinging round the buoy in Malta. We would be away at every opportunity to visit the many interesting (and quite often beautiful) ports in the countries bordering the shores of the Mediterranean. I had visited many of them before but usually under wartime conditions when they were not looking their best. Some of these were our North African ports of call such as Benghazi, Tripoli, Tangiers and Port Said while the most attractive ones were on the opposite shores of the Mediterranean. The first was Naples, in Italy, where we also enjoyed the fascination of Pompeii, the ruined city at the foot of Mount Vesuvius, then on to Calvi in Corsica which was really attractive. In the days before Yugoslavia started to destroy itself we visited the beautiful city of Dubrovnik on the Dalmatian coast, with its sixteenth-century fortress and lovely harbour where we sipped wine in the outdoor cafés while all the locals tried to talk to us with their few words of English. We then went to Split which is the largest Dalmatian city, a major port and naval base on the Adriatic. The entire Fleet congregated at Las Palmas Bay in Sardinia where the Annual Fleet Regatta was to be held and, on completion of the Fleet Exercise Programme, *Glasgow* went to visit Villefranche, a lovely little place on the French Riviera.

My little crew was kept pretty busy on all these visits because there was always some sort of reception for the local dignitaries – either cocktail parties or dinner or dances held on the Quarterdeck – and each time, after the awnings were spread, the QD had to be decorated with flags and bunting and, of course, stripped again on completion. It was all rather hectic because Mountbatten himself loved entertaining and, of course, everybody in the Mediterranean wanted to meet him. He would also bring one or two of his friends out from England so that he could entertain them for a few days – his two favourites for this were both famous British actors of the time, namely John Gielgud and Noel Coward. The latter, of course, had portrayed Captain Mountbatten of HMS *Kelly* in the wartime movie *In Which We Serve*. Mountbatten was, and always had been, keenly interested in the making of movies – possibly because there was a bit of an actor in him somewhere. He was also a very keen, and quite expert, snorkel diver and it was a common sight to see the Admiral's barge at the gangway, very early in the morning, waiting for the Admiral and his party dressed in swimming gear and carrying masks and spear-guns.

Whatever his theatrical leanings, Mountbatten was a very competent officer and a born leader and, before very long, he was to demonstrate this in no uncertain terms. The occasion was to be a visit to the Fleet by Emperor Haile Selassie of Ethiopia, a small man with a fierce black beard and known as 'The Lion of Judah'. In 1935 Mussolini's troops overran Ethiopia and the Emperor and his family were exiled to Britain and I remember for many years they lived at Warne's Hotel on Worthing's seafront and I saw them around town on many occasions. Now, it was October 1954 and, after almost twenty years, he seemed not to have changed at all. Anyway, Mountbatten decided to perform for his friend a complex and spectacular manoeuvre known as 'The Gridiron' which, when carried out at high speed, could be very hazardous, not only to ships but also to the career of the Admiral concerned. The manoeuvre entailed two columns of ships, steaming on a parallel course, turning inwards (towards each other), passing through the lines on opposing courses, and eventually resuming the original course together so that the columns had changed sides. It was a manoeuvre that was still in the books and therefore still taught and occasionally exercised but always with great caution, because the danger came from the different turning circles and the variations in speeds, even when the same engine revolutions were used by every ship. Sixty years previously, in 1893, the then C-in-C Med. who was Admiral Tryon attempted this same manoeuvre which resulted in the loss of his flagship *Victoria* and himself with it!

For a week prior to the 'big day' the entire Fleet was at sea practising 'Gridirons' – slowly at first but then increasing speed as the characteristics of all ships became more compatible until, finally, we were executing the manoeuvre at twenty-four knots. On every ship the bridge personnel were holding stopwatches as they noted speeds, engine revolutions, distances, bearings and time elapsed for each alteration. Of course, on the day everyone performed brilliantly and the whole thing was a roaring success and most gratifying for Mountbatten because, although it was not mentioned, we all knew that this was his 'swan song' in a seagoing command. At the end of the year he was to leave us to become the First Sea Lord at the Admiralty. This was the post held by his father at the commencement of World War I and everyone in the Navy knew that it was the height of Mountbatten's ambition to achieve the same status.

Promotions must have been in the air at that time because on 15 October 1954 my papers came through for promotion to Chief Yeoman of Signals which, of course, was a cause for celebrations all round. Because it was decided to keep me on *Glasgow* until our return to UK it meant that *Glasgow* was the only ship in the Navy carrying two Chief Yeomen. Bill Giddings and I were good friends so there was no problem on that score and, when I moved into the Chief Petty Officers' Mess, there was a lot of kidding for both of us from the other members. The first one to offer me his tot was my old friend 'Mitch', the PO Cook from *Sirius* days in Bermuda who was now a Chief PO Cook also serving on *Glasgow*. Of course, my biggest celebration had already taken place on 1 August when I received a telegram to say that our daughter Karen had arrived. Because Karen was a little bit late, all the Department had been asking me what was going on so now this was the only excuse they needed 'to wet the baby's head'.

The two other notable events in that year were the Ship's Company Dance in December, which, like the Communicators Ball, was held at the Phoenicia Hotel and with Admiral Mountbatten in attendance. It was a very successful evening even though, for most of us, there was something lacking in not having a wife or girlfriend to accompany us – even though someone had thoughtfully rustled up a bunch of Wrens and nurses. The second event was the Ship's Concert, held on board in December and this was also pretty successful because it is an occasion when everybody lets their hair down and has a good laugh. Certainly a good laugh was what we needed at this time because it was now that 'the buzz' had been confirmed that we would not be returning to England in the New Year as originally planned but would remain in the Mediterranean for a further three months!

Perhaps in an effort to soften this nasty shock, the Admiralty now relaxed their rule that would not permit families of personnel on seagoing ships to join them on foreign stations. It was announced that any *Glasgow* man could bring his wife to Malta to live for the remainder of our time in the Mediterranean. Not many responded to this, for one reason or another – a few officers had their wives come out and my friend 'Mitch' was also able to have his wife join him. I had no option in the matter because Eileen, with two young children, could not leave home. Mitch and his wife had taken a flat in Floriana and, very generously, invited me and a couple of others to join them for Christmas dinner. As it turned out we did not go on Christmas Day (we did not want to miss the celebrations on board) but we did go on Boxing Day and I was amazed at the quantity and variety of food laid out on the table. There was turkey, pork and ham, every imaginable vegetable and several fancy desserts, not to mention all the 'snackies' etc. Mitch had obviously been very busy and we all really appreciated the effort but whether we did justice to the food I am not sure – I just know we stuffed ourselves until we couldn't move.

Since 1952 Admiral Mountbatten, in addition to being

the Royal Navy's C-in-C Med., had also held the post of Allied Naval C-in-C for the NATO organisation and was therefore in command of six other Navies in the Mediterranean. When he was due to leave Malta in December of 1954 all these very distinguished Naval and Military NATO Commanders, including Field Marshal Montgomery, came on board *Glasgow* to speed him on his way. In fact, they did just that when six NATO Admirals manned the oars in the Admiral's galley and rowed him ashore from *Glasgow* to the Customs House.

In January *Glasgow* was due for a short refit to be undertaken in Malta Dockyard and it was arranged that, during this three-week period, the ship's company would be sent ashore, in two watches, to participate in an Assault

Bob, Hank Brown, Bill Giddings, Andy Edge, Alf Songhurst.

Course and Rifle Range programme at the RMTC at Ghajn Tuffieha. I really enjoyed this time and, of course it brought back a lot of very nostalgic memories for me. I completed the Assault Course (without doing any damage to myself this time) and also got good results in the Rifle Range programme. In the evenings, of course, there was much getting together in the Sergeants' Mess and I was pleased to find a couple of RM Instructors still there from my previous time at RMTC.

Although it seemed the day would never come when we turned for home it did finally happen and, on 7 April 1955, we left Malta Grand Harbour for the last time and were on our way to Gibraltar and, ultimately, Portsmouth. Our stay in Gibraltar was very pleasant and gave me a chance to stock up with some presents for Eileen and our girls. On the Main Street in Gibraltar there are endless stores stocked with virtually the same items – so the scheme is to start at one end and compare all the prices before actually going in and buying something. I remember that I could not resist a large doll, about two foot tall, that was dressed in beautiful Spanish costume and I knew Julia would love it.

Our passage home through the Bay of Biscay was calm and pleasant and was notable for one incident concerning myself. It was a Sunday afternoon, calm and clear, when we passed a large merchant ship, outward bound from England and, as is the custom, exchanged identities with her by signal lamp. Having found out who we were, the merchant ship continued to signal us and Captain Dawnay, thinking it was some chatter for him, asked to see the message and was a bit shocked when he read, 'To Chief Yeoman Adams from Captain Denyer – Welcome home again.' Unfortunately I was attending a cinema show on board, unaware of all this 'till later; I would have loved to send a reply. Captain Denyer and his wife lived on Goring Way also – immediately opposite to Eileen and me so that we knew them both quite well.

It was a beautiful sunny morning on 22 April 1955 as we steamed into Portsmouth Harbour and found a large crowd of friends and relatives on the dockside waiting to welcome us home. I knew, of course, that Eileen was somewhere amongst them because she had written to say that she would be leaving the girls at home with a friend and would catch the early train to Portsmouth. As soon as the ship was secured and the gangways in position we were allowed ashore and when I found Eileen in the crowd I brought her on board where we had some coffee in the Chief's Mess. We did not hang around very long because we were anxious to get back to Goring Way to see our girls. As soon as I had collected my bag and all my parcels we were on our way. I remember I was carrying a pair of blue budgies in a little wooden cage, which I had bought on leaving Malta and I felt a bit like 'Jolly Jack Tar' coming home with a parrot on his shoulder.

When we reached 261 Goring Way, Karen (who was now nine months old) was in her pram in the back garden and I could hear her howling before I got there. I was wondering what sort of reception I would get from this little girl when she found a strange man coming into her life. As I leant over the pram to look at her she suddenly stopped crying and began to smile – I began to think I had some magic power until Eileen told me that it was not me but the sun glinting on my gold cap badge that was fascinating her. Anyway, we quite soon made friends and, thankfully, there was never a problem between us. Julia, to my surprise, was a very different story and would not have anything to do with me for the longest time, even though she had been asking, 'When is my daddy coming home?' I was now a stranger to her and she refused to look at me or talk to me. Even the large and glamorous Spanish doll, which I had thought would be a winner, was pushed aside for some time but, in the end, it did win her over.

Of course, it was just wonderful to be reunited with all my family again and I know we all enjoyed a very happy leave – I was entitled to about three weeks Foreign Service Leave – which passed all too quickly. When I returned to the *Glasgow* in the middle of June I found that I was to be drafted back to the Signal School at Leydene 'for disposal'. This was not entirely unexpected because now that I was a Chief Yeoman I was 'supernumerary to ship's complement'. On the day that I was to leave the ship I was asked by Lieutenant Martineau, who was *Glasgow*'s Signal Officer, if I would like a ride with him to *Mercury* where he had some business. Of course, I accepted and therefore arrived at *Mercury* in style because, only the day before, he had taken delivery of his brand new 1955 MG Magnette and wanted to try it out.

So, for me, it was goodbye to HMS *Glasgow* whose next port of call was to be Gdynia, in Poland.

The ship survived until she went for scrap in 1958.

CHAPTER TWENTY-FIVE

HMS Coquette

Coquette: a woman who plays with men's affections
(Webster's Dictionary)

I WAS ALWAYS FASCINATED BY the name of *Coquette*; it was so stylish and the definition was, I felt, equally applicable to a ship as to a woman. What I could not understand though was how it had come to be selected for a warship, because men-of-war names had always been rather macho and aggressive – I know we had digressed during the war when we had Flower Class corvettes – but, even so, I could not picture a stuffy and traditional committee at the Admiralty saying, 'This ship will be called *Coquette.*' Anyway, it happened and I am pleased it did and I was so taken with the name that, many years later, I wanted to name my boat *Coquette* but, for some reason, Eileen would not hear of it!

When I rejoined the Signal School in mid-June 1955 after leaving HMS *Glasgow* I was hoping for a decent spell at HMS *Mercury* in an Instructional capacity and, to me, this did not seem an unreasonable expectation after spending a year abroad in a seagoing ship.

At the end of July I was beginning to feel secure when I went home for two weeks Summer Leave. During that fortnight Eileen and I were to travel to Ireland to attend the wedding of her brother Nick in Belfast. We were accompanied by Eileen's brother John who was back in England after a spell in Borneo with the RM Commando. Our trip was made possible by John's wife Margery, with her children, coming to stay at 261 Goring Way to look after Julia and Karen while the three of us headed out to Ireland.

The journey itself was memorable enough because it was so long and tiring; we travelled by train from London to the port of Heysham (just north of Blackpool) to catch the overnight ferry to Belfast. We were tired enough at this point – it was about ten p.m. when we boarded –

and it did not help that we had been unable to obtain sleeping cabins and therefore had to spend the night sitting in the lounge. Before the bar closed at 1 a.m. John and I had the good sense to lay in a few beers for the trip and spent the rest of the night talking and watching people being seasick (the Irish Sea is <u>always</u> rough, even in August). We arrived alongside in Belfast at 6.30 a.m. and were pleased to disembark and find Nick there to meet us with a car and we drove to the home of the bride where we were expected for breakfast.

Since returning from his training in South Africa Nick had been a pilot with Coastal Command, flying Shackletons out of Londonderry. One day, at a dance I believe, Nick met Marina who was then a young nurse and they have been together ever since.

When we arrived at Marina's home on that early morning in August 1955 we were not ready for a few surprises that awaited us. The Melvilles lived in a very nice bungalow in the Belfast suburb of Glengormley and it was here that we had a very warm welcome from all of Marina's family. Mr Melville was an ex-police sergeant, retired from the Royal Ulster Constabulary, and his wife was a very sweet and grandmotherly lady. Also there were Marina's brothers – I am not certain but I think there were seven of them. After the introductions we sat down to a huge table absolutely laden with breakfast foods but, because it was Friday and they were strong Catholics, there was no bacon or other meats and I recall having a delicious meal of salmon. While this was going on Mr Melville was circulating with a bottle of Scotch and pouring very generous helpings for those who would accept.

When we insisted that we could not eat or drink any more, we were led into the next room for a small concert – all the brothers had their own band with Marina as singer. When we had exhausted the repertoire, somebody suggested we should walk to the pub to sample a few glasses of 'porter' (the local brew which is rather like Guinness). Finally, some time in the afternoon, it was decided that we should head for our lodgings which were to be in a boarding house at Bangor, a delightful little seaside town at the mouth of Belfast Lough. Our landlady, Mrs Patterson, a widow, after a little initial confusion (she wanted to put Eileen and John together and me on my own) got us sorted. Because we were about twenty miles from Belfast, the Melvilles had very kindly loaned us the family car to use during our stay. One night, quite late, we were returning to Bangor along deserted streets when suddenly there were lights flashing ahead and we were surrounded by a squad of armed police. A huge sergeant came to the car and, as I opened the window, said very sternly 'Will you be coming quietly, or shall I send for the wagon?' – I guess the look on our faces just made his night because he just broke up laughing and, when we were on our way, I remember thinking, 'What a wicked sense of humour,' but I know we had many a good laugh about it later.

Anyway, the wedding was just perfect, the Nuptial Mass very impressive and a wonderful reception afterwards at Belfast Castle. It was a marvellous visit for the three of us but, nevertheless, we were happy to get home again to the children.

On completion of my leave in mid-August when I returned to HMS *Mercury* it came as a bit of a shock to learn that, one week later, I was to join HMS *Coquette*. Not only had I not been expecting such a move (to another seagoing ship) but it was also unusual to be given such short notice. In wartime, of course, it would have been perfectly normal but now that drafting had settled into a full peacetime routine it was a surprise to get 'a pierhead jump'. I started making a few discreet enquiries and soon learned (unofficially) that I was being sent to replace a Chief Yeoman whom the Captain of *Coquette* deemed 'unsuitable' and wanted replaced without delay. The next surprise came when I learned that the man I was being sent to relieve was none other than Bill Dickinson who had been Chief Yeoman of my watch for three years in Malta. This made me wonder what the future held for me.

During the week before I joined *Coquette* I also made every effort to discover all I could about the ship and the type of duties on which she would be employed. I found that *Coquette* was an Ocean Class minesweeper and was employed primarily in Northern waters on Fishery Protection Duties with a secondary role of minesweeping during any NATO exercises. She was the Flotilla Leader of eight similar ships which formed the 'Fifth Fishery Protection and Minesweeping Squadron' and was commanded by a 'four-ring Captain' (which entitled him to a Chief Yeoman)

with the abbreviated title of 'Capt FMS5'. The other ships of the Flotilla were commanded by a Lieutenant or Lieutenant Commander and carried a Leading Signalman. I soon realised that I knew little about Fishery Protection and nothing about minesweeping; the former did not bother me but I was very concerned about the latter as I felt that I must know not only the signals involved, but also the whole business of how it was done. I soon learned all about the signals relative to 'sweeping' by studying the appropriate publications but as regards the actual methods of minesweeping I could not find anybody in the Signal School to help me because none of them (like myself) had any practical experience of the job. Of course, we all knew that 'paravanes' were streamed and ultimately recovered but there was much more I felt I should know about the equipment and exactly how it was used. I later realised that it was not really surprising I could not enlist any help; minesweeping was a vital operation in wartime and there-fore minesweeping vessels were manned by wartime ('Hostilities Only') personnel.

On the morning of 22 August 1955 when I joined HMS *Coquette* I was very fortunate in one respect: she was in Portsmouth Dockyard on a rare visit to her 'home port' and this saved me a long journey to Scotland. My first impression when I saw her alongside the dockyard jetty was 'this is a small ship' – which, of course, was very true. A happy Bill Dickinson met me on the gangway and, after a lightning tour of the ship, grabbed his bag and departed on the same transport back to *Mercury*. He had not told me of any problems and I felt it best not to ask but when I reached the Chief's Mess I soon learned all the details of the friction. It appeared to have been a personality clash more than anything else, although I did hear the Captain had been rather upset when he found that his Chief Yeoman knew nothing about minesweeping. This con-firmed my feeling that I would not be similarly caught out and therefore, at the first opportunity, I sought out the Minesweeping Officer and told him that I wanted to know everything about 'sweeping'. Lieutenant Wemyss was a very pleasant man and was only too happy to teach me – he took me on the sweep deck, explained all the equip-ment and how it would be used and when we had finished I felt quite confident about handling any situation of 'sweeping'.

The following morning when I went to the Captain's cabin for the first time I was really wondering what to expect but the Captain greeted me very civilly, shook hands and welcomed me to *Coquette*. He did not mention my predecessor nor any problems in the past; neither did he comment on my own rather sudden appearance on board but I did have the feeling that he would be watching me pretty closely for a while and I had better watch my step.

Captain A. D. Robin RN was a tall, slim, distinguished looking gentleman, quietly spoken and somehow reminded me more of a headmaster than a senior officer. I soon discovered that, on the bridge, he was stern, meticulous about every detail and liked everything to run smoothly and quietly. I soon realised that this was the root cause of the trouble – he would (and obviously did) object strongly to Bill Dickinson's foul-smelling pipe (he was a non-smoker), his loud 'barrow-boy' voice and generally casual and laid-back attitude.

A couple of days later we sailed from Portsmouth and headed up Channel to the East Coast and then up to Scotland which was our regular operational base. Port Edgar was a small, purely naval, harbour on the Firth of Forth and was tucked under the southern end of the mighty Forth Bridge. It was the traditional base for mine-sweepers in the area and at that time was used solely by ships of our Squadron – not that any of us were allowed to spend much time there because we were usually away on patrol or on a visit to some northern port. Typically, we now had a brief spell for refuelling and replenishing and were then on our way to another Fishery Patrol – the first one for me – and this time to Iceland.

I soon learned that the Fishery Protection business was essential for our fishing Fleets but, for us, was mostly tedious work, broken occasionally by a spot of excitement and almost always carried out in foul weather because of the locations. Because, in those days, the ocean seemed to offer an unlimited supply of all kinds of fish (cod was favourite) our trawlers would fish wherever the fish were most plentiful, invariably in northern waters because the cod (and other types) were essentially 'cold water' fish. Therefore our patrol areas would stretch from the North of Norway to Greenland, and anywhere in between. Our job was to keep an eye on the British fishing trawlers and try to keep them out of trouble – or try to assist them if they were in trouble. The biggest problem was to prevent them from fishing inside territorial waters which they were often tempted to risk, in spite of the heavy penalties imposed by the courts in Iceland and Norway if they were caught. Of course, their excuse would always be that their navigation was faulty but, knowing they were very experienced seamen, we knew it to be a rather feeble defence. Iceland especially had a very vigilant and aggressive fishery patrol and we had our work cut out trying to prevent the arrest of our 'strays'.

We were not always popular with the trawlermen because, although we were there for their benefit, it was like seeing the local policeman whenever we appeared on the scene. At the same time, if they were in other sorts of difficulties they were very grateful for our assistance. For instance, trawlermen lived and worked in very dangerous conditions and it was all too easy to lose a couple of fingers, a hand or a foot in the constantly moving wires and winches on a wildly rolling deck. They were fortunate we carried a doctor and he was often called away to treat an injured man who might otherwise bleed to death. Likewise, an engine or equipment breakdown might require an engineer to be rowed through choppy seas to assist. The trawlers were not slow to show their gratitude for this kind of help and many times I saw our whaler return alongside just loaded to the gunwales with fresh fish.

A month later it was a change of scene when we were back in the North Sea and in command of the minesweeping force for a large NATO exercise to be carried out over a very wide area. Our part of the exercise involved day and night minesweeping operations and, when it was over and declared a success, I was very thankful for the effort I had made in acquiring some rapid knowledge of the subject.

On completion of the exercise programme the Fleet split up and proceeded to their various destinations – to make courtesy visits to ports of the participating nations. I think *Coquette* was lucky here because we drew Amsterdam which I found to be a beautiful and endlessly interesting city because there was so much to see and do there, but mostly because the people were so friendly and welcoming. I really remember one day when I was sitting in a dockside bar with a couple of friends and just sampling the local brew – the radio was blaring and Englebert Humperdink was singing the latest hit which was *Unchained Melody*.

This was only the first of many such visits to unusual ports – places which vessels on normal naval duties would never see – and this was one of the features that made my time in *Coquette* so interesting and enjoyable. Interspersed with our fishery patrols were visits to Norwegian ports – Stavanger, Tromsø and Narvik where we watched incredibly fast cross country ski-ing, to Reykjavik in Iceland, Copenhagen in Denmark and, to the north of Scotland, the remote Faeroe Islands (part of Denmark). The population there seemed to be part Viking and part Celtic, which made them a very sturdy and independent people. Also to Kirkwall in the Orkney Islands and many more visits to the more traditional ports further south such as Aberdeen and Dundee, Inverness, Leith (the port of Edinburgh), and down to the Humber where we visited Hull and Grimsby and further south again to Great Yarmouth and Lowestoft.

During the summer of 1956 we put into Hull for a weekend visit (I think it was Friday to Monday night) and because leave was granted for a 'short weekend' (i.e. from noon Saturday till 0800 Monday) I thought I would take

5th Fishery Protection and Minesweeping Squadron on manoeuvres, Scotland 1956.

advantage of this to pay a visit to Nick and Marina. They had now moved from Ireland and Nick was piloting Lancasters from a base in Lincolnshire and they were living in a village called Tealby. Before setting out I could not find Tealby on my map but I knew it was near the town of Market Rasen and thought that, if I could get that far, it should not be too difficult to find. I set out with two friends who were also making for Market Rasen and we got the ferry across the Humber to Grimsby and managed to catch a bus for somewhere in the right direction but eventually we had to get off and then were lucky enough to hitch a ride with a couple of salesmen who were going to Market Rasen. From there I managed to get a local bus that would be going through Tealby but when we got there it was dark and it took me a while to find their cottage. They had recently had their firstborn, Christopher, and Marina was bathing him when I knocked on the door. Of course, they had no idea I was coming to see them but, nevertheless, made me very welcome and we enjoyed a lovely weekend together

On the Sunday morning we went to Mass in the church which was right next door and, later in the day, Nick phoned Grimsby to confirm the time of the last ferry that night, reputedly at 10 p.m. After driving me to the ferry terminal it was a shock for all of us to find that (being Sunday) there was no 10 p.m. ferry! There was no alternative for me but to wait for the first one in the morning at 6 a.m. but here I was lucky – there was also an end-of-the-line rail station there and the sole railwayman on duty took pity on me and let me sleep in a train compartment, promising not to let me oversleep. He even woke me with a cup of tea at 5.45 – good man!

During my summer leave of 1956 I went on another trip to Tealby because Nick and Marina wanted to see Eileen and the girls and so they invited us to stay with them for a few days. This time I drove our car from Worthing and it was a very successful trip and I found them again without any difficulty. While we were there Nick asked me if I would be interested in going up in his plane, if it could be arranged, and, of course, I jumped at the chance. The problem was that it was not legal to take passengers so it had to be arranged 'unofficially'. At six a.m. one morning I had to be at a certain spot on the perimeter fence and, when Nick taxied this monster plane over to the fence, I had to crawl under and then be hauled on board by his crew. The event was a day's low level navigation exercise and, because we were in sight of the ground, it was very interesting as we did a complete circuit of England. What really put me off that type of flying though was the incredible amount of noise and vibration – not to mention the lack of passenger comforts in a Lancaster!

Over on the west coast *Coquette* also visited Fleetwood which is close to famous Blackpool. All of these ports were very intensive fishery centres and the visits were designed not so much for our recreation, as for forging a close liaison with the local fishing industry. Also, whilst on the West Coast of Britain we were fortunate enough to visit the city of Dublin, capital of the Republic of Ireland and situated on the River Liffey.

I well remember, during our visit to Copenhagen, which was in October 1955, a very important date occurred in the naval calendar – possibly the most important – the 21 October which was the anniversary of the Battle of Trafalgar when Admiral Lord Nelson had beaten the combined French and Spanish Fleets at the Battle of Cape Trafalgar in 1805. Every year on this date, the Navy celebrated the occasion in very traditional fashion i.e. ships were 'dressed overall' and the order was given to 'splice the mainbrace'. Of course, the latter had nothing to do with a rope's end – it meant a double issue of rum to all those so entitled. Previous to the day, Captain Robin realised that, even though this would be the 150th anniversary of the battle, it might possibly cause some embarrassment to our Danish hosts if *Coquette* were to 'dress ship overall' in view of the fact that Nelson had also, in the Napoleonic Wars, beaten the Danes in the famous Battle of Copenhagen. It seemed that a decision could not be reached locally and so the matter was referred to the Admiralty for an answer. Well, we were kept in suspense until half an hour before 'Colours' on the 21st – the answer was 'go ahead' and, thankfully, we never heard a murmur after that.

In between these visits our patrols were long and sometimes arduous, particularly during the winter months when the weather in the Arctic could be really miserable and a lot of time was spent chipping ice off the superstructure because, if this were not done, it could cause a vessel to capsize due to excessive top weight. On these trips catering would become a problem because, a few days out, the fresh meat, bread and vegetables were exhausted and it was back to canned goods unless we were lucky with a boatload of fresh fish from one of the trawlers.

During these first few months I had come close to liking Captain Robin although our relationship was always on a formal footing. I had found him to be fair and pleasant and, without a doubt, a good Captain for the ship although, I must admit, he was rather distant with the ship's company. Early in the New Year of 1956 he was to leave *Coquette* to take up an appointment at the Admiralty and was to be relieved by Captain E. A. S. Baillie. Captain Baillie was a very different kettle of fish and he soon made his mark on the ship and her company. He was a bluff, cheerful and outgoing sort of man, very keen on all sports but above all an excellent ship handler because he had been a captain in destroyers. A typical example of this was on our visit to Dublin where the berth we had been allocated was not the easiest to get into, being inside a basin and involving a 180 degree turn. Captain Baillie decided to demonstrate how it should be done. After a careful study of the charts, he made a rather showy entrance and eased the ship alongside without any assistance from the tugs who were standing by. He and I soon struck up a good relationship and I never looked back from then on. I remember, shortly after he joined *Coquette* and was inspecting Sunday Divisions on the jetty, he stopped in front of me and, with a smile on his face, said, 'Chief Yeoman, you are the only man in the ship who wears more medals than me.'

I found Captain Baillie to be remarkable, not only for his capabilities in ship handling, but also in his willingness to share his expertise with anyone who was interested. For instance, when I was at *Mercury* prior to joining *Coquette* I had sat (and passed) the Navy's 'Higher Educational Test' which would have qualified me for promotion to commissioned rank – it was simply a challenge and I thought it would be nice to have the certificate in my file. When Captain Baillie became aware of this (and that one of my subjects had been Navigation) he arranged for me to keep watches as '2nd Officer of the Watch' (with Lieutenant Wemyss) so that I could obtain practical experience in the subject. Also, on quiet days, he would organise 'ship handling competitions' involving myself, the Coxswain, the Chief Stoker and a couple of junior officers. This meant that each of us in turn would have control of the ship when the alarm would be given 'Man Overboard' and a lifebuoy dropped to represent the man. It was then our job to manoeuvre so as to pick up the man in the fastest possible time. At first it was a bit scary to be in total control of a seagoing ship but, after a while, it got to be a lot of fun. There were four obvious choices: (a) put the helm hard over, maintain speed and allow the ship to complete a circle back to the lifebuoy; (b) stop engines and then reverse engines and go astern to the lifebuoy; (c) put the helm over and stop one engine; or (d) to reduce speed on the inboard engine with the helm hard over. I favoured the last one and did quite well with it – but it was a bit scary with the Captain holding a stopwatch.

In the Fall of 1956, when the Squadron assembled at Invergordon for the Annual Regatta and Sports, following an intensive exercise programme, *Coquette*'s crew were feeling very confident – something that had never happened before because *Coquette* had usually finished somewhere near the bottom. Suddenly there was a spirit of competition in our ship and everyone wanted to do their best. I was the stroke oar for the Chief & POs' racing whaler and was also on the tennis and field hockey teams plus dinghy sailing. Well, thanks to a lot of practice, we managed to win the Chief & POs' whaler race and, best of all, *Coquette* won the Squadron Trophy.

In the spring of 1956 we paid another visit to Amsterdam and, after securing, the Captain sent for me and told me that his wife was also to be in Amsterdam during our visit. He then surprised me by saying that, owing to official business the next day, he would be unable to accompany his wife and asked me to act as her escort and guide for the day. Mrs Baillie proved to be a charming lady and I know we both had a very pleasant day. In the morning we went out to the tulip fields which are an amazing sight – like a quilt of many colours for as far as the eye can see. We also attended a tulip auction where the growers would sell their product. After lunch we toured the city, both by bus and also on the excellent tourist boats on the canals which run all through the city.

The Chief's Mess, like everything else in *Coquette*, was small but this was not a problem because there were only six of us and, because of that, we came to know each other pretty well. For instance, the Coxswain, who was the senior man on the lower deck, was a good friend of mine and because of his age (about ten years older than me) was generally known as 'Dad'. He was also very serious and conscientious and, probably as a result of that, I could not resist playing the odd practical joke on him. At one time, we had returned to port somewhere after a long spell at sea and were all enjoying the luxury of fresh foods again. The Cox'n was the Mess Caterer that week (we took turns at it) and we all appreciated a nice salad for supper. After the third night of salad though I thought we needed a change – so I made five sets of rabbits' ears out of cardboard and string and when we all trooped in, wearing our rabbits' ears we all enjoyed a good laugh. All except the Cox'n – I thought he was going to have a fit because he did not think it was funny and his reaction was a threat to resign as Caterer! Well, we did calm him down and even got a smile later on but he still would not admit it was just fun and well meant. The second occasion was a discussion about the ship's future movements. When I came into the Mess one day the Cox'n was telling the others that *Coquette* was going to be returning to Portsmouth in the near future – a 'buzz' that I knew to be wrong because I had just handled a Confidential signal ordering us elsewhere. Of course, I could not even whisper this in the Mess but the Cox'n was so sure he was right that he rather rashly bet me his tot next day and naturally I accepted the challenge. Next morning, our movements were officially announced and, of course, he was proved to be wrong but, even so, I would never have taken all his rum – especially as I had an unfair advantage, but I could not resist teasing him. I warned the other mess members what I was up to and so they were all there to witness the action.

I made sure I was in the Mess early and drew my own tot which I set aside, out of sight. When the Cox'n arrived for his rum I said, 'You owe that to me,' and he did hand it to me, thinking I would only take a sip – which would be the gentlemanly thing to do – but I said, 'Cheers,' and downed the whole lot. Well, he was shocked and amazed that I would do such a thing so, when I thought he had suffered enough, I produced my own tot and gave it to him. Of course, the rest of the mess were having a good laugh by now but it was quite a while before the Cox'n forgave me for that little episode. My other special friend in the *Coquette* was the Chief Stoker – he was a typical farm man from Hampshire, slow moving and soft spoken with a strong Pompey accent, who was very efficient and had been in *Coquette* for a couple of years. On Sunday mornings when we were in Port Edgar he and I used to go for long walks along the foreshore, discussing everything under the sun.

Towards the end of my spell in *Coquette* I was home on leave and rather surprised Eileen by taking her to the drapery department of Bentall's in Worthing where I purchased some yellow and some blue material and, after returning to the ship, amused myself by using the sewing machine to make up three miniature flags – replicas of the Fishery Protection Flag which was flown continuously at our masthead. One of these I presented to the Captain, one to the Signal Officer and the third is on the wall in the den.

During the summer of 1956 I was involved in an event which could have changed the rest of my life. An Admiralty Fleet Order was received concerning the brand new Royal Yacht *Britannia* which was now fitting out in Portsmouth and would soon be commissioned. The order called for volunteers, from all ranks, to form the new ship's company. Although the Royal Yacht is part of the Royal Navy and flies the White Ensign, men accepted for the Royal Yacht Service (known in the Navy as 'yachties') are subject to a few slightly different conditions. First, they are paid a special allowance, minimal and not a factor to be considered. Secondly, once accepted they will serve the remainder of their service in the Navy on the Royal Yacht – which sounds attractive at first but will mean frequent, and often long, absences from home on foreign cruises and royal visits abroad. Anyway, I lost no time in applying to serve as the Chief Yeoman in *Britannia*. Captain Baillie forwarded it with what I heard described as a 'glowing recommendation'. Shortly afterwards *Coquette* was on a rare visit to Portsmouth for a short refit and Summer Leave when I was told that I was on the short list for the Royal Yacht and, at 0900 the following morning I (and two other Chief Yeomen) were to report on board the *Britannia* to face the interview board for the final selection. The Board consisted of two Admirals and a Commodore and they asked endless questions until I felt they must have my complete history (both Naval and personal) at their fingertips. A few days later when I heard the result I was very disappointed because I had not been selected – but it was some consolation that the post had gone to an old friend of mine – Bill Giddings from *Glasgow*.

About the middle of September 1956 when on one of our Northern Patrols we received a signal stating that, on our return to Port Edgar, I was to be discharged back to the Signal School at Leydene.

So, on 22 September 1956 (just thirteen months to the day) I was to leave *Coquette* – also on the same day, quite by coincidence, that my friend Dick Barton (the Chief Stoker) was also to return to Portsmouth for 'discharge to pension' having completed his twenty-two years service. On the day, Dick and I left the Mess, having sampled a couple of rums, to make our way to the gangway where we had left our bags. Little did we know that the rest of the crew had decided to give the two of us a right royal send-off. The ship was tied up at the end of a long wooden jetty and running the length of it was a single-gauge railway – used for transporting mines during the war, using a four-wheel flatbed railway truck. When we reached the gangway we could see our kit was already on this truck and then, the next thing we knew, we had both been hoisted off our feet and were being carried down the gangway. When we reached the jetty they laid us on top of our kit, flat on our backs, and then raced the truck along the tracks all the way to the end and, while all this was happening, the entire ship's company (officers and men) were lining the rails and cheering us on. Not a very dignified send-off but one that I shall always remember and appreciate.

A much wiser man than I, when writing about warships, said:

> sailors have always been prone to claim that different ships have different characters. Happy ships, where the line between wardroom and messdeck is flexible, ready to adapt, and others where the opposite is equally obvious. Men under punishment, with lists of defaulters as further proof of the discontent which can harm any ship.

On the eve of my departure, pacing the upper deck alone, late at night, and just reminiscing, I knew that *Coquette* was a happy ship and that, as far as I was concerned, she had lived up to her name – I loved that ship!

CHAPTER TWENTY-SIX

Hong Kong

THE TWO AND A HALF YEARS that we spent living in Hong Kong were, understandably, the most interesting and exciting period of my life and I am sure the same can be said for Eileen, Julia and Karen. Hong Kong was and, I am sure, still is one of the most exciting and fascinating destinations in the world and I would love to return there today to see all the changes that have occurred in the past forty years.

However, I think it is rather interesting to look now at how we came to finish up there – because we almost went somewhere quite different.

Upon returning to the Signal School after leaving HMS *Coquette* in late September 1956 it was only a few short months before I heard that I was to be on the move again. I think it was some time in February 1957 when I was told, quite out of the blue, that I was being drafted to take charge of the Main Signal Office at the naval base of Trincomalee in Ceylon. This, of course, was before Ceylon gained independence and became Sri Lanka and the Tamils there disrupted life with an ongoing civil war. This move came as a complete surprise for me but not an unpleasant one because, being an overseas shore base, it meant that it was an 'accompanied' posting and I would be able to have Eileen join me there. Having spent a considerable chunk of time there during the war, I was not especially thrilled with the place but it was, after all, an exotic location and I knew Eileen and I (plus Julia and Karen of course) would make the best of it and enjoy ourselves out there.

Trincomalee was at the northern end of the island and consisted of a huge natural harbour which made it ideal for a naval base. When I had been there during the war, the naval base installations consisted of a few wooden huts and it was very much in its infancy.

I could not wait to get home to break the news to Eileen so I telephoned her from Leydene and, before telling her anything else, I asked, 'How would you like to have elephants at the bottom of your garden?' At first she thought I had completely flipped but, when I explained, she was equally excited and wanted to know everything.

At this stage I knew when I would be travelling (by troopship) and I also knew the name of the Chief Yeoman whom I would be replacing so I wrote a long airmail letter to him asking him to let me have everything about the place such as accommodation for our family, schools, shopping, etc. Whilst waiting for a reply, I decided that we should proceed with all the arrangements at our end so that when I departed Eileen and the girls would be more or less ready to follow me.

From our experience in Malta we knew that a family would not be allowed to leave England for an overseas station until such time as suitable accommodation had been arranged for them at their destination. So we went ahead and Eileen and the girls had medical examinations and all the necessary inoculations; I was surprised to find that we needed one for yellow fever and, for this, had to attend a special clinic in Portsmouth. There was the problem of what to do with our bungalow (after our previous experience of the policeman/tenant we were a bit wary of letting again) but we were very fortunate here – a couple we knew were returning from Ghana and were only too happy to take possession and rent from us while we were away. There was also the question of what to do with our beloved Morris Minor and, of course, the obvious answer was that we should sell it.

This was quite a busy time for us and we were pleased with the progress we were making until one day when the balloon went up – we got a reply from my man in Trincomalee which was a real shock. The Chief I was supposed to relieve out there was flabbergasted when he got my letter because he had his family out there with him and was not due to return to England for another year! This was terribly disappointing for us, especially as we had done so much preparation already, but it was obvious now that my draft to Trincomalee would have to be cancelled.

The rules for overseas service then were eighteen months for a man on his own and two and a half years for one who was accompanied by his family. It was obvious that whoever was responsible in the Drafting Office had goofed rather badly, but that was not much consolation to me and I was determined to find out more about the situation. I knew the problem was not at *Mercury* (they merely acted on instructions issued by the Drafting Office). The Drafting Office was 'an ivory tower' located at Haslemere in Surrey where civil servants and Secretariat Branch people issued movement instructions for everyone in the Navy. For obvious reasons it was strictly 'out of bounds', both for visiting and even telephoning. However, I went to see the Divisional Officer at *Mercury* and told him a very sad story – how we had rented out our house and sold our car (both of these were <u>almost</u> true) and that my family was all packed and ready to leave. Well, he was very sympathetic and did make a couple of phone calls and then told me that 'the drafting people were very sorry for the mistake and that I was now at the top of the list for the next accompanied draft, wherever that might be.' Well, that was encouraging but it was also a bit nerve-racking not to know where it might be or when – and so I started to make a nuisance of myself by bugging the Divisional Officer every day for information. Finally he said, 'Go ahead and phone them yourself – but I don't know anything about it!' It did not take me long to find the right person at 'Drafting' – he was a Chief Writer and seemed quite understanding so I did not give him a hard time – I just kept in touch with him by phone until eventually he was able to tell me that I was now going to Hong Kong.

So now the cycle started all over again – making preparations for the move and, of course, I wrote to the Chief Yeoman in Hong Kong – and then held our collective breaths until I got a reply.

This time there were no apparent snags and he was very co-operative, giving me all the information he could. With several weeks still to go before my ship sailed I began toying with the possibility of getting Eileen and the girls to accompany me on the voyage. When I broached the subject with the Divisional Officer at *Mercury* he did not argue – he just told me that he did not see how I could get round the 'suitable accommodation' clause, but otherwise, why not? Although my opposite number in Hong Kong was very helpful and co-operative I obviously could not ask him to rent a flat for me and also get it approved by the local Naval Welfare people. Nor was there any chance of 'official' accommodation because, although there were some Naval Married Quarters in Hong Kong, there was a fifteen month waiting list for them. Finally, I knew that I could not look for any assistance from any naval authorities – the Admiralty policy was that, having allowed the option of taking one's family, it was up to the man to do all the legwork. It was here that I envied the Army and Air Force where transport, housing and everything else were laid on for them.

I managed to overcome these obstacles by getting my friend in Hong Kong to make reservations for the four of us at a small but respectable hotel which he knew was already on the approved list locally. Armed with this written confirmation I once more attacked the Naval Drafting Office with a request for them to arrange passage for my family in the same ship as myself. At first they tried to put me off by saying that the ship was now fully booked, but finally, my persistence and powers of persuasion won out and, wonder of wonders, I eventually had in my hands written orders for myself and my family to embark in the Troopship *Nevassa*, sailing from Southampton on 12 May 1957 and bound for Hong Kong.

Finally, all the last minute arrangements had been taken care of and the big day arrived; we all trooped down to Worthing Central Station where we were to catch the 10 a.m. express to Southampton Docks (because it was an express it would not stop at West Worthing). I know there were a few tears shed on each side but it was not until very much later that I realised what a very sad day it was for my mother, to be watching her eldest son and his family leaving for the other side of the world and knowing that in two short months, Jack and Vivien and their two boys would also be leaving for Canada. June, of course, had married Harold in 1951 (while we were living in Malta) and they had set up home (and a business) in Horsham which, although only 22 miles distant, was a long way for someone without transport. June was very good though and used to come to Worthing every week to visit my mother. Neither, on that day of departure, did I think that I might not see my mother again.

By noon that day we had arrived at Southampton Docks and were admiring the beautiful ship that was to be our home for the next six weeks. TS *Nevassa*, with her gleaming white hull with the broad blue band denoting a troopship, was a very impressive sight and, of course, I could not help comparing her in my mind with the old *Dilwara* which had taken me to Hong Kong to join the *Eagle* in 1939.

Nevassa was a new ship, purpose-built for trooping, and had very sleek and elegant lines. She was about 25,000 tons and, outwardly at least, could have passed for a cruise ship – in fact she was quite similar to the *Loveboat* and other Princess cruise liners of that era, before the greed of shipowners turned cruise ships into those floating monstrosities – ugly, top heavy and looking more like a downtown office block than a vessel of beauty.

The scene on the dock alongside the ship would, to a civilian eye, appear to be chaotic – with mountains of Army equipment and baggage, squads of soldiers stamping about and everybody seeming to be shouting instructions. We managed to ignore all this activity and made our way up the gangway and were eventually shown to our cabins, and here we had a nice surprise – we had been upgraded to first class cabin accommodation. We did not waste much time down below but, after a quick freshen up, went on deck to watch all the activity as it came close to sailing time. A couple of hours after our arrival at the docks all the bodies and baggage had been swallowed up by the ship and their place on the dock had been taken by an Army Band, in full dress uniform, who were playing all the old nostalgic tunes (like *Goodbye Dolly Grey*) to cheer us on our way. There was also a crowd of friends and relatives on the dock, very busy waving (and using) their handkerchiefs. As we leaned over the rail we watched the lines holding us to England being let go and then we were moving, guided by tugs, out into the Solent and, in the beautiful sunshine, we slipped past the Isle of Wight and headed down the Channel.

The next morning all the naval personnel were assembled for a meeting to discuss and allocate duties during our voyage. The Officer in Charge of the naval draft was going to Hong Kong to become the Staff Communications Officer and, as such, would be my boss there. He was Lieutenant Commander Atkinson and we got on well all during our association. It was a small naval group (probably about twenty-five including six Chiefs & POs) so everything was pretty informal for us. A very high percentage of the passengers were Army (as was normal) and most of these were a regiment of Gurkhas going to relieve the garrison in Hong Kong. It was here that Lieut Comdr Atkinson told me that my main duty during the voyage would be 'to look after' the dozen or so naval wives going out to join their husbands. When I asked exactly what was involved he told me to visit them all to make sure they had no problems or complaints and, should anyone be short of money, I would arrange with him for an advance. This all sounded very simple and attractive and was certainly the easiest duty I had ever been detailed for. That is until I started visiting their cabins and then I found that, instead of being their friend as I thought, I was their enemy. I found that I was about as popular as a pork chop in a synagogue and it did not take long to find out why – they were all very anti Bob Adams 'because he had his family on the ship with him and they didn't!' They were led by Peggy Kesterton (wife of a Chief ERA who was already in Hong Kong) and were all quite vociferous on the subject. After I had managed to explain all the details of my particular situation, they did calm down a bit but I don't think they ever really forgave me for having the nerve to bring my family with me!

Our accommodation in *Nevassa* proved to be very comfortable even though we could not all be in the same cabin – Eileen and the girls were in a three-berth outside cabin and I was next door, sharing a two-berth with an Army WOII and, next to that (all in the same passageway) were his wife and two boys. Bill and Joyce Webb were a very nice couple, from London and naturally we got to know them very well and we continued to see a lot of them while we were all in Hong Kong. Now, forty years later, we still keep in touch with Joyce who now lives in a retirement village at Kingston-upon-Thames. Bill, after retiring from the Army, worked at Selfridges in London as a maintenance engineer but, shortly after they had bought a retirement villa in Spain, he had a heart attack and died.

When we checked out the rest of *Nevassa* we were very impressed with what we found. The second class dining room where we were to eat was huge and beautifully kept – there was a large and comfortable lounge and bar for Senior NCOs – there was a school where the girls would attend every morning – a library and, of course, the upper deck was well equipped with deckchairs for lounging and sunbathing. There was also a swimming pool but, because it was below decks, not too many people used it.

The *Nevassa* was owned and operated (on behalf of the War Office) by the British India Steam Navigation Company who had been carrying British troops backwards and forwards for the past hundred years or more. The crew, typically, were British officers with a Lascar crew and the stewards and waiters were Indians from Bengal and they were working on a strange roster system. Because employment was scarce at home and because 'trooping' with BISN was a good and well paid job for them, they would only be employed for one year and then return home to allow somebody else from their province to take over the job. They were hard working, polite and pleasant and I know we all got quite attached to our table waiter whom we overworked shamelessly because the food was so good; there were multiple choices on the menu and the only limit was on the amount one person could eat.

At that time the Suez Canal was still blocked with wreckage from the Suez War and was unusable for passage so we were obliged to go round the Cape of Good Hope which would add an extra week to our voyage – but I never heard of anybody complaining!

Our first port of call was at Freetown, Sierra Leone on the west coast of Africa and here we were allowed ashore to stretch our legs for a couple of hours. I remember it as being a very dusty and dirty place and very 'African' – not too exciting. From there we sailed on down the west coast until we reached the Cape but, to our dismay by-passed Cape Town (we did get a glimpse of Table Mountain) and then turned up the east coast of Africa until we reached the lovely city of Durban where we were to spend a couple of days. I remember we spent a wonderful day ashore with Bill Webb and his family, who particularly enjoyed the rickshaw ride, pulled by a huge Zulu. Just this year we received from Joyce Webb the photograph, taken by Bill, of Joyce and Eileen in the rickshaw.

From Durban we headed out across the Indian Ocean and, by-passing Ceylon, had our next stop at the huge commercial docks of Singapore. Here we enjoyed another day ashore – first, swimming in the huge pool at The Britannia Club (built for servicemen since the war) and then we took the girls to visit the famous Tiger Balm Gardens. When we sailed from Singapore it was only a few more days up to Hong Kong where we arrived towards the end of June, six weeks after leaving Southampton. It had been a wonderful passage and a voyage we all remember to this day.

As we entered harbour and secured alongside at the P&O pier in Kowloon it was all very familiar to me but, at the same time, I was realising that this was going to be very different for me. I would be living and working ashore and, being responsible for a family, I would have to cope with all the unknown problems of our living together in Hong Kong.

After disembarking from the *Nevassa* I got a taxi to take us and our bags to the Ritz Hotel on Austin Road in Kowloon where reservations had been made for us. The Ritz was not as pretentious as its name suggested but it was located in a very respectable residential area and, although quite small, it was clean and comfortable and we were very pleased to settle there, even on a temporary basis. I remember we enjoyed our supper there in the hotel's very pleasant restaurant and then, after getting the girls settled for the night, decided to call it a day ourselves; I had an early start next morning and we were both a bit

Eileen and Joyce Webb in a Zulu rickshaw, Durban, 1957.

weary after an exciting day. Being late June the Hong Kong weather was quite hot and humid and the Ritz Hotel, like most buildings at that time, did not boast air conditioning so, when we went to bed, we opened wide the window and the drapes in our room which, we had already established, looked out on an alley and a blank building opposite and everything was in complete darkness. In spite of the temperature we slept soundly and when I next opened my eyes it was broad daylight and, to my horror, saw a Chinese gentleman in the building exactly opposite our open window – he was quite motionless and without expression but was staring in fascination at Eileen and me lying on our bed without a stitch on!

CHAPTER TWENTY-SEVEN

HMS *Tamar*

AFTER BREAKFAST THAT MORNING I caught a bus (red double-decker) on Nathan Road to get to the Star Ferry Terminal in Kowloon where I had to get the 8 a.m. liberty-boat for Chief & POs which would take me across to Hong Kong Island where I was to report for duty to HMS *Tamar*.

The Naval Base at Hong Kong in those days was, like the Colony itself, in three parts. *Tamar* was the Naval Barracks, located right on the harbour and close to downtown Victoria, and just along the road was the Naval Dockyard with its huge dry dock which was capable of holding a heavy cruiser. The third section (and a fairly new edition) was the Naval Headquarters Building, which was where I would be working and, like many buildings on the island, was cut into the side of the steep hill and about a third of the way up. Victoria Peak rose very sharply up from the harbour, reaching a height of 1,800 feet. The best way to reach the Peak was by the Peak Tram (a funicular rail car) which ran straight up from the base in Victoria. There was also a road to the top but, because of its zig-zag route, it was much slower

Tamar was a very pleasant environment, considering it was a barracks. The buildings, mostly two-storey, were typical colonial, painted white, with long, arched colonnades to keep them cool and lots of overhead fans. The Chief Petty Officers' Mess was large and comfortable and, on a hot day, the ice-cold Carlsberg was always welcome. *Tamar* was mostly run by what the Navy termed 'Locally Entered Personnel' (LEP's).

All the domestic duties such as cooks, stewards, messboys, boat's crews and drivers were local Chinese, entered in the Navy under special conditions but wearing a uniform and subject to Naval Rules & Regulations. After completing my 'joining routine' in *Tamar* I was to proceed to the Headquarters and I found that, for Chief & POs, we were provided with an Econoline van and driver to get us there and back. It seemed that we always managed to get the 'other ratings' watch keepers in the van – it was a bit hot for walking. Our driver was a young Chinese called Wing Tak. Unlike most he was very self-confident, spoke excellent English and, unless he was restrained, drove like a maniac!

The Headquarters Building was quite spacious and airy and a very pleasant place to work. It was the Headquarters of 'Commodore Hong Kong' and his Staff who were responsible for the operation and administration of all Naval interests in the Colony. 'Com. HK' was Commodore Gregory who was a very pleasant, approachable and efficient man to work for and I could not find fault with any of his Staff Officers either. My boss, the Staff Communications Officer, of course, was Lieutenant Commander Atkinson who had travelled out with me on the *Nevassa* and his Assistant SCO was Lieutenant Frank Denny.

The Communications Department was located on the top floor of the building and I found that I was to be one of two Chief Yeomen – one was in charge of the Main Signal Office and my job was in charge of the Cryptographic Department. This suited me fine – it was a very interesting and responsible position and I knew that I would enjoy the work.

Having established myself in my Naval environment, I then turned my attention to finding a place to live. Like Malta, accommodation here in Hong Kong was in short supply, although for a different reason – there was no war damage here but just a huge, and rapidly growing, population. One of the attractions of Hong Kong is that it is a very cosmopolitan community where almost every nation is represented but it soon became obvious that there were five different levels, or categories, of population here. First came the very rich Chinese (and there seemed to be quite a lot of them) who lived in mansions on the top of the Peak and travelled around in chauffeur-driven Rolls or Mercedes. There could also be included in this category a handful of particularly affluent British such as bank presidents and top colonial service people. The next echelon was the balance of the British community, which could very generally be classed as supervisors, who lived in houses or apartments only halfway up the Peak, on places like Garden Road. After these there was a very strong contingent of Portuguese who had settled in Hong Kong very long ago – probably an overflow from the Portuguese island colony of Macau which was near. Next was a large Indian community who were mostly shopkeepers and also a lot of Sikhs, tall and dignified with a turban and a beard, they were unmistakeable. In pre-war days they had formed the Hong Kong Police Force but were now relegated to bank guards; they would sit at the door of the bank with a large shotgun across their knee – and I don't remember anyone challenging them! Finally the Chinese themselves who, naturally, formed the bulk of the population and here again there were several subdivisions. There was an army of bank tellers, office workers, shop assistants and the like. There were thousands of bus drivers, taxi drivers, lorry drivers and such. Construction was a thriving industry (both roads and buildings) and employed thousands of workers. Being an island, the ocean was also a major fact of life – there were huge junks everywhere, either fishing or trading up and down the coast, there were hundreds of smaller sampans where the owners scratched a living anyway they could – they were born, lived and died on their boats and a thirty-foot sampan would accommodate a family of five or six people. Last in the pecking order came the 'shanty people' who lived in shacks of cardboard, tin, tar-paper or anything else available. These homes were 'stuck' onto the hillside in a shantytown above Causeway Bay where it was considered too steep for any regular building. There were continual tragedies here – in the monsoon season huts would be swept away by the downpour of rain and, when the cooler weather came, there would be outbreaks of fire as they tried to warm their homes with an open fire.

It was typical of Hong Kong that there were such tremendous extremes of living conditions and cultures in the Colony. Many districts were so civilised and really attractive but it was not long before one was driving through just the opposite – a slum area where life was almost impossible – but the Chinese still thrived on it.

After unsuccessfully responding to newspaper advertisements for apartments – there were very few and these, upon inspection, always proved to be below standard, I also asked about vacancies from everyone I met – and then heard of one from our friend Peggy Kesterton (yes, we did become friends). She and her husband Len were living in an apartment complex in a quite respectable part of Kowloon and invited us to come and see. It consisted of three two-story buildings with six apartments each and they were all rented to British servicemen and their families. The rent sounded reasonable and I think they were partly furnished. The Chinese landlady was very pleasant and I think she finally approved us because she offered to rent an apartment to us should we be interested. We did not jump at it though because, in spite of the obvious advantages, Eileen and I had reservations about it – it seemed to us rather like living in a holiday camp with everyone in close proximity and not a great deal of privacy. Anyway, the following day while we were still considering the matter, I happened to be talking to a man at work and telling him our problem. He was a civil servant who worked as assistant to the Staff Officer (Intelligence) and he and his wife were very English – they played bowls at the Kowloon Bowling Club and cultivated pretty window boxes on their balcony. He suggested there might be a vacancy coming up in the building where he lived and then very kindly invited Eileen and me there for a cup of tea – partly for us to see the accommodation and partly, I suspect, to see if we were suitable. It was a very smart building, four stories high, and only two hundred yards from the Ritz Hotel. But the biggest bonus was that all the apartments overlooked the beautiful greens of the Kowloon Cricket Club and Kowloon Bowling Club. Of course, we both fell in love with it and knew we could not be happier anywhere else.

The apartment in question ('our apartment' as we were already thinking) was on the second floor (or first-floor if you are English) and was currently occupied by an Army Medical Officer and his family who were due to return home. I went to see him first and discussed the situation – he was happy for me to take over the apartment and even more delighted when I agreed to buy the furniture which he would have to get rid of. Of course, I still had to meet the landlady and get her approval and so I arranged an appointment one evening with Miss Chan and I remember it was a very long interview which took place in the ground floor apartment (i.e. below 'ours'). Miss Chan (probably in her forties) was a very glamorous and exotic Chinese matron (it was not until much later that I realised that 'madam' would be more appropriate). I don't know what she was thinking but I know she asked a lot of questions and finally said 'she would think about it' and

I had to meet her a second time before she finally agreed to rent the apartment. We soon moved in and were extremely happy with our find – so much so that, a year later, when we were offered an official Married Quarter we decided to turn it down in favour of staying where we were on Austin Road. One odd thing was that we were the only Naval family in the whole block – all the remaining units were occupied by British civilians who were either Dockyard employees or civil servants; we must have passed their selection criteria, although we did not realise it at the time. The only exception to the tenant situation was that the ground floor apartment immediately below us was occupied by two very attractive young Chinese females – we did not think anything of this at first but, as time passed, we learned a bit more about their lifestyle.

Having established our home, my next priority was to get an 'Amah' – a female Chinese servant who would live-in and do all the housework and cooking. To do this I had to visit 'The Naval Families Office' in *Tamar* one morning when all these Chinese females were paraded before me and I had to select one to come and live with us.

This was, I found, a difficult choice to make, even with the benefit of their employment record and references which were available to me. The routine was that the Admiralty provided an amah to all naval families and paid them a fixed wage (I think it was $75 HK per month) but if the husband was prepared to add to that figure, out of his own pay, then he would get a more qualified or experienced amah who did not want to work for the flat rate. Anyway, I think I finished up adding fifty dollars (HK) and brought home a young and attractive Chinese girl called Elaine. I think she was seventeen at the time and I chose her because she had been educated and could speak pretty good English and, although not very experienced, I felt we could teach her our ways of doing things.

Quite rapidly our life in Hong Kong settled into a pattern – and a very easy-going and pleasant pattern it was. I was very happy in my work and the hours were very good – I would catch the 8 a.m. boat in the morning and return on the 4 o'clock in the afternoon. That was on Monday to Friday and then I was off for the weekend and the only additional duties were an occasional 'Duty

CPO' in *Tamar* and, on the first Monday every month, I spent the evening teaching Cryptography to young RNVR Officers.

I soon realised that we needed a car, mostly for getting to the beaches on the weekends. We were very fortunate to have a large, open-air swimming pool just across the road at Gun Club Hill Barracks and also an indoor one at the YMCA near to the Star Ferry Terminal. Both of these we made good use of but we longed to get in the ocean and, of course, all the beaches were out of town and not accessible by public transport. For instance, the best beaches were Repulse Bay, Stanley Bay and Big Wave Bay, all on the far side of Hong Kong Island, and Clear-water Beach and Silverstrand Beach, both on the Kowloon side. Big Wave was our favourite and, once we were mobile we used to pack a picnic and head for one of them on most Sundays.

When looking for a car, I once again found the most satisfactory way was to purchase from somebody who was returning home. One day, on the notice board in the Chiefs' Mess, was an advertisement of a car being sold by a dockyard civilian who was due for going home. It was a real vintage car and I could not resist it – it was a huge 1937 Armstrong Siddeley *Sapphire* convertible, sort of Wedgewood blue with a black top. This was before the days of automatic transmissions in English cars but this one had the next best thing called a 'Pre-Selector Gear Shift'. I am not sure how long we kept it, but most likely about nine months, and we had an enormous amount of pleasure from it. Eventually I passed it on, to another civilian, when I bought a brand new 1958 Vauxhall Victor when they first came on the market and with the object, like Malta again, of taking a new car home when we returned to UK. The Victor was canary yellow, with lots of chrome and black upholstery. While we were in Hong Kong I never had to wash my car because, like everybody else, I had a 'car boy' who would clean it every day.

Although our girls were very young when we arrived in Hong Kong (Julia was almost six and Karen almost three) we soon had them both fixed up with schools. Here again we were very fortunate because Julia was entered in the Junior School just across the road in Gun Club Hill Army barracks and Karen was accepted at a Kindergarten (or Nursery) School which was run by one of the Army wives in the married quarters of the same barracks. They both seemed very happy in their schooling and I never felt that their education suffered by being abroad. Just a hundred yards down the road from our home was the Catholic Convent with a lovely chapel where we attended Mass every Sunday and, after instruction there, Julia made her First Communion.

Shopping in Hong Kong seemed to fall into three categories for us and none of them presented a problem. First was the household shopping which was made easy by the owner of a large general store, just around the corner, who would come to us once a week to pick up a list of groceries we needed and then deliver them to us next day. Also, once a week after work, I would go to the huge market for fresh meat and fish (usually grouper or red snapper) and it was always a whole fish with the head and tail off. One day our amah asked me what had happened to the head and tail and, when I told her I had asked for them to be cut off, I was in trouble – in future I always brought them home for her supper! It was not advisable to buy vegetables from the market because one could never be sure of the conditions under which they had been grown. Fruit and vegetable were always purchased from a large company called The Dairy Farm (at a slightly higher price) who guaranteed their purity. The second form of shopping was 'the look-see man' who was an Indian gentleman who came to the door once or twice a month and, from a large suitcase, produced all kinds of small wares such as brass, china, pictures, statues etc. When he was faced with the initial response of 'not today thank-you' he would always reply, 'Just look-see, Missy,' and, of course, we usually finished up buying something as his prices were usually better than the stores and his payment terms were always very flexible. Of course, there were an incredible number of regular stores of all descriptions, ranging from tables in an alley, through tiny shops in doorways to large and brightly-lit stores on the main thoroughfares. On Nathan Road, which stretched for several miles in Kowloon, there was an endless blaze of neon signs, day and night, and all mounted on what looked like a flimsy structure of bamboo. Their range of goods was enormous and came from all over the world but, of course, the bulk of it was either made in Hong Kong or came from Japan, Taiwan, or mainland China.

The Hong Kong weather had just enough variation to make it pleasant and bearable throughout the year. The summers were scorching hot, even in the monsoon season when there would be torrential rain and sometimes a typhoon would hit the Colony. I remember the streets being flooded almost to our knees and, wearing flip-flops, we went to the cinema. The cricket and bowling greens opposite were always immaculate and, even after two days of heavy rain, the groundsmen would be out there with

Karen and Julia at a
birthday party.

hoses! In the winters it got pleasantly cool enough for us to change into blue uniforms for a few months but heaters were never required. For this reason, many people visited Hong Kong from Singapore where there was no such winter respite.

About six months after our arrival we had really settled down and had made a lot of new friends and then, as we got into the New Year of 1958, several things happened which were to affect our lives in Hong Kong. Unfortunately, at this stage, I cannot vouch for the chronological sequence of these events but it will not make a lot of difference.

My friend, and opposite number in the Main Signal Office, Chief Yeoman Bill Trotter, was coming due to return to the UK. We had become quite good friends with Bill and his wife Eve who, having no children, lived in the Married Quarters on Argyle Road in Kowloon. Bill asked me whether I would be interested in earning some extra cash by taking over a couple of spare time jobs he was doing and would soon be leaving – of course, I jumped at the opportunity! The first one was teaching English literature to Chinese students, one night a week, at a private Chinese college in Kowloon. I went for an interview and, when they asked what qualifications I had, I was pleased to be able to produce my Naval HET certificate, and so I was accepted. This proved to be a rather interesting and sometimes hilarious occupation when I got to know the students more closely. One of their first projects was always to write an essay describing their life, themselves and their ambition and, when correcting these for spelling and grammar, some were really quite amusing because they were not at all bashful and did not hesitate to describe what wonderful people they were. Mostly, they were in their early twenties, male and female, and were dedicated to their studies because English was needed for any decent job in the Colony and also for emigration. I remember at the end of the school year one young man in my class insisted on taking me to see a Chinese opera with him. At 10 p.m. that night we went to this Chinese theatre and I am sure I was the only white face there – but no matter. I had been worried about not understanding the Chinese dialogue, but I need not have worried for there was no dialogue – none was needed because the whole thing was enacted with extremely dramatic actions and, with their highly painted faces, it was not at all difficult to follow the story. Another feature of my school experience was that Elaine (our amah) had enrolled at the school because she wanted to improve her own English so that she could go to England to become a nurse. I know she was very proud to arrive at school in my car with the rest of her class watching.

In Kowloon we had a very good Service Club for Warrant Officers and NCOs which, of course, included the Navy and RAF equivalents and therefore was known as the 'Wo's and Jo's Club'. All kinds of excellent entertainment nights were held there and one of the most popular was the twice weekly 'Tombola Night'. Tombola is the service equivalent of Bingo where the rules are a bit different but basically it is similar. This was operated on behalf of some ladies' organisation (I think it was the WVS) by a Tombola Committee under the charge of the RSM of the Military Police. Bill took me one night and introduced me to the committee and proposed me as his replacement. Being a paid job it was much sought after but, I am happy to say, I was accepted and, before I knew it, I had been nominated as the 'Caller' and never looked back after that. Another factor in Bill Trotter's departure was that the Chief Yeoman sent out to relieve him was Ben Hilton, a friend of mine since early days at *Mercury*.

About this time also, Eileen was getting terribly bored with her days – with an amah to do all the cooking, cleaning, washing and ironing and with me at work and the girls at school it did not leave much for Eileen to do except an endless round of 'coffee mornings'. This problem was solved one day by Margaret Leach who was a friend of ours. Her husband Jack was a Petty Officer Telegraphist who worked watches at the Headquarters and he and I used to play hockey for *Tamar*. Margaret worked full-time as a cosmetics sales assistant at Watson's English Pharmacy and suggested she should try to get Eileen a job there. Watson's was the biggest, and most exclusive, drugstore in the Colony and was located in the heart of Victoria on Hong Kong Island. They employed some Chinese and some European staff and they were all strictly controlled by a female battle-axe type. Well, Eileen got the job and was very happy there for the rest of our stay in Hong Kong – selling cosmetics (mostly Avon) and perfumes to rich American tourists who visited the Colony in regular cruise ships.

A change in our life occurred when Elaine (our young amah) was finally accepted for training as a nurse at Lewisham Hospital in London, We were very sorry to see her go and I think she was reluctant and not a little apprehensive about leaving us and Hong Kong. However, it all worked out very well because, after we had returned to England, we went to visit her at Lewisham Hospital and found her off-duty and playing tennis. She had settled in very well and was really enjoying her new life.

Now, of course, we were faced with the prospect of finding a replacement amah. This time, however, I did not have to go through the 'talent parade' at the Families Office – I had heard through the grapevine of a family returning to England who were trying to arrange employment for their amah before leaving. When I spoke to them for references they were very enthusiastic and praised her highly and so an interview with us was set up. When we met Ah Kwai we found her to be a very gentle and pleasant woman with a ready smile and, although she did not speak a great deal of English she could understand us well. She was quite a bit older than Elaine and was a very experienced amah and so we took her on without hesitation and never regretted it. Ah Kwai proved herself to be competent, clean and conscientious and was a real treasure as far as the girls were concerned because she loved both of them and treated them as her own although it was obvious that little Karen was her very best favourite. We soon found that Ah Kwai had a son of her own – I think he was about ten – although she did not bring him to the apartment. Ah Kwai had her own little room at the back of the apartment where she slept and did all the ironing; on washday the clothes were threaded onto a couple of bamboo poles and stuck out of her window to dry.

The biggest factor in making life in Hong Kong so pleasant was the tremendous schedule of social activities which went on throughout the year and I know we attended as many as were possible. The Army NCOs and the Navy C & POs' messes cooperated fully and put on some very outstanding functions; we did not have much to do with the RAF who had a relatively small unit out at Kai Tak. Each Mess had an Annual Ball which was a full evening dress affair, dancing with a good band and some of the most fabulous buffet suppers I have seen anywhere.

Three of the most memorable of these events were, first of all the Hallowe'en Ball, in October 1958, given by *Tamar* CPOs' Mess where the guest of honour was Commodore Gregory and his wife. A month later it was the Annual Ball given by the Sergeants' Mess of the Lancashire Regiment who were then stationed at Gun Club Hill Barracks in Kowloon. It was a matchless evening, only partly because they managed to hold it at the Kowloon Cricket Club which was next door to them. This was November 1958 and, at that time, there was a film crew in the Colony busy making a movie called *Ferry to Hong Kong* and so the stars of the film were invited to the Lancs' Ball as guests of honour. The next month, December 1958, it was the turn of the Royal Hong Kong Defence Force and they

Bob, Eileen, Karen, Julia with our Amah, Ah Kwai in our apartment.

held their Annual Ball at the world famous Peninsula Hotel in Kowloon and, of course, it was an outstanding success. One further memorable occasion was when the new P&O liner *Chusan* visited the Colony and was secured at the Kowloon pier and the Hong Kong Red Cross arranged to hold a Charity Ball on board the ship. Because it was not a Service event I could not wear my uniform evening dress but had to go and have a dinner jacket made. It was worth it though because it was certainly a tremendously successful evening which we all enjoyed.

In addition to all those top-notch evenings there were also many lesser events which we found nonetheless enjoyable. At the Wo's & Jo's Club there would be a Pub Darts Night or a 'Tramp's Ball' and there would be Mess Dances at the least excuse.

Of course, all this was fine for the Senior Ratings but, in *Tamar*, we had a great many younger 'other ratings' who formed the bulk of our Communications Staff at the Headquarters. I think it was Lieutenant Denny who first suggested we should do something for them in the way of entertainment and so we got together and formed 'The Communications Welfare Committee' for this purpose.

RMS *Chusan* leaving Kowloon Wharf in Hong Kong.

Frank Denny was elected President and Bob Adams was elected Secretary – which meant that I was the one who had to make all the necessary arrangements for whatever events we decided to hold. It proved to be a very successful and popular move and we finished up with quite a variety of functions. Most of these were held at The China Fleet Club and included dances, pub nights, bowling nights etc. In addition to the indoor activities we would arrange evening BBQs on a beach, or on a Sunday we would 'borrow' a boat (with Chinese crew) from *Tamar* and head out to one of the tiny islands for a day's picnic.

During the course of Eileen's employment at Watson's Pharmacy she would meet very many of the tourists who came to the Colony on the cruise ships. One of the more interesting ones was a man named Malcolm Muggeridge who was very famous in Britain as a television personality – he was an interviewer and also involved in a couple of game shows and was notorious for his acerbic wit and often downright rudeness. However, when he met Eileen he was at his most charming and wanted to know all about her and how she came to be living in Hong Kong. Another of Eileen's famous persons was Orson Welles who had come to Hong Kong to star in the movie being made there – *Ferry to Hong Kong*. Eileen always remembers that she sold him a tube of Colgate's toothpaste – not a very large purchase for such a large man!

During the winter it was not cold but it was just not beach weather and, on Sunday afternoons we would drive out of the city to explore the New Territories and quite often finish up at Sha Tin where we could get tea in the garden. Also at Sha Tin was a small airstrip from which the Army Air Corps operated daily flights over the New Territories to make sure the Communists were not planning any mischief along the Chinese border. Through an Army contact of mine I managed to arrange to go along on one of these flights and it was very interesting and informative. We were flying in an Auster which was a small observation plane and I enjoyed the flight but would have been a bit happier if there had been a door beside me to close!

Security in the Colony almost never seemed a problem because the very efficient Hong Kong Police Force seemed to keep a tight rein on everything and seemed to know everything that was going on. However, we all knew that there were two days (at least) each year when there was sure to be trouble. They were 1 October which was 'Communist Day' and, shortly after, on 10 October it was 'Nationalist Day' and on these two days there would be riots, fighting, looting and burning in the streets.

The Police would be out in full force and all Service establishments on standby while all European families were advised to stay indoors. When it was all over and everything was back to normal we knew we would not have to worry again until next year. Like most organisations in the Colony the Hong Kong Police were very British and very well trained. They had British officers and Chinese constables, always armed, their uniforms were always immaculate and they always impressed me as being very efficient. Perhaps never more so than on the night they got me out of bed at 1 a.m.! We were sound asleep when there was a loud banging on the apartment door and when I opened it I found an inspector and two constables, all looking very serious, which I thought was a bit much for a couple of parking tickets. They never really told me what they wanted; just asked me endless questions about who I was, what I was and, most of all, what I was doing at that address.

I finally got the feeling (they never told me) that they just wanted to find out if the person living in my apartment had anything to do with the activities of the two Chinese girls who lived in Miss Chan's ground floor apartment.

Field hockey was a very popular sport in Hong Kong, especially among the Services, and *Tamar* boasted a good team. I think it was January or February of 1959 when we were involved in a Hockey Tournament which was to be held over one weekend in Macau, the neighbouring Portuguese island colony. Eileen and I travelled on the night ferry from Hong Kong – we boarded about 10 p.m. and sailed about an hour later; we had a small but very clean two-berth cabin and, when we awoke in the morning, we were tied up in Macau harbour. The tournament was a great success but I remember the weather was bitterly cold (much more so than HK). We were all together in a small, comfortable hotel and, when we returned from the games, all shivering, the owner introduced us to 'Whisky-Macs' (Scotch and Ginger Wine) which was very effective in the prevention of hypothermia! Macau was a very pleasant and interesting place to visit but, like so many of these old colonies, there was an air of neglect and decay. In the evenings we visited the local casinos which seemed to be the mainstay of the local economy.

Field hockey, as I said, was a very popular sport but, as so often happens, there was a shortage of umpires so I took a course with the Army Physical Training School and got myself qualified as a hockey umpire.

An event which had a considerable influence on our life in Hong Kong was when my cousin Victor arrived in the Colony to take up a position with the Hong Kong & Shanghai Bank, accompanied by his new bride Anna. They had married just prior to leaving England and had enjoyed their honeymoon on the sea voyage to Hong Kong. Although we did not see a great deal of them for the first year as they got settled into their new life and new job it was, nevertheless, nice to feel that we had some family nearby. Included with Victor's job was a fully furnished apartment which I think was on Garden Road on Hong Kong Island. After about a year Victor was promoted and elevated to a luxurious apartment, on top of the Peak, which also included three Chinese staff. They entertained us there very royally and we also enjoyed some very pleasant evenings out together. When Victor and Anna had their first baby, Sara, in 1959, we were very happy to be asked to act as godparents. The christening was quite a large and formal occasion and I know we all enjoyed it immensely although, due to a health problem of Eileen's, we nearly missed it. Eileen had already been into the Royal Naval Hospital for an appendicitis and then, shortly before the christening, had to be admitted for a thyroid operation. She did manage to get out again before the christening date but was now sporting a large scar across the base of her throat. Fortunately, she did manage to wear a white bead necklace to disguise the result of her operation.

As the summer of 1959 began drawing to a close Eileen and I started to have thoughts about our return to UK but, also at this time, I received the tragic news that my Mother had died suddenly and unexpectedly. One evening, after a visit by Aunt Nellie, she had suffered a cerebral haemorrhage and had died instantly. Of course, I immediately applied for compassionate leave to attend the funeral but had another shock when my request was, in effect, denied. I would be allowed to fly home for the funeral but, because my Foreign Service was almost completed, I would not be returned to HK. This would mean that Eileen would have to pack everything up and return home by sea with the girls. Obviously this was not at all practical and so I elected to remain in Hong Kong until my normal return date. It was all very upsetting but not much of a choice.

As time slipped by I was delighted to find that our departure date from Hong Kong would coincide with the return sailing of the troopship *Nevassa* – we could not have been happier about this arrangement because we had so much enjoyed the outward trip. We decided that we would spend the final two weeks before sailing at our old favourite, the Ritz Hotel. This would enable us to clear the apartment and sell furniture etc. without a terrible panic at the last moment. However, when Victor and Anna were told of this arrangement they would not hear of such a thing and, very generously, invited us to spend the final two weeks with them in their apartment. This was a very pleasant and happy arrangement and our stay with them made the two weeks before sailing very relaxing for Eileen and me.

My most outstanding memory of our departure was the incredible amount of stuff we had accumulated to take home with us. Of course, I was responsible for packing it all and, in this, I was very fortunate to be a friend of the Chief Shipwright in *Tamar*. In the end, the 'Chippy's Shop' constructed for me, to my measurements, no fewer

Instructing cryptography to Naval Reserve Officers of Hong Kong Defence Force, Naval Headquaters, 1959.

than seventeen wooden packing cases. It said a lot for the most popular sport in Hong Kong – shopping! – at which Eileen had become an expert. There was furniture, bedding, linen, lamps, vases, ornaments – not to mention clothing. I was rather surprised that nobody complained when all this had to be loaded in *Nevassa* and even more surprised when we reached England and the Customs did not ask me to open one case.

The voyage home in *Nevassa* was every bit as enjoyable as we had hoped it would be. The trip was one week less than the outward voyage because the Suez Canal had now been re-opened and therefore we did not have to go all round South Africa. It was early October when we left Hong Kong and I remember it was a very sad and tearful farewell – we had enjoyed our stay so much and we were leaving so many good friends (who all came to see us off). We were no less sad at having to leave Ah Kwai, who had been such a treasure to us all. I remember she was delighted with all the stuff we had unloaded onto her and also that I had been able to find her a new job before leaving.

For the voyage home we were all together in a comfortable four-berth cabin and, when we first saw it, it was filled with beautiful flowers – a farewell from all our friends. It was a wonderful voyage, lots of parties and dances, the food was still outstanding and, although we longed to see England again, we did not want the voyage to end. The weather was great all the way and even the infamous Bay of Biscay behaved itself, but as we turned into the English Channel we were hit by a sudden and violent storm. It was so unexpected that most furniture and fittings had not been secured for bad weather. It was about nine in the evening when it happened – the girls were safe in their bunks and I managed to grab the bar but Eileen, in an armchair, flew from one side of the lounge to the other. Incredibly, someone in the library went smashing through the glass doors without getting a scratch – just a shock I guess.

When we arrived at Southampton (I think it was 11 November) it was a lovely autumn day and my sister June was there to meet us. We disembarked surprisingly quickly and managed to get ourselves and our baggage into her car – the seventeen crates would follow us by rail. We enjoyed the ride to Worthing and catching up on everything as we went but, of course, our homecoming was overshadowed by the loss of my mother.

I was now due for seven weeks Foreign Service Leave which would take me to the end of the year. By then I would have just three more years to serve in the Navy before I became due for pension and, at this point, I was naturally wondering what might be in store for me, although I felt pretty sure that my next move would be to a ship.

I did not have too long to wait before finding out. Before completing my leave I received a telegram ordering me to report to HMS *Tyne* on 4 January 1960.

CHAPTER TWENTY-EIGHT

HMS Tyne

WHEN I JOINED HMS *Tyne* in Portsmouth Dockyard on 4 January 1960, I must confess that it was with mixed feelings, and not all of them connected with the ship.

With barely three years left to serve in the Royal Navy I was beginning to think seriously about the future and wondering what civilian life would be like after so many years as a sailor. I was not especially worried about the transformation because I knew that I would be able to adapt to whatever role I chose and it would, after all, be a new adventure. Even so, I was always wondering what would I be doing? Where would we be living? Most importantly, would my family be happy in our new life?

Walking through the dockyard on that day, and many days to come, I was more occupied with thoughts of the Navy, past and present. I found it very sad to see so many empty berths which I remembered being filled with warships of all types, most of them swarming with 'dockyard mateys' with rivet guns and welding torches, as they were repaired or refitted. There had been lines of frigates and destroyers, either preparing for sea or perhaps returning, weather-beaten and battle-scarred from a long spell away. Now there were so few ships and the whole dockyard was without the former sense of urgency, as the previous chaotic noise and action was no longer required. All of the capital ships had disappeared – the battle cruisers, battleships and aircraft carriers – and all that was left was one 'Commando Carrier' and a few destroyers. In the midst of this, as though to inspire us still, stood Nelson's famous flagship HMS *Victory*, proud and magnificent in dry dock as though to say, 'Wars may come and wars may go but *Victory* goes on forever.'

After six years of war, Britain was virtually bankrupt and therefore it was essential to reduce the enormous manpower of the Forces – men were 'de-mobbed' to 'civvy street' and equipment was either sold, scrapped or 'mothballed'.

In Portchester Creek, at the north end of Portsmouth Harbour, there were literally hundreds of vessels, of all shapes and sizes, which had been, or were in the process of being, 'mothballed'. This was the 'Reserve Fleet' – there in case they should be needed again because, at that time, nobody could see how the Cold War would be resolved. Of the ships in the Reserve Fleet, a few would be sold to foreign Navies but most would remain mothballed until it was their turn for the scrapyard.

It was obvious that Britain would never again need to maintain the Royal Navy on its pre-war scale when it had been the largest in the world. The British Empire was now also shrinking as Colonies rapidly became independent territories. Therefore, the Government of the day shrank the Navy to what was considered an acceptable level.

On another train of thought I was considering the ship that was to be my home for the next eighteen months. After returning from my two and a half years ashore in Hong Kong I knew, without a doubt, that I would be sent to a seagoing ship in the Home Fleet and therefore it came as no surprise when I was ordered to join HMS *Tyne*. It was, after all, a prestigious appointment because *Tyne* was the Flagship of the Home Fleet and I knew that it would be a very busy and demanding task for me. Although *Tyne* was a fine ship, which I knew from my days in Alexandria, I would have been much happier to be joining a different type of ship, such as a cruiser. *Tyne* had been specially designed and built, before the war, as a Destroyer Depot Ship and, as such, would provide maintenance, repairs and support services for destroyers wherever she was needed. She had huge machine shops, spacious and comfortable accommodation, a huge bakery and galley and everything except armament because, not being a 'fighting ship', she carried the minimum of guns. Due to the drastic Naval reductions I have already mentioned there were few capital ships still in commission so it was a sign of the times that the Commander-in-Chief, Home Fleet was forced to fly his flag in a Depot Ship rather than a Battleship or Cruiser. However, that was not my problem and, as it turned out, did not seem to be a problem at all to those directly concerned.

The Commander-in-Chief of the Home Fleet at that time was Admiral Sir Philip Vian who had been in the *Indomitable* with me when we were in the Pacific. The years did not seem to have improved his temper and I now found him to be arrogant, unpleasant and rude – not to me but certainly to his Staff Officers and especially his Flag Captain who, of course, was the Captain of HMS *Tyne*. They seemed to be totally opposite characters and therefore incompatible. Captain Crawford was a mild-mannered gentleman with rosy cheeks and a pleasant manner (I could imagine him as a farmer). His second-in-command was different again but nonetheless pleasant and popular. Commander Tom Fanshawe was a big, bluff and cheerful man who had spent most of his time in destroyers. Thanks to these two officers, *Tyne* was a happy and pleasant ship in which to serve.

Because of this happy relationship, the Chief Petty Officers' Mess decided to go all out and invited Captain Crawford to dinner. I had never heard of such a thing happening before but the Captain accepted our invitation and I will always remember what a pleasant and relaxed evening it was for everyone concerned

I soon settled in and, once again, adapted to the peace-time routine of a big ship. Due to the volume of signal traffic to and from the C-in-C, the Communications Department was quite large, even for a ship of that size. I found that I had a V/S Staff of thirty-six men who were employed on continuous watch-keeping duties. I was also happy to find an old shipmate of mine in the CPOs' Mess – it was 'Mitch' the chef from my days on *Sirius* and *Glasgow*. He was now the Chief Baker on *Tyne* and, because he had a large bakery and only a limited amount of bread to bake for the ship's company, he was always creating little 'goodies' for the Wardroom and the Chiefs' Mess.

HMS *Tyne*, together with other ships of the Home Fleet, went through all the usual peacetime routines such as exercises (both at sea and in harbour), drills, training and ceremonial occasions. Obviously, for economy reasons, we did not spend a great deal of time at sea but I did not complain because, when in harbour at Portsmouth, I was able to get home every night which suited me fine. There were, however, two occasions when we were involved in major NATO exercises.

The first of these events was in the late Fall of 1960 when we were at sea taking part in a large NATO naval exercise being held in the North Sea and Norwegian Sea.

Part of *Tyne*'s role in this was to transport a large group of Royal Marine Commandos who were to be landed in Norway where they would undergo winter training in the mountains. When they were embarked many of us were wondering where they were to be accommodated for the voyage – but we need not have worried because they simply unrolled their sleeping bags and slept on the upper deck! I remember coming off the bridge late one night and thinking, 'I know Royal Marines are meant to be tough but to be sleeping on the deck while it was snowing and blowing seemed to be a bit too much.' Another feature of this exercise was that Eileen's brother John was one of the RM officers on this jaunt – since being with us in Malta he had been promoted to commissioned rank. Although it was not possible for us to spend a lot of time together I do remember we managed to share a couple of tots and to catch up on the family news.

The second memorable occasion was in the spring of 1960 when *Tyne* (I should say Admiral Vian) was in command of a large NATO naval force, which was engaged in combined manoeuvres and exercises in the Atlantic. On completion of the 'working-up' programme we retired into Gibraltar for a breather. While we were there a tragedy hit the holiday resort of Agadir on the Atlantic coast of Morocco. They were hit by a sudden and severe earthquake which virtually destroyed the city and killed twenty thousand people. Obviously they needed every kind of assistance and needed it as soon as possible. Because *Tyne* was a large ship and conveniently located at Gibraltar we were ordered to act as 'rescue ship'. Every kind of emergency supplies were embarked as quickly as possible, including commandeering every piece of useable lumber so that our 'Chippies', working on the upper deck, could pre-fabricate buildings while we were *en route* to Agadir. When we arrived there was nowhere for us to go alongside so all our equipment was off-loaded by a Spanish landing craft who had also responded – it was not easy work with the Atlantic swell rolling into the anchorage but they did it very well and were rewarded by loud cheers from our ship's company as they took their final load to the beaches. I remember the seafront there which had been a long row of luxury beachfront hotels – the shore had just opened up and swallowed them and only their rooftops were now visible.

The following year we were again at Gibraltar after

combined exercises with the Mediterranean Fleet when once again there was a Moroccan tragedy when the King of Morocco died very suddenly.

I remember hearing this news item on the BBC news at four o'clock and my first thought was that the 'colours' would be halfmasted, the following day and that, whenever possible, the flag of the country concerned should be used at the masthead as a mark of respect. All naval vessels carry a complement of some foreign ensigns but this is dependent on the area of operations. This meant that *Tyne*, as a Home Fleet ship, would not be equipped with the flags of any Mediterranean countries but, not to be outdone, I telephoned the Naval Stores Depot in the Dockyard and managed to order one. I also managed to persuade them not to close (at 4.30) but to wait until my signalman could get there to pick it up. I did not tell anyone on board about what I had done so, at 'Colours' the next morning, there was total amazement on the Quarterdeck as the Moroccan Ensign was broken at *Tyne*'s masthead.

It was not until later that I learned of the consternation in C-in-C Med's Flagship, and also at Flag Officer Gibraltar's HQ when they saw that the only Moroccan Ensign in the Colony had been cornered by an interloper from the Home Fleet! The Signal Officer sent for me and congratulated me 'on the best piece of one-upmanship he had seen'. Quite recently (in fact, only a couple of weeks ago) I was reminded of this incident when I read a small paragraph in the *Sunday Sun* announcing that the King of Morocco had died – after ruling his country for thirty-eight years.

When we returned to Portsmouth on completion of that Spring Cruise we were greeted by news that was not entirely welcome – we were told that *Tyne* was to be 'paid off' to go into the Reserve Fleet and that the entire ship's company was to be dispersed elsewhere. It was now April 1961 and, with a little more than eighteen months left to serve, I felt fairly confident that I would spend the balance of my time at *Mercury*.

The 'rundown' of our complement did not waste any time getting started as both officers and men were sent without relief to other ships and establishments. One day Commander Tom Fanshawe sent for all the Executive Branch Chief Petty Officers (there were probably seven or eight of us) and told us that, as the ship no longer had enough Executive Branch Officers, we would be required to take over the duties of Officer of the Watch on the Quarterdeck.

One day when I was on duty as OOW and greeted Sub Lieut Wales as he came on board I could see that he was quite excited about something and could not wait to tell me. Pete Wales was the Assistant Communications Officer of *Tyne* and had been on a duty visit to the Drafting Office to discuss the dispersal of *Tyne's* Communication ratings. He and I got on very well together as I had known him since he had been promoted from a Petty Officer Telegraphist. Apparently he had overheard a conversation at Drafting about 'who could we get to relieve Chief Yeoman Cox at HMS *Sussex*?' He knew that I lived in Worthing so Pete Wales jumped in and volunteered me for the job. Of course, I jumped at the chance of being an RNVR Instructor at the RNVR Sussex Division which was at Hove, Sussex and only eight miles from my home. So finally, on 23 May 1961, I left HMS *Tyne* for the last time, not without considerable regret, and went to take up my new position as an RNVR Instructor.

HMS Sussex

M Y FINAL SHIP in the Royal Navy was, in fact, no ship at all; only as far as the designation 'HMS' which was applied to all naval ships and shore establishments in commission.

The Royal Naval Volunteer Reserve (Sussex) Division was located on the seafront at Hove, Sussex and consisted of a series of wooden buildings (pre WWI era) surrounding a parade ground and the requisite mast with White Ensign. These were stores, workshops, classrooms, offices and a Wardroom Mess. There was one permanent house that contained the Commanding Officer's office and the Administration Office. The site was enclosed on three sides by a six-foot iron fence with Main Gate and on the fourth (to the east) by the massive structure of the neighbouring swimming pool complex which had been built just prior to the war in 1939. During the war it had been used by the Admiralty as a training facility for thousands of young RNVR officers and became famous as HMS *King Alfred.*

Hove in Sussex was a very select residential community of tall Regency houses and elegant seafront hotels and the RNVR Division, being located right on the Hove seafront promenade, could be (and often was) described as 'a very desirable property' or, as we would say in Canada, 'a piece of prime real estate'. I am sure the Admiralty found it very difficult to resist offers from developers who would love to build a hotel or condominium block on the site.

The Commanding Officer of HMS *Sussex* was Lieutenant Commander Moen RN who was a very pleasant officer and was there to ensure the efficient running of the establishment and, I suspect, to maintain harmonious relations between the Regulars and the Reservists. I never did hear of any significant disagreements between the 'professionals' and the 'amateurs' and I know for a fact that the Instructors did everything conceivable to ensure that the Reservists received the best possible training and encouragement.

My own part of this little kingdom consisted of a large classroom with an adjoining office where I would work during the day. This involved keeping the Communications Publications up to date, setting and marking examination papers and preparing lectures for the twice-weekly training sessions. On Monday and Thursday evenings the Reservists would attend for training in their particular branch of the service. My Communications classes were both male and female (about fifty-fifty), they were very keen to learn and, once again, Cryptography was the main subject.

In addition to the twice-weekly evening training, we were also able to provide sea training on weekends and a two-week training cruise in the summer. This was possible because, attached to the RNVR Division, we had a Coastal Minesweeper – HMS *Curzon*. These vessels, about the size of a small trawler, were developed during the war and built of wood to combat the magnetic mines.

Curzon did not have a permanent crew and was only manned by the RNVR when they took her to sea on weekend training and the 'summer fortnight'. At other times she was berthed in Shoreham Harbour at Portslade (about a mile from HMS *Sussex*) and was maintained and kept ready for sea by the eight of us who were CPO Instructors at the RNVR Division.

Happily, it was not all work and no play for us because each summer there would also be an 'Instructors' Cruise' for one week in the *Curzon* when we would sail for a favourite destination with Lieut Comdr Moen as skipper and eight of us for crew.

During the two summers I was there we went first to Jersey (Channel Islands) and the following year to Guernsey. Naturally, it was always a very relaxed and easy going week and I know it was greatly enjoyed by all concerned.

To compensate for the evening training sessions our hours of work were very relaxed – we did not have to be there until ten each morning and we were free to leave at four p.m. except on the two training nights.

Our official transport was a Royal Navy Econoline van and I was one of the two official drivers. To do this I had attended the Dockyard Motor Pool to take a driving test which qualified me as a 'Naval Driver'. Most of the trips were to and from the *Curzon* and an occasional trip to Portsmouth or to Bisley with the RNVR Rifle Team. My personal transport was also something new for me – a *Vespa* motor scooter which I bought from June and Harold's motorcycle dealership. Although it was only eight miles from home, public transport would have been very inconvenient and running our car every day too costly.

Of course, while all this was going on in my 'naval life' I was also enjoying my life at home with Eileen and our girls. We could not have been happier at the terrific bonus of being able to spend my final eighteen months in this fashion.

Wonderful though it was, we knew it would soon come to an end and so we had to do some serious thinking about my future after leaving the Navy. Opportunities were still not great in England and, when I made a few tentative enquiries about work, the usual response was to the effect that I was a bit old to be starting something new – I would only be forty!

There were a couple of options for people like myself – I could join the police force or the civil service (they had just opened their new Tax Headquarters nearby) but I could not see me pushing papers around for the rest of my life. Eileen tried to persuade me to take up teaching but I was not keen at the time although I must confess now, it might not have been a bad idea.

We finally decided on following in June and Harold's footsteps and to go into the retail store business. That was all very well but the difficult part was finding a suitable store with adequate turnover and also accommodation for a family of four. During my 'final year' we spent many weekends travelling to see businesses that we had seen advertised for sale but, no matter where and no matter what, we never did succeed in finding one that met all three criteria so essential to us.

Whilst we were prepared for a major change in our lifestyle, neither of us was looking forward to leaving our lovely home at 261 Goring Way but it was a step we must take in order to provide the capital necessary for starting a business of any sort. Therefore, at the end of the summer of 1962 we put our bungalow on the market and, not surprisingly for us, it sold very quickly.

Prior to my final discharge from the Navy I found I was entitled to a month's vocational training course which, depending on the subject chosen, could be taken at a number of schools and colleges. Alternatively, it could be done on a 'hands-on' basis with any employer who was willing to accept the candidate; and this was the option I chose. This meant that I spent the month of November 1962 working as a civilian employee of Harold Lines Motorcycles Ltd in Horsham, Sussex. This arrangement worked quite well for both parties – the Navy continued to pay me while I was being trained for civilian life and

His character was† .... 1939 – 1962 Very Good

His ability to supervise was .... Excellent

His efficiency as an Instructor was .... Superior

His efficiency on discharge was assessed as† .... Superior

Special Remarks:—(To include power of command, initiative, energy and any other qualifications not recorded above).

Adams was one of the most loyal, conscientious and efficient chief Petty officers I have met for many years or that I could wish to serve with. As an instructor he was excellent, showing patience and tact but with complete control. He carried out many jobs apart from communications and in them all he used his initiative and common sense – and always remained cheerful.

H.M.S. Sussex

Date 25 October 1962

Signal Officer.
Lieut. Cdr RN.
Captain.

†Compiling Officer should consult Q.R. & A.I. App: 10, Part 2.

N.5221/52.
N.4296/52

Wt. 39499/D14514 1M (I) 10/60 We. & S. Gp. 805

5th November, 19 62.

You are leaving the Royal Navy after twenty-two years'
service or more. You have served your Country, in peace
and war, at Home and Overseas, and have visited other
countries of our Commonwealth and many foreign lands.
Thus can you rightly claim to have played your part,
not only as a member of Her Majesty's Forces, but also
as an ambassador in upholding the good name of the
Country and of the Service to which you belong and in
strengthening the bonds which bind together the British
Commonwealth of Nations.

The Board of Admiralty take this opportunity of conveying
to you their appreciation of your long and faithful service
and their hope that all good fortune will attend you in
the future.

BY COMMAND OF THEIR LORDSHIPS

To   Robert Alexander ADAMS.

Rating   Chief Communications Yeoman.

Official Number   P/JX. 156474.

Harold benefited from having an extra employee (albeit a trainee) cost free for a month.

Before the end of November I was notified by the Navy that, instead of rejoining HMS *Sussex* as I had expected, I was to report to the Royal Naval Barracks at Portsmouth 'for release'. It was then that I began to realize that finally leaving the Navy was not going to be the occasion of joy and celebration that I had somehow imagined. My final few days were, in fact, rather depressing – going through the 'leaving routine' of signing papers, getting medicals, and returning kit – and all among people I did not know. Had I been leaving from *Sussex* or *Mercury* I would have been with friends and I am sure there would have been a little party and a few people to wish me luck in the future. As it was, the whole procedure was very impersonal and uninterested and, for me at least, quite disappointing. On my final day, 4 December 1962, I had a ten-minute interview with the Commodore of the RN Barracks (an officer I did not know) who shook my hand, thanked me for twenty-five years and wished me luck – and that was it!

As I walked out of the Main Gate and saluted the Officer of the Watch for the last time I was not feeling on top of the world as I had perhaps anticipated.

But, tomorrow was to be my fortieth birthday and I was now beginning my new life as a civilian again.

Part Three
Civilian Again

CHAPTER THIRTY

Civilian Again

As the year of 1963 began for me it was a feeling of big adventure as a whole new life was ahead of me and I was in control of it (or at least I thought that I was). I was feeling confident about the whole situation because I believed that whatever came along I could handle it and make a go of whatever my final vocation proved to be. I knew also that, inevitably, there must be some period of moving and change until we were finally settled. It is just as well that we cannot see into the future because if I had known at that time that we were facing eight years of very unsettled and changing conditions in our lives then I would not have felt so happy. I have always believed that a life which is constant and unchanging must be very dull and I must say that our situation was entirely the opposite – but that is what life is all about sometimes. However, I must not give the impression that those years were all doom and gloom because that would be far from the truth. There were many periods in those years when we were very happy with our lives and really thought that we had settled down at last.

Horsham, Sussex

AT THE START OF 1963 we had, of course, moved from the bungalow in Goring and were now settled in June and Harold's flat over their motorcycle business in Horsham. It was a bit cramped for the four of us but we did not mind because we knew it was only temporary until we found permanent accommodation (wherever that might be). It was located in the heart of Horsham which is a very pleasant country town and we enjoyed settling in there – it was convenient for shopping and Julia was now enrolled at the Weald High School for Girls in Billingshurst and Karen was attending the Junior school in

Horsham which was only a hundred yards away. But the biggest convenience of all was that I was now living right above my place of work – in the morning all I had to do was walk downstairs and I was there (no excuse for being late!). I enjoyed working in the motorcycle business – there was so much to learn and we always seemed to be busy. In twelve years Harold had worked hard and had built up a very respectable sized retail business. He now had an additional store in Crawley (about ten miles away) and at each store he employed a manager, a mechanic and a parts man. I spent most of my time working at Horsham but occasionally went to Crawley when an extra hand was required. My duties were varied and included a little bit of everything – sales, spare parts, deliveries, a bit of ac-counting and payroll – in fact wherever I could be useful. One responsibility I do particularly remember – every Tuesday I drove the small pickup truck to London where I would tour all the big London motorcycle dealers (one for each make) picking up spare parts ordered by our customers. I would start about six-thirty in the morning and aim to be home by six in the evening.

This was very popular with the customers because, in-stead of waiting several weeks for a part to come from the manufacturer, they could order it on Monday and receive it on Wednesday.

Life settled into a very happy pattern during this year and when the summer came and I was due for a week's holiday we decided to get away for a vacation and the final choice was to rent a small motor-home (they called it a Dormobile in England) in which we would tour the West Country (Dorset, Devon, Cornwall). Strangely, perhaps, we had never bothered much about going away on vaca-tions because having always lived at the seaside, there did not seem much point. Anyway, we thoroughly loved this one as we drove all along the north coast to Lands End and then back along the south coast and across Dartmoor.

June and Harold were living just outside Horsham in a beautiful property called 'Violets Farm' where we used to visit them quite often. When they had bought it, many years before, the whole property was in a terrible condition – the farmhouse (which was about four hundred years old) was totally derelict and had not been used for many years and the huge garden was like a jungle. The house had now been professionally rebuilt (one brick at a time), the barn and stables renovated and the garden licked into shape, complete with a swimming pool. They had both taken up horse riding and had a couple of lovely horses and a donkey called Toffee grazing in their fields.

Adversane, Sussex

OUR OWN HAPPY EXISTENCE continued for about a year and I think it was probably quite early in 1964 when we found Gess Gates. For some time we had been searching for a suitable home for ourselves and, when we found Gess Gates, we both fell in love with it and I knew it was for us. It was a black and white, timbered farm cottage. with an orchard and a pretty garden and was something over three hundred years old and this was obvious when one went inside because the floors were all angled and some of the beams were rather low. Of course, we bought it and couldn't wait to move in. It was located in the hamlet (not even a village) of Adversane which was just south of the village of Billingshurst. Adversane consisted of one corner store, one very nice pub called the Blacksmith's Arms and Lavender Cottage, which served teas.

It was a very exciting day when we moved into our cottage after spending every moment we could spare in re-decorating it throughout. We had also engaged a local builder, Mr Blewett of Billingshurst, to do some recon-struction work. Although the cottage boasted a bathroom and small kitchen we decided to totally refurbish the former and to demolish the latter, so that we could build on a modern kitchen. We were more than happy with the results and we looked forward to spending many years of our lives in this idyllic setting. We felt that living in the country it would be nice to have a dog around the place and we had always fancied an Irish setter, ever since my cousin Yvonne had owned one when we were young, so now I started to make a few enquiries.

Without letting anyone know what I was doing I then checked around all the breeders in the area and found one in Crawley who had a one-year-old female available so, after getting the vet to check her out, I paid five guineas for Millie and promised to collect her after Christmas. I then bought a nice dog collar and plaited leather lead which I gift-wrapped for Eileen's Christmas present. I always remember her expression when she opened the package – pleasure, then very puzzled and finally asking 'what is it?' She told me later that she wondered if it was some new fashion accessory. When I explained that she was now the owner of a lovely Irish setter she was thrilled and could not wait to get home to collect Millie – who was immediately re-christened Cindy and became a much loved, and very loving, member of our family.

Not too long after this our carefree existence abruptly changed when, at work one day, Harold and I had a disagreement which we could not resolve and, in the heat of the moment, things were said which I felt made my position untenable with the result that I gave a week's notice that I would be leaving. I was very sorry to leave the motorcycle business because I enjoyed the work and liked the people I worked with. Very soon I regretted my decision even more as I realised that alternative employment was not easy to come by and, having left by my own choice, I was not entitled to any form of unemployment insurance.

I cannot remember how long this situation lasted (it seemed ages) as I checked the newspapers every day and followed up any possibilities. At one point I felt I had the answer – Pearl Insurance Company in Horsham needed an agent for the area to replace a man who was retiring. After a couple of interviews with them I was told the job was mine – subject only to a clean medical, which did not bother me in the least. For a few weeks I did not hear any more until I really pestered them and then they reluctantly told me that I could not be employed because my blood pressure was too high – not surprising.

Shortly after this I found an advertisement in the *Daily Telegraph* which sounded interesting and promising – an un-named company was looking for 'a few good men' to work in the field of education and promised excellent prospects for advancement. Details were very few but interviews would be held at the Excelsior Hotel which was opposite London Airport. Upon arrival I found there were about thirty other applicants but instead of interviews we were all grouped in a large hall and two men spoke to us all very enthusiastically about the work, although, once again, details were not forthcoming. Finally, we discovered that this marvellous opportunity involved selling the

Encyclopaedia Britannica and, at this point, many applicants left but, being desperate to do something, I decided to follow it through. I guess today we would be known as tele-marketers but then we were just known as salesmen. The work was not hard or difficult but I found it boring and rather depressing. We started at ten in the morning and spent several hours on the telephone trying to set up appointments, usually in the evening, when we would do our best to sell somebody a set of encyclopaedias, quite often finishing about ten in the evening. I soon learned to accept rejection on the phone but, in the end, I was successful a few times and they offered me a job as a supervisor, but I wanted out and prepared to take my chances elsewhere.

On my way home from Guildford (where I had been working) I stopped in Horsham to buy a local paper and check the Situations Vacant section. As usual there was very little available but there was one advertisement that made me stop and think – at Curry's branch in Horsham they wanted a van driver/salesman. Obviously not a very prestigious job and so the pay would not be great but I remember thinking to myself, 'What the heck – let's have a go.' I had to be doing something and I could not face sitting at home just waiting for something better to turn up; in any case I had always believed in starting at the bottom. When I walked into Curry's store that day and asked to see the manager, the assistant who approached me must have thought I was somebody important because I was wearing a smart business suit and carrying a briefcase – he must have got a surprise when he finally heard I was there for a job. The Manager proved to be a tall, quietly spoken man about my own age and we seemed to hit it off right from the word go. He questioned me very closely about my background and why I would be applying for such a low-grade job – he even tried to talk me out of it but I was now determined to go ahead and have a go at it.

He and I seemed to be very compatible and soon found we had a common bond because he had also served in the Navy during the war. Anyway, he took me on and I started work the following day and it was a relief to be doing something useful and enjoyable.

Curry's was (and is) a large and successful retail chain selling electrical products – major appliances, television, radio plus bicycles. At that time they operated a chain of 360 stores across Southern England and their Head Office and Distribution Centre was located in Winchester in Hampshire. I soon discovered that the secret of their success was that all their operations were very well organised and strictly controlled. Although they could never be accused of being generous I found they were always fair and I enjoyed working for them. We were paid a salary plus commission on what we sold and, although I would not get rich on it, it was a relief to have a regular income again.

Arthur Burrett was the Manager in Horsham and his wife, Alice, ran the office side of the business. They had two children and lived in a very pleasant flat above the store. They were both very pleasant, genuine and friendly people and both Eileen and I became great friends with them and we used to go out to dinner together after closing up on a Saturday night. Of course, they are retired now and live in a bungalow in Seaford in Sussex and we still keep in touch with them. Just a couple of years ago they visited Canada on a coach tour and we were delighted to be able to meet them at Niagara Falls.

Curry's were fortunate to have Arthur Burrett – he was a very good manager, totally honest, intelligent and good to his staff and customers alike. He had been at Horsham many years and had turned down quite a few offers of promotion to bigger and better stores because he had built up a good business and was happy and settled there. Next up the ladder above Arthur was Mr Middleton who was our District Manager who would visit the store once a week to make sure everyone was following company policy – I liked him and we soon had a good relationship. Above him came Mr White who was the Area Controller and he ruled over the entire area of South East England for Curry's and so had a lot of power and influence.

Mr White was probably about sixty, small and a bit rumpled with grey hair and an unsmilling face. He was very strict but, like the Company, was also fair and I had no problem with him and he was always very polite to me.

I soon realised that, without any effort on my part, I was being guided towards better things – I was being invited to stay behind in the evenings to find out all about stock ordering and control and the accounting procedures in the office. Eventually I was left on my own in the office, on a Sunday morning, to complete the dreaded BWR. This was the Branch Weekly Return, a book about two foot square with a box to account for every penny or activity of the branch that week. Then these figures had to be compared with the corresponding week in the previous year to see how we were doing.

It had to be completed (in triplicate) and mailed to Head Office by Sunday night.

Next came the time when Arthur and his family were going on vacation for two weeks (they used to drive to Spain every year) and, rather surprisingly, I was told that I was now the Assistant Manager and would be in charge while they were away. This raised a few eyebrows among the rest of the staff but, I am happy to say, everything went off very well. In addition to myself there were five other salesmen, a female cashier in the office and a part-time mechanic for cycle and moped repairs.

While all this was going on there were also developments on the home front. We loved living in our beautiful cottage and the girls were happy in their schools – Julia was still at the Weald High School and Karen was also now at school in nearby Billingshurst. It goes without saying that Cindy loved the freedom of running in the adjoining fields and often coming back a bit smelly after falling in a cow pat!

It was about this time that I decided to change our car for an estate car (in Canada that would be a station wagon) in order to accommodate Cindy more easily when we were travelling. I found the ideal car at a local garage and made a deal to trade-in our 1958 Vauxhall Victor for a 1964 Vauxhall Victor Estate – it had a white body and a dark green roof and trim. It was a lovely car and we enjoyed it until we left England.

It was now the summer of 1965 and over the past two years our finances had taken rather a beating so that, even with both of us working (Eileen worked half-days in a farm office and a couple of nights a week babysitting), it was proving more and more difficult to make ends meet. Finally, when we started getting pressure from the bank manager, we were forced to face the awful, but inevitable, conclusion that we would have to leave Gess Gates. This dreadful realisation was softened a bit by the fact that my work situation was improving as I had now successfully completed a Management Course at the Head Office in Winchester and with several seminars with manufacturers under my belt, I felt confident enough to ask Mr White to give me my own branch. He promised to do this, just as soon as one became available – encouraging news but, unfortunately, there was no way of knowing where or when it might be.

Very reluctantly we put Gess Gates on the market and, because it was now such an attractive property, it was not too long before we found purchasers for it. They were Sue and Tony Davy who were retiring to England after working

Karen at school in England.

for an oil company in the Middle East. A few years ago we were in Adversane and we were able to visit the Davys who, I am pleased to say, are still very happy living at our Gess Gates. And so it came about that we left Gess Gates – very reluctantly and not without a few tears – to move into a flat in Horsham above a hairdressing salon. No matter how we consoled ourselves with the thought that it was only temporary because we would soon be moving again when I was promoted to my own branch, which would have accommodation, it was still not a happy situation but it was necessary. One advantage, however, was that we were now located immediately opposite Curry's store on West Street – no more travelling to work and I could even dash home for lunch. We were also able to continue our activities as before as Eileen remained in her job at the farm office and the girls were able to continue in the same schools.

Deal, Kent

AFTER ABOUT TWO OR THREE MONTHS Mr White arrived in Horsham one day to announce that he had a branch in Deal which would soon be needing a new manager – and offered it to me. Of course, I was delighted and quite excited about the prospect of running my own store, even though I knew it was not as big or as prosperous as Horsham. When I discussed the offer with Arthur Burrett I found he was a bit less than encouraging; which I found a little surprising in view of his past help and encouragement. He told me that I would find Ronnie Fisher, the District Manager there, to be somewhat different to our Tom Middleton at Horsham, a man I both liked and respected.

We also discussed how I would arrange to move my house and family and he agreed to give me two days off to travel to Deal so as to find a house. Deal is a small seaside town in Kent on the south-east coast of England. Although less than a hundred miles from Horsham it was directly across country and involved several hours of driving. Leaving the girls at home, Eileen and I set off for Deal and, upon arrival, arranged to spend two nights 'Bed & Breakfast' at a pub there. We then had a couple of hectic days chasing estate agents and looking at houses they had to offer and, just when we were running out of time (and prospects) we found just what we were looking for. It was quite a modern three-bedroom house, in excellent condition and with a garage and quite a large garden. It was located on the outskirts of Deal, in a nice little village called Sheldon, but was still only ten minutes from town. The vendors were a Royal Marine Bandmaster (who was due to leave the RM School of Music in Deal) and his wife who happened to be Maltese. They were very pleasant people and we found we had a lot in common so that it was not long before we struck a deal and I was on the phone to our solicitor in Worthing, asking her to rush it through (she thought I was crazy because we were on the move again – I must admit I was beginning to feel a bit like a gypsy by now).

Whilst visiting Deal on this occasion there was one thing that I would have liked to do, but didn't, and that was to visit the store where I would be working when we moved so as to get the feel of it.

Normally, I would not have hesitated but, in this instance, I had been specifically told not to have any contact with the outgoing manager, nor any of the staff until I had taken over. Thinking about it later, I suppose this should have been a warning of things to come but, at the time, I was not too bothered and therefore obeyed the rules.

Our actual move to Deal went very smoothly and we were very quickly settling in our new home there. I do remember that, for the long car journey, we had to give Cindy a couple of tranquilliser pills and so she slept most of the way. One of the first things we had to do was to arrange for the girls to attend school and, when we found there was not a Catholic school in Deal, we chose to send them to the Catholic High School in Dover. This was a mixed school and was about twenty miles away so they would travel by bus every day.

Having moved into the house and congratulated ourselves because everything seemed to be going so well we were unprepared for the problems that the first Monday would bring. It was to be my first day at work and the girls' first day at school.

I had been told to be at Curry's store in Deal at 8.30 when it opened on the Monday morning and Mr Fisher, the District Manager, would meet me there at that time. I had also been told not to talk to the staff until he arrived, which did not seem a big deal at first but, when he did not arrive until noon, it had become a bit embarrassing for me. When he did arrive, he said, 'Let's go to lunch,' and I thought, 'This is a good sign,' but, as soon as we sat down, he spoiled it by saying, 'This is the only time I will buy you lunch.' He talked for an hour, about all his expectations, while I dutifully listened and tried to take it all in – in the end, I had decided I did not like him much but it did not bother me then.

When I got home from work that evening I found Eileen and the two girls very upset and all in tears. They finally told me that their first day at their new school had been a terrible disaster – not so much at the school but on the journey home on the bus. Apparently, some of the students (boys and girls) had been using absolutely foul language and, with nobody in charge of them, had been most objectionable and obscene. Well, the next morning I telephoned the Headmaster and explained what had happened but, to my surprise, he did not seem too concerned and even suggested that Julia and Karen were making it all up.

Julia, Karen and Cindy
at Deal, 1965.

It was then that I told him they would not be attending Dover Catholic High School. We then decided that they should go to the Catholic Convent School for girls in Deal. It was not an easy decision to make because it was a fee-paying school and we would have to outfit them with new uniforms but we were delighted when the nuns agreed to take them.

I soon found that the Curry's branch I had inherited was not in the best of shape – the sales were way down and, worst of all, there was a large number of delinquent accounts which seemed to have been neglected. In Curry's the policy was that should accounts not be collected by the branch they would be written off as 'Bad Debts' and, of course, would be taken off the branch profit picture and this, in turn, would affect the Manager's income.

I could not entirely blame the staff for these two problems because Deal was undoubtedly a depressed area – there was no local industry or commerce and, although Deal had many attractive residential areas, there were also a lot of low income areas and from these came the bulk of our Hire Purchase customers. I spent quite a few evenings, after work, collecting money to improve this situation and, in time, I also achieved a fair improvement in the sales figures. Curry's is very sales oriented and every branch is working in competition with others in the area so, unfortunately for Deal, we were up against quite affluent towns like Dover, Folkestone and Canterbury. In spite of this I did manage to place Deal first in an Electrolux vacuum cleaner sales contest.

Unfortunately for me, the one fly in the ointment was always our own very unpleasant District Manager, Mr Fisher. As time went by I was always hoping that our relationship would improve but it never seemed to happen – in fact, it got worse because he proved to be a very difficult man and, something that had never happened in my life before, I was forced to the conclusion that I could neither work for him, nor with him.

Accordingly, I wrote to Mr White and told him that Mr Fisher and I would have to go our separate ways and tendered my resignation as of the end of the month. Typically, this created a big stir in the Company and immediately brought in a team of auditors but, when they found everything in order, they suspected I was being recruited by the competition. I had, in fact, been offered employment by Civic Radio who was their closest competitor but decided I would not be comfortable in accepting. I did not mention my future plans to anyone until my final day at Curry's, Deal, and then I took all the staff along to the pub for a farewell drink – and then I let them into the secret.

I was sorry to be saying goodbye to the staff because they had served me well, proving themselves both reliable and sympathetic. George, the van driver, was in his thirties and rather overweight and I had met him previously when he was serving in the Royal Marines as a Wardroom Mess Steward aboard HMS *Tyne*. He seemed very popular with the customers and, at first, I was a bit puzzled by the number of little old ladies who came to the store and asked for George but, if he was out, would not talk to anybody else. Finally, I caught on – these were people who could not afford to buy a new washing machine so George had promised to find them something for a couple of pounds from the trade-in appliances we had from time to time. Curry's was not in the used appliance business and these machines would be consigned to the scrapyard. Even so, George could have been fired for running a sideline like this – but I chose to ignore it and, although never mentioned between us, he knew that I knew what he was doing. Then came Ed, whom I had employed as a salesman when he came in one day looking for a job, even though I had not advertised for anyone. He had been a Radio Officer in the Merchant Navy and was a survivor of the *Princess Victoria* disaster of the previous year – a Scotland to Northern Ireland ferry which sank in heavy seas with terrible loss of life. He was a quiet young man and proved to be an asset to the business. Then there was John, a young boy who was competent at his job but not memorable. In the office I had two very pleasant and efficient ladies – Donna was the cashier, newly married and very reserved and therefore I did not get to know her all that well.

The other one was Rose, who was about my age and a nice, friendly person and both Eileen and I got on well with her and her husband, who was also a Bandmaster at the RM School of Music in Deal. Just prior to our leaving Deal we were honoured to be invited, as their guests, to the RM Sergeants' Mess Annual Ball. It was a 'black tie' dinner and dance affair; very large, very formal and seemed to be the highlight of Deal's social calendar.

In spite of all our worries and problems at Deal we also enjoyed many happy times whilst living there. During my time off which was a half day on Thursday and all day Sunday (obviously I worked every Saturday which was our busiest day at Curry's) we would often have trips to places of interest in our part of Kent. We saw the beautiful, ancient city of Canterbury with its enormous cathedral, and stood on the spot where Thomas A'Beckett was martyred for his faith. We had visits to Dover and Folkestone, usually for shopping because they both had bigger and better stores than Deal. We went to Sandwich, a lovely little town which, in ancient times, used to be an important seaport. We spent several happy days at Ramsgate, a pleasant town with its attractive harbour which became famous during the war when 'the little ships' evacuated our troops from Dunkirk. Now it was a lot brighter, with the harbour given over to the operation of pleasure and fishing boats and the whole area festooned with the usual trappings of the tourist trade such as ice cream stalls, amusement arcades, fish & chip shops and some very pleasant seafront pubs. More locally, we would take Cindy for walks on the cliff tops to the south of Deal where she would wear herself out chasing rabbits (real and imaginary) among the gorse bushes. If the weather was poor on a Sunday we would call at the newsagents on the way home from Mass and, armed with newspapers and a large bag of chocolate, we would go home and relax for the day.

When the time came for us to leave Deal it was, naturally, quite a wrench for us all – besides leaving behind a few sad memories we would also be leaving many happy ones and, even though we were heading for a new and more settled life, we were, inevitably, sorry to leave our home and all its pleasant surroundings. Even though we had enjoyed them for only six months it did not make the parting any easier.

There is a little postscript to Deal – just a couple of months after our move from there I heard, from Arthur Burrett, that Mr R. G. A. Fisher had died of a heart attack. If you believe in fate, it will show you how strangely it can sometimes affect our lives.

Lowestoft, Suffolk

IT WAS TOWARDS THE END OF 1965 when we moved from Deal to Lowestoft. Lowestoft is, and always has been, a large and important fisheries centre located on the East Coast of England at the mouth of the River Waveney. It has a good harbour and several large fisheries operate their trawlers from there. The town itself is not large but it is located at the southern extremity of that huge recreational area known as the Norfolk Broads. This comprises a series of large inland waters, all inter-connected, which provide wonderful opportunities for recreational boating, both motor and sail. Oulton Broad, one of the largest, is just outside Lowestoft and is home to many marinas, boat builders and boat rental agencies.

Given all this, I must admit that Lowestoft is not the place I would choose to live but, once again, the need for earning a living to provide for my family was what dictated our relocation there. This was how it came about. As my work situation at Deal steadily got worse and I became more and more depressed I was forced to face the fact that there must be a major change in my life, no matter how difficult or unwelcome it might be. I realised that it had to involve a change of employment and, should that also mean a change of location, then so be it. For quite a while I was racking my brain, trying to find alternatives and then analyse what would be involved. I did think, much later, that it might have been possible to request Curry's for a change of branch, even if it meant losing the manager's job for a while, but at the time, I did not consider this as an option.

I must confess that, by this time, I was almost wishing I was back in the Navy but that was not worth thinking about because, even if they would take me, I could never face leaving my family again. However, this led me on to a new train of thought and one that led me to the Coastguard Station at Deal.

Whilst thinking about the Navy I remembered that a friend of mine from the old days was now the Station Officer at HM Coastguard Station in Deal; Nick Carter was a quiet and serious type and had been a young Acting

Yeoman of Signals when I was on the *Eagle* at the beginning of the war. One day I spent my lunch hour from
work on a visit to see Nick Carter – I very briefly outlined
my problems and asked him all I could about his work.
What he told me that day sounded very interesting and,
although he did not push it, he did advise me as to how
and where to apply should I still be interested. After some
consideration, I did write to the Board of Trade in London
requesting an application form and full details concerning
conditions of service in HM Coastguard. What I received
by return proved very interesting and so I completed and
sent off my application to join. To cut a long story short,
I was accepted and, after passing one more medical examination, I was offered a posting to the Coastguard Station
at Lowestoft.

Before committing myself to anything I decided it would
be a wise move to visit Lowestoft to check out the place
and, without being hampered by any 'gag order' this time,
to talk with a couple of the staff there. Although Lowestoft
is only about 75 miles from Deal 'as the crow flies' it is
probably about double that distance by road. This is
because one has to drive nearly into London (Woolwich
in fact) in order to negotiate the Blackwall Tunnel under
the River Thames, and then it is still a long haul up
through Ipswich and into Suffolk. Anyway, one Saturday
evening, after work, Eileen and I set off for Lowestoft,
having left the girls and Cindy at home in Deal. Late that
evening (nearly midnight in fact) we had arrived close to
Lowestoft and then pulled off the road into a field and
settled down for the night in the back of our station wagon.
We woke to a bright and sunny Sunday morning and,
after a quick face wash and a cup of coffee from our flask,
we headed into Lowestoft, arriving at the Coastguard
Lookout Station at about 7.30 a.m. I introduced myself
to the man who had just come on duty and explained to
him what I was doing there – his name was Ted Field
and he invited us to his house later that day so that we
could see what the accommodation was like. The Coastguard houses (there were five) were located about a quarter
of a mile up the road at a place called Battery Green.

On the drive home that Sunday evening Eileen and I
discussed everything we had seen and heard that day and,
although I was now in favour of taking the posting, Eileen
did have a couple of reservations about it. First was the

house which, although quite spacious and well maintained, was Victorian vintage construction and therefore, not particularly attractive from the outside appearance. There were four houses in a terrace for the four watch-keeping officers and a fifth, detached, house for the Station Officer. The SO was a small, scruffy looking and rather ignorant little man who immediately reminded me of the cartoon character *Andy Capp* – and so that is what I named him. Eileen's idea was that I would not be happy serving under him but he proved to be no problem at all.

Without any further delay I accepted the posting, was given a date when I should report for duty at Lowestoft and ultimately moved house to No. 2 Battery Green. On the Saturday of my first week there I experienced an initiation that was unexpected and quite exciting. On that day a previously arranged joint exercise took place to simulate the rescue of the crew of a ship supposedly run aground. Involved were the Coastguard, the Coastguard Auxiliaries (these were civilian volunteers who would turn out to assist the Coastguard officers in such an emergency), the Lifeboat crew, and RAF Rescue helicopter. At one point, when we were all assembled on this deserted, white sandy beach, the RAF said they wanted to practise hauling somebody up from the beach and, because I was now the junior coastguard, I was nominated for the job. On my way up to the helicopter from the beach, as I dangled in space on the end of this wire, I was thinking, 'I would rather be on a ship in a rough sea!' I then found out that the whole thing was being filmed by Anglia TV and would be shown on the six p.m. news that evening, and so Eileen and the girls were able to see my initial exploits in my new job.

The Coastguard work was interesting because there was quite a lot to learn, even though my naval service made me well qualified in many respects (naval service was a requirement for all 'new entries'). The watchkeeping routine was easy to adapt to – we usually did 'two days on' and then 'two days off'. Inevitably, though, there were periods of boredom but, because these were interspersed with bursts of excitement, we did not get too complacent about our work. Essentially, our job was to keep our eyes and ears open when on watch, listening to the radio tuned to the 'Distress Frequency' and to keep a sharp lookout for any boat or swimmer in trouble. In any case of emergency the CG on duty would have to deal with the situation until reinforcements arrived to assist. This could involve calling out the Rescue helicopter (by telephone) and in minutes the helicopter would be hovering over the lookout to find the trouble (usually a swimmer in distress). The lifeboat was manned by civilian volunteers who, when required, were called out by the CG on duty who would fire a maroon. This was very much like an Army mortar – a tube fixed in the concrete and when a shell was dropped in it the charge would fire it straight up in the air, to burst overhead with a very loud explosion, loud enough to be heard all over town and would bring the lifeboat men to their boat in double quick time. Unlike many stations, the Lowestoft lifeboat remained in the water and so would be very quickly away and out of the harbour.

Unfortunately, Cindy just hated that explosion (she was rather timid and not at all like a gun dog) and every time we fired that maroon she would be over the seven foot wall at the back and disappear somewhere in the town for the rest of the day – but she did come home in the evening when she got hungry.

Because the Coastguard kept a particularly close watch on the many trawlers coming and going from Lowestoft the owners (who often phoned to find out when one of their trawlers was due in) would show their appreciation every Monday morning without fail – at 7 a.m. a fisherman would arrive at the lookout station with a large bucket of very fresh fish, to be shared among all the Coastguard officers. It really was beautiful and I think we ate fish, in some form or other, almost every day.

Another responsibility of the Coastguard at Lowestoft was to patrol the coastline to the north and the south of the town, approximately five miles in each direction. The north patrol finished at Gorleston, near Great Yarmouth and the south one at Southwold and these patrols had to be completed once every month. This duty was not terribly popular and was shared between us on a rotating basis and we could select our own day for doing this. The shoreline in each direction was quite deserted and desolate and the object was to note anything unusual. We would start out in the morning and, having reached the limit of our patrol, would return to Lowestoft by bus. We would then write a report on what we had seen – any significant erosion of the shoreline, any unusual wreckage or debris (or bodies).

When it was my turn to patrol I used to take Cindy with me and she just loved being able to run wild and free all day – chasing seabirds and all kinds of wildlife to her heart's content. By the time we got on the bus to return home she would be exhausted and just flop out on the floor of the bus – that was fine but then she would often bring up some of the seawater she had swallowed.

Happily, both the girls seemed to be settled in at the local High School and appeared to be doing well. Fortunately, this school was within walking distance of our home. Julia soon had a best friend called Lesley whose parents owned a Radio & TV business in nearby Oulton Broad. After we moved to Canada, Lesley came out to visit us for a week and brought David her boyfriend with her. Shortly after, when she married David, Julia and Karen travelled back to England to be her bridesmaids.

The house we lived in at Lowestoft was, of course, Government owned and therefore any repairs, alterations and decorations were undertaken by the Board of Trade who would employ a local contractor for the work. The only snag was that any work needed was subject to funds being available for the purpose but, shortly after we moved in, I did manage to get approval for one bedroom to be redecorated. I made friends with the contractor, got him to teach me all I needed to know about paperhanging and then did the rest myself. We also spent quite a tidy sum of money on having the whole house carpeted throughout. This, and a few other small jobs, made our house a very comfortable place to live and we soon felt very happy and settled there.

After living in Lowestoft for about six months we had visited, by car, several of the very attractive places scattered around the Norfolk Broads and it started me thinking about how nice it would be to own a boat in the area. Accordingly, I began to study all the boating magazines and also visited a few boatyards in Oulton Broad. It did not take too long to find what sounded a very attractive boat which was advertised for sale in one of the periodicals. It was lying at Wroxham, not far from Norwich and, after making an appointment to inspect, we set out to see it. The owner was a schoolmaster and he and his wife were on board when we arrived. I thought the boat was in good condition and appeared to have been well cared for so, after a trial run, we had soon decided to buy.

It was a twenty-six foot motor cruiser, twin engines, fiberglass construction and with good accommodation which included a shower. I am kicking myself now because, for the life of me, I cannot remember either the maker's name nor the name of the boat when I bought it. I do know that it was my intention to change the name to *Puffin* but somehow I never got around to doing so.

My next task was to find somewhere to keep the boat at Oulton Broad (the nearest point to Lowestoft). Because this was such a popular boating area, spare berths were pretty scarce and, of course, rather expensive. I was lucky enough to find a man who lived in a big house (he was a local builder) on the edge of Oulton Broad and he had a private dock which he did not use (he did not own a boat himself) and agreed to rent it to me at what seemed a reasonable sum – I seem to remember it was sixty pounds per year. Having achieved this, we wasted no time in going back to Wroxham (I got an off-duty CG to drive us there) and successfully brought our boat 'home'.

During that summer of 1966 the four of us enjoyed a wonderful vacation just cruising around the Broads in our floating home and I soon realised why renting a Broads Cruiser (either motor or sail) was such a very popular holiday option. The whole area was there to be enjoyed by boaters and was well serviced with plenty of food and fuel stops for their convenience. I thought it was great, after a day on the water, to stop and secure the boat right outside one of the lovely little pubs and then enjoy some refreshment before supper.

After a few months at Lowestoft, our life and my work schedule had settled down to a routine which I was happy with and had no wish to change. I knew that I was doing a good job of work and *Andy Capp* (the Station Officer) did not bother me in the least – in fact, by then I was on pretty good terms with his two superior officers. They were both stationed at the Coastguard Area Headquarters which was at Great Yarmouth – the District Officer (a Lieutenant) would visit us weekly and his boss, the Area Controller (a Lieutenant Commander) came to see us once a month. They were both officers whom I liked and respected and I knew that, had I stayed there, I would soon have been in line for promotion.

In the autumn of that year I was told that I was going to be sent to another CG Station for a week to relieve the

Station Officer there. He was required in London to give evidence at a Board of Enquiry, which would be investigating the circumstances of a shipwreck the previous winter which had resulted in some loss of life.

The Station I was being sent to was at North Somercotes which proved to be a very lonely and desolate spot on the coast of Lincolnshire but, nevertheless, important because it was right on the shipping lanes in and out of the River Humber with its major ports of Hull and Grimsby. I left home on Sunday morning for the long drive north as I had to be there for eight a.m. on the Monday. I was to be accommodated in the local village pub because I suppose the Board of Trade thought it would not be appropriate for me to live in the SO's house while his wife was living there. I arrived at the pub in early evening and found the accommodation comfortable and the food good (also the beer). I remember one evening when the landlady asked me if I liked Yorkshire pudding and, of course, I said 'yes' but I was a bit surprised when I sat down for supper and she put in front of me a large soup plate with a Yorkshire Pudding about the size of a tea plate just floating in a mass of gravy! I thought, 'Is this it?' and was quite relieved when she gave me the next course – roast beef and veggies, of course.

The Station Officer's wife was a very pleasant lady, probably a couple of years older than me, and we spent lots of time, over cups of tea, talking about our lives. I remember her telling me that, when her husband left the Navy, they had emigrated to the United States and lived in Georgia. Apparently she could not stand it there so her husband bought a brand new convertible and they drove to Florida to settle there. It seems she could not bear to leave England so they packed up and returned home.

I had a lot of time to spare when I was there because, even when I was off duty, there was nowhere to go so I spent a lot of hours just walking and exploring the seashore which was pretty wild in that area. The Station Officer had a dog (some sort of terrier) which seemed to me to be hyper-active so I used to take it with me to try and wear it down a bit – but never succeeded.

Early in 1967 we were devastated by the news that Eileen's best friend, Hilda, had been diagnosed with cancer and, because it was in the liver, she only had a couple of months to live. Eileen and Hilda had been friends for twenty-five years (they had met when they both served in the Air Cadets in Worthing) and she had been Eileen's bridesmaid when we were married. Hilda was married to Clem and they lived, with one little boy, at Shoreham in Sussex. Until we had moved from that area we had been very close and had done everything together – picnics, beach parties, celebrations and even went on holiday together (to Warner's Holiday Camp at Hayling Island). During that awful couple of months Eileen would split her time between her own family and Hilda. On my off-duty day I would drive Eileen down to Shoreham, leave her there and then drive back to Lowestoft and then, four days later, reverse the procedure – drive to Shoreham, pick up Eileen and bring her home for four days. We covered a lot of miles at that time because it was about a hundred and fifty miles each way. When she died (I think it was late February or early March) we went to the funeral in Shoreham but found it difficult to believe that we had lost our lovely friend when she was only forty years old. It was not too long before Clem remarried – a lovely girl he had known slightly for many years – but, incredibly, he also contracted cancer and died very quickly.

A few weeks later we had another bolt from the blue – but this time it was not an unhappy one. This time it was a totally unexpected telephone call from my brother Jack, in Canada. It was so totally unexpected because, in the eleven years since we had seen each other, we had not been in contact except for exchanging Christmas cards.

Jack and his family had left England and emigrated to Canada in 1957, just a couple of months after Eileen and I had sailed for Hong Kong. In that time Jack had only returned to England once and that was when our Mother had died in late 1959, and that was only a brief visit for him. I knew, of course, that he had worked very hard in Canada and had made a success of his life there. I knew also that, a couple of years earlier, he and two partners had successfully bought and set up their own steel fabri-cation business – which told me that Jack was very settled in Canada, just as I now thought I was very settled in England. So it was quite a shock when Jack threw the cat among the pigeons and asked me when I was coming to Canada! At first I thought he was simply suggesting that we visit Canada and I remember responding that he and his family should visit us in England but gradually it sank in that he was suggesting that we should move to Canada permanently. I know I was quite taken aback by the idea and from thereon I am not quite sure what I said. I do recall that Jack was very persuasive but at the end of that telephone call everything was left in the air and no decisions had been taken, either way. However, Jack was not going to be put off that easily and over the next few weeks we had several letters from him and all explaining how great it was in Canada and how good the living was. I remember replying that, even so, we were now finally settled in England and, quite honestly, had never considered leaving England. Jack persisted and wrote letters detailing how much everything cost and he did it as he had been trained to do, i.e. Time and Motion Study – and told me how many hours I would work to buy a car, to buy a bottle of rye, to put food on the table for a week. It was a very comprehensive list but there was one thing missing – what would I be doing in order to earn this money to buy all these things?

I remember Jack's response to my question – he said, 'I think it is time we were working together in some sort of business,' and I think it was that statement which made me seriously consider his proposal. I know that all this time Eileen and I were having endless discussions, both with and without Julia and Karen. We were kind of forced to make a decision, one way or the other, when Jack told us that he had found a business for us and that, if we decided in favour of coming, we should arrange to get there as soon as possible. When the final vote was taken it came out three to one in favour. Eileen and I were keen to do it. Julia would be happy enough to go but Karen, at twelve years old, was very definitely against going to Canada.

Once the decision was taken we wasted no time in getting things organised and I remember thinking, 'Wow ... here we go again,' and, 'I hope we are right this time.' We went to the local travel agents and booked our passage on *The Empress of England* due to sail from Liverpool to Montreal on 15 May 1967. We also booked train tickets to get us from Montreal to Oakville.

I can well remember the day which the four of us spent in London in order to attend Canada House so as to complete the formalities to be accepted for emigration to Canada. It was not a simple procedure then and took several hours to complete – forms to be completed, questions to be answered, passports produced, verification of employment on arrival and evidence of a sponsor who would be responsible for us in Canada. We had to prove that we could read and write English, had no criminal record and that, eventually, we would be an asset to the country accepting us. Today, it amazes me when I hear of the hundreds of illegal immigrants who enter this country without permission – and then are allowed to remain here – what sort of people are running the country nowadays? Finally, we all had to undergo a medical examination and, all of us being in good health, took it as a formality and figured it would be a piece of cake. As we were about to leave the office I was told that the doctor wanted to see me again and, when I complied, he gave me the devastating news that he could not possibly allow me to go to Canada because my blood pressure was far too high! I tried to persuade him but he would not budge from his decision so I asked him what I could do about the situation. He said the only alternative was for me to go home and see my own doctor and when he was able to produce three satisfactory blood pressure readings, taken on three consecutive days, then my application would be reconsidered.

I wasted no time in getting to a doctor next day (I had not needed a doctor until then) and explained the situation to him, stressing the urgency of getting something done. He replied that medication could be prescribed to control it but first I would have to see a specialist and undergo tests to determine the underlying cause. When he told me that I could get a specialist's appointment in about two months I am sure it did nothing for my blood pressure – so I agreed to pay five guineas to see him 'privately' – in two days! I remember the specialist asking me reams of questions and then sending me to Norwich Hospital to undergo more tests. Nothing showed up and it was finally decided that mine was a hereditary problem; which meant that I was now able to start taking medication.

From then I was attending my Lowestoft doctor every day to have my BP checked – he told me it was improving, but very slowly – he was a good man and could see my impatience and recognised the need to get something done quickly. He told me that the only way we could do this was for him to check my BP, on three consecutive days,

before I got out of bed! So he came to my house at eight
o'clock every morning and, sure enough, got three satisfactory readings so that, thanks to him, I came to Canada.

Obviously the next few weeks of our lives were very
hectic, sometimes distressing, often exciting and always
very tiring. The physical effort of packing and leaving our
home was one thing but parting with some of our treasured
possessions was sometimes quite upsetting. I would have
loved to employ movers to pack everything in a large
container and so ship it to Canada but, unfortunately, the
cost of doing so was beyond our means – and so we were
faced with a 'do-it-yourself' type of move. Looking back
now, I think everything went remarkably well and, once
we were on the way, many of the sad moments were soon
forgotten.

Located on the Lowestoft shoreline, just to the north of
the Coastguard Lookout Station, was a very large factory
owned by Birds-Eye who were the leaders in the fairly
new, but rapidly growing, frozen food business. It was here
that they processed their 'garden peas' and, to do this,
employed a large number of local women in the plant. In
case you are wondering what is the point of this apparently
useless bit of information, I should tell you that some of
these women were our lifesavers when it came to selling
up our home. One of these workers at Birds-Eye was our
good friend Lorrie (Ted Field's wife) who offered to put
a 'for sale' notice on the notice board to advertise the
articles that we wanted to dispose of. I typed up a list with
all the details of what we had to offer and it was not long
before some of these women started knocking on our door
to see what was available. I remember Eileen described
some of them as 'a bit rough and tough but with hearts
of gold' because, having selected what they wanted and
paid for it, they insisted we should keep it until we were
ready to leave in a few weeks time.

Incidentally, Birds-Eye also provided (unknowingly) another bonus for the people at the Coastguard Station. In
August, when the pea crop was being harvested, there
would be a continual stream (about one an hour) of large,
open tractor-trailers (in England they are known as
'articulated lorries'), which were brimming over with all
these peas which were still on the vine. As they passed the
lookout we would wave to the drivers and many of them
would stop and drop off a large pile of peas-on-the-vine

for us. This meant the CG on duty would spend the rest of his watch picking off the pods and disposing of the vines.

When we had sold most of the smaller stuff we then had to get rid of some of the larger furnishings. We had a beautiful bedroom suite in rich cherry-wood with little brass handles – it was manufactured by Stag, a well-known maker of good quality items. It was less than two years old but we had only purchased it when we moved to Deal. Our advertisement was answered by a young lady, about to be married, who knew and loved that particular suite but could not afford to buy it new and was delighted to get it at a reasonable price. It made it a little easier for us to part with it – especially when she said we could keep the furniture until we were ready to leave. Another item was a lovely three piece lounge suite, also purchased when we went to Deal, which I remember was snapped up by a local dentist. We also had to dispose of our houseful of almost new carpet – it was a lovely soft 'Teal Blue' – and, when we advertised it, it was taken by a man who owned a boarding house and, happily he lifted it off our floor and took it away in his van.

For all our remaining possessions (in other words – whatever we would be taking to Canada with us) I had to make arrangements for the packaging and transport to the dock in Liverpool from where we would be sailing. I managed to find a woodworking shop in Lowestoft where they would custom make packing cases for me at a cost that was not too exorbitant. I think I ordered four to start with, but, as I found a need for more and more, I think I made two more visits and finished up with eleven wooden packing cases. With these, and a lot more stuff in suitcases and trunks, I managed to fill the truck that I was going to drive to Liverpool and back.

Our final travel arrangements did not include all four of us because Julia had decided she wanted to remain in Lowestoft for six more weeks in order to complete her GCE examinations. So, reluctantly, we agreed to leave her behind and accordingly made arrangements for her to travel by air and join us in Canada early in July. Very kindly our friends Lorrie and Ted Field had offered to accommodate her and look after her until the time for her departure. Also, they were very hospitable and accommodated all of us on our final night in Lowestoft and in England.

The *Empress of England* was due to sail from Liverpool in the early evening of 15 May 1967 and I believe we had to be on board by four p.m. To do this we got an early train from Lowestoft to London in order to catch the boat-train somewhere about 1.30 in the afternoon. This was all straightforward and there should not have been a problem but I (and my blood pressure) nearly screwed the whole thing up. The previous day I had made my final visit to the doctor who told me I was fine, just as long as I kept on taking the medication. Knowing that I was off to Canada, he pointed out that I would not have any medical insurance at first and, because the tablets were quite expensive, he would give me a prescription for an additional supply. For some reason I could not get to the chemist (drugstore) that evening and so figured I would pick them up somewhere *en route* to the ship (obviously the prescription would be no good after leaving England). Well, we had got to the boat train (I think it was from Liverpool Street Station) when I remembered the prescription still in my pocket. I bundled Eileen and Karen and our bags into a compartment and took off at a run to find a chemist because the train was due to pull out in about thirty minutes. Of course, when you really need something it can never be found and I think I must have run a mile before I spotted a chemist's shop. The chemist, who was not in a hurry, glared at me when I told him I was – but he did get moving when I explained why. With the tablets safely in my pocket, I started to gallop back to the train, thinking all the time, what would happen if the train left without me. I think I made it with about three minutes to spare, with a very worried looking Eileen leaning out of the carriage window looking for some sign of her errant husband!

It was, of course, a tremendous relief when we walked up the gangplank of *Empress of England*, with her gleaming white paint and her Canadian Pacific markings. I had something of a surprise though when I looked at the mast, expecting to see a Red Ensign flying there, but instead I saw a strange ensign with a red and white design and what I later learned to be a maple leaf.

We had a very pleasant voyage across the Atlantic and, being May, even the weather was good. Karen, who had been upset when we left Lowestoft, found lots to interest her, made friends and really enjoyed herself while on board.

I was a bit put off by one man who was travelling to Canada – he had a big beer-belly, wore cowboy boots, jeans, a black T-shirt and a cowboy hat and forever had an open can of beer in his hand. Fortunately, we made friends with a nice, elderly lady who was returning home after a visit to England and she hastened to assure us that not all Canadians were like that one!

Part Four
Canada

CHAPTER THIRTY-ONE

Canada

O N THE MORNING OF Friday 21 May 1967, as the *Empress of England* sailed majestically up the St Lawrence River, it was an exciting day for me. After a pleasant and comfortable voyage we were close to arriving in our newly adopted country and, of course, I was very keen to get an early glimpse of it and so I was up on the foredeck, with my binoculars, scanning the northern shoreline as it swept past us. I realised this was Quebec and I remember thinking how bleak and rugged it looked, with its little individual houses and small fishing villages, all looking very isolated and rather desolate. This image was not helped by the huge areas of snow along the shoreline and this was something that my English brain took a little while to adjust to – how could there be so much snow about on such a warm and sunny day? I was on deck with just a jacket and not feeling at all cold because it was a day that I would later learn to be rather typical Canadian weather. The sky was very blue and very high, the sun was warm and there was just a gentle breeze which scarcely put a ripple on the water.

Early afternoon on the same day the ship secured alongside in Quebec City and we all had to go ashore to be processed through the rather lengthy Immigration and Customs procedures. When it was all done I think we felt a little more secure in the knowledge that we were now officially 'Landed Immigrants' of Canada.

After our final night on board, the ship arrived in Montreal and it was thrilling to see, from the ship, the interesting structures of Expo '67 which reminded us that, being Canada's Centennial Year, it was an appropriate time for us to commence our new life in our new country. We docked in Montreal about eight in the morning and, having already completed all the formalities, disembarkation was a fairly simple operation. We were taken by special buses to Montreal railway terminal where we were due to catch the afternoon train to Toronto and all our heavy baggage would follow on later. It was now that Karen, once more, became terribly upset and, no matter what we did, or said, or promised, we were unable to console her. Whilst on board she had been fine but, as soon as she left the ship, her distress overcame her once more. Because of this Eileen had developed a headache and asked me to try and buy some aspirin or such like. Not realising that, in Canada, I needed a 'Drugstore' (and not a 'Chemist') I remember having some difficulty in making the local population understand what I was looking for but was finally successful when I switched to '*Pharmacie, s'il vous plâit?*' As we had a couple of hours to wait for our train time we decided to get a snack in the station buffet and, having ordered a 'chicken salad sandwich' each, were amazed at the size of the platefuls that were served to us. This was something that took a long time to get used to and was equally so when we later had visitors from England.

The train journey to Toronto seemed slow and rather boring because, even though we looked out the windows, we could not see much of real interest. Therefore we were very pleased to arrive in Toronto (I think it was about six p.m. because it was just getting dark). We were also very pleased that Jack and Vivien had driven into Toronto to meet us and thus saved us from catching another train from Union Station to Oakville. Of course, we were all delighted to meet again after so many years and it was quite a while before we ran out of questions and answers. I remember on the drive to Oakville, along the QEW, being amazed at the size of Canadian cars compared to English. Jack's car was a brand new 1967 Ford Galaxie – dark green with a black interior and very large and comfortable. His previous vehicle was a 1963 Rambler which I agreed to buy from him for five hundred dollars.

Jack and Vivien were very hospitable in welcoming us into their home and, I remember, he quite soon introduced me to something called rye & ginger. They lived in a very nice bungalow at 512 Lees Lane and their children were Martyn and Paul, who were both at school, and Debbie who was just six months old.

We were surprised and delighted, when we found that Monday 24 May was a holiday – 'Victoria Day' to celebrate Queen Victoria's birthday, which was something we had never done in England. Already I was beginning to like Canada with its tradition of 'long weekends'. The weather remained clear and bright and we did not stray far from home on those first couple of days.

121 Allan Street, Oakville

ALTHOUGH JACK AND VIVIEN insisted that we could stay with them as long as we wished, Eileen and I were keen to be settled in some sort of place of our own again.

So, after the weekend, Eileen and Vivien set out to find us an apartment and very quickly found one that we liked in a complex of three apartment buildings at Allan Street and Lakeshore Road in downtown Oakville. It was a nice, one-bedroom unit on the ninth floor and, from our balcony, we could see Lake Ontario. Best of all, the rent seemed to be affordable – I think it was about a hundred and sixty dollars a month which sounds ridiculous now.

We wasted no time in getting into Toronto to buy some furniture for our new home. I remember we borrowed Vivien's car – a nice Ford Falcon convertible in white with a blue interior – to drive to Consumers Distributing on Castlefield Road. I can still hear Jack saying, 'Stay on the 401 but don't miss Trafalgar Road or you will finish up in Milton.' We bought bunk beds for the girls, a bedroom suite for us (which we have still got), a dinette set and a bed/chesterfield and chair, which was huge and very heavy. By this time our numerous wooden crates had arrived at Oakville Station and I arranged for them to be picked up and delivered to us. I remember Eileen and I were very busy getting this stuff unpacked one evening when Jack and Vivien arrived unexpectedly and we were very pleased to see them – and not just because they were carrying a bottle of gin, a bottle of tonic and a bag of ice!

At the beginning of July, as arranged, Julia came by air from England, having successfully completed her GCE examinations and expecting to start work in Canada (just as she would have done in England). However, because she was still one month short of sixteen, she was told she would have to attend high school for one more year and did spend that time at White Oaks High School – repeating secretarial subjects in which she had already qualified. It was arranged for Karen to attend Blakelock High School where she did not do well because she hated being there, mostly due to teasing and bullying by other students. Subsequently, we took her away from Blakelock and sent her, privately, to Sylvia Gill Secretarial School where she settled down and did exceptionally well.

Upon our arrival in Canada one of the very welcome things we noticed was how polite and pleasant all Canadians seemed to be – although it took a while to get accustomed to 'Have a nice day'. It was not long before we realised that Canadians, whilst very polite and friendly, were not people who made friends easily. One instance of this was a couple we met soon after arriving in Oakville – Bill and Betty Pettigrew lived in a nice house on Riverside Drive where we were invited once or twice. They were pleasant people and both went out of their way in their efforts to get us settled here in Canada but, on the other hand, we never really socialized with them. Betty was senior secretary to a Toronto lawyer (Cel Weiler) who also lived in Oakville and Betty managed to get Julia a job with him when she left school and thus began her career as a legal secretary. Bill Pettigrew had been in the Canadian Army and, for his part, tried hard to find a recreational pursuit that would hold our interest. He took us bowling and he took us curling and he took me to the Oakville Canadian Legion where he was a member.

In our apartment building we got to know a few people. There was David Schooling and his wife – he was a young doctor, over from England about a year and doing very well at Oakville Hospital and would soon have his own practice. There was another English couple we knew quite well but I cannot remember their name – Jack had been an engineer in the Royal Navy, which gave us some common ground. They had a young daughter – about one year older than Karen (which would make her 13–14) but who seemed very mature for her years and I remember we were a little concerned for their friendship, but we need not have worried. From a very attractive young girl she grew into a very plain young lady and, last we heard, she had become a missionary.

Our first summer in Canada in 1967, from a recreational point of view, was fabulous and this was due to two things. Firstly, the weather was continually gorgeous and, secondly, Jack would propose that we should all go for a picnic and swim – on every Sunday. Remembering the unsettled climate of England – even in the summer – I could not believe it was possible to arrange an outing so far ahead and not be disappointed! We would travel to various swimming places – like Elora Gorge, Crystal Beach on Lake Erie, Glen Eden or Emerald Lake. The last was undoubtedly our favourite and we spent many happy Sundays, swimming, barbequing and generally relaxing. It was a private property (due west from Carmbelleville) and there would be a nominal entrance fee.

When the winter of 67/68 came we were to find out what winter was really like and we had to get used to snow tires and anti-freeze – things we never had to think about in England. In the New Year of 1968 came a bad winter storm which hit Oakville on the weekend – there was heavy snow on Friday and Saturday and, that night, there was continuous freezing rain, which was another new experience for us. When we went for a walk on Sunday the Reynolds Street area was like a winter wonderland – all the trees looked as though they had been cocooned in glass, and were just as brittle so that many of them suffered severe damage as heavy branches just snapped like twigs.

Our life in Canada began in Oakville, simply because my brother had settled here and therefore it seemed the natural thing to do. We soon found that Oakville was a very pleasant place to live and, for that reason, we have never had any wish to live elsewhere in Canada. In 1967 Oakville was still very small time. With a population of only 52,000 it had not begun the rapid expansion that has put it on the map in recent time. The Queen Elizabeth Way seemed to be the northern boundary of the town because the only thing above the QEW was farmland. Oakville's main claim to fame seemed to be that the Ford Motor Company had established their Canadian manufacturing plant here and most of the population seemed to be employed there or at Mack Trucks, just across the QEW. Oakville was always proud of its long and interesting history when the harbour had been one of the most important shipbuilding and industrial centres on Lake Ontario. In 1967 both of the harbours were, as yet, undeveloped for modern boating but it now has three of the finest recreational boating harbours in the area. Shopping facilities were very limited and comprised the downtown core and a few strip plazas. Oakville Place had not been thought of and indoor shopping malls were still a thing of the future. What is now Bronte Village Mall was then a rather rundown motel property with lots of dilapidated cabins scattered around. The property opposite Bronte Village Mall was a rather grim looking Junior School, before being re-developed with Lick's and The Coach & Four. Hopedale Mall was then Hopedale Plaza with the two 'anchor stores' being Dominion and a rather insignificant S.S. Kresge. Another early memory of Oakville was that it was the Area HQ of the Canadian Army, located in Ortona Barracks on Kerr Street which has now become the Kerr Street Senior Citizens Centre.

Another oddity of life in Canada which struck us as rather outdated and even unnecessary was the strange method of controlling sales of beer and liquor. Stores for the sale of liquor were grim looking places where it was first necessary to fill out an order form, complete with name and address, before a suspicious looking assistant would disappear out to the back of the store to fetch the bottle of one's choice. Fortunately, modern, self-serve outlets have replaced this archaic system. I can also remember one Saturday evening when the four of us went to the new Holiday Inn in Oakville for a drink. Eileen and Vivien found a seat but, because there were not seats for Jack and me we were not allowed to buy a drink.

Thorco Manufacturing Limited

I DO NOT WANT TO GET TOO INVOLVED in describing my brother's business affairs but it is necessary to give an outline here, simply because his company proved to be such a major factor in the course of my life in Canada.

Jack had trained with an engineering company in England and had become something of an expert in the art of 'Time & Motion Study' and, with this qualification, had managed to obtain employment in Canada with McGraw Edison Limited who were then one of the major manufacturers of both large and small electrical appliances. They had a large manufacturing plant on Browns Line in New Toronto and after Jack had been with them a few years he was doing very well. I believe it was in 1964 that the company decided to sell off part of their manufacturing operation in order to concentrate their efforts on what were obviously the more profitable lines of production.

The outcome was that Jack, with two partners, took over the operation and set up their own business, in the same building, for the fabrication and painting of steel products. They also took over existing contracts for supplying parts for a variety of equipment including washing machines and driers, gasoline pumps, vending machines and drug-store shelving and dispensary cabinets. Three years later, when I arrived in Canada, the company, although proceeding cautiously, was doing well and almost ready to expand.

Zip-Grip International Incorporated

THIS WAS THE COMPANY that had lured me from England so that Jack and I could work together. Unfortunately, it was an enterprise which was ill-fated from the start.

The business, which had been dormant for a few years, involved the manufacture and sale of a quite ingenious wire clothes-line for drying the laundry and this was to be sold, in kit form, to the general public. Initially, I had doubts about the general practicality of the idea because of the Canadian climate and also the availability of driers, but I did not express them forcibly because, being in England, I was not knowledgeable enough about conditions over here. I was also persuaded by the fact that Zip-Grip had proved successful for the previous owner, who had made a lot of money with the system.

Doug MacKenzie was the current owner but, when I met him, I knew that he was not a man I would ever get to know, or like. He was small in stature, wore a long overcoat and drove a big car and was out to impress what a great businessman he was. There were intended to be four partners – MacKenzie, Jack, myself and a fourth man (who was to be the Sales Manager) but who backed out just prior to my arrival. The deal was that each would provide five thousand dollars and, having forwarded mine from England, I felt committed before I arrived but, being very keen to get going, was not too unhappy.

I was naïve enough to assume that the funds provided were for operating the company – until MacKenzie arrived one day to show off his new Cadillac Eldorado. He was to be a silent partner but would sign all cheques while I would be paid a salary of $125 a week to work the company and Jack would oversee day-to-day running of Zip-Grip.

The first physical obstacle we came up against was the location of where the business was to operate. Initially all the equipment and spare parts were stored in a large and windowless, corrugated steel shed in Alliston near to Doug MacKenzie's home. At first, Jack seemed to think we could operate from there but, because it was fifty-two miles from home, I was strongly in favour of moving it nearer to the Oakville area. Being unable to find any suitable, or affordable, premises near home we finally arranged to rent space and locate in the McGraw Edison Building (alongside Thorco) on Browns Line.

The actual move was completed in about five days by recruiting three 'wino's' from the Employment Office to do the packing and loading and with me flogging back and forth in an old Chev. pickup truck borrowed from Jack's brother-in-law Arnold. It was invariably overloaded and I think I was lucky to complete the move without any serious incident. Well, there was one incident – I had just driven my little helpers home to Jarvis Street and (because Jack had warned me) I was careful about the speed limit on the Gardiner Expressway (70 mph then) but coming off the highway onto Browns Line (with only two hundred yards to go!) I got pulled over by a large yellow police cruiser with all the lights and siren going! The large policeman seemed a little confused when I produced an International Driving Licence (issued in England) and explained that I had only been in Canada for one week. Strangely, he did not give me a ticket there and then – just wrote all my answers on a long pad and told me I would be hearing more about this later. He also noted the name on the truck door – 'Vermeltfoort RR1 Caledonia' because, about a week later, the police arrived at Arnold's farm and questioned him about this Robert Adams. Somehow Arnold convinced them that he did not know me – so they left and I never heard any more about it!

Jack and I got the equipment set up and functioning and also built an office (around a desk borrowed from Thorco). We managed to find a replacement salesman after a while and, working on commission, sent him off with a bunch of 'qualified leads' in his hand to find distributors on the US East Coast, especially Florida. After four or five weeks of driving his back gave out and he phoned to say goodbye. We were now left with sales obtained from a continuous running advertisement in the *Financial Post*.

During this time Jack and I, besides working hard, attended regular weekly meetings with our President, Mr MacKenzie, which always seemed to take place, in the evenings, way out in Scarborough where he operated a 'nursing home' for old folks. In those days I don't think there was much in the way of regulations and I soon realised that, for him, it was just a way of making easy money. I remember he often boasted of 'living on other people's money' and I soon learned what he meant. Every time we arrived at the nursing home the Matron was engaged in a discussion with him about paying bills, which he would not do until the last possible moment. It was a case of, 'The butcher refuses to deliver any more meat unless he is paid tomorrow' or, 'The cook is going to quit unless she gets paid.' After about a year Jack and I realised Zip-Grip was not going to make it and so we decided to bale out. The company was taken over by a young and energetic engineer who moved it to new premises but, in spite of his best efforts, it eventually failed.

517 Lees Lane, Oakville

AT THE END OF OUR FIRST YEAR in Canada our apartment lease at Allan Street was about to expire and we felt that, rather than renew it, we should make a move toward a more permanent home. Although we had thoroughly enjoyed our apartment living, we desperately wanted a permanent home of our own again and knew that, until we achieved it, we would continue to feel rather like gypsies. The big problem was that, at that time, there was no way we could afford to buy a house and so we set about looking for rental properties. As we searched we were getting a bit depressed because we could not seem to find anything suitable – at least not within our price range. We looked at basement apartments, above-store apartments, a couple of rental bungalows and shared apartments in private homes.

By a tremendous stroke of good fortune, it was Vivien who found the answer for us. She had a friend who lived in a small bungalow which was immediately opposite Jack and Vivien's home on Lees Lane and she told Vivien that she was about to move out (I forget for what reason). We all felt that, if we could get it, this would be ideal for us. Cute was not a word that I used in those days but that is how I would describe it today. It was a quite small, wooden construction, painted white and with quite a large and attractive garden. It had two small bedrooms, a living room and a very large kitchen which, we learned later, had been added when the building was converted from a chicken house! There was an oil-fired furnace and we had to provide our own appliances. First, though, we had to overcome one obstacle, namely the owner of the property who regarded us very suspiciously and questioned us very closely before deciding that perhaps we were not going to wreck his bungalow. The previous tenant had been his own daughter and he was now reluctant to allow strangers to live in his bungalow. Gus Dreger and his wife were, I believe, from Eastern Europe originally and both were stern faced and unsmiling people but, once we were accepted, they were as good as gold although they always kept a close watch on the state of the garden. Gus, who owned a local construction business, was a large man and he and his wife lived in a correspondingly large house not far away on Rebecca Street.

During the time we were in the bungalow, which was about fifteen months, we enjoyed very much having the feeling of somehow 'belonging' once more. Quite soon we found that Eileen was pregnant and, although she was now 42 years old, Dr Bykerk felt that was acceptable but unfortunately it ended when she had a miscarriage. It was just at this time that we were visited by Eileen's brother Nick and his wife Marina who had been on vacation in New York. Later that same year (in the fall) I went into Oakville Hospital for emergency surgery to remove my gall bladder.

The Christmas of 1968 was quite memorable because we were now able to offer some hospitality in return and, thanks to our oversize kitchen, managed to seat thirteen or fourteen people to help with the turkey on Christmas Day.

However, we were always longing for the day when we would have a real home of our own again, but with our present income, the prospects were not too bright. Eileen even got herself a job in the factory at the GEC plant in Oakville. It was a boring and uninspiring job – cleaning the print off thousands of light bulbs – and it was not very well paid. However, fate was kind to us again when, in the April of 1969, a lady knocked at the door and asked Eileen for a donation (I think it was Red Cross or The United Way). They got chatting about life with the result that Eileen was asked if she would be interested in a secretarial job and, if so, to phone soon for an appointment. The lady at the door was Mel Carey who was then the Personnel Manager for Procor Limited. The outcome was that Eileen was taken on as 'Assistant to the Contracts Administrator' – who was then Frank Westlake – and she remained in that job until she retired thirteen and a half years later.

This rather sudden and unexpected improvement in our financial situation made a tremendous difference to our dreams of a home and so we lost no time in doing a bit of house hunting. It proved to be a long and tedious process and, at first anyway, the results did not seem to be encouraging. By now we knew our way around Oakville and were very much attracted to the older areas of the town where there were many beautiful homes but, of course, most of them were beyond our reach financially. Even the modest ones were stretching it for us and there was the added disadvantage that most of East Oakville was not yet connected to the town's main sewer system. Thenceforth we were to concentrate our search in West Oakville but still without success until we hit upon a new housing project, in quite early stages, in the area just below Rebecca Street and a little west of Hopedale. Some homes were built and occupied and they also had several model homes, fully furnished and open to the public. It did not take us long to select our own ideal home and from then on Eileen, at every chance she had, would visit the model home and sit on the chesterfield in the living room – just pretending that we were living there.

It was early July of 1969 when we finally took the plunge, paid our deposit and, almost unbelievably, placed an order for the home of our choice to be built. We were told that this would take six weeks to complete which, at first, sounded incredibly fast but then, of course, time seemed to drag by. I remember the agent for the project was a Mr Winters, a very inoffensive and helpful man, who 'lived' in one of those office/trailers on the site. We had to choose the building site and selected a rather large corner lot which, amazingly, was the same price as the smaller lots, and also gave a lot of thought deciding on various colour schemes and materials to be used for flooring and bathrooms and such.

We could hardly wait for the day when the builders 'broke ground' for our new home and thereafter we would visit the site every day to see what sort of progress they were making.

2132 Sunnyvale Drive, Oakville

WE HAD GIVEN NOTICE that we would vacate the bungalow on Lees Lane on 31 August 1969 and arrangements were made for us to move into Sunnyvale Drive on the same day. Before that day arrived, however, there were a couple of amusing incidents that I think are worth recounting here.

Mr Weiler, who was Julia's employer, was acting for us in the purchase of Sunnyvale Drive and, because he lived in Oakville, we asked him to visit the site with us so as to give an opinion on the quality of materials and construction, bearing in mind that we were pretty ignorant about Canadian building methods. Of course, he agreed and, on the appointed day, we all met at the 'model home' because ours was not yet started. I do not remember if that was a particularly wet summer but I do remember the area in front of the house was just a sea of mud and the builder had placed duckboards up to the front door for the benefit of visitors. Eileen, dressed for the occasion with high heels and nylons, managed to slip off the boards and went into the mud which covered both of her ankles! Well, Mr Weiler thought this was the most hilarious thing he had seen and could not stop laughing and, in later years, never missed an opportunity to remind Eileen of her 'slip'.

The second event did not seem so funny when it happened but we had many a good laugh about it later. Our house was to be a 'split level' and so would have two staircases (one to the upper level and one to the basement) installed side by side and we had a choice of the arrangement. We made our decision, which was duly noted on the plan, but one day when visiting the site to check progress, we were horrified to find they had installed them the wrong way round. Well, it all ended OK for us but the builder was not too thrilled about ripping out two staircases and changing them round!

There was one glitch immediately prior to our moving date when the crew installing the hardwood flooring went on strike. Most of our floors had been completed but the living/dining room had not been started and the builder said he couldn't get anyone else to do it and, very generously (?), offered us a discount of one hundred dollars off the purchase price if we accepted plywood flooring instead. Because we were so close to moving in – and knowing we intended to have broadloom anyway – we accepted the offer.

In our search for a home we had decided that our financial limit was to be thirty thousand dollars (wouldn't that be nice today?). For that reason Sunnyvale Drive seemed just made for us because the purchase price was to be twenty-eight thousand five hundred dollars – that is until we started looking at the 'extras' that were offered. There was available, at an additional six hundred dollars each (I could never understand how they could all be the same value but figured it made the accounting easy), several options. There was a double garage, a bay window in the living room, a floor to ceiling brick fireplace in the family room and the 'crawlspace' could be excavated to provide additional basement space.

Well, we finally decided on going for the first three of these options.

In the couple of weeks prior to our move Eileen and I were busy shopping for additional furniture, carpets and drapes etc. and, of course, this was made possible by Eileen's improved income situation. We went to Danny & Jean's Interiors in Bronte on Lakeshore Road where we selected carpeting, drapes, sheers, a chesterfield suite and a gold chair – all of this was to be paid, by Eileen, at one hundred dollars a month. We also went to Home & Rural Furniture on Kerr Street where we purchased a nice Diel-craft dining room suite. Once this lot was delivered and installed we were all set because we already had bedroom furniture and, of course, all our appliances.

The day of the move did not go quite according to plan because, being the last day of the month, the movers were, typically, double booked. This meant a lot of wasted time, with Eileen at Lees Lane and me at Sunnyvale Drive, each without a phone and wondering what was happening. I think we finally completed our move-in just after ten o'clock that evening.

Initially, of course, there was no landscaping on the property and so we were very pleased when a couple of guys arrived to lay sod all around the house and, when it was finished, it was a tremendous improvement. A couple of days later (on the Sunday) we were surprised to see a man and a woman walking around our garden with a tape measure and, when I asked what they were doing I found they were the owners of the sod company and could not believe the huge amount of sod used to landscape one property!

We were then faced with the problem of what to do with this enormous garden and, more important, the most economical way of doing it. We could not bear to leave this space looking rather like a vacant football field so we decided to fill it with fruit trees (cheap to buy and fast to grow) and finished up with fourteen apple, two pear and a couple of peach trees. Of course, they were tiny little things, as were the two blue spruce I ordered from Sears catalogue (2 for $5.00) and, at first, I had to be careful not to run over them with the lawnmower but later they grew into enormous trees.

It was not too long before we started thinking about recreational pursuits – or, in other words, how were we going to be spending our free time, mostly weekends. The obvious choices seemed to be a cottage, a boat, or a swimming pool and it was not easy to decide. We had already had a little experience of vacation cottages and we really loved the country/lake environment. After a great deal of deliberation on the subject, we turned down the idea for one reason – we could not face the thought of all the travelling involved – racing to get there Friday night and joining the traffic jams coming home again on Sunday night. Boating seemed very attractive to all of us but, in those days, boating was nothing like as popular as it is today – so that one was dropped also.

So we were left with the swimming pool in the garden idea and, although we were all enthusiastic about the project, we realised that we knew little about pools and, because they were still quite new in Canada, we had to tread carefully.

In February 1971 we attended the Pool & Patio Show, held in the CNE buildings, and persuaded Jack and Vivien to accompany us. They had recently moved from Lees Lane to a nice home on Watersedge Drive which was not too far from us. I recall spending the whole evening, going from one manufacturer or distributor to the next, asking endless questions of them and collecting numerous brochures. Finally, we decided we were most impressed by Willow Pools (a division of Willow Construction) who were the Canadian distributor for an in-ground pool they were importing from Los Angeles. I think what really decided us was that they had a fully functional pool installed, complete with water and a couple of very attractive 'mermaids'!

Having both decided to 'go for it', we then set about getting a good deal and placing the orders. 'The deal' was that we each got a fifty dollar discount for placing a double order for two pools to be installed in the same vicinity. They were to be put in during early May and I know we all went home very happy that night. This was a decision that Eileen and I would never regret because it provided endless fun for the two of us, for our children and their friends – and all without any tedious travelling!

During the twenty-three years we lived at Sunnyvale Drive our pool was the focal point of so many barbeque evenings and garden parties which were always very popular and well attended. In addition, there was one particular night when there was a pool party – and Eileen and I knew nothing about it 'till the next day. Although our bedroom was at the back of the house, overlooking the pool, the air conditioning was running so all the windows were closed and we never heard a sound. Bill and Stephanie were our friends and neighbours at the back and they heard all the splashing going on and, knowing it was not us, called the police but they were not too interested and did not show. The first I heard of it was the next morning (Sunday) when I went to introduce myself to a new next-door neighbour who had moved in the previous day – he said, 'You had a really good party last night.'

There was another incident which was also attributed to high school students on summer vacation and looking for mischief. It was a Friday evening and Eileen and I had gone to bed earlier than usual and the house was in darkness. Before we were asleep we thought we heard a strange noise from downstairs and, when we saw Lulu our Siamese cat sitting, fully alert, at the bedroom door, we knew there was something up. As I jumped out of bed I heard the distinctive sound of the back door being opened and reached the kitchen just in time to see a couple of shadowy figures leaping over the fence. This time I called the police and when they arrived, twenty minutes later, we had been joined by Bill and Stephanie and were all enjoying a drink to calm our shattered nerves. The break-in was our own fault because, until that time, we had not bothered to put any locks on the sliding windows. We soon realised that entry had been gained by sliding the dining room window open and then, because Eileen had numerous small ornaments along the windowsill, they had very carefully placed each one on the grass outside before climbing through. The only thing missing was a twenty-dollar bill, taken from Eileen's purse which had been on the kitchen table. They then left through the back door.

Julia and Karen

Since their arrival in Canada, the girls had rapidly developed from schoolgirls into attractive and well-adjusted young ladies but obviously not without a few of the inevitable problems that all youngsters have to go through. Older people will often envy the youth of younger people but they also tend to forget the difficulties of growing up. I really believe that until youngsters reach maturity and find their own slot in life, the transition period can be (and usually is) quite traumatic for them because they are faced with situations to deal with, and decisions to be made – all without the benefit of wisdom and experience that comes with age.

Both girls had their own share of youthful problems – some home-related, some at school or work, and, of course, a few connected with romantic associations. One of the early problems was that for a long time Julia and Karen seemed to be really bitter enemies but I think this changed about the time Karen left school and now it gives us great pleasure to see how their friendship has grown and strengthened over the years.

In the summer of 1968, when Julia left school, she went to work as a secretary for Mr Weiler in Toronto. She was very fortunate in being able to get into a car pool but I know she hated the travelling – she liked her work, Mr Weiler was an excellent employer and, of course, she enjoyed having some money to spend. I think it was early in 1969 she decided to buy herself a car and after quite a bit of searching, we found a very smart Volkswagen Beetle at Oakville Volkswagen on Kerr Street. It was a dark green 1968 demonstrator, which had been jazzed up with wire wheels and some racing stripes and was a really sharp looking car.

After two years of working in Toronto Julia decided that she wanted to go and work in England for a year. This was quite a bit of a shock to us, and some people believed that we should not allow an eighteen-year-old to go off on her own, but knowing Julia to be a sensible and responsible person, we reluctantly gave her our blessing. She was to share a flat in London with Sally, a former school friend, and we soon learned that she had landed a job with a fashionable and exclusive firm of jewellers in Kensington. Julia really enjoyed her year in England – so much so that she decided to stay an extra six months. However, she admitted later that, in the summer of 1971 when she was at London Airport to see Aunty Eve and Aunt Gertie off to Canada to visit us, she would have dearly loved to be going with them.

Just about the same time as Julia went to England, Karen finished her time at Sylvia Gill Secretarial College and set about finding herself a job. Without telling us, she answered a newspaper advertisement for a secretary and came home early one day to announce that she was now working for a lawyer in Oakville. It was also at this time that Karen started driving and could not believe her luck when she found that Julia was going to entrust her with the *Beetle* while she was away. Karen proved herself to be a good driver and there were no problems.

It came as no great surprise to us when we realised that our girls were growing up to be quite adventurous young women, keen to see something of the world. About a year after Julia's return from England (I think it was in 1973) they decided to take a vacation together in Hawaii and I think they enjoyed it so much that all their holidays were joint efforts after that.

I think their next big event was when they both decided they wanted to go and live, and work, in Montreal. This was a really big wrench for us to let both of them go but, after making sure that this was what they really wanted, we had to agree with it. The plan was that after arriving there by train, they would stay at the YWCA until they found their own apartment and, as regards work, they were confident they could at least get temporary employment through an agency. Of course, their baggage contained virtually all clothing and everything else would have to be 'found' once they were established there.

I remember that, after seeing them off at Union Station, I stopped at Sears in Sherway Gardens and arranged for a small colour television to be sent to them. It was supposed to be delivered to them at the YWCA but somehow it never materialised – somebody must have diverted it for their own use – and Sears had to come up with a replacement for them.

The first accommodation they found was an apartment in quite a large, older home on Pine Avenue but, of course, it was not self-contained. Later on they were rather lucky to find a very nice apartment in a large, modern building in the Mount Royal area. Julia soon settled into a permanent position with a large corporation but Karen was happier with temporary positions through the agency, even though many places she worked offered her employment on a permanent basis.

During the couple of years they were there Eileen and I visited them twice – once by air and once by road. Our first visit was to Pine Avenue and we were due to fly out of Hamilton at 5 p.m. on the Friday and, although I left work early, we almost missed the plane. I had never driven to Mount Hope before and so finding my way in the heavy traffic and heavy snow was not too easy and I think we arrived with just a couple of minutes to spare – the plane was ready for take-off but they were holding the door for us and, as soon as we flopped into our seats, we were off the ground – next stop Dorval. I will always remember the cost of that flight – it was a special – ninety-nine dollars return!

The second visit, by car, was less nerve-racking because it was in the summer and I remember driving out to the

Laurentians and thinking how attractive the little towns and ski resorts would be in the winter.

I well remember one snowy Christmas which proved to be a near disaster, not for us but certainly for Julia and Karen who had planned to spend Christmas at home with us and intended travelling by train from Montreal on the evening of that Christmas Eve and Eileen and I would meet them at Union Station in Toronto at about ten p.m.

However, the awful weather changed these plans – the snow in Toronto was bad enough but in Montreal it was ten times worse which, of course, made their journey home nearly impossible. Eileen and I arrived in Toronto early and spent four hours alternating between Union Station and the Royal York Hotel, via the underground tunnel. Each time at the station we would enquire about the train only to be told it was delayed by weather and a time of arrival was not available. Each time at the Royal York we would try to distract our minds by watching all the comings and goings in the spacious lobby. Finally, we were told that the train from Montreal was due and eagerly went up to the platform, only to be disappointed because, when the train pulled in, there was no sign of Julia and Karen. We asked one of the station staff who said, 'No – everybody is off the train.' Then we saw, down at the far end of the platform, two forlorn little figures, loaded with parcels and struggling through the snow – what a relief it was! On the drive home we heard the sorry story – Julia had been working all day but Karen had not so they arranged to meet at Montreal train station and Karen was to bring their luggage and the Christmas presents. Due to the severe storm Karen had difficulty getting on a bus and finally had to leave their suitcases at home and come on with just the gifts. Of course, we all had a wonderful Christmas together, even if it was a 'dressed down' event for the girls.

After two years of living and working in Montreal, Julia and Karen felt it was time to return home and I planned to drive there, with a U-Haul trailer, to bring their stuff back to Oakville. Then Jack volunteered to help me and, because he was then driving a big Thunderbird, it was decided we should use his car. We drove to Montreal, picked up a 12 ft trailer, and then spent the night at the girls' apartment. Next day we loaded up and drove home, arriving early evening to unload the contents in my garage. On the following day the girls were booked to fly off on another adventure – this time a vacation in Barbados. I know they thoroughly enjoyed their holiday except for Karen coming home with terrible sunburn – trying to get a final last minute tan.

Subsequently they were to enjoy other exotic vacations together including one to Acapulco where Julia and Karen managed to go para-sailing on their last day by trading their beach bags for a trip. Julia also took her camera aloft with her, to get a bird's-eye view of the beach.

They were also fortunate later on, when Julia was working for Mr Weiler again, in being able to visit Sanibel Island in Florida when Mr Weiler let them use his 'time-share' condominium there.

Inevitably, there were a few 'junior romances' for both of them but, just when they seemed to be getting interesting, they would fizzle out. Nevertheless, Eileen and I got a lot of pleasure from seeing these young people enjoying the pool, the BBQ and each other. All of the boys were very pleasant and a couple of them quite interesting. One of them even offered to help me paint the house but, although very willing, did not prove to be the greatest of helpmates.

My little helper would arrive about ten a.m. and I would get him started but he was not the speediest of painters – you could picture him painting the Sistine Chapel instead of my eaves – and, half an hour later, would suggest we should have a beer. One young man, when we were on a cottage vacation, brought his powerboat from two lakes away and purchased new ski equipment because he heard we were into water ski-ing.

Ultimately, of course, both girls chose (or were chosen) wisely and well. Karen was the first to ring the wedding bells when, after meeting John on a 'blind date', they became very close and finally became engaged in 1981. There was no talk about a wedding because, both being very private people, they could not face the exposure of a family wedding and had decided to elope. Eileen and I knew nothing of their plans – we were just told that they were going to a cottage for the weekend 'to help a friend build a dock'. In fact, their arrangements were a bit more elaborate and the first Eileen knew was a telephone call from Karen saying that she and John had been married that morning in a church in Saint Croix in the US Virgin Islands. Karen was very worried that Eileen would be upset because she had not been told but, in fact, we were both so very happy for Karen and John and wished them all the luck in the world. That evening, which was Saturday 22 May 1982, Eileen and I went out to dinner to celebrate the occasion and invited our friends Bill and Stephanie to join us. We went to the Windjammer restaurant in Clarkson and Bill, who had been a heavy smoker for many years, marked the event by giving up smoking – and, to the best of my knowledge, has not smoked since that evening.

John and Karen did not immediately produce a family because they had a very carefully thought out 'five-year plan' in which they were going to enjoy travel and vacations before settling down to family life. Their most ambitious one was to Australia where they flew out to Alice Springs (John had always had an ambition to do this) and climbed Ayers Rock. After returning to Sydney they embarked for a cruise on the new P&O liner *Oriana*. They visited Hong Kong, Singapore (where John was anxious to visit the famous Raffles Hotel) and also Bangkok.

John and Karen,
Wedding Day, St Croix,
Virgin Islands, 22 May
1982.

Karen on her Wedding
Day, St Croix, Virgin
Islands, 22 May 1982.

On 4 November 1988 (right on schedule) Karen produced their firstborn, Britt, in Oakville Hospital and followed this with two more lovely babies – Signy on 22 January 1990 and Olivia on 21 October 1993. All three girls were a real joy to us all and are now rapidly growing into delightful young ladies.

After the girls returned from Montreal Julia apparently decided to have a change of pace because when Mr Weiler offered her the job back (even though she liked him and knew him as a generous employer) she wanted to try something different. She got herself a job as a secretary with the Halton Board of Education, working at the General Wolfe High School in Oakville. I know she enjoyed the time she spent there – no doubt due to the younger and more active environment. She also changed

John Andersen on his Wedding Day, St Croix, Virgin Islands, 22 May 1982.

her image with a change of car – this time it was a very sporty Triumph TR6, in navy blue and I thought it suited her very well.

I think it was after another couple of years that both girls got itchy feet again and decided to find themselves an apartment in Toronto. After some searching they were successful in getting a nice unit in the High Park area of Toronto.

By now the TR6 had been changed for a very tiny Morris Mini which caused Eileen to have a fit every time Julia took it on the QEW. I remember driving it myself and thought afterwards that I would never be able to straighten my legs again. A couple of years later this was replaced by a Ford Capri in chocolate brown.

Not too long after Karen's wedding we found that Julia

was to follow suit and we could not have been happier. Julia met Jim at a Hallowe'en party in Toronto where she was giving an impressive imitation of Superwoman – it must have impressed Jim because it was not too long before they announced their engagement. This time it was to be a traditional affair in a church with a reception to follow. When these arrangements had been made the date was fixed for 14 July 1984. Julia and Jim had booked a very nice church in Toronto and the reception was to be held at the Old Mill. Invitations went out to all our friends and relatives and we were all pleased when we heard that Aunty Gertie and Aunty Eve would be able to attend from

Eileen, Jim, Julia and Bob at Julia's wedding.

England. When the big day arrived it proved to be the hottest day of the year but I think we were all too excited to notice it. John had volunteered to be our 'chauffeur' and drove Julia and me to the church in Toronto. The reception was held in the Garden Room at the Old Mill so that we were able to walk outside to have a drink and take photographs in the fresh air. The only glitch was at dinner when a young waitress, carrying a very large tray of melon balls, slipped and fell – melon balls everywhere. Somehow they managed to replace them very quickly. Julia and Jim had made arrangements to spend their honeymoon on the beautiful islands of Fiji but another snag occurred when, after a long flight, they were unable to land in Fiji due to a strike of air traffic controllers. They continued on to New Zealand and, after a few days, they were able to continue their honeymoon in Fiji,

Julia and Jim did not have a five-year plan and so Emma, the first of our five grandchildren, arrived in this world on 3 October 1986. Not too much later, on 29 November 1988, she was to be followed by Heather to complete their family.

Julia and Jim are now happily settled in a very nice home in nearby Clarkson and, happily for us, Karen and John are even closer, on Devon Road in Oakville.

All the girls are now growing up very rapidly and Emma has just become the first teenager in the family. Eileen and I are so very proud of Julia and Karen and their two lovely families.

We always remember the old saying:

Eileen and Britt.

A son is a son, till he takes him a wife,
but a daughter's a daughter for the rest of your life.

Thorco Manufacturing Limited

I THINK IT IS TIME TO GET BACK to my working life
in Canada, which we left rather abruptly in 1968.

When our endeavours with Zip-Grip folded up I felt
very much out in the cold again and while I was still
wondering what sort of company might be interested in a
forty-five year-old 'jack of all trades' Jack came to my
rescue. He had arranged for me to be employed by his
company, Thorco Manufacturing Limited. I was particularly grateful for this because, apart from being saved from
a period of unemployment, I realised that I was being
taken on as a charity case, especially because there was no
specific job for me. I remember deciding that, to show my
appreciation, I would tackle anything and everything which
I was capable of. The first task was sweeping the factory
floor and I remember this raised a few eyebrows and curious
remarks from some of the employees.

It is not always easy to recall events of thirty years ago but I do have some vivid memories of my days with Jack's company. Jack had two partners who seemed to be opposites in so many ways. Harry Voisin, who was Canadian, was small, noisy and just bursting with energy while John Toop, who was Estonian, was large, quiet and rather slow moving. They were both very pleasant and I got on well with both. John retired due to ill health and, tragically, both died about ten years later.

One of the punch-press operators was Victor Boyko who was Ukranian and happened to live close to me in Oakville. He did not like driving to work for some reason (I think his wife liked to use the car) and so I was persuaded to take him as a passenger and for this he gave me five dollars a week (quite a lot in those days of cheap gasoline). Victor was a very taciturn man and would not speak to me on our journeys unless I asked him a question. In those days he seemed quite old and a bit frail but now, almost thirty years later, I still see him around Oakville. I remember one occasion (it was a Friday) and I was going to be out of town so Victor drove his own car that day. As luck would have it, we got hit by a severe winter storm that day and, by the time I reached home, it was getting quite late but I got a frantic phone call from Victor's wife because he had not made it home. About eleven that night Jack and I set out in Jack's car, equipped with blankets and a bottle of rum, to search for the missing Victor. I remember driving through horrific snowdrifts and, when we were almost back at the plant, I got a message on my pager, to say that Victor had turned up – apparently he had taken shelter, with a lot of others, in the Esso station on Steeles Avenue until the storm had abated.

At Thorco in 1968, Jack had quite a large inventory of drugstore shelving which was a legacy from when the Bulman Corporation had gone bankrupt. This material was on racks in a separate area but was rather neglected because there was not much demand. My first real task was to sort it, list it and label it – this was my introduction to store shelving equipment, which in a few years time was to become my livelihood. There were still two or three of the Bulman salesmen in the business who would occasionally order small quantities of this material but there was no longer any steady demand for it.

There was, however, an increasing demand for steel

shelving for the rapidly expanding chain of K Mart stores which were replacing the obsolete S.S. Kresge department stores. Jack, Harry and John decided that, in order to keep up with the demand, they would have to expand their operation and so, in 1969, placed an order for a new, larger independent plant to be built on virgin land out in Bramalea which was a newly developing area and therefore offered the best tax base.

Not too long after moving we were involved with supplying a large new K Mart store in Ottawa and, because it was due to open the following morning, it was imperative to get some 'last minute' fixtures to them that night. Leaving the plant about seven I managed to reach the store at midnight which made everybody happy. After unloading and getting a bite to eat, the plan was to find a motel but, thinking of saving time and the cost of a room, I decided to head home again. I was driving Harry Voisin's Oldsmobile Vista Cruiser station wagon which was very smooth and powerful. On Highway 401 near Cobourg at six o'clock in the morning, not a vehicle in sight in either direction, I was sailing along happily until an OPP cruiser appeared from nowhere and pulled me over. He was a bit upset with me because he said I was doing ninety-six miles per hour! He gave me a lecture and a ticket which resulted in a fine of $160 which, thankfully, was paid by Thorco Manufacturing. I regret to say that, in those days, I was something of a lawbreaker as far as speeding was concerned and managed to collect quite a few tickets.

It was also about this time that I started to move up the ladder when I was appointed as Production Manager. By now I had learned all I could about the fabrication of steel products, I was familiar with the materials and tooling used and had met most of the suppliers and customers. The actual move into the new factory in Bramalea was just a bit tricky for me because it coincided with the weekend when I was to move into our new house on Sunnyvale Drive and so I had to split myself in two!

Before actually moving to Bramalea I can well remember our association with another company, also in the business of store fixtures. At that time Ontario Store Fixtures was a well established, and well respected company with large premises on the Lakeshore Boulevard not too far from Thorco. They were known more for their woodworking expertise and would undertake very large (and very expensive)

jobs like hotel lobbies and restaurants. At that time they were not into steel shelving so, when they landed an order requiring this, they would come to Thorco for it. This arrangement worked very well for both of us and I remember a couple of the projects concerned. By now they had employed a new operations manager and Bill Sloan was quite a live wire, knowing what he wanted and how to get it. He was well educated, smart and efficient which made him good to deal with. He landed a couple of supermarkets for Loblaws and the paint colour we had to provide was Kumquat – as you can guess, this was Canada's 'orange era'! We also had to produce a new design of steel shelving for them to install in the new North York Central Library. But most memorable of all was when Ontario Store Fixtures landed the contract to complete the interior of the new McLaughlin Planetarium being built on University Avenue in Toronto – and this was a really major undertaking.

Our involvement in this one was to paint the hundreds of special ceiling panels (provided by OSF) which would form the ceiling and represent the universe. They specified very special paint for this which had to be imported from the US at a cost of forty dollars per gallon so, needless to say, great care was exercised in the painting and shipping of these panels. Unfortunately, when they arrived at the Planetarium, they were left sitting on the floor and got covered in dust so somebody was detailed, at the site, to clean them but, not being too bright, washed them with a cloth and a bucket of water! Total disaster. We had to order another batch of paint for them which was applied by hand, on the site.

About a year after Thorco moved to the new plant in Bramalea, Ontario Store Fixtures decided to do the same and established themselves in an enormous building where they were able to centralise all the manufacturing (including steel shelving) so our period of co-operation came to an end, and thereafter we were just competitors.

In order to cope with all the added workload, it was necessary to provide additional fabrication equipment and this was done upon arrival in the new Bramalea plant. The main additions were an automatic roll-forming machine and a multi-spot welder – and, of course, a completely new paint spraying shop. It was also necessary to hire additional operators to provide a second shift from four p.m. to midnight. I remember one young man who, half an hour into the shift, must have dozed off while operating a small brakepress and managed to chop his fingers off. I recall racing him to Brampton Hospital where they somehow managed to stitch them back on – but probably he would never play the violin!

Starting in October 1973, in an endeavour to improve my professional skills, I embarked on a 'Management Development Program' with Humber College of Applied Arts and Technology. It was a six course program consisting of:

1   Marketing for Manufacturers

2   Managing Human Resources

3   Understanding Cost Accounting

4   Purchasing

5   Effective Supervision Administration

6   Management for Results.

It was a rather rough six months, especially for Eileen, because I was often at school five nights a week, not getting home until ten-thirty but, in May of 1974 I was granted a 'Certificate of Management Studies' and felt it had been worth all the effort! Especially when I was promoted to Plant Manager for Thorco Manufacturing. This was a very proud moment, especially as an announcement was made in the Toronto *Globe & Mail* complete with a photograph.

By now my job was getting rather hectic because, since the deaths of Harry and John, I was involved in purchasing the steel (and most other materials), issuing the work orders and generally dealing with both suppliers and customers. By now I had my own office in the plant and had been allowed to employ a secretary to help me keep track of all the paper. Nancy was quite young and proved to be a great help to me.

One good customer for our shelving was Williams Food Equipment Ltd in Windsor who used to specialise in grocery, variety and deli stores.

Dick Williams was a large, gruff man but I got on well with him so I had a shock one day when he came on the phone so mad he was fit to be tied. He was installing our shelving in a grocery store down beyond Chatham and when the shelves were loaded, many of them collapsed which, of course, resulted in a big clean-up job. In order to pacify him (and his customer) I guaranteed he would have replacement fixtures that night and, to do this, I had to get a new set of wall uprights made because, by now, I realised the original ones had been badly welded. When these were ready, I borrowed John Toop's big Ford Country Squire, loaded them in and set off from Bramalea shortly after seven p.m. and arrived at the town of Bothwell about ten p.m. It was a small town and I had no difficulty in finding the store because it was the only place with lights on! We both set to work replacing the defective material and had the store finished about 1.30 when I set off for the return trip with the old equipment in the back of the station wagon. About an hour later I was feeling a bit hungry, having missed supper, and pulled off the 401 at an Esso service centre to eat. I was on the way out again when a young man, carrying a large rucksack, approached me and asked if that was my station wagon and, if so, could I give him a lift. By a rather weird coincidence he proved to be Dick Williams' son; he was on a camping trip, and had recognised the shelving equipment in the back of the vehicle! This turned out to be a valuable meeting because, years later when Dick retired and I had my own business, his son Rick, having inherited the business, became a good customer.

Although I was working hard and enjoying what I was doing I began to realise that, as far as Thorco Manufacturing was concerned, I had now reached the pinnacle of my achievement and therefore began to give some thought as to how I could improve my prospects. I remembered Jack saying, more than once, that he would like to be in 'sales' because that was where the money was and, although I was not keen at first, I began to see that the rewards could well be related to the amount of effort put in. But, where to start – and in what line? The more I thought about it, the more I was convinced to stay with something I knew – like store shelving equipment! Gradually I focussed on the old Bulman line of shelving which was still in use in a small way. Jack now employed an industrial designer, experienced in store fixtures, who had done a lot to improve this shelving by eliminating obsolete features and adding new ones.

Thorco Sales (Eastern)

IN THE SPRING OF 1976 it was all arranged and I went into business for the purpose of planning store layouts and supplying and installing all kinds of store fixtures but principally steel shelving. At this stage I felt that I needed some guidance in setting up, and preferably from someone with experience in all aspects of the business. I therefore formed a partnership with Bob Mavins whom I had known for a few years and judged to be honest, reliable and encouraging. Bob was the owner and operator of Mavins Store Equipment in Winnipeg and, up to that point, had been a good customer of Thorco Mfg. Bob was a widower with a fourteen year-old son and liked to make regular visits to Toronto, ostensibly to visit Thorco, but more to enjoy a two or three day break from home. I used to pick him up at the airport – he invariably stayed at the Skyline Hotel because he really enjoyed Diamond Lil's bar with sawdust on the floor and no shortage of attractive girls.

To get started, we each put in ten thousand dollars which, for my share, had to be borrowed from the bank. There were, of course, one or two problems before we got going but nothing that delayed us unduly. For instance, the company name we would use – I was very keen to retain the connection with the Thorco name but no matter how I tried, I was not allowed to register anything even close to it. We had wanted to use 'Thorco Sales (Eastern)' and 'Thorco Sales (Western)' for our respective companies but, because this was unacceptable for incorporation, we had to be satisfied with using these as trading names and incorporate under 'Adams Shelving Products Limited'.

I spent endless hours in putting together price structures for the two lines of shelving available to us – one suitable for drugstore or variety store use and a heavier duty one for use in food stores. The prices had to be sufficient to reimburse Thorco for manufacturing, provide a reasonable profit for ourselves and still be competitive in the market. When we were finally ready Bob came to Toronto for a couple of days and we spent them together doing an awful lot of calling on potential customers which, I remember, was great experience for me but I don't think it resulted in many orders. At least a lot of companies now knew who we were and what we were doing.

And so began my new career (and final one) as an independent, and busy, businessman which was to last for the next fifteen years and which I enjoyed immensely. Naturally, there were some headaches as well, especially in the early days, when I would be wondering where the next order was coming from; or, how could I twist a certain customer's arm to make him pay up! These were all part of the game as I soon realised.

I think my first contract for a store, although a very small one, was perhaps the most memorable. One day I received a call from a young Chinese couple who wanted to open a new drugstore in Guelph and needed a quotation for shelving and counters etc. They arranged to meet me on the campus of Guelph University – at first this seemed odd to me but eventually became appropriate because the store was to be called 'Campus Drugmart'. Vicki and Malcolm Au were from Hong Kong; Vicki was a qualified pharmacist and very smart in every way while Malcolm was some sort of executive with Campbell's Soups in Toronto. We spent the entire afternoon going over and over prices and layouts 'till we achieved the absolute minimum acceptable for the store – she would be opening it 'on a shoestring'! It was a tiny property, wedged in between a supermarket and a restaurant, and miniature by drugstore standards – because of this, many people said it could not work, but it did. By astute ordering and stock control Vicki made it work and a couple of years later I got her moved to larger premises in the same plaza and very soon she also took over the store next door. All this added work for me made my initial efforts worthwhile and, in addition, she was continually placing orders to alter or renovate areas.

During the first couple of years of my operation there were many things to occupy my attention. When I was not out chasing customers for orders, I was getting things set up for a smooth operation so as to make a professional presentation to a potential customer.

I had arranged to have comprehensive price lists printed and attractive brochures designed and printed; I purchased a drafting table and taught myself to draw, accurately to scale, floor plans with equipment layouts for various types of store. Shortly afterwards I felt the need to expand my activities and decided to move to my own premises where I could control my own inventory, thereby streamlining the packing and shipping process. Therefore, I rented an industrial unit nearby, bought a truck and a lift truck, installed racking for the shelving equipment and, after employing a couple of strong young men for the warehouse, it was all systems go.

I do not remember the total number of stores that I equipped but I do know there was a wide range of stores – from A&P supermarkets down to the smallest variety store. There were health food stores, drug stores, toy stores, hardware stores, gift shops, dispensaries, women's fashions, discount stores, hairdressers, even an automotive service centre where they wanted racks in the service bays for their lubricants. Also, the locations of all these stores varied tremendously: many, of course, were in the Toronto area but others ranged from British Columbia to Newfoundland. In many cases I would be dealing with the distributors who were spread across the country; in Vancouver, Edmonton, Calgary, Winnipeg, Windsor, North Bay, Montreal, Moncton and St Johns. This was good business for me because the distributor would deal directly with the store owner and do the layout and installation and I would get paid by him in reasonable time. Installations closer to home, where I was dealing directly with the store owner, were more of a problem because the installation process was time consuming and not usually very profitable and therefore was something I would prefer to avoid. Sometimes the owner would undertake the installation himself, sometimes I would employ an outside contractor and at other times I would do it myself.

Worthy of a particular mention here was 'my man in Newfoundland'. Colin Strong was a true 'Newfie' – very patriotic, honest and outspoken and one of the nicest people I've met. We became very good friends, drawn together by our mutual interest in the Royal Navy, which Colin had joined on the outbreak of war (Newfoundland was not part of Canada until 1949). Colin was a past president and staunch supporter of the Royal Canadian Legion and insisted on joining me up – so, for many years, I was an invisible member of Pleasantville (Branch 26) of the Royal Canadian Legion. On one of my trips to the East Coast I took Eileen along with me when we visited Moncton and Halifax and then up to Newfoundland.

Colin was very hospitable when we arrived and I remember, after a sight-seeing tour, stuffing ourselves with fresh lobsters at his home.

Going back to the installation problem, this situation was changed when, some years later, I landed the contract to supply and install equipment for an extensive modernisation programme to be undertaken by the Canadian Oxygen Company (otherwise known as Canox) which was the Canadian subsidiary of British Oxygen Corporation. Canox was the major supplier of welding supplies and, as such, had branches scattered all across the country that, until now, had been operated as an industrial warehouse type of business. The object was to convert these branches to modern, self-serve retail stores.

The object of this conversion was to increase their customer base by attracting 'non-professional' customers and promote 'impulse buying' from attractive shelving displays. The man behind this scheme was their Operations Manager at the Head Office in Toronto. Des Wright was, to me, a typical English gentleman – he smoked a pipe, was always polite, never raised his voice or got excited but nevertheless had a way of getting things done. Initially, I was asked to provide sample shelving units at the Head Office and it was much later (when I began to think it was a wasted effort) that I got a call to meet the Operations Manager to discuss his pet scheme.

From that day Canox became my best customer and I found it a pleasure to do business with Des Wright; he was well organised, gave me specific instructions of what he wanted, usually gave me a good lead time and did not dicker over nickels and dimes. The cost of equipping these stores ranged from five thousand to ten thousand dollars each – not great when compared with other major stores but here the advantage was that these orders were repeated on a very regular basis (about every six to eight weeks). We started with a couple of older locations (Orillia and Bracebridge) where it involved setting up a store somewhere in the existing premises and, when they found the plan was working, they started building new premises to locate larger stores. Initially I employed a young man who was keen and energetic to do the installations but, after several complaints about his work, I recognised the danger of losing this customer, and resolved to personally take care of these installations in the future. I was very lucky to find the ideal man to assist me. He came to the plant one day to pick up an order for another customer and I got talking to him – he was driving a large pickup truck and was towing a horsebox. I asked if he was interested in helping me in the future and, from there on, we became good friends as well as co-workers. Bruce was a very pleasant, quietly spoken man with a good sense of humour but, best of all, he was a very good worker with a knowledge of shelving and a good set of tools, I think he was the black sheep of his family – they operated a large car dealership in Hamilton – because he never seemed to associate with them. He lived, with his girlfriend, in Thornhill where he also operated a small business repairing and selling used commercial refrigeration equipment.

The first Canox job we did together started out as a bit of a nightmare. It was a new store in Chateau Gai, a small town on the south side of the St Lawrence just opposite Montreal. The arrangement was that Bruce would pick up the shelving in the afternoon and, the following morning, I would leave home at four a.m., drive to Thornhill and from there we would be on the highway for our destination at four thirty. This would enable us to be at our store early afternoon and, by working till ten or eleven p.m., to complete a day's work instead of wasting it on the road. This arrangement worked so well for us that we adopted it for all future jobs, mostly in Quebec, where we were bound. Unfortunately, on this trip, Bruce was using the horse trailer, but the weight of the equipment was too great so that by the time we reached the outskirts of Montreal we had changed two wheels on the trailer and had to stop to buy new tyres which, because they were an oddball size, we had to go to the factory for. Thereafter we had no such problems because Bruce used a bigger trailer and also bought a new and powerful Dodge pickup with a diesel engine.

After this we did many Canox stores in Quebec, always using the same routine and almost always successful. The one exception was, I am happy to say, not our fault. The information provided by Canox regarding their building programme was very reliable – except when they sent us to one store which was still under construction. It was in Granby, Quebec, and when we arrived around midday we were horrified to find that the building was in no way fit to receive store fixtures and so, reluctantly, we had to turn round and drive home again. It was in February with thick snow on the ground as is often the case in Quebec. We returned two-weeks later and finished the job, and without the need for haggling we were paid for both trips.

A couple of the more memorable Canox stores were Vancouver and Calgary; both of these were large stores and because they were too far to drive we shipped the equipment by transport and we hopped on a plane. I took Eileen with me to both of these (also to Saskatoon). It was early October in Vancouver and when we arrived the weather was mild, so it was something of a surprise to look out of our window the next morning and see a lot of snow on the ski hills across the Stanley Bridge. We made time to go to the top via cable car and we both thought it was really beautiful. Before returning home we also took the ferry across to Nanaimo and drove through the gorgeous scenery of Vancouver Island down to Victoria, planning to have tea in the famous Empress Hotel, but unfortunately it was closed for renovation. When we went to Calgary we also took Bruce's 'significant other' and made up a foursome. We stayed at the Skyline Hotel and, on a Sunday, we drove out to Banff and, this time we were luckier, because we did enjoy a meal at the Banff Springs Hotel.

This happy state of affairs lasted several years but sadly came to an end when Des Wright retired and at the same time Canox got a new President.

There were, of course, other memorable installations, too many to cover here, but worth a mention was a large drugstore we were completing in a large, new, shopping mall in St John, NB. We had finished the work late on the previous night and went to the store in the morning just to pick up our tools on the way to the airport. There was suddenly a terrific explosion as one wall blew in and wiped out a section of the store – a workman had been installing ceramic tiles in the public area of the mall when, inside the store, a young lad had plugged in a vacuum cleaner which created a spark and caused the explosion from the other side of the wall! Fortunately (and surprisingly) nobody was seriously hurt, but it meant that I had to leave one man behind for a couple of days to put things together again.

I remember another store, this time in Winnipeg, where there were no accidents but the weather was so incredibly cold I could not believe anyone would want to live there. It was the end of January with lots of bitter wind and snow and I remember how lovely it was to get back to the Holiday Inn and jump in the swimming pool.

Cars I have known in Canada

MY FIRST CAR IN THIS COUNTRY was, as I mentioned earlier, a 1963 Rambler Classic with a standard shift and not much else but it served me well for my first four years here and, considering I only paid Jack five hundred dollars for it, it was a good deal. However, over those four years I was impatient to get a new car, especially as I admired so many beautiful vehicles on the highway.

In June of 1971 I decided the time had come and so paid a visit to the local GM dealer, Kerr Cadillac/Pontiac who was then in very cramped premises at Robinson and Dunn. It had been a toss up for me between the Chevrolet Monte Carlo and the Pontiac Le Mans. I thought both were rather sporty looking but finally decided on the Pontiac. The dealer had just received a large number of these from the factory but, due to lack of space, they were parked in a long line at Trafalgar Village outside the Dominion store. I remember inspecting these more than once until I found just what I was looking for – it was gold in colour, a two-door model and with a V6–250 engine. When I went back to the dealer and told the salesman (Mr Rasmussen) he said they had no such vehicle in stock and I had to take him to it in order to prove my point. It was easy to see the mistake – the GM logo on the side of the car said 'V8–350' but, when I opened the hood, it was, in fact, a V6. It was a lovely car, served me well and I was always very proud of it.

The next car to come into my life was always a bit of a joke with family and friends because I won it in a raffle for twenty-five cents! It was in 1972 when Julia was working as a school secretary at General Wolfe High School in Oakville, which was a semi–vocational establishment and therefore had all sorts of interesting workshops and courses. This included a very well equipped and supervised 'automotive repair shop' and it was here that the car, obtained from a wrecker's yard, was stripped down and rebuilt over a period of a year. The occasion of the raffle was the annual 'Open Day' which was very popular and Eileen and I always attended. The car was on display, in its new coat of blue paint, and was drawing a lot of attention so I blew a whole dollar and bought four tickets. Towards the end of the evening Eileen and I went home and, when Julia phoned to say that my ticket had won the car, I thought she was kidding – but it was true! It was a very early model of Isuzu, four doors and a standard shift and with it came a large placard in the rear window announcing the car was a product of General Wolfe Auto Shop. Eileen, who had been getting a ride to work, was delighted with her little car, especially as it seemed to run on fresh air and she could fill it for a couple of dollars. With some tender loving care from Jimmy Alexander at the Texaco station on Third Line it took Eileen to and from work for several years.

When the Isuzu finally gave up the ghost (even Jimmy said it was no longer worth repairing) Eileen decided she would like to have an AMC Pacer – and everybody laughed about Eileen's greenhouse! It was a two-year-old model, which we bought privately from an ad. in the local paper. I think this would be 1979 or 1980 and Eileen drove and enjoyed that car for six years until it got traded-in for a new vehicle.

In 1985 I decided Eileen should have a new car which started us on quite a lengthy search. Although I made several suggestions as to what might be suitable, Eileen had her own ideas about what she wanted in a new car. I know we finished up at Lockwood Chrysler (on a Sunday afternoon when it was closed) and were busy browsing through the lot when, suddenly, a salesman popped out of his office where he had been working. I know it made his day when he sold us the car – it was a 1985 Plymouth Duster which had just been introduced with a rather sleek and sporty body. It was a two-door and was finished in a beautiful deep metallic red – so the next stop was the drugstore because Eileen wanted nail varnish to match! It was a lovely car and a pleasure to drive and we parted with it six and a half years later when I retired and we no longer needed a second car. We sold it, with an incredibly low mileage on it, to Tony and Jean, who are still using it.

When I started up my own business it made sense to

me that I should lease a car, at company expense, so that is what I did for the next fifteen years. Leasing then was not as complicated as it is today and I had no trouble getting started. My first one was a 1976 Chrysler Cordoba which was new on the market and getting very popular. The one I chose was certainly attractive – two-door, of course, finished in Jamaica Blue with a white vinyl top and I loved driving it. At the end of the three-year lease I bought it for two thousand dollars, having already decided that my next one would be another Cordoba. This time I went to Oakville Chrysler Dodge on Fourth Line where they gave me three thousand dollars for the first one and I leased a Mk II model (1979) for the next three years – it was Midnight Blue with a leather interior and very luxurious.

Three years later and due for a replacement I then chose another Chrysler. This was the new 1982 New Yorker – Fifth Avenue very large and very luxurious and finished in dark grey with black vinyl trim and 'opera windows'. A week after taking delivery we set out, with Aunty Eve and Aunty Gerty in the back, for a fairly extensive trip around Manitoulin Island, crossing from Tobermorey on a new car ferry *Chi-Cheemaun* and returning via Gravenhurst to pick up a cruise of Lake Muskoka aboard SS *Segwin*.

In 1985 I felt it was time for a change of pace and decided to switch to Ford – in fact, their 1985 Special Anniversary Edition of the Thunderbird. This car was quite different from the regular model (as I found when I drove both of them) and had many additional features – all of which was reflected in the price, as they say. It was a very sleek and very powerful car and was a wonderful car to drive – when the road was dry! Unfortunately, it was about the last of the rear wheel drives and, even with oversize tires, had a tendency to 'fishtail' – even on damp grass. I drove it for two years, but was never really comfortable in winter conditions, and then decided to make a change – a year early. One deciding factor was that the Aunties were visiting again that summer and I did not want to subject them to struggling in and out of a low-slung, two-door vehicle.

The changeover was done very smoothly because a good customer of mine – Pat Mendoza, who operated J&J Display Sales – had always admired my Thunderbird and so we arranged for her to take over the remaining portion of the lease.

This was now 1987 and I had fallen in love with the re-styled Buick Le Sabre which was new on the road. I ordered one from Sherway Ford, who had also handled the Thunderbird, and when it arrived I could not have been more pleased. I felt the design was up to date but had not sacrificed the traditional look. It was finished in silver grey clear coat and had all the features I could have wished for. It was to prove reliable, comfortable and attractive in appearance.

Early in 1989 I made a decision to get another vehicle. I liked the Buick so much that I wanted to save it for my retirement and therefore did not want to put too many miles on the clock; besides which I found it was being used too much for carrying all kinds of shelving materials. So, I bought a truck. This time, though, it was a little one. From the Mazda dealer in Brampton I purchased a 1989 Mazda B2200 pickup truck – it was charcoal grey and had a five-speed standard shift. From then until I retired I really enjoyed driving that vehicle and was quite sorry when I no longer had a need for it. I had no difficulty in selling it privately, for a good price.

So nowadays, I am still driving the 1987 Buick Le Sabre and am still enjoying it but not putting too many miles on it these days. The Buick, like myself is getting a bit long in the tooth but, as long as we both keep going, I shall be happy.

Vacations from Canada

EILEEN AND I ENJOYED MANY GREAT VACATIONS from Canada including many to visit friends and relatives in England. I believe every one was happy and successful – all, that is, except the first one which was a total disaster.

It was in April 1971 that we first got itchy feet and, after reading all the brochures, settled on a Wardair package holiday to Nassau in the Bahamas, probably because the price was right. Besides our flight, it included seven days at the Britannia Beach Hotel on Paradise Island. We had invited Jack and Vivien to join us for this one and they were happy to come along. I remember driving to Pearson

Airport at six in the morning – and then returning by bus, through Oakville, to get the plane at Buffalo, owing to a strike. I had previously visited Nassau and Paradise Island when I was in the Navy and now, twenty-three years later, the town had not changed much but Paradise Island was almost unrecognisable due to the high rise hotels and casinos now occupying most of the island. Our hotel was great and the food, in the many restaurants, was certainly first class. We enjoyed five days and nights of this and then, on the Thursday, we rented a car and went on a tour of Providence Island which is quite large. Jack particularly wanted to visit the Bacardi Rum plant on the South side – in Canada the Bacardi Rum plant was right next door to Jack's own plant in Bramalea and so he was quite friendly with the Bacardi family. Anyway, we did the rum bit where the Nassau branch of the family were very hospitable. Later, we found a beautiful sandy beach, very deserted and inviting, so drove the car onto the sand, changed into swimsuits and went in the water, having left all our clothes and valuables in the trunk of the car which was in full view. Somehow, somebody got into the trunk (unlocked, of course), scooped everything up and disappeared without a trace.

We had not seen or heard anything and the first we knew of a problem was when I couldn't find my trousers. We ran out on the road but found nothing and then an odd thing happened – a large police sergeant arrived in a car and, having ascertained we were physically OK, proceeded to give us a lecture for being so stupid. Apparently, a young Canadian man who lived in Nassau, had found a couple of our belongings dumped along the road and, realising the danger, had promptly called the police who feared the worst. The articles recovered were my wristwatch and some medication. The following morning Jack and I patrolled both sides of that road on foot but found nothing else. Of course, we both lost cash (but not too much) and American Express Travellers Cheques which were quickly replaced. The tragedy was that Eileen had lost all her jewellery, to which she was very attached, – she had put it in her purse rather than leave it in the room. She was devastated and quite inconsolable and, from that moment, we could not wait to get home. The only redeeming feature (which we still laugh about) was that, before we left, we went in the casino and Eileen put all her money (two quarters) in a slot machine – and walked away with fifty dollars! After we got home I put in a claim, not very hopefully, on our house insurance and, much to our surprise, got one thousand dollars.

After that we seemed to drop into a routine of visiting England one year and then having a Caribbean holiday the next. Anyway, I suppose a couple of years later, we ventured forth on our next overseas adventure. Whether it was England or elsewhere, we usually managed to go in early April. This time, on a recommendation from Julia and Karen, we booked a trip to Acapulco where we stayed at a small hotel, the Tropicana and enjoyed a very relaxed and pleasant holiday. Before leaving I had to go to the market and buy a model sailing ship, which are a well known export of Acapulco. I bought the largest one I could find and, once it was crudely packed, I had difficulty getting the ship, and Eileen, into the very small taxi. Fortunately, I did manage to get it home for Julia.

A couple of years later, also on Julia and Karen's recommendation, we booked to go to Barbados, which we thoroughly enjoyed. Already an independent nation, Barbados has still retained all the customs and traditions from its British heritage. We stayed at the Southern Palms Hotel where we had a lovely room overlooking the beach and sea. Touring the island, driving a Mini Moke, was fun and all the restaurants were great.

Julia and Karen had also been enthusiastic about a holiday they enjoyed on Sanibel Island in Florida, where they were able to use Mr Weiler's time-share condo. Accordingly, in 1981, Eileen and I went on vacation to Captiva Island (next to Sanibel) and stayed in a condo on a very large and very exclusive estate called the Plantation.

In 1983 we went on vacation with our friends Sheila and Roy Stewart and went to St Lucia. As we stepped off the plane we were approached by the tour guide and told that, because our hotel was overbooked, we would be accommodated elsewhere. We did not complain and soon found we had no reason to – they put us in the Holiday Inn with rooms right on the beach and an altogether superior hotel. I remember a great day we had cruising on *The Jolly Roger* – somehow Roy and I were quite merry – good rum.

In 1985 we went to Antigua and this time it was a two-week vacation; the first week on a very small cruise ship and the second week ashore in Antigua. The ship

(I wish I could remember her name) was Dutch owned and operated and was really nothing like a modern cruise ship. I particularly chose it because it was so small – it could carry 160 passengers but, on this voyage, there were only 120 on board. Because of its size it could visit some of the lesser known islands where the bigger vessels could not get in. We sailed from Antigua on the evening of our arrival and, as we were having a drink in the bar, the Captain walked in, addressed me by name and then proceeded to make a message to me by semaphore – the message was, 'I like girls, do you?' He was quite young and was very proud of the fact that he had been a signalman in the Royal Netherlands Navy. From then on we were firm friends and, a couple of times, were invited to join him and his wife for dinner. The morning following our departure, we arrived in Montserrat – when it was still a very beautiful and hospitable island – i.e. before it was destroyed by the recent tragic volcano eruptions. The following day we spent at Saint Eustace and the one after at the tiny, rocky, island of Saba. Next, on to St Kitts where we enjoyed a day of cruising on a large catamaran and finishing with a beach barbeque on the island of Nevis. Then on to the island of St Marten, which is half Dutch and the other half is French. I think our final port of call was the very attractive island of St Barts and then we were on our way back to Antigua. We were sorry to leave the ship – we had enjoyed every minute of that week, but the good news was, we still had another week's vacation at a hotel.

When we disembarked from the ship we were taken by bus to our hotel, the Blue Water Beach which was right at the top of the island and on arrival we, and three other couples, were told they had no bookings for us. Of course, everyone was gunning for the tour guide who told us, a couple of hours later, that she had made alternative arrangements for us all at the Blue Heron Hotel. This proved to be the best thing that could have happened to us because we had not liked the Blue Water as soon as we had seen it – it was large, cold and impersonal and more like a barracks than a hotel. On the other hand, the Blue Heron was a delightful place – quite small, right on the beach, accommodation in cabins (with TV) and the restaurant was one of the best I have known. Last but not least, the owner and his wife were charming and friendly and, by the time we left, we had got to know them very well. Quite by chance the eight of us off the ship, although an assorted group, bonded immediately (we had never really met on the ship) and that week became a truly shared and wonderful experience. One was a Toronto dentist, one owned a jewellery store in Cambridge and the third was an investment analyst and, after returning to Canada, we did keep in touch for a while.

The final episode of this wonderful holiday was, for me at least, a little bit depressing. We were at the airport, waiting to board our Air Canada flight home, when I noticed some of the ship's officers and crew sitting at another table and, thinking they were going home for a spot of leave, I went over to talk to them. They told me they had been recalled to Holland because, returning to Antigua the previous night, the ship had run aground and was now out of action. My sympathy was with the charming young Captain who would now be facing a Board of Enquiry.

At the end of 1987 (in fact, on New Year's Eve) Eileen and I flew to Puerto Vallarta, Mexico for a week and stayed at a Holiday Inn, right on the beach. When we checked in, the young lady on the desk tried to tell me that our room was still being cleaned and not yet ready but somehow it came out as, 'Your room is filthy!' That night we were to attend a huge festive evening on the roof to celebrate New Year and, at four p.m., decided to have a rest in preparation but, just as our heads touched the pillow, a Mexican Mariachi Band struck up, right below our window – it was now 'Happy Hour'.

Early in 1988 we decided to do a repeat visit to Barbados and, because it was a good deal, booked for two weeks at the Barbados Hilton at the beginning of April. Unfortunately, at the end of February I had to go into Oakville Hospital for surgery due to cancer of the colon. All went well but the surgeon (Dr Brabant) insisted that I should check with him, at the hospital, on the day scheduled for our departure. Well, he did say 'Go' but I did not dare to think about the alternative! We spent that night at the Constellation Hotel and, next morning, boarded our plane (it was Odyssey Airlines – an excellent carrier) bound for Barbados and a truly wonderful vacation.

In April of 1989 we spent two weeks in Aruba (one of the 'ABC Islands' which are Aruba, Bonaire and Curacoa

Fiesta Time! New Year's Eve, Holiday Inn, Puerto Vallarta.

— they used to be known as Netherlands Antilles but are now independent). Located just fifty miles off the coast of Venezuela, Aruba is always hot and windy — the wind never seems to change and, for this reason, Aruba is the wind-surfing capital of the world. I remember cruising the island on a large catamaran, which was moving pretty well, when a group of wind-surfers would just leave us standing. The island still retains a lot of the Dutch atmosphere, the people are very friendly and honest, and most of them are proud to speak good English. The hotels are first class and the food on the island is excellent. I think the highlight of this holiday was when we took a trip in the *Atlantis*, a miniature submarine, which gave us a tour of the coral reef and the tremendous colour and variety of the local tropical fish life.

As a contrast to all the exotic, tropical places we took a mini-vacation in February 1990 when we visited Sault Sainte Marie in Northern Ontario. While there we went on an exciting trip on the famous 'Snow Train' of the Algoma Central Railway which runs through incredible winter scenery up to the Agawa Canyon and back.

In June of 1990 we had our final 'overseas' vacation and, appropriately, it was one we had always dreamed of – a return visit to Malta where we had lived for three and a half years and where we had welcomed Julia into the world. It took quite a lot of planning and was not too easy to arrange because, at that time, Malta was not a holiday destination from Canada – now, of course, it is becoming very popular from here. I had made all the arrangements with the help and co-operation of a small travel agency in Lydney, Gloucester where Aunty Eve lives. They sent me brochures and made all the flight and hotel bookings plus a car rental in Malta. On 6 June we flew with Worldways from Toronto to Cardiff and, after a couple of days with Aunty Eve, we flew with Air Malta from Heathrow to begin our vacation.

It was just wonderful to be back in the country where we had such happy memories. It was then thirty-eight years since we had left Malta and we could not wait to visit all the places and people we had known However, we soon realised that we should have made our pilgrimage earlier because many of the people we wanted to see had died and many of the places had changed, some beyond recognition. Nevertheless, we did enjoy driving all over the island and the first place we visited was Birzebbuga on Pretty Bay where we had our first little apartment. On this little country road we did find the house, only because Eileen recognised the door knocker, and while we were sitting in the car, a Maltese lady came from the house next door and spoke to us. She told us that Sam (our landlord) and his wife had both died but, amazingly, she did recognise Eileen because, as she said, she had been eight years old and Eileen used to wave to her and that Eileen used to wear a striped dress! We were staying at the Imperial Hotel in Sliema which was one of the older and more traditional hotels but very comfortable and we enjoyed our stay. The next place on our list was Mosta, where we had made our second home (apartment next to the cinema) and here we had a couple of disappointments. The quiet little town, although unchanged, was now very busy with traffic. We went into Mosta Dome which was still the same. Our 'cinema home' had changed drastically – the cinema had gone and been replaced by a bank and the adjoining apartments now looked rather shabby. We had a chat with the bank security guard and learned that he was now living in 'our' apartment.

We visited Johnie's Bar in the square, to find it now run by his son because Johnie had suffered a couple of strokes, and was not in good shape.

We drove out to Ghajn Tuffieha to find the Royal Marine Training Centre now operating, on a part-time basis, as a training centre for the local militia. We tried to reach the 'House on the Hill' – it was now impossible to reach because the whole area was so overgrown with scrub but we could see that the lovely house was now deserted and derelict. We drove to the top of the island and took the car ferry across to neighbouring Gozo – it was something we had always wanted to do but never managed when we lived there. We also had a long and memorable day when we took a trip to Sicily – something else we had not done – in our day it had meant an overnight trip on a small steam ferry. Now, the seventy mile voyage was done in an hour and a half on a very fast Express Ferry (a catamaran) which was very comfortable but also very noisy. We landed at Pozallo on the west coast and, after breakfast (we had left Valletta at six a.m.) boarded a nice coach for a tour of the island. We visited Palermo, drove up Mount Etna, finished in Taormina and finally returned through Catania. Palermo was interesting, Taormina beautiful and Catania rather scruffy. We arrived in Malta about ten p.m., feeling very tired.

Other days during our Malta visit were spent just lounging around the pool or else driving to one of the lovely beaches around the island – or shopping in Valletta or Sliema. We spent a very interesting day on a visit to the Malta War Museum which is in Fort St Elmo in Valletta. They had many authentic exhibits but most moving of all was a film of Malta during the war which showed the harsh conditions and terrible destruction which the people of Malta were forced to endure – they certainly earned that George Cross. Needless to say, we had enjoyed every wonderful minute of our holiday in our 'Maltese home'.

CHAPTER THIRTY-TWO

Retirement

THIS WAS SOMETHING WHICH I KNEW must happen one day but, until the summer of 1991, I had not given it much thought and certainly not made any plans for it. Then, it just seemed to creep up on me and suddenly, it became the prime focus of my life.

The first indication was, strangely enough, a boat. In that July, Aunty Eve was visiting us and one day, walking along Bronte Pier, our attention was attracted to a very smart looking motor cruiser tied up alongside and the owners enjoying tea (or something else!). On the way home we discussed how much it might cost and a few other relevant details – all of which set me thinking it would be a great retirement project and I was soon looking for a similar boat. Surprisingly, I found one in Bronte which looked ideal and displayed a 'For Sale' sign on it. It was a Chris Craft 32 ft Sea Skiff and was obviously well cared for but I had a surprise when I phoned the owner – he lived right opposite me on Sunnyvale Drive. We arranged a meeting, took the boat on the lake and had soon agreed on a price. I paid a deposit and, of course, set up a survey of the boat which, much to my dismay, revealed a rotted transom with a replacement cost of six thousand dollars.

Shortly afterwards Aunty Eve, Eileen and I were spending a few days in Muskoka and, as we drove through Gravenhurst, I saw a sign for 'Bob Clift's Marina – Specialising in Wooden Boats'. Of course, I could not resist a visit during which I saw and liked a boat lying in the slings there. It was a 1968 Chris Craft 30 ft Cavalier for which the owner was asking $18,000. I inspected it, arranged for it to be put in the water and took it out on Lake Muskoka and once again arranged for a survey. This time it was pretty good and, after a few repairs (and payment of $14,000) *Knot Enuff* was mine. It was transported by road to Bronte, launched there and I took it directly across the lake to Newport Marina where I had

Knott Enuff cruising off Bronte.

arranged for a berth. The following year I was lucky enough to obtain a berth in Bronte Harbour.

The second nudge toward retirement came shortly after when I found (quite without looking) somebody who was keen to take over my business. I had known Bill Harkness for a few years – he was a sales rep. with Atomic Transport in Oakville and I had always found him to be reliable and efficient. He obviously thought I was doing pretty well and could not wait to get in my seat. We worked out a deal where, starting in October, he would gradually assume more responsibility for the business so that, by the end of the year, he would have total control and I would be retired. Up to this point all went well and, when I left, he seemed very keen but, after a couple of return visits, I was to form the impression that he felt he had done his time 'on the road' and now wanted to run the business from a desk and just take orders over the phone. I knew this would not work and it did not surprise me when the business started to deteriorate.

The third factor in my run-up to retiring occurred in October of 1991 when Julia phoned me to say, quite out of the blue, that she thought she had found the ideal home for us in our retirement. This was rather a surprise because we were still living at Sunnyvale Drive and, up to then, had not really considered moving anywhere.

Pier Twelve

JULIA HAD FOUND, and saved for me, an advertisement in the *Toronto Star* which said, under a picture of Bronte Harbour, 'Bronte Bargain', but did not give much detail about it. More out of polite curiosity than any real interest I telephoned the agent, who was Pat Knox of Century 21, and made an appointment to see the place during my lunch hour the following day. When we arrived in Bronte I still had no idea which condo building we were heading for but, when I found we were entering Pier Twelve, my interest perked up because I had watched the building go up a few years earlier. I had even visited the Sales Office and inspected their model suite which I found very impressive – which also applied to the prices they were asking – end of that story!

Now, as we entered Suite 214, I was again very impressed and really liked what I saw. The suite was owned by a single young man who appeared to use it as a place to sleep only because the fridge contained a few beers and the other appliances were unused. Apparently he had bought it six months earlier as an investment but, sadly for him, market prices had gone down instead of up and he stood to lose fifty thousand on it. The asking price was $159,000 and, when I took Eileen to see it next day, Pat Knox must have made the easiest sale of her life at $156,000.

At this point we felt that everything was coming together very nicely and were looking forward to the upcoming events of the next few months. It was a pity we could not see into the future – we would not have been so happy had we known that the next eighteen months would be a very traumatic period for us due to two disastrous real estate deals with unscrupulous buyers. Although we longed to move into our new condo we could not do so until 2132 Sunnyvale Drive had been sold.

Having got the Pier Twelve deal all signed and settled we then faced the problem of putting our house on the market. We were confident there would be no difficulty

Pier Twelve, roof patio.

in finding a buyer and, when Pat Knox asked if we would list it with her, we saw no reason to refuse – up to that point we had no idea that we were dealing with a totally inadequate real estate agent. The low point came a month later when she told us she was going on vacation – to India for six weeks! Assuring us that we would be well looked after while she was away, she then produced a young boy, just entering the business with the sole qualification that his uncle was the boss. He visited us a couple of times but his only interest seemed to be admiring himself in our hall mirror.

In February of 1992 we met Peter Clark and his fiancée Deborah who both loved the house and were very keen to have it. Peter Clark seemed a good prospect – he was an independent computer programmer, drove a Porsche, agreed a good price and paid the required deposit. The fly in the ointment was that he owned a nice house in East Oakville which was not yet sold. We moved out of Sunnyvale Drive and into Pier Twelve on 1 April 1992 and, although still worried, were feeling a lot better about the situation and, every day, prayed that it would soon be concluded.

Subsequently, Peter Clark and Deborah moved into the house on a 'rent-to-own' basis but, when he failed to come up with the rent, I had to turf them out. I felt very bad about it because, although I was mad at Peter, it happened to be the week Deborah gave birth. During their few months in the house they owned a fairly large dog (it was a German Wimmerammer) which they kept outside and, when they left, I found the dog had virtually destroyed the back garden and also the rear garage door, kitchen door and screen door – so I was kept pretty busy cleaning up and replacing stuff.

Meantime we were thoroughly enjoying our life at Pier Twelve but were getting worried by the financial burden of carrying two homes.

Then it seemed our prayers were answered – along came Mr Cunningham who had recently joined my brother Jack's company as Financial Controller. He let it be known that he was looking for a house in the area so naturally, Jack sent him to me. Later he brought his wife (a medical secretary) and his two sons (21 and 10) to the house and they all loved it. The deal was made but from there everything went downhill. I don't want to go into all the sordid details here (it would take too long) but suffice it to say that after a long and bitter struggle we did manage to collect our money. But, finally he was evicted from the house by his mortgage company and the house, which was a mess, was sold by the company at a loss.

Having got all the horrible stuff out of the way, let us turn to the good part. That is what we said to ourselves at the time and, although it was not easy, we did not let it spoil our enjoyment of living at Pier Twelve. We loved our building and our own unit and all the people we met in the building were pleasant and friendly. After a year there I was approached by Willie Sims who, as President of the Board, asked if I would consider serving as a member of the Board of Directors and I agreed to give it a go. At the Annual General Meeting in June I was a little surprised to be elected because I did not have a lot to qualify me for the job. I found it all very interesting and, after attending a couple of courses in Condominium Management, I felt more confident about what I was doing. During the seven years of living at Pier Twelve I spent six years on the Board with five of those as President and, upon my departure, I was honoured to be given a wonderful party and lovely farewell gift by all the residents.

I had become good friends with Willie because, over the years, we had worked well together on the Board and shared a keen interest in the welfare of the building and its residents. Our Superintendent was Mike Walker, a very pleasant and helpful young man although sometimes a little forgetful. The building was managed by Lounsbury Real Estate Management and our Property Manager was Pat Kummer who was herself very efficient but, when Lounsbury got into trouble, we decided to make a change. We settled with an Oakville company, Trafalgar Management, and welcomed Gerry Sheahan as our new Property Manager. On a more personal note, I must say that our time at Pier Twelve was an extremely pleasant and enjoyable experience for us.

During the summers we found ourselves spending all our spare time on *Knot Enuff*, either cruising on the lake or perhaps just sitting in the harbour to watch all the other boating activities. When the boats came out of the water in October I could find plenty of work on the boat to keep me busy until the snow came and it was time to put the tarpaulins on 'till the Spring. It was great, all year, to see the boat from our condo balcony.

In October of 1995 I decided, at the age of 72, to get myself a job. Partly, it was to occupy my time but also, I must admit, to provide some extra cash. I decided that a local car dealership was the place to look so, after hours of coming up with a suitable resumé, I made the rounds of each one asking if they needed a 'parts driver' or 'lot man'. Every one was negative but, after I got home, I received a call from the Sales Manager at Kennedy Ford, asking me to come in and see him. Rick Grainger was a very pleasant young man, we got on well from the start and I enjoyed working for him. The job (and the pay) were not the greatest but I liked what I was doing. The job involved receiving new cars from the factory and, ultimately, preparing them for customer delivery. The young man in charge of this Department when I joined was Ralph but I think he was 'two planks short of a load' as they say. Shortly after, the boss got suspicious of Ralph and, when the police raided his garage at home, they brought back two vanloads of stuff belonging to Kennedy Ford, mostly tape players and radios that he was selling on the side. That was when I got promoted – I had two young guys working for me and we were always kept busy and, especially at first, the days seemed very long. At Christmas we were rewarded with a turkey and a delightful dinner and dance at the Richview Golf Club.

Unfortunately, in the following March I ran into a major problem when, on three consecutive weekends, I experienced a heart attack – each successively worse than before. After the third one I left work and went to the doctor on the Monday morning – it was 1 April 1996 – and straight away he sent me to Oakville Hospital where I stayed for a few days. Then I was sent to Toronto Western Hospital, where I had an angiogram which showed that I was in need of a quadruple heart bypass. I was sent home to await my turn but towards the end of July I experienced a bad attack during the night so Eileen called an ambulance and packed me off to hospital. I was told that I would remain in Oakville Hospital until they had a date for my surgery at the Toronto General Hospital. This turned out to be ten days and then I was transferred by ambulance to Toronto where I found the surgery was scheduled for the next morning which would be 8 August 1996. Needless to say, everything went very smoothly and, six days later, they sent me home, minus a few pounds and very tired but I never looked back and soon was as good as new.

After this I decided it was time to slow down a bit and, as a first step, put my beloved *Knot Enuff* up for sale and, as a result, it crossed the lake to Rochester NY. I also started considering alternative living accommodation, even though I did not want to move and knowing that Eileen was very much against the idea. I looked at many different places – condos, rentals, re-sales – but nothing seemed to fit the bill. Until one day, towards end of November 1998, I was attracted by a notice on Marine Drive: '2 bed apt available.'

Marine Towers, 2220 Marine Drive

I STARTED BY VIEWING THE APARTMENT which was advertised and, although I liked it very much, I would not make any decision on it before the whole family had seen it and approved it. So, at the beginning of December I signed the lease and started paying rent, at the same time hoping it would not be too long before we sold our Pier Twelve condominium. It did not take any hesitation on my part to ask Willie to list it for us and to handle it in her usual capable way. Eileen and I both felt that Willie did an excellent job of advertising and showing our unit: even so it was three months till we found a firm buyer.

Very reluctantly I might say, we moved from Pier Twelve on 27 April 99, after seven happy years, and moved into our new home at Marine Towers. Once again we are on the 2nd floor (#204) and overlooking the garden, the tennis courts of Ennisclere next door and also the lake. The apartment is almost the same size as Pier Twelve except that we do not have a solarium and now have only one bathroom. After eight months in residence here we are both very settled and very happy here and we are convinced that we shall not be moving again.

The residents here are very pleasant and always friendly and we now feel very much at home. We have a very pleasant and efficient couple as Superintendents here and the building itself is undergoing a major renovation programme.

The Millennium

IT IS APPROPRIATE THAT I SHOULD FINISH my story here because it is now five p.m. on the last day of the old year. Tomorrow we shall be starting a New Year as well as a New Century and a New Millennium.

Certainly sounds very impressive – I wonder what they will bring?

Conclusion

So, we come to the end of this over-long and somewhat rambling tale. Should you have reached this point, then I must congratulate you on your patience and perseverance. Also, you may have thought, 'Well, this is not a very good story of Bob's life and family,' and, in reply I would like to emphasise that this is not, nor was ever intended to be, an accurate history of the Adams family. Such a project would have involved a tremendous amount of time-consuming research and this I could not do – not because I am planning to go anywhere but simply that, at the start, I promised myself a completion date of the year end (i.e. 1998) but have already overshot my target by one year because it is now the end of 1999!

Therefore, instead of a history we have got just a collection of memories of people, places and events with whom, or with which, I have been associated in the first seventy-five years of my life.

Having said that, I can now look forward to the second seventy-five and, who knows, it may prove to be more interesting than the first.

Finally, mainly for the benefit of my younger readers, always remember:

Life, in the end, is nothing but a collection of memories – so make sure they are good ones.

THE END